THE
HARPER & ROW
RHETORIC

WRITING AS THINKING
THINKING AS WRITING

Wayne C. Booth
The University of Chicago

Marshall W. Gregory
Butler University

1817

HARPER & ROW, PUBLISHERS, New York
Cambridge, Philadelphia, San Francisco, Washington,
London, Mexico City, São Paulo, Singapore, Sydney

For

Alison and Katherine

and

Melissa and Holly

Sponsoring Editor: Phillip Leininger
Project Editor: Donna DeBenedictis
Text Design: Barbara Bert/North 7 Atelier, Ltd.
Cover Design: Karen Salsgiver
Production Manager: Jeanie Berke
Production Assistant: Brenda DeMartini
Compositor: ComCom Division of Haddon Craftsmen, Inc.
Printer and Binder: R. R. Donnelley & Sons Company
Cover Printer: Lehigh Press

THE HARPER & ROW RHETORIC: Writing as Thinking/Thinking as Writing

Library of Congress Cataloging-in-Publication Data
Booth, Wayne C.
    The Harper & Row rhetoric.

    Includes index.
    1. English language—Rhetoric. I. Gregory,
Marshall W., 1940–. II. Title. III. Title:
Harper and Row rhetoric.
PE1408.B6128 1987   808'.042   86-22743
ISBN 0-06-040837-5

86 87 88 89 9 8 7 6 5 4 3 2 1

Acknowledgments

We gratefully acknowledge the following authors and publishers for allowing us to reprint their materials.

pp. 41–42: Letter to the editor by John J. Jones, *The New York Times,* July 17, 1985. Reprinted by permission of the author.

pp. 87–88: From *Thomas Jefferson* by Gene Lisitzky. Copyright © 1933, renewed 1961 by Gene Lisitzky. Reprinted by permission of Viking Penguin, Inc.

pp. 106–107: From *Selected Letters of James Thurber,* edited by Helen Thurber and Edward Weeks and published by Atlantic-Little Brown. Copyright © 1980 by Helen W. Thurber.

pp. 124–130: "Enemy Evenings" from *Letters from the Country* by Carol Bly. Copyright © 1975 by Carol Bly. Reprinted by permission of Harper & Row, Publishers, Inc.

pp. 174–181: "Thinking as a Hobby" by William Golding, *Holiday Magazine,* August 1961. Copyright © 1961 by William Golding. Reprinted by permission of Curtis Brown, Ltd.

pp. 186–187: From *The Educated Imagination* by Northrop Frye (1962). Reprinted by permission of the publisher, Indiana University Press.

pp. 268–269: Excerpt in "Home-Coming" from *Essays of E. B. White.* Copyright © 1955 by E. B. White. Originally appeared in *The New Yorker.* Reprinted by permission of Harper & Row, Publishers, Inc.

pp. 292–293: From "Bedfellow" Turtle Bay, February 6, 1956, in *Essays of E. B. White* by E. B. White. Copyright © 1956 by E. B. White, renewed 1984 by E. B. White. Originally appeared in *The New Yorker.* Reprinted by permission of Harper & Row, Publishers, Inc.

pp. 296–297: From *I Know Why the Caged Bird Sings* by Maya Angelou (1969). Reprinted by permission of the publisher, Random House, Inc.

pp. 300–302: From *Killers of the Dream,* Revised, by Lillian Smith. Copyright © 1949, 1961 by Lillian Smith. Reprinted by permission of W. W. Norton & Company, Inc.

pp. 319–320: From *The Descent of Woman* by Elaine Morgan. Copyright © 1972 by Elaine Morgan. Reprinted with permission of Stein and Day Publishers.

pp. 323–324: From *The Poet in the World* by Denise Levertov. Copyright © 1961 by Denise Levertov Goodman. Reprinted by permission of New Directions Publishing Corporation.

pp. 372–373: Letter to the editor by Joseph Feldman, *The New York Times,* June 29, 1985. Reprinted by permission of the author.

Contents

CHAPTER **8**

The Power of Words   219

CHAPTER **13**

Supporting Your Thesis III: Deduction, Fallacies, and Rhetorical Reasoning 393

CHAPTER **14**

The Rhetoric of Research Papers: Weaving Other People's Ideas into Your Own 431

Preface

We have long been convinced that Freshman Composition can be the most important of all college experiences. More than any other, this course will determine whether students ever discover what college is *for,* whether they survive beyond the freshman year, and—most important of all—whether they will have *learned how to learn* and thus continue their own educations after leaving their teachers' care. What is more, the character of this course will determine whether teachers continue to work with freshmen or retreat—out of boredom or burnout—to easier courses to teach. In short, the writing course should not be merely a "service course" in which the teacher serves and the students focus only on skills that will get them by. Rather, it should, and can, be an engaging and rewarding experience for both students and teachers.

It will be that, however, only if teachers work to make the course intellectually challenging in its fundamental conception. In re-thinking what such an aim might entail, we found ourselves having to re-think much of what we had taken for granted in our past teaching experiences. Our results cannot be summarized briefly; they are best reflected both in the organization of the book and in the design of writing situations within each chapter. Here we underline only the more important purposes that became clearer as we moved through our various drafts of the manuscript.

Perhaps our most important goal, as our subtitle suggests, was to underscore that all the writing tasks are based on thinking. We suggest repeatedly in different ways and in different contexts that writing is one of culture's most important means of accomplishing real tasks; that it may be viewed as a kind of reflective speech, in which words are thought about, taken back, exchanged, and shaped before being "uttered"; and that the reflection that goes into writing, when combined with the writer's concern for logic, control, and precision, constitutes a powerful kind of mental training and discipline. Though we suggest some forms of "free writing" that are in a limited sense unpremeditated, we stress strongly that putting hard thought into multiple revisions can be one of our most important educational experiences, not only about "writing" in any narrow sense but about how to think *in* writing. In short, we try to help students practice and reflect on their language, to help them to see writing as a supple and powerful instrument for serving a vast array of social and personal needs. We see writing as a kind of thinking that is simultaneously social and private.

In other words, writers do not think in a vacuum. They usually address an audience, and we have stressed throughout the "rhetorical" dimension of writers' thinking. By treating writing as "conversation" with potential readers, we have found traditional topics like "invention" and "design" transformed into explorations of ideas that writers share, or might share, with readers. Thus, though we do not cite many rhetorical theorists, classical or modern, our work was inspired at every point by the desire to put their fundamental insights into a practice that would be intelligible and useful to any serious student. It is a practice based on the premises, first, that writers can never write effectively until they have clear notions of audience and purpose; second, that all of the other variables in writing—invention, design, tone, voice, figures of speech, use of evidence, reasoning, and so on—will be determined by the combination of audience and purpose; and, finally, that all the variables, including purpose, will shift and alter as writers go through the writing *process,* continually rethinking and reshaping as the looping process of revision takes them over already traveled paths, and shows them how to make the bends and twists less tortuous for the writer and clearer for the reader.

Though we do not discuss current controversies directly, we hope that both specialists and non-specialists will find here an approach that capitalizes on the best insights of each major contemporary theory. Theory and research have much to teach us all —they continually nourish our thinking—but finally the teacher must be able to translate theory and research into pedagogical practice. Every teacher faces the questions, "Which issues do I focus on first?" "Where do I go next?" "How do I help students get from here to there?" By providing a focus on these issues in both its organization and content, *The Harper & Row Rhetoric* aims not only to help launch the course but to ensure that the direction and destination make practical sense—to both teachers and students.

This book does not preach, then, a given line to the exclusion of all competing ideas, nor does it try to convert all teachers to a single writing "approach." Instead, we simply tried (although it has not been a simple task) to rethink the basic issues afresh. Why *is* it important to teach students how to read and write? How do we take the newly fashionable term "invention" and make it immediately and practically useful in "finding something to say"? What do we *mean* by such terms as purpose, thesis, voice, tone, and logical fallacy? What do students need to do, think, or believe in order to care about their writing and to work in order to improve? What sequence of topics and issues will help teachers keep their objectives and strategies clearly in mind? How can they make the "research paper" achieve broader educational ends than merely "learning how to use the library"? How can students be helped to see that day-by-day writing practice is not an isolated, discrete activity but an influence on their intellectual, social, and ethical development?

There is no question that this rethinking of fundamental questions was useful to us both as teachers and writers. It gave us our greatest rewards and toughest challenges. When we began we were somewhat jarred to discover what a large portion of our own teaching and views about writing relied on rule-of-thumb experience, and how little of it had been earned by first-hand thought. This discovery did not lead us to conclude that everything we had been doing and thinking was wrong, but we came to realize how little time and energy we teachers of writing have for the kind of fresh thinking about basic issues that doing a book like this requires. Of course, no amount of time will be enough for a task of this magnitude. We assume that much that we say will have to be revised later, and we know that the book is less comprehensive than we would like it to be. But we have tried to think every issue afresh, and we will, of course, welcome suggestions from those who discover the book's weaknesses.

We also worked to make our thinking accessible to students. We try to engage students' interest and commitment by placing before them both utilitarian arguments ("Yes, writing really is important in other college courses and in the working world beyond college") and intrinsic arguments ("As word creatures, the quality of our social lives and our very concepts of 'self' are grounded in words; we also take a natural pleasure in words used effectively"). We attempt to sustain that interest by using hundreds of varied, lively examples of good writing, selected to illustrate the largest possible variety of purposes and tones. We are convinced that students learn how to write better if they have the sounds of well-used language reverberating in their heads. Talk about writing is necessary, but the advice must be supplemented by examples.

In a further attempt to engage students' interest we address them directly. Though we cannot pretend to know their current interests or address them "personally" (like those "personal" carsort advertisements), we have tried to maintain a tone that will engage them in thinking through the issues with us. This may occasionally lead to the impression that you, the teacher, have been shut out of a dialogue among Booth, Gregory, and the students. You, no doubt, do not need our assurance that the book leaves more than enough for you to do.

To allow for practical applications of the concepts and guidelines we discuss, we have constructed two kinds of assignments: notebook writing and sentence /paragraph/essay practice. These assignments appear and are tied in with various sections in the text where we felt that practice or reinforcement would be helpful. Notebook assignments encourage "private," informal writing, allowing students to gain confidence in translating their thoughts into words without the pressure of a public forum. Sentence/paragraph/essay assignments, on the other hand, are intended as hand-in assignments or as the subjects of class discussions.

Finally, we place writing in the larger context of "cultural literacy." We hope that students will see that the character of the world they live in is determined in large part by the quality of discourse shared by its citizens. Some kinds of writing are purely private—reserved for the eyes of the writer alone. For such writing there are no criteria for better and worse since it produces no effects on the world beyond the writer's ego. But most writing is public writing; it is addressed to someone who will read it. And all such writing, from presidential reports to student essays, carries some potential power to shape the world by influencing the opinions and feelings of its readers. If we can help students see clearly that this "rhetorical" point is also a political point, and to *care* about it, they will see that they have a stake in learning to write, a stake far more important than merely making grades, earning money, or having a fund of cocktail conversation. And when students become covinced of this potential, they will be eager to learn.

We would like to express our appreciation to those reviewers who analyzed drafts of our manuscript: Victoria Aarons, Trinity University; Ann E. Berthoff, University of Massachusetts–Boston; Wilma R. Ebbitt, The Pennsylvania State University; Janet M. Eldred, University of Illinois at Urbana–Champaign; James L. Kastely, University of Hawaii, Manoa; Charles I. Schuster, University of Wisconsin at Milwaukee; Linda B. Spoerl, Highline Community College; Richard L. Larson, Lehman College–CUNY; Gregory H. Mason, Gustavus Adolphus College; and Mary K. Wallum, North Dakota State University.

Wayne C. Booth
Marshall Gregory

1

Overview

Introduction

Beginnings are hard

WAYNE BOOTH: Marshall, how's this for an opening?

The purpose of this book is to see that students in a college writing course will be given a complete overview of the problems faced by each and every inexperienced writer, along with giving them practical advice about how to solve each troublesome problem. In this first chapter, just to get things started, a complete outline of the topics to be discussed will be provided, and the reasons for learning to write will be discussed. The fourteen chapters of the book have been organized so that by the end of the term every student will have been given "hands on" practice in dealing with the major problems any writer faces, whether he or she is experienced or not. Though no promise can be given by the authors that every student will be a good writer by the end of the term, the promise can be made that doing the assignments each week will produce great improvement by the end of the term.

MARSHALL GREGORY: That's a terrible opening—just won't do. It just won't do at all.

1

BOOTH: Why not?

GREGORY: Surely you know why not. Didn't you write it as an example of how *not* to begin a book?

BOOTH: Well, that's not how I began. I had to get started somehow, so I just began with a couple of offhand sentences. They didn't seem terrific, but not terrible either. "Well," I said to myself, "why not just go ahead and at least get something down on paper?" That's what I usually do when I write my first drafts anyway. You have to admit that I easily could have made it a lot worse. I may have used too many passive verbs, but I didn't commit any obvious grammatical or spelling errors. Every sentence is on the same subject. What's so bad about it?

GREGORY: Well, with or without errors, it's boring. It doesn't make me want to continue reading. It doesn't even sound as if you're convinced that writing the book is important. If the students reading our book learn to write like this, nobody will want to read *their* work either.

BOOTH: That's easy enough for you to say. You haven't tried yet to write a first paragraph for this book about how to write. Beginnings are always hard. Why is this one especially boring?

GREGORY: Well, for one thing, you use a lot more words than you need. We all do this in our first drafts, but extra words are like muddy ground to a runner: They make the going tough and slow. Having to work so hard makes a reader annoyed or bored, even if the writer finally says something important. Let's do some simple cutting.

• Instead of

complete overview

just say

overview

because an *over*view is in itself complete.

- Instead of

each and every

say

every

"Each and every" is a cliché.

- Instead of

troublesome problem

say

problem

because all problems are by definition troublesome.

- Drop

just to get things started

because we're *obviously* just getting started.

- Instead of

complete outline

say

outline

because no one will know whether our outline is really complete until they read the whole book.

- Just drop

hands-on practice

because "hands-on" duplicates practice and has become a cliché.

- Instead of . . .

BOOTH: *(interrupting)* But none of those changes seems to make the paragraph more interesting. Even if you made more of them, it would just move a bit faster. It wouldn't say anything different.

GREGORY: Well, faster writing is livelier writing, even if the content remains the same—at least up to a point. Go *too* fast, of course, and nobody will be able to follow you.

But let's keep working at it. Another big problem is that you don't show real people actually *doing* any of the activities you refer to. Though you mention students, they don't *do* anything, and you make all of *our* jobs—our planning, organizing, writing, revising, and editing—sound as if they just happened by themselves. You and I often tell our students that they should try to get *people* into their sentences and use active rather than passive verbs. But because your mind was on other things, you forgot your own advice as soon as you started out on this difficult writing task.

• So let's change

that students should be given

to

to give students

That saves words and makes things clearer.

• Instead of

a complete outline will be provided

say

we will give a complete outline

This identifies where the outline is coming from.

• Instead of

The fourteen chapters of the book have been organized

say

We have organized

This makes it clear who organized the chapters.

- Instead of

> every student will have been given practice

say

> every student will have practiced

- Instead of

> No promise can be given by the authors

say

> The authors cannot promise

- Instead of

> the promise can be made

say

> they can promise

Now let's see how it sounds, cutting a few more unnecessary words as we go.

> The purpose of this book is to give students in a college writing course an overview of the problems every inexperienced writer faces, along with practical advice about how to solve them. In this first chapter we provide an outline of the topics to be discussed and reasons for learning to write. We have organized the fourteen chapters so that by the end of the term students will have worked on the major problems all writers face, whether they are experienced or not. Though we cannot promise that you will be a good writer by the end of the term, we can promise that if you do the assignments each week you will improve rapidly.

BOOTH: Over forty words cut—and the meaning still intact! Okay, I agree that you've made it a bit better, but now that I look at it more closely it *still* seems boring. I'm afraid that no matter how we rewrite it, it will always be boring.

GREGORY: Why?

BOOTH: Maybe because it's all description with no problem or question to engage the reader directly. Writing is a complicated activity learned by first-hand practice, not by second-hand description. We *tell* the students that we have tried to organize the book well. So what? If I were in their shoes I'd assume *that* about any textbook. But we give them no purpose of their own. The question is: What do *they* get out of learning to write better? The paragraph says nothing about that—it's just transferring some information we care about from our heads into theirs.

GREGORY: So what do we do?

BOOTH: I think we have to start over, and this time try to get some action and purpose into our prose.

GREGORY: How do you think it would work if we opened our book by presenting this paragraph of yours and our efforts to revise it—then our ultimate decision to scrap it—so that students can see even experienced writers going through the same process of rethinking and rewriting that we're recommending to them?

BOOTH: I don't know. Let's try it, and if it fails we can always start over again. Beginnings *are* hard.

Starting over: The importance of practice

The two problems we have just dramatized—"How should I begin this piece of writing?" and "How do I begin to revise my first drafts?"—are just two of dozens of problems that you will encounter whenever you write. A writer attempting anything other than an exact copy is always trying to make something new. Like a cook whipping up a new recipe or a musician composing a symphony, a writer sets down words that have never been put together *just that way* before. And whenever we try to make anything new, we are forced to work in ways that cannot be defined precisely ahead of time. Writing isn't achieved by following formulas, but by using skills that can be adapted readily to new tasks. Such skills are developed only through steady practice.

Nobody expects to become good at piano or guitar playing, gymnastics or chess simply by taking a few easy lessons. Mere competence in any of these activities requires long hours of practice and discipline. Beginning violinists can expect to spend a year or two of daily practice before anyone else can stand to listen to them. Beginning gymnasts expect to spend years of training before they can hope to start winning any prizes. Beginning writers, too, require the same kind of long—and sometimes painful—practice. Nobody can make you a better writer merely by spelling out a set of rules. Like violinists or gymnasts, you also must learn to accept many false notes and spills along the way. They may hurt but are never fatal, and they afflict the best writers as well as the worst.

Whether you consider yourself just a beginner or advanced, you will face problems of the kind that we faced as we started this chapter: How do I begin? What do I really want to say? How can I be not just accurate but interesting? Where do I go after this opening? How can I tie all these scattered thoughts together? How can I make sure that I'm not committing some fault I've never even heard of? (You can't. Nobody can.) How do I improve my first drafts?

We assume that you will be assigned essays frequently, but doing an essay once every week or two is not enough practice to guarantee much improvement. Concert pianists and pole vaulters do scales and general calisthenics every day to keep in shape. In the same way, you need regular practice. Two of the most useful kinds of practice are free writing and notebook writing. Together they need take no more than thirty minutes a day; the important thing is—if you do them at all—to do them regularly.

Free writing. Free writing practice involves writing on any topic you choose and simply putting down whatever comes into your head for ten minutes each session. What's important is that you keep this ten-minute appointment with yourself *every day.* If you run out of things to say, then write something like, "Now I have run out of things to say. When will I think of what to say next? Should I switch topics? I never knew ten minutes could pass so slowly." And so on. Do not pause in your writing or fake writing during the ten minutes. At the end of each session, you can either throw the pages away or—if something looks interesting—save them in a folder.

Free writing will rarely yield good writing. It simply gets your words flowing. Free writing builds up your confidence to face those accusing blank pages, and it sometimes turns up ideas that you can develop later into essays.

Notebook writing. Another kind of practice is to write, for about twenty minutes a day, in a notebook that you reserve for this purpose. Unlike free writing, notebook writing offers you the opportunity to pause, reflect, and reconsider your ideas. This writing probably should be more than a diary-like record of your day's activities or personal problems. It offers you the opportunity to include observations and reflections about what you've been reading or thinking. Of course if you get stuck for something to write about, you can always try some free writing. You will learn something even if you do no more than copy a piece of writing that you have enjoyed. Or you can read a favorite paragraph, and then put it aside and try to copy it from memory. Benjamin Franklin claimed to have taught himself to write with this exercise, using the works of writers he admired. Many other professional writers copy and preserve sentences or paragraphs as aids to further thinking and as writing models. When the poet W. H. Auden became famous, he actually published his collection, called *A Certain World: A Commonplace Book* (1970), with alphabetical entries like this one:

Bores

Who on earth invented the silly convention that it is
    boring or impolite to talk shop? Nothing is more
    interesting to listen to, especially if the shop is not
    one's own. [Auden himself]
We are almost always bored by just those whom we must
    not find boring. [La Rochefoucauld]
What is more enchanting than the voices of young people
    when you can't hear what they say? [L. P. Smith]
The most intolerable people are provincial celebrities.
    [Anton Chekhov]

Like a railroad yard where cars are separated and connected to make departing trains, a notebook can become a sorting house for different ideas and feelings. You might include, for example, any of the following in your notebook:

- descriptions of people: funny, threatening, puzzling
- reactions to political, educational, or social issues
- agreements and disagreements with the ideas you meet in literature or in classes
- various solutions to personal and social problems
- criticisms of some of your own ideas, opinions, or behavior

Free writing and notebook writing are simple and brief exercises. But if they are performed regularly—and that is the key—they can condition your mind just as physical exercise conditions your body. Henry David Thoreau, the author of *Walden,* makes the point that genius comes when it wills, not when it is commanded. Notebook writing so conditions the mind that when inspiration comes, you will recognize it for what it is, and be able to pick up on it productively.

Why write, anyway?—the power of language

Every successful writer recognizes the immense power of language. If you believe that words are always a poor substitute for action, then you may see little reason to work at improving your verbal skills. But if words *are* in themselves deeds—if the American Revolution was fueled in part by the writings of Patrick Henry, Thomas Paine, and Thomas Jefferson; if slogans such as "Remember the Alamo," "Hell No, We Won't Go," and "Yankee Go Home" can galvanize dissimilar individuals into single-minded groups; and if baptisms, marriages, inaugurations, retirements, graduations, and funerals would be barren without words—then both history and everyday experience show that the potential power of the writer is rooted in the actual power of language.

This power demonstrates itself most clearly in its capacity to fill the mind with images. The actions that make up our lives—our efforts to meet responsibilities, to get the things we want, and still to have time left over for play—mostly begin with mental images of possibilities that largely come from other people's words. As people tell us about their feelings, describe their childhood homes, or tell stories from the past; as we read books, stories, essays, and articles; and as we listen to sermons, jokes, song lyrics, and speeches, we create mental images based on words. Through these images we "see" places that we will never visit, and meet fictional people whose feelings and histories we can remember as easily as we can remember our own. Through words, other people ask us to look at the world from their point of view, to climb inside their skin, to feel the world through their nerve endings, and to accept their judgments. Many of the images that language puts in our heads become permanent additions to our imaginations; they show us other lives that we might lead, other feelings and desires that we might have, and other selves that we might choose to be. (Of course words share some of this power with photography, painting, television, and film; later you may want to write about the powers of the different "media.")

The potential power that you possess as a writer is based on this ability to put images of the world *you* see, and ideas about these images, into other people's heads. When Abraham Lincoln wrote the Gettysburg Address, he did not merely describe the Civil War; he created a version of it in the imaginations of his countrymen that helped them not only to keep on fighting but to imagine a newly united nation as the goal. Other persons were trying to place competing versions of the war in the minds of Americans, but Lincoln's simple eloquence gave his words the power not only to carry the day, but to endure. Many of his expressions, such as "Government of the people, by the people, and for the people," are fixed permanently in the imaginations of most Americans. In the same way, the novelists or short story writers who draw verbal pictures of whole worlds not only enter- tain you, they give you images that you automatically compare to your own world. And when the scenes you imagine seem more desirable than the reality around you, then you begin to alter the world you live in. None of us wants to be saddled with the world as it is if we can pursue a better one that now exists only in the imagination. When the images of "better" that move us to action come from writers, as they often do, it is fair to say that writers become agents of change in the real world. Even when that does not happen, our "internal worlds" have been changed nonetheless just by the addition of images we did not have before. In the words of Northrop Frye, "Imagination gives us both a better and a worse world than the one we usually live with, and demands that we keep looking steadily at them both."

One reason for learning to write better, then, is to help create the kind of world—presumably a "better" one—that you will want to live in. We all may not be Lincolns creating the national character, but all of us create the character of our own social lives primarily through words, whether in the dorm, on the job, in the frat or sorority house, in the family, or in the classroom. Whether you are writing memos at work, letters to your family, or essays, the relationships you have with other people are created largely by the kind of language that you and they exchange. And the life you live, hour by hour, is largely made up of the words—spoken or silent—that run through your mind.

Thus, even if you are not intending to specialize in English or one of the many writing trades, learning to write will be one of the main objectives of your college education. If you are in college to become a better thinker and to gain greater control over your own life; if you are in college to increase your skills in dealing with people, to acquire knowledge, and to grow emotionally and intellectually; and if you feel that your sense of well-being, self-respect, and future security are somehow tied to how much you know and how mature you become, then you will want to develop your general sensitivity to language. Doing so will help you acquire knowledge through reading, listening, and conversation. It will enable you to catch nuances and implications that you would miss otherwise. And finally, it will help you resist shoddy reasoning and illegitimate emotional manipulation.

Perhaps more important, any increase in verbal power changes who you will be. As we all learn early in life, the unending task of deciding who we are and who we want to become depends to a surprising degree on our ability to use language effectively, both in talking with others and in carrying on that internal dialogue that everyone conducts almost constantly, while awake as well as asleep. The "self" you are is the "self" you make—in words. Every choice of one word rather than another not only shapes the world around you—your "circum"-"stances"—but reinforces your tendency to be the kind of person who imposes upon the world *that particular* shape, or who at least makes the attempt. And the world *does* change its way of treating you in response to your verbal clues.

If you don't believe this to be so, try the following experiment: Engage, for one full day, in nothing but nasty, blunt talk, telling people off in the strongest language you know; then, the next day use as much "sweet talk" as possible, buttering people up, even when it seems a bit dishonest; finally, on the third day, talk in your normal way, using whatever mixture of tough-talk, sweet-talk, and straight-talk seems natural. On second thought, perhaps you'd better just *imagine* it, but *don't do it:* You will make so many enemies, if not on the second day then surely on the first, that you won't have anyone left to talk to on the third day.

At the end of E. B. White's *Charlotte's Web,* Wilbur the pig says of Charlotte the spider, who saved his life by spinning words into her web, "It is not often that someone comes along who is a true friend and a good writer. Charlotte was both." What we have been trying to say about writing and language is a bit like that: "It is not very often that learning any single skill offers the users a chance to improve themselves and society at the same time. Learning to write does both."

The difficulty of using language well

Although we all are immersed in language from birth, few of us can claim to use it with notable clarity, force, or grace. Those who use language mostly in extemporaneous and routine ways, however, frequently fail to see how difficult it is to use it well, even when "only" conversing, reading the newspaper, or writing business letters. They get through the day's chores all right, but they may not realize how much trouble they create for themselves with their carelessness. Not only do they often fail at the most practical language tasks—giving street directions or teaching others how to sew, drive, or cook—but they often hurt other people or are hurt themselves because of accidental, unintended meanings. When we find it difficult to express clearly our loves or our hates, when we grope for words in a heated discussion, or when we receive a returned essay with "confused," "unclear," or "obscure" written on it, then we may feel that the powers of language cannot be taken for granted.

PARAGRAPH PRACTICE

To reinforce the point we have just made about fumbling and inaccurate uses of language, take thirty minutes or so to write a paragraph on one of the following topics. Describe:

- an occasion when you inadvertently used confusing language
- an occasion when you *knew* you were using language poorly but couldn't seem to do anything about it
- an occasion when someone accidentally misled or confused you
- the most *malicious* speaker you know, a person who always seems to know which words will wound others' feelings or splinter a group
- the most *productive* speaker you know, a person who always seems to know which words will heal others' feelings or bring a group together

Direct your paragraph to your classmates, and make your description as vivid as possible. Try to remember (or create) precise uses of language. Then share the paragraphs in class, considering together how they illuminate everyday failures with language.

ESSAY ASSIGNMENT

We come now to your first essay assignment. (Remember that "to essay" means only "to attempt"; see the opening paragraph of Chapter 3.) You may be one of those people who enjoys writing, or you may be a bit anxious about your abilities. Either way, you should avoid the idea that this or any other essay will prove how good or how bad a writer you are. Writing is a skill in which you work for improvement draft after draft, essay after essay, and not all at once.

First, we ask you *not* to write this paper to your teacher as the reader. Instead, we suggest as your audience or reader that person who, in your previous schooling, was most helpful or friendly to you (perhaps a former teacher, classmate, coach, or counselor). You will "essay" to write the best letter you can write.

What you are going to write about, your subject, will be your experiences so far in one of your college courses (not this one).

Your purpose will be to make your correspondent feel your feelings with you, experiencing through your account a concrete and lively sense of this one part of your college life.

Your thesis will be that the course you describe is either the best or the worst that you have taken, the most interesting or the most boring, the most educational or the least educational. (If extremes like "best" and "worst" make you nervous, just make it "a good one" or "a bad one.") You will not only want to show your correspondent how the course works and how it feels to you, but also to give evidence to support your judgment of it as educationally good or bad. Possible titles (and it's always a good idea to think of a title, even though you don't intend to put it on your letter) might be "A Waste of Time" or "Why Can't They All Be Like This One?"

Since we hope never to stifle your independence with our instructions, please feel free to reshape your purpose and thesis on this assignment—even to choose another audience—if you have a clear idea of what you would like to attempt. Unless your teacher says otherwise, treat all of the assignments in this book in this same way; you often may improve them by thinking about your own special concerns.

Do not try for any special length. In itself, length is never an automatic virtue or vice; length is good or bad as judged against the writer's objectives. "Too many words" will seem windy and redundant; "too few" will seem skimpy and undeveloped. In short, proper length will vary as writing tasks vary. Still, to allow for careful revision you probably will do best to keep your account no longer than two pages—something like 500 well-chosen words that really "capture" the course you choose to attack or praise.

As you write your first draft, don't worry about grammar or spelling. Follow the flow of your thoughts, with or without an outline in mind (whichever feels more comfortable). But before you make your final copy, be sure to do one last check for grammatical and spelling errors. *Remember:* Every essay will receive closer attention from readers (including your teacher) if you give the impression—with clean, neat, legible copy—that *you* care not only about what you are saying but about every aspect of the project. If you can type your papers, or write them on a word processor, do so. If you can't, it might be worth your while to have them typed, even at a little expense.

Carefully follow your teacher's directions about format: such matters as margin sizes, double spacing, and so on.

Some points to keep in mind

Before we go into more detailed discussions of writing, here are nine general points about the writing process.

1. *Writing is a round-robin process.* Descriptions of writing, such as those that occur in this or in any other textbook, cannot avoid giving the misleading impression that the different steps of the writing process occur one after the other in some kind of linear sequence. The truth, however, is that all writers make decisions about audience, purpose, thesis, design, voice, tone, and so on in a round-robin kind of way. As you will see when we discuss purpose in Chapter 3, no writer makes just one decision about purpose. We all make many decisions and revisions, each one made *in process.* And each one modifies the previous one and affects choices about everything else, even sometimes down to details of punctuation. We don't punctuate a humorous essay or gossip column, for example, in the same formal style that we would use in a scientific paper.

2. *Revision is essential.* It follows from this first point that the writing process is a kind of looping or spiral activity: two steps forward, one back; two steps forward, one back. The heart of the process is **revision**: constantly going back over what you did before in light of what you have done since. Good writing thus is usually re-writing. And revision is re-vision: "seeing" the topic in altered ways as you go along.

3. *Writing is based on thinking.* If you approach writing in this way, you can see that learning how to write is not the same thing as learning word tricks; rather, writing pulls you into the world of *hard thinking.* Gene Fowler, the novelist, once said, "Writing is easy. You just stare at a blank piece of paper 'til drops of blood run down your forehead." In writing and rewriting your words, you exercise your mental powers. Intellectual strength is developed just like muscular strength—by constant exercise. In "testing" your ideas on paper, you discover what you really believe, and how to make what you believe sound convincing to others.

4. *Public writing goes beyond self-expression.* All this suggests that the kind of writing you will be doing in this course will go beyond "self-expression." Of course all writing is in a sense an expression of the "self" who is responsible for it. Diary writing and free writing are self-expression in another sense: They express your private feelings, written for your own amusement or reflection, and usually in unrevised form. Such writing can be highly valuable. But in the public worlds of college or the workplace, you are constantly asked to write in such a way as to make your "self" available to others—to address readers who either need or want to hear you. Public writing requires that writers climb out of their egos and their private feelings in order to think about issues, ideas, and audiences.

5. *Improvement is always possible.* No matter how skillful you now are, even if you have found it easy to get A's, you have only just begun. There is no point at which you can allow yourself to stop working, and no point at which you will have learned all you need to learn.

6. *Take assignments as invitations, and not as inhibitions.* This advice about *working* can be especially important whenever you consider an assignment to be dumb or Mickey Mouse. Sometimes you will be asked in college to perform chores that initially don't make sense. Even in this book, where we have tried hard to avoid all pointless requests, you are likely to find some assignments that strike you initially as dull, meaningless, or weird. When that happens, always try to poke around in the general subject long enough to find related topics that will be interesting and manageable *for you.* Whenever a subject seems too large—Booth was once asked to "Compare and contrast the Old and New Testaments, in four pages"!—hack away at it until you can break off a chunk suitable for a short paper. If, on the other hand, someone gives you a subject that seems petty, vague, or dull—"Analyze the data on page 27"—ask yourself "Why? Why?" until you can think of some good reason for analyzing those data and sharing your results. In short, always try to put aside your initial objections, and discover some *point* worth making. You'll have more fun that way, and fewer of your essays will be boring.

7. *No native speaker starts from zero.* If you have not had much writing experience and are anxious about it, remember that you already possess many powerful verbal skills. You've been "talking your way through the world" for a long time now, and most of your skills in speaking will prove useful in your writing. Even the least-talented persons in gym class have more athletic ability than they realize, but they must be willing to work hard enough to develop it. The same holds true for writing. No one who is willing to work can fail to discover unsuspected abilities.

8. *Writing improvement goes up and down.* Do not expect entirely consistent results. Everyone has good days and bad days. If you get an A on one essay followed by a C on the next, you are not necessarily losing ground. Writing improvement cannot be measured in one-essay increments, nor does it follow a straight, upward path. Everyone is subject to a common-sense "law," sometimes called "regression to the mean," which says that after you do your best job at any task, you almost certainly will lose ground on the next try. The better today's essay, the higher the probability that tomorrow's will fall short. (If you don't believe that performance goes up and down, take a look at the day-by-day batting averages of your most admired baseball player.) Expect a long-term, not a day-by-day, improvement of your "batting" average as a writer.

9. *Word processors create some dangers.* If you use a word processor (as we do), you must edit and proofread your copy *even more carefully* than when you write by hand. Computers create the illusion that a writer has unlimited space and clean paper. This offers two temptations: to just run on and on (because producing words is so easy), and then to trust what comes out (because it looks neat and finished). Typed or hand-written drafts have the advantage of becoming so messy that writers have to go back and re-copy each draft, and in doing so they accomplish some of their best additions and prunings. Even if you work carefully at a computer, you need to run off *at least one* printed copy (preferably two or three) before you print the final draft, so that you can do extensive revision and proofreading with pencil in hand.

To illustrate this point, we present an earlier draft of points 3 and 4 in this section. At that point every page in the manuscript of this book had already been rewritten about six times and combed for errors, but we were still finding it necessary to cut, reword, insert, and reshape what we were saying—in short, to re-see and revise what we were doing. The entire manuscript—all 600 pages of it—went through three more complete revisions.

PARAGRAPH PRACTICE

Choose one of the following.

1. Select any one of the nine points we have just discussed and write a paragraph or two either disagreeing or agreeing with it. Use your own past experience with writing as the main basis for your position, but if you happen to know what other people have said about the particular point you chose, feel free to use them to support your position.
2. On the basis of your past experience, add a tenth point that you think we have failed to consider, and write a paragraph developing it as we have developed the first nine.

   Share your paragraphs in class to see how others' past experiences affect their present attitudes about writing.

Correctness and errors

For centuries people have claimed that the English language is in danger of corruption and decay; hundreds of books and articles have deplored its decline. In 1924, for example, R. W. Chapman, speaking of "the decay of syntax," said that "the morbid state of modern English prose can be only the beauty of decay." As early as 1712, the great satirist Jonathan Swift suggested that to combat the threat of change, which he saw as the threat of decline, an academy should be formed to establish and preserve the correct forms. Some nations have established such bodies, and, to this day, in France and other nations, such official or semi-official academies issue formal decisions about which words or expressions will be given a badge of approval.

(text continues p. 22)

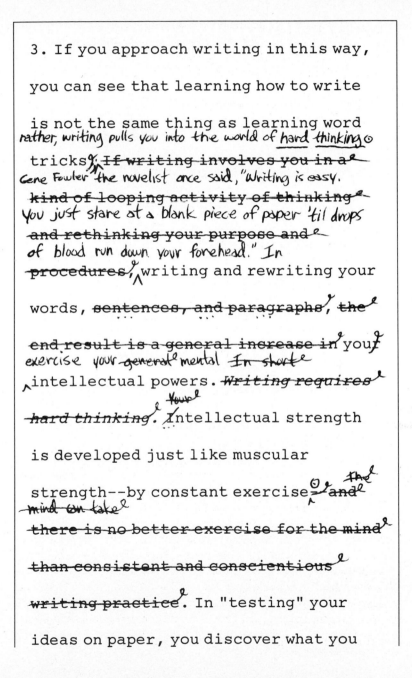

3. If you approach writing in this way,

you can see that learning how to write

is not the same thing as learning word
rather, writing pulls you into the world of hard ~~thinking~~⊙

tricks~~.~~ ~~If writing involves you in a~~
Gene Fowler the novelist once said, "Writing is easy.

~~kind of looping activity of thinking~~
You just stare at a blank piece of paper 'til drops

~~and rethinking your purpose and~~
of blood run down your forehead." In

~~procedures~~, writing and rewriting your

words, ~~sentences, and paragraphs~~, ~~the~~

~~end result is a general increase in~~ your
exercise your ~~general~~ mental ~~In short~~

intellectual powers. ~~Writing requires~~

~~hard thinking~~. *Your* Intellectual strength

is developed just like muscular

strength--by constant exercise⊙ ~~and~~ *the*
mind can take
~~there is no better exercise for the mind~~

~~than consistent and conscientious~~

~~writing practice~~. In "testing" your

ideas on paper, you discover what you

really believe, and how to make what you really believe sound convincing to others.

4. All this suggests why the kind of writing you will be doing in this course

Insert 1/9 *

will go beyond "self-expression." ∧

Diary writing and much of the free writing we have suggested might be called self-expression; ~~it~~ they expresses your private feeling for your own amusement or reflection only ~~and it~~ can be highly valuable. But you will never be asked to do diary writing in the real worlds of college or jobs. You will be asked to do *public* writing, writing that addresses readers who either need or want to hear you. Public writing requires that writers climb out of their egos and their private feelings in order to think about external

issues, ideas, and audiences, not just
their internal feelings.

Insert 1/9 above:

Of course all writing is in a sense an

expression of the "self" who is

responsible for it. Diary writing and

"free writing" are "self-expression"

in another sense: they express your

private feelings, written for your own

amusement or reflection, and usually in

unrevised form. Such writing can be

highly valuable. But in the public

worlds" of college and work, you are

constantly asked to write in such a way as to make your "self"

available to

others--to address

readers who either need

Nobody has succeeded in establishing such an academy to oversee the development of the English language. Many have tried, and many others have bemoaned the seemingly chaotic way in which new and formerly forbidden expressions make their way from being outlaws—termed as "slang" or "foreign" or "vulgar" or "colloquial"—to being used by careful writers.

Many linguists have claimed that these purifying efforts are entirely misguided. Since all languages are constantly changing, and since there is never any clearly established authority to say which changes are good and which are bad, our ideas about good English must shift according to the usage of whatever group we address.

The warfare between the linguists and the purists often has been bitter and confusing. It has been marked by much name-calling, and it has revealed a good deal of puzzlement and anxiety on both sides. (See, for example, the controversy about the inclusion of slang—and especially the permissive view of it—in *Webster's Third International Dictionary,* as recorded in *Dictionaries and That Dictionary,* edited in 1962 by Wilma Ebbitt and James Sledd.)

Few of us can hope to figure out the rights and wrongs of such an elaborate and prolonged controversy. But we can profit from it by becoming aware of the issues and thinking about our own practice or usage. Our choices must always be dictated both by our effort to address different readers successfully and by our own knowledge, or lack of knowledge, about what expressions hinder our communication.

We soon learn that "correctness" is, at best, a mere beginning. Observing correctness in writing is like observing the speed limit while driving: Following the rules may have the "negative" virtue of keeping you out of trouble, but it cannot produce, in and of itself, the "positive" virtue of good writing. Every beginner soon learns, moreover, that there is no end to the number of mistakes teachers can find in an essay; almost all of us have experienced a sense of hopelessness when we've seen our manuscripts marked again and again with corrections that seem endless.

Should teachers and students stop worrying, then, about correctness, as some permissivists have argued? We all know that if we do so, we will make a lot of trouble for ourselves. Some people will refuse to read what we write if they find it full of errors, even when linguists point out that many of those very "errors" have been accepted by great authors from Shakespeare's time to the present. But deciding to concentrate on avoiding errors will not work either. For one thing, it takes our minds off the main business of writing. For another, it can never be fully successful. As we have worked on this book we have constantly discovered "errors," real or imaginary, in each other's writing, and we know from experience that, even after careful correction by editors at Harper & Row, our readers will still discover faults and infelicities.

Thus our choices in this matter are complicated. If we wrote, "Neither one of us don't know nothing about grammar," or if we comited many mispellings, and if you decided that we didn't know any better, you would probably stop using this book. But if we worried too much about catching every conceivable error, we would have to stop writing. So we all have a problem here—the problem of finding a liveable mean between an over-anxious vigilance on the one hand, and the carelessness that will confuse or alienate readers on the other.

Like many problems in life, this one cannot be dodged. With every word we utter, we either meet those we address or we fail to meet them, and our success will depend in part on learning how, in any given situation, to be as "correct" as that situation requires. This in turn means that to learn to write well, we must learn to think hard about the standards of correctness in different situations. The kind of language accepted as correct English in a college essay may be fatal in a dormitory bull session, and vice versa. As you struggle to find appropriate language for your various writing tasks, you may at times become almost immobilized for fear of committing undreamt of errors. When this happens, you should remind yourself of five things.

First, you are not alone. Every author mentioned in this book has depended on the corrections of other people; most authors show their writing to friends before sending it to a publisher, and all of them depend finally on copy editors whose professional task is to improve manuscripts. That you need help with your writing is thus no disgrace.

Second, although possible errors in writing may seem infinite in number, the really crippling ones are relatively few. If you think hard about the *kinds* of errors you find flagged in your papers, you can soon learn to avoid those that give you the most trouble.

Third, remember that reading carefully helps you learn cor-

rect ways of writing. Even when you are not thinking about errors
at all as you become absorbed in a good book, you are learning to
avoid them as you pay attention to how professionals write. If you
had to memorize a list of all the possible bad ways of writing, you
would have reason to be discouraged. But by engaging attentively
with people who write well, you will automatically take in their
ways. Thus, the more you read, the better you will write.

Fourth, don't forget that correctness is only a means to much
more important ends. As you write you are learning to say things
worth saying, and, if you face up to the challenges offered in this
book, your writing will clean itself up to a surprising degree. Most
of the errors you now commit you yourself would recognize, *if* you
really concentrated on your words as closely as the authors whom
we quote in this book have concentrated on theirs. By emulating
the close attention they practice, you will learn what it means to
choose the right words for specific purposes.

Finally: Nothing helps quite so much in spotting errors as
reading your work aloud, slowly. Your worst errors often will
jump out at you when you hear yourself saying something that
fails to make sense.

How to take criticism—and how to use it

By now your teacher will have returned some of your hard-
worked pages, perhaps marked with glowing praise, but perhaps
with some troublesome objections. Some of you may feel that
other students in the class know a lot more about writing than you
do. Or perhaps the amount of hard work that writing requires has
discouraged you. In your darker moments you may even wonder
whether you'll *ever* learn to write a really polished essay. How can
you deal with all these critical voices, both external and internal?

First, it is worth remembering that all writers live under
steady critical fire. The very act of publishing one's work—and to
hand in an essay is to publish it, or to make it public—invites
critical response. Since none of your readers would ever say what
you say in exactly the same way, some of them will *always* differ
with you. Words never settle down on your page with a once-and-
for-all certainty, and some of your readers, trying on your ideas,

will think they fit badly. Your readers will be complex and unpredictable. Thus, you can expect to draw fire from some of them, especially if you try to say something challenging.

Even professional writers receive negative criticism. William Kennedy's *Ironweed,* a novel that won the American Book Award, was flatly rejected by many publishers before Viking accepted it; and Madeline L'Engle's Newbery Award-winning novel, *A Wrinkle In Time,* was turned down almost thirty times before it found a publisher. But we as authors don't have to look elsewhere for examples. When we sent this book in manuscript form to our Harper & Row editor, he sent copies of it to eight reviewers, all of whom suggested some changes. The reader who gave us the most help in improving our final draft was the one who graded us most severely! Even our highest "grader" had many objections. Such criticism is what most writers can expect most of the time. (We long for the day when we'll write something and everybody, just everybody, will say "Marvelous! Don't touch it. It couldn't be improved!"—but we're not holding our breath.)

If you look at journals that carry book reviews, you'll find that reviewers often give even the best writers an implied F. The *Times Literary Supplement* (London) recently carried the following criticism of a second volume of an autobiography by one of the most famous living philosophers, A. J. Ayer. Ayer had said in his book that when he was in college he often heard the sound of a fellow student's typewriter "spinning out his commentary on Thucydides." The reviewer, Alan Bell, objected.

> "Spinning *out"* is a lapse from the author's normally lucid and accurate prose; if typewriters can indeed spin, "spinning" by itself would have been a suitable word. . . . One cannot help feeling at the conclusion of this further installment of Sir Alfred Ayer's autobiography that it would have better been conceived as, or reduced to, a closely woven single volume.

How would you feel if you had written two books, only to have a critic tell you that you had written one too many? Actually Professor Ayer, *Sir* Alfred Ayer, who was knighted for his important writing, has been attacked far more negatively than that. What's more, if we look closely at Alan Bell's own prose, we have to say that he also deserves some criticism. Surely he should have written "would have been better conceived" instead of "would have better been conceived." Criticism (and possible improvement) is endless.

How you deal with those outside voices will depend in part on your temperament and even more on the aptness of the criticism. That great, zany 18th-century novelist, Laurence Sterne, said, "Of all the cants which are canted in this canting world,— though the cant of hypocrites may be the worst,—the cant of criticism is the most tormenting!" And he spent many delightful pages in his novel, *Tristram Shandy* (1759–67), teasing imaginary critics who were—he claimed—misreading his work. Modern authors occasionally write angry counter-attacks, but while these let off steam, the writer runs the risk of sounding merely defensive and silly.

Some authors protect themselves by simply ignoring negative criticism, and sometimes they are right to do so. In some instances it is better to plow ahead, trusting your own instincts. George Eliot (Mary Ann Evans), one of the greatest of all novelists, was so upset by negative reviews that her lover, George Henry Lewes, simply censored the mail and allowed her to see only the favorable reviews. Since she was a genius, she did not seem to suffer much harm from this method, though we can suppose that she might have made good use of some of the negative criticism. For those of us who lack her genius, however, pretending to be blind and deaf can cut us off from important ideas that can help us improve what we say.

While some authors avoid or reject negative criticism, others take it so seriously that it leads them to anxiety and intense self-doubt. Their diaries are full of laments about how badly they write. At the age of fifty, when Virginia Woolf had long been established as one of this century's important novelists, she wrote the following in her diary:

> . . . since we came back, I'm screwed up into a ball; can't get into step; can't make things dance; feel awfully detached. . . . All is surface hard; myself only an organ that takes blows, one after another . . . hatred of my own brainlessness and indecision; the old treadmill feeling, of going on and on and on, for no reason . . . shall I write another novel; contempt

for my lack of intellectual power; . . . worst of all is this
dejected barrenness. And my eyes hurt: and my hand trem-
bles.

Better than to suffer such agonies yourself is to *learn from your
critical voices.* Develop a tough hide—not so tough that no barbs can
penetrate but too tough to be wounded fatally. You cannot write
without laying yourself open to suggestions, objections, and even
hostile attack; vulnerability comes with the territory. You may as
well take an oath, right now, to profit from negative criticism
whenever it is justified, and to ignore it when it is not. Use your
critics as friends, even when they don't sound friendly.

The hard truth is that most of us are not the best critics of
our own work. Like indulgent parents, writers are protective and
defensive about their children, even to the point of liking the
brattiest ones best. Mark Twain, for example, always thought that
his book on Joan of Arc—a book that hardly anyone reads today
—was his best. All of us can be blind to the faults of sentences,
paragraphs, or essays that we have worked hard to produce, so we
all need the help of our reader/critics who, even when their objections sting, can help us improve.

Giving credit to your sources

While getting help is almost always legitimate, it is important, of course, to acknowledge any help that makes up a significant part of what you "publish." If your main idea has come from
someone else, either in print or in conversation, or if someone has
corrected a lot of your errors, it is both honest and gracious to say,
in a footnote, something like, "I got the original idea for this essay
from Louise Hanson, when we were trying to make sense out of
the assignment"; or "The structure of my argument here is borrowed from Stephen Toulmin, *The Uses of Argument,* pp. 27–45."
You might look at the "Acknowledgments" pages of a few scholarly books in the library to see how others give thanks for help
received.

The complete debt that any writer owes to others never can
be fully acknowledged. Nobody thinks or learns alone. The great
poet and critic Goethe once said that 98 percent of his ideas were

borrowed. Probably most of us would be lucky if we could claim even 2 percent as our own. Even when we "think for ourselves," the very thoughts we think have been assimilated from others whom we have met in person, in books and articles, on television, and in the classroom. Nobody expects you to provide footnotes that say, "I owe this idea to my sainted Mother, who taught it to me when I was three"; or "The structure of this essay was suggested to me by my teacher, Ms. Deborah Thatcher"; or "I got this idea from *The Harper & Row Rhetoric,* Chapters 2 and 3." Yet if you borrow in the wrong ways, without giving proper acknowledgment, you will rightly be accused of **plagiarism**: using someone else's work and passing it off as your own.

How do you decide when to mention your helpers? Although we will discuss this point in more detail in Chapter 14, a good rule of thumb for now is this: *Whenever you consciously borrow any important element from someone else—any sentence, any colorful phrase or original term, any plan or idea—say so, either in a footnote, bibliography, or parenthesis.* Don't forget that many a promising career has been destroyed by a moment of heavy, unacknowledged borrowing, but *no* career has ever been harmed by openly embraced collaboration.

Conclusion

In this chapter you have explored some specific problems that all writers meet as they try to improve their writing. As you continue to work on these sometimes burdensome problems, you should occasionally remind yourself just how much is at stake for *you* in learning to write and speak well. Language is your birthright —human beings are the only creatures who wield its immense powers. But like any other birthright, its value can be diminished or enhanced. The legacy you inherit from those who have spoken and written before you can be turned to dust or gold, depending on what you do with it.

But to view language as inherited property may be misleading. Language is more like the air we breathe, the medium that sustains our very life. Can you imagine a life without words? Or a world in which most speech was so garbled that only the speakers knew what they meant? Such imaginings suggest that language is more like health than property. We desire physical health because without it most of what we care for in life becomes impossible or painfully difficult. But we also desire health because it is an intrinsic joy—just plain good in itself. Similarly we seek linguistic health—competence and control in our use of language—both because it is useful and because it is enjoyable for its own sake.

Such talk may seem excessive to you—mere hot air. But every human being has experienced good health, or recognizes it as desirable, and every human being has learned to use at least one language. Whenever we observe an infant who is learning to talk, or a four-year-old who has discovered how to rhyme, or a ten-year-old who "talks" to computers, we see that they do what they do because it is fun, not just useful. Their sheer joy in the process itself spurs them on. Something like that natural pleasure is what you can hope for in the weeks ahead as a compensation for the labor pains that almost always accompany the conception and delivery of good essays.

Whenever your assigned tasks seem artificial or your results seem painfully inadequate, and you find yourself wondering if the gain is worth the effort, step back for a moment and ask two simple questions that may help clarify your commitment to many different kinds of activities, including learning how to write: "What is my life *for*?" and "Can I ever be satisfied with that life if I fall far short of realizing my potential with language?" Since the answer to the second question will always be "no," no matter how you answer the first, your moment of reflection may help you meet your challenges with determination and enthusiasm.

PARAGRAPH PRACTICE

Listed here are the divisions within Chapter 1. Write two paragraphs in which you attempt to summarize the main point of two of them. For number 3 you may select one of the nine points discussed in that section.

Introduction

1. Beginnings Are Hard
2. Starting Over: The Importance of Practice

Why Write, Anyway?—The Power of Language

The Difficulty of Using Language Well

3. Some Points to Keep in Mind
4. Correctness and Errors
5. How to Take Criticism—And How to Use It
6. Giving Credit to Your Sources

Conclusion

In each paragraph try to restate something new that you learned, and indicate how it might help you in your attempts to improve your writing.

ESSAY ASSIGNMENT

Here is a list of assertions, one from each division of Chapter 1. Select any one of these and write an essay, directed to us, offering reasons designed to prove or disprove our claims.

You might want to follow this rough organizational scheme: First, clarify in your own words what you think the claim means. Second, marshal all the good reasons you can think of for viewing the claim as true or false (or as a good or bad piece of advice). Third, indicate what practical use you might make of the content of the claim (if you think it is true), or how we might have made the claim true, or improved it (if you think it is false or weak).

Try to draw as much as possible on your own experience with reading and writing.

1. "Writing is a complicated activity learned by first-hand practice, not by second-hand description." [p. 6]
2. "Like violinists or gymnasts, . . . [the writer] must learn to accept many false notes and spills along the way." [p. 7]
3. "Whether you are writing memos at work, or letters to your family, or essays, the relationships you have with other people are created largely by the kind of language that you and they exchange." [p. 11]
4. "Those who use language mostly in extemporaneous and routine ways . . . frequently fail to see how difficult it is to use it well, even when 'only' conversing, reading the newspaper, or writing business letters." [p. 12]
5. "Writing improvement cannot be measured in one-essay increments, nor does it follow a straight, upward path." [p. 17]

6. "Observing correctness in writing is like observing the speed limit while driving. Following the rules may have the 'negative' virtue of keeping you out of trouble, but it cannot produce, in and of itself, the 'positive' virtue of good writing." [p. 22]
7. "Use your critics as friends, even when they don't sound friendly." [p. 27]
8. "Even when we 'think for ourselves,' the very thoughts we think have been assimilated from others whom we have met in person, in books and articles, on television, and in the classroom." [p. 28]
9. "Similarly we seek linguistic health—competence and control in our use of language—both because it is useful and because it is enjoyable for its own sake." [p. 29]

2

Writing as a craft: Making choices

Introduction

Everything we have said so far—especially the emphasis on practice—suggests that writing is a learnable skill, a craft. This might lead you to expect us to provide a set of clear procedures or rules, "tricks of the trade," something like "five easy steps from apprenticeship to mastery-of-the-craft." We would if we could, but writing is possibly the most difficult of all skills, and nobody can give you a single method or formula that will guarantee full success on all occasions. Even gymnastics coaches can't do that, and the variables in gymnastics performance are far simpler than those in writing essays.

First of all, your special strengths and individual problems will differ somewhat from those of other students, and they will change rapidly as the year progresses. Perhaps even more importantly, the nature of the writing process-as-craft varies enormously from task to task. We don't work in the same way when writing an essay about a subject like "The typical American family and its problems" as we do when writing about a subject like "The creationism-evolution debate" or "The mess in Washington."

The complexities are so great that some writing coaches refuse to offer any general advice at all. "Just plunge in and *write*," they say, "and then write some more and some more, and in some mysterious way you will improve—if you have what it takes." Though there is much to be said for the advice to keep on writing, regardless of anyone's specific advice, you will almost certainly progress more rapidly if you *think* about your problems, not just while writing but before you start each draft. Instead of moving blindly by trial and error, like some badly programmed robot, try to analyze what has gone right or wrong in your drafts so far, and determine how you might work more effectively on the next one.

As we do that kind of personal analysis on our own essays, whether before, during, or after completing a never-quite-final draft, we find it generally useful to ask seven questions (p. 34). Sometimes when a piece of writing comes easily, the first draft will itself seem to answer the seven questions almost automatically. But at other times, when nothing seems to come right, or when a draft has *something* wrong and we feel stumped, then solid thinking about each question can frequently reveal fresh paths of inquiry. And we always find that at some stage, early or late, it is useful to run through the whole list, to make sure that our essay can look us in the eye and offer a good answer to all seven questions.

Warning: By all means do not expect to have clear and simple answers to all of the questions before you attempt a first draft. Try to become clear about *audience* and *purpose* as early as possible—but don't let the questions immobilize you. Few of us could hold off writing until we have answered all the questions. The point is to move *toward* answers as we go through various drafts. *Another thing:* The answers will seldom be simple propositions. To say, for example, that "My audience is the dean of the college" only *begins* to address the issues about audience. Who *is* the dean after all, and what will appeal to *her*?

In the end, then, the answers to the seven questions do not exist outside an essay but are embodied in it. The essay's intention, arguments, design, tone, and voice *are* the essay. But every writer needs some way of approaching these important issues without becoming paralyzed. Our seven questions thus are not a formula for "how to write," but a way of reminding ourselves of the kinds of issues that *at some point* we will have to confront and resolve in order to bring our task to completion.

Seven fundamental questions

1. Who are the members of my *audience*? What do I know about them? Who do I address here? Can I appeal to their interests?

2. What is my *purpose*? What is my essay's function? What are its intended effects? Why am I bothering to write this thing in the first place? What is my *point*?

3. What are my *strategies of argument*? Do my resources of persuasion exhaust the possibilities? What further kinds of argument —logical proof, factual evidence, examples, personal appeals, analogies—would be useful and appropriate?

4. What is my *design*? How shall I organize my essay? What blueprint shall I follow?   ORGANIZATION

5. Have I achieved *cohesion*? Have I made the connections among the parts clear to my readers?

6. What is to be my implied *character*? Whom do I choose to be in this essay? What kind of ethos do I project? What is my distinctive "voice"?

7. What are my *stylistic resources*? What graces and subtleties of language shall I use? What figurative language shall I employ for vividness and concreteness?

These seven questions offer writers the security of knowing the fundamental issues that any writing task will require them to face. They are important enough to justify a detailed look.

Examining the seven questions

Audience refers to your intended readers, who will vary widely from one writing task to another. ("Audience" implies hearing, not reading; the suggestion that you are talking to someone can in itself be helpful.) Certainly the audience you address in a letter to the editor is not the audience who reads your semi-annual office report or your letter to a distant family member. No writer can get any writing task effectively underway without developing some clear notion of the most likely readers and the traits that may influence their responses: their prejudices, beliefs, passions, religion, education, income, sex, and previous knowledge about the subject. Not all of these will be important every time, but they are all potentially crucial.

Purpose refers to the responses you hope to elicit from your readers, your basic reasons for writing and then "going public." Your purpose in this sense is different from your motives, though we sometimes use these two words synonymously: "My *purpose* [my motive] in drinking a glass of water is to quench my thirst." Regardless of our *motives*—perhaps to earn an A or to make money or to show off a skill or simply to get an assignment out of the way —writing *purposes* always center around some point to be made and some overall effect to be achieved.

Consider another example. You may have several motives for fixing the starter motor on your car—to save money, to test your mechanical skill, to regain transportation, to prepare the car for sale, and so on—but none of these motives will help you decide which move to make first, which wrench to start with, or in what order to approach the different parts of the task. Your *motives* as a complex person are usually multiple; your *purpose* as a mechanic is to fix the starter motor, and that purpose, unlike your motives, will point to a relatively precise order of tasks: first disconnecting the coil wire, then loosening the housing bolts, and so on. Thus when we talk about purpose in writing, we are not referring to motives like "blowing off steam" or "winning the prize for the best essay." We refer, rather, to objectives that (like fixing the starter motor) define a particular task with particular, hoped-for results.

As writers we frequently fail to achieve our purposes. Our actual readers, some of whom might yawn in the face of a Shakespeare, may remain unpersuaded. But this does not necessarily mean that we have written badly—as long as we have done *all that might be done* to share our purposes. Martin Luther King's "Letter From Birmingham Jail," written at the height of the civil rights movement in 1963, is one of the most moving and effective pieces of rhetoric in modern times. It does *all that might be done* to make his case for peaceful integration—yet so far as anyone can tell, it did not convert segregationists in Birmingham at the time. Nevertheless, King was trying to do the *kind* of task that we will stress throughout this book: to "publish" essays (or speeches) designed to accomplish some significant purpose in the company of other human beings—if they will only listen.

Strategies of argument refer to all the means for making one's case clear and compelling to the audience. In writing this book, for example, we authors had to "invent" *topics* (Chapter 5) for achieving *our* purpose: to help you improve your writing. We then had to seek in those topics appropriate *reasons,* or *lines of argument*—sound logic, compelling analogies, factual evidence, examples, and so on (Chapters 11, 12, and 13). Later we'll discuss in more detail how good reasons vary considerably from one instance and one audience to the next. However they may be defined, they always play a crucial role in gaining an audience's assent. Though we may get annoyed when our readers insist on good reasons from *us,* we don't feel embarrassed about insisting on them when *we* are readers. Even when we agree that good reasons are not necessarily limited to factual or scientific data, we still insist that they be present.

Design refers to the arrangement or organization of the various parts of an essay. *Parts* can be defined in many ways, of course; paragraphs, sentences, and words may all be viewed as parts. But if we asked you to identify the design of parts for some machine —an automobile, say—you would not simply refer us to a parts catalog. A catalog would include many non-essential parts, such as floor mats, and, most importantly, it would not show how the essential parts, such as the engine and transmission, should be connected. In writing, design refers to the arrangement or organization of the essential parts: the reasons, arguments (including analyses), and evidence (facts, examples, statistics, and so on) that we identified above as strategies of argument. Our reasons simply cannot be thrown together at random. Design is the arrangement that writers use to support their purposes. The design of a bicycle is the organization of the wheels, handlebars, and frame for a particular purpose: to be ridden, or at least to be ride-able. In writing as in riding, the parts must be organized appropriately; otherwise the essay—like a bicycle with one wheel above the handlebars—will never roll.

Cohesion is achieved when writers *connect* their organized parts with sufficiently clear and numerous signals—like the words "finally," "thus," "however"—to make the development of their cases intelligible and to lead the reader safely along the emerging lines of their arguments (Chapter 7).

Character refers to *voice* and *tone* (Chapters 9 and 10), the "self" that you create for any given writing task. Your readers will read your voice as well as your words—or rather they will read your voice *in* your words—and they will decide whether they like or respect *you* at the same time that they decide whether they like your arguments. All readers react not only to the explicit content of an essay but to the implied character of the author. In reading as in real life, we simply like or trust some people and dislike or distrust others. Some writers strike us as pretentious and snobbish or disorganized and superficial, while others strike us as warm and wise or coherent and profound. Writers cannot avoid eliciting these kinds of responses about themselves as persons. In a sense, the words on the paper *are* the person: Few readers ever have access to an author's character beyond the words on a page. Part of your power as a writer thus will lie in your ability to create, or discover, a version of yourself appropriate to the purposes, the persuasive strategies, and the design of a given writing task.

When you have done so, when you sound like a real person with an identifiable character talking about a topic that you find genuinely interesting, you will have achieved what many people call **voice** (Chapter 9), a distinctiveness of utterance that can be modulated and expressed in many different **tones** (Chapter 10). If you are writing about social injustice, for example, you may wish at different times and for different purposes to sound aggrieved, outraged, indignant, angry, lofty, reserved, scholarly, or personally injured. If you are writing about childhood experiences, you may range from tones of nostalgia through irony to aloofness. On different occasions you may want to sound colloquial, formal, schoolmasterly, friendly, or inquiring. Sometimes you may want to sound like a friend and companion, addressing equals, and, at other times, like an instructor or judge, addressing inferiors. Each of these tones will be appropriate for different writing tasks and for different audiences. No one can really finish a writing job without having established an effective character using an appropriate tone of voice.

Stylistic resources refer to uses of language that create intensity, vividness, evocativeness, suggestiveness, or beauty (Chapter 8). Basically, **style** is the quality that makes your prose sound different from that of careless or hasty or dull writers. It is obviously the chief means for conveying voice and tone. Every football quarterback, basketball center, or marathon runner performs the same moves, yet different athletes don't all look alike even when they do the same things. Larry Bird's jump shot and Joan Benoit's running style are distinctive. The same thing is true of musicians or dancers.

How is stylistic vividness achieved in writing? Style is first of all the result of effective word choice based in part on a sensitivity to the **connotations** of words, their capacity to *imply* suggestions not found as part of their **denotations**, or dictionary definitions. The wrong connotations—such as those in this epitaph published in a newspaper upon the death of Queen Victoria—can fatally undercut any writer's purposes.

> Dust to dust and ashes to ashes,
> Into the tomb the great queen dashes.

Both the literal meaning and the connotations of "dashes" are inappropriate to anyone's burial, but when applied to the fat and sedentary Queen Victoria, they destroy the writer's (apparent) intended solemnity. (There is always the possibility, of course, that an irreverent wag was making a joke, which would mean that the writer did know the connotations and exploited them for a laugh.)

Second, effective style depends on using **concrete** rather than **abstract** words. "Concrete" comes from the Latin word that means "to grow together," to become dense and hard. The concrete in sidewalks becomes dense and hard as it sets. When your teachers write, "Be concrete!," in your page margins, they mean, "Don't use words that float in the air; use words that evoke experience of the five senses."

"The young man showed satisfaction as he took possession of his well-earned reward" seems a perfectly respectable sentence (borrowed from Will Strunk and E. B. White's *Elements of Style*), but it contains no concrete information, nothing that can be felt by the senses or pictured in the imagination. How young is the "young man"? In our culture one can be "young" from 8 to 30 years of age. (In fact, politicians are considered still young in their fifties.) Does he "show satisfaction" by doing cartwheels and heel kicks? By launching into a high-flown speech of thanks? By writing a letter of gratitude? By blushing or weeping for joy? The reader has nothing to picture. How does the young man "take possession"— and of what? As readers we don't know whether to picture a thirty-year-old carting off a piece of sculpture in a wheelbarrow, or a fifteen-year-old caddy pocketing a tip. This writing is grammatically correct, but *empty:* abstract instead of concrete. Abstractness serves some occasions, of course, as in writing treaties or settling labor negotiations or writing laws; we could never function at all if every word had to be "concrete." But frequent abstractions usually undermine a writer's purposes. "The skinny, freckled lad tried to conceal a grin as he pocketed the coins," or "The pimply but muscular teen-ager shouted 'Right on!' when the loudspeaker announced that he had won the broad jump": These are not sentences worth carving into stone, but they at least give the reader a chance to construct a picture.

Third, stylistic power can be increased by the skillful use of metaphors and other forms of **figurative language** (Chapter 8). Metaphors, similes, hyperbole, metonymy, personification, and other figures of speech help writers avoid abstractions. To say, "He's a tyrant!" is intelligible but vague. To add, "He's a Hitler!" calls up a picture with an emotional charge. Like any other good thing, figures of speech can of course be overdone. Used by the cartload, they will seem obtrusive, even comic. And we must be careful to keep our vivid pictures coherent. The newspaper headline in 1985 that read "Politician's Tunnel Vision Falls on Deaf Ears in Newsroom" achieved, with its mixed metaphors, an unintended comic effect, as did the man who wrote "Now let's turn the tables to the other side of the coin." But avoiding figures of speech because they can work against you is no solution. A writer refusing to use figures of speech would be like a mechanic refusing to use the hoist because it might some day drop a car on him. We must learn to use all available aids, even if learning to use them *correctly* presents dangers.

Using the seven questions

Every writing task requires hundreds of decisions, conscious and unconscious. Each word, as we have said, represents a choice made from many competing alternatives. Some choices you will make automatically, but others you will need to ponder. Using the seven questions will not make everything easy, even if you can finally produce essays that answer each one satisfactorily. But they can be profitably asked at any stage in the complicated process of traveling from first notion to final draft.

Each writer must discover by experience just how and when the questions will be useful. Some writers freeze if they ask them prematurely, but most of us can save ourselves hours of fruitless work by asking at least the first four early on. At some stage one can then hope to leave off consciously thinking about them and just move forward. Later, the questions can come into play again. It is hard to imagine any writer who could not improve an essay by running through all seven questions one last time before typing up a final draft.

All this talk about doing many drafts implies an amount of labor that may threaten to eat up all your time. Time is almost always limited, and when an assignment is due "next Monday," just how many drafts can one attempt? We can only repeat what is perhaps the most important single piece of advice in our book: No matter how you go about writing essays, do your best to squeeze out time for *just one more serious revision,* a revision based on asking the seven questions.

NOTEBOOK ENTRY

Without looking back over what you have just read, take fifteen or twenty minutes to jot down in your notebook the seven questions we have discussed in this section, attaching to each question two or three sentences that explain what the question means to you. Then reread this section and jot down any additional ideas that you think are significant. You can use your notebook entry as the basis of participation in class discussion.

Such an exercise is always useful in two ways: It seems to hook ideas more firmly in your memory, and it reveals to you, upon review, which ideas have dropped out of memory altogether. This in turn simply points out two of writing's most basic functions: to aid memory and clarify thinking. Though we'll seldom ask for notebook entries that merely summarize, you will find systematic summarizing useful in all of your college work.

Sample analysis based on the seven questions

The best way to test the helpfulness of the seven questions would be to walk through the writing of your next essay with you, referring to the questions as we go. Since this is impossible, we'll now work in reverse, showing how a completed essay "replies" when the questions are applied to it. Clearly this is not the same thing as working with you "in process," but it is the next best thing. Here is a letter to the editor that appeared in *The New York Times* on July 17, 1985.

To the Editor:

On July 6, 1535, 450 years ago, on Tower Hill in London, (1) Sir Thomas More, once the King's Lord Chancellor, laid his head on the executioner's block. He succumbed to the ax rather than deny his conscience. Today we read that some American politicians, New York's Governor Mario Cuomo among them, claim Sir Thomas as a source of inspiration. But the lesson More's martyrdom may teach to the modern public servant could be unsettling, especially to any who misemploy conscience as a convenience.

A few words would have spared More's head. He refused (2) to swear to the Act of Succession, the law whereby Henry VIII's marriage to Catherine of Aragon was declared null, and his union with Anne Boleyn was pronounced lawful matrimony. More refused to swear, even though he acknowledged the succession and so stated to Henry's First Secretary, Thomas Cromwell. For to swear to the oath's clever wording was to approve also the Act of Supremacy, bowing to Henry as the supreme head of the Church of England.

Here is where conscience chafed at More, like the hair shirt (3) he often wore as penance. Sir Thomas, though not a cleric, was a defender of the Roman Catholic Church, and he could not abide a layman's seizing power over its teaching and sacraments. In the apt image of Richard Marius, a More biographer, he could not bear the thought of Henry rising from the corrupt bed of Anne Boleyn and laying his stained hands on the Holy Church. And as a lawyer, More would have denounced Henry's abjuring in one act the liberties guaranteed the church under Magna Carta. So More did not swear the oath as commanded, though others did, even members of his own family.

Four-and-a-half centuries later, elected and appointed (4) officials frequently quarantine their consciences from their public acts. An extreme example would be the South African official who privately abhors apartheid, but who publicly administers that law, because it is the law. In the United States, we find governors who say their private belief is that abortion is wrong, but who swear publicly to execute laws that administer the practice.

Politicians then should choose their saints carefully. More (5) gave up his life rather than separate his conscience from his public acts. His conscience was not a convenience. If Thomas More's tragic death teaches the modern world anything, it is that conscience is the same, public and private.

John J. Jones

As we apply our seven questions to the letter, we can reconstruct some of the fundamental steps that led to its composition.

The writer's audience. Writers of newspaper letters clearly have a less specific target audience than many other writers, but because the letter is addressed to *The New York Times* rather than the *Enquirer* or a local weekly, a fairly high level of education among readers is assumed. And it is clear that in choosing this form of publication, the writer wishes to reach the widest audience possible and gain the widest understanding and acceptance. Notice how he rides the "line" between sounding like an authority who knows more than the general public and sounding like an authority whose expertise is accessible to that public. He desires the credibility that goes with being a true expert, while gaining an audience much wider than just "other experts."

The writer's purpose. Clearly, the purpose is to expose what the writer considers the hypocrisy of state officials agreeing to support laws that do not square with their private beliefs. The writer can rely on most readers (in New York, at least) knowing that Governor Cuomo, who as a Catholic disapproves of abortion, had several months earlier defended his administering those laws in the state of New York. The writer's particular purpose is to expose Governor Cuomo. (For Governor Cuomo's earlier statement, see *The New York Times,* Sept. 14, 1984, Section A, p. 21.)

The writer takes it for granted that if he can make readers agree that when modern politicians support laws against their consciences they are being hypocritical, they will also agree that politicians deserve to be condemned for such behavior. The assumption made is that if a basic contradiction or inconsistency in Governor Cuomo's thinking is shown, it will give us good reason to view the Governor as at least unreliable, and, at worst, as dishonest. Whenever such a strategy works, it is powerful because the assumption behind it is sound: Whenever we find people speaking out of both sides of their mouths, we do indeed regard them with suspicion.

The question is: Can the writer make the hypocrisy charge against Governor Cuomo stick? He will have to provide readers with more than mere assertion, for this letter is trying not merely to inform us—to give us information that we can take or leave— but to persuade us to condemn the Governor, and all other such politicians, as basically dishonest. And most people will feel that before they can agree to call the Governor a liar, they must be given good reasons.

The writer's strategies of argument. The most important argument is an *analogy* based on an historical example: Sir Thomas More's refusal to swear allegiance to Henry VIII's Act of Succession. (See Chapter 12 for a fuller treatment of analogy.)

As   (a)   is to   (b)

As Sir Thomas More behaved : in relation to his conscience : :

so   (c)   is to   (d)

so modern politicians should behave : in relation to theirs.

The strength of the analogy depends in part upon the reader's being convinced that Sir Thomas More is an appropriate model for modern politicians. The writer cleverly emphasizes that More is not merely an exemplary politician but a "defender of the Roman Catholic Church." Since Cuomo is himself Catholic, even a reader who does not personally find More a commanding figure might think that *Cuomo* should, either on political grounds or religious grounds or both. By slipping in the suggestion that Cuomo's political positions ought to be judged by specifically Catholic standards, the writer thus attempts to lead readers to blame Cuomo for not following More's example.

A second strategy is to use More's story as a kind of testimonial from authority. Clearly the writer thinks that More's indirect testimonial will do his or her case good because More has been viewed for 550 years as a vivid symbol of the firmest kind of moral integrity: He defended his principles at the cost of his own life. His image has been popularized in recent years by Robert's Bolt's award-winning drama, *A Man For All Seasons,* which in the 1960s was turned into an Oscar-winning film. In short, the writer can count on most readers of the *Times* not only knowing about Sir Thomas More, but viewing him favorably, even if they only know of him from stage or screen productions.

The writer's third strategy is to use another example, this time a negative one: "the South African official who privately abhors apartheid, but who publicly administers that law, because it is the law." Just as the writer can count on most readers of the *Times* viewing More favorably, so he can count on most of them viewing apartheid, the legally enforced system of racial segregation in South Africa, not just with disfavor, but with deep moral repugnance. To cite the example of a South African politician supporting apartheid (against the dictates of his conscience), and to claim that *that* example parallels Governor Cuomo's position on abortion is an attempt to condemn the Governor by association. The writer wants the reader to respond, "Oh, I see; Cuomo is no better than those South African politicians who piously disclaim support of apartheid, but who reap the benefits of it anyway." The writer implies that a politician who separates private conscience from public duties *on any issue* is as guilty as the politician who performs that separation on the *worst* issues. Does it seem to you that the writer's allegations are fair or unfair?

The fourth argument is a *deduction* of the kind discussed in Chapter 13:

Major Premise: All public officials who "quarantine their consciences from their public acts" are dishonest.
Minor Premise: Governor Cuomo, in his position on abortion,
has quarantined his conscience from his public acts.
Conclusion: Governor Cuomo is therefore a dishonest man and
an immoral public official.

The writer's design. In this short essay, the design is fairly
simple. The writer spends paragraphs 1–3 developing the example
of Sir Thomas More. Paragraph 4 establishes the contrast we have
just described, between modern officials who "quarantine their
consciences from their public acts" and More, who did not. Paragraph 5 expresses the conclusion.

The writer's cohesiveness. The design is immediately accessible to the reader; thus it exhibits cohesion. The paragraphs
would stand up under what we'll later describe as the "fan test":
If they were recopied onto 3 × 5 cards, thrown into a fan and then
picked up, a careful reader could figure out their actual order [see
pages 98–99]. There are no fancy moves here, but the straightforward arrangement of parts does keep the writer's position coherent, and the connections help make it clear. This does not guarantee that the writer's position will be universally believed, and it
certainly does not guarantee that it is right. But he is not likely to
lose readers simply because they cannot follow the letter's organization.

The writer's character. The writer of this essay clearly intends to be seen as an authority, probably a scholar, certainly an
intellectual. He is in command of dates and names that most of us
could not produce without using an encyclopedia or history book.
The writer knows not only that More was executed in 1535, but
that the event occurred on *July 6,* 1535. He also knows the name
of the document that More refused to credit, the Act of Succession, and the names of Henry's first two wives and his First Secretary. He knows that the "clever wording" of the Act forced all who
swore to it to deny the authority of the Church, and that More
often wore hair shirts as penance. He has read at least one biogra-
phy of More and is capable of separating More's objections to the
Act into their religious and legal components. In short, the writer

commands a lot of knowledge that the rest of us possess only spottily, if at all, and this easy command of such details, the voice of a scholar, is the main device used for establishing his character as an authority.

The writer's argument, however, is basically about morality, not history: It is an argument about what makes public officials honest or dishonest, not about the accuracy of the date of More's death or the names of Henry's first two wives. But it is clear that the writer expects his knowledge about history to support the argument about morality. Whether it does or does not will depend on how critically the reader scrutinizes the writer's strategies, but it is clear that the writer would like to be credited with all of the virtues that go along with intellectuality: superior thoughtfulness, insight, and wisdom.

Although the writer speaks with a scholar's authority, his *tone* conveys passion. On the surface the writer is restrained, but deep feeling is shadowed forth in ominous warning: "But the lesson More's martyrdom may teach to the modern public servant could be unsettling." In this context "could be unsettling" really means "could teach them what hypocrites they are." (Would the charge be stronger if he had said "a bitter one" rather than "unsettling"?)

Through paragraphs 2 and 3 the tone is dry and distant, but the beginning of paragraph 4 expresses disappointment: Here we are, the writer implies, 450 years after More's martyrdom, still not having learned the lesson about conscience that More gave his life to teach us. And a tone of explicit censure appears in the image of officials "quarantining" their consciences. The writer's allegation that Cuomo's stand on abortion is equivalent to support for apartheid is inflammatory—although not expressed in inflammatory language. It reveals the depth of the writer's feeling. (A critical reader will want to ask whether the writer is being fair.) The writer clearly assumes a tone of moral superiority, one that he hopes will condemn politicians without alienating the reader.

The writer's stylistic touches. The first heightened use of language appears as the last four words of paragraph 1: "conscience as a convenience." This becomes the writer's tag-phrase, an identifying label applied to any politician who (in the writer's opinion) unscrupulously separates private conscience from public acts. The tag is repeated in the letter's conclusion, thus underscoring the writer's final condemnation. It is difficult to overestimate the power of such phrases; they grip us immediately and powerfully, especially if they seem to express an opinion that we already accept. Our minds are always on the lookout for tags to reinforce our prejudices. The catchiness of "conscience as a convenience," as with many such phrases, is produced by its **alliteration** and **rhythm**: the repetition of not only the consonant, "c", but of the whole syllable, "con," and the rhythm of the stressed and unstressed syllables. Note also the rhythmical repetition in the second sentence of paragraph 1: "More *sucCUMBED to the AX* rather than *deNY his CONscience."*

In other cases, the catchiness of a phrase is produced by a visual or physical image, as in the writer's reference to "elected and appointed officials [who] frequently *quarantine* their consciences." Not only does this phrase repeat the alliteration of "conscience as a convenience," but the visual image of quarantining, of separating things into non-communicating rooms or buildings—as people with smallpox or typhoid used to be separated from the public—concretely captures the writer's charges against modern politicians. The image connotes contamination or sickness. By using the image of "quarantining" rather than, say, "damming things up" or "storing them on a shelf," the writer manages to suggest that such behavior is a kind of disease, not a mere difference of opinion among healthy opponents. The image also implies that Cuomo's disease is disguised, hidden; Cuomo is free to run around and infect others. (Again, the critical reader will want to ask whether this is fair.)

The writer repeats an image of contamination in the picture borrowed from Marius, More's biographer, of Henry "rising from the corrupt bed of Anne Boleyn and laying his stained hands on the Holy Church." Altogether he is consistent in using images that suggest something diseased about people who violate their principles to serve their desires, especially when those principles are taught by the Roman Catholic Church.

Finally, the writer relies on alliteration once again in the concluding phrase of the essay, "public and private," depending on the repetition of the explosive "p" sound to give the essay something like an authoritative cymbal clash at the end.

Conclusion

In this chapter we have asked the kinds of questions that every successful writer must answer, consciously or unconsciously, in order to complete any writing task. Of course we all ask ourselves many questions besides these seven, but they will remain fundamental to most of your writing tasks. (Obviously if you write poems or short stories, some of the questions either will be useless or will require extensive re-statement.)

ESSAY ASSIGNMENTS

Write on only *one* of the following assignments:

1. Choose an essay that you have written recently, and, in a new essay of two or three pages addressed to your instructor, discuss how adequately your earlier essay responds to the seven questions we have just reviewed. You may want to use our analysis of the letter in *The New York Times,* not as a model to duplicate, but as a source of ideas about how to proceed.
2. Choose a recently composed essay and, after probing it with the seven questions, rewrite it. If it seems too weak to be salvaged, or if you are bored with it, you may want to start over, with a sharpened purpose and perhaps a changed audience. Indicate which of the seven questions revealed the essay's weaknesses.
3. Choose a published article and write an essay on how it does or does not respond to the seven questions. Include a copy of the essay you are analyzing when you hand in your own. You might address your essay as a letter to the author.
4. Listed below are some quotations dealing with learning and language. Choose a quotation or two for *one* of the following reasons: (a) because you think it is particularly insightful and true; (b) because you think it is foolish and untrue; or (c) because you think the two quotations "speak" to each other in either a complementary or a contrasting way.

   If you choose (a), write an essay that builds upon and offers evidence to support the truthfulness of your selection.

   If you choose (b), refute the selection, offering evidence for its falsity.

If you choose (c), create a dialogue based on your two selections. Simply invent words to put into the mouths of each speaker, without worrying about historical accuracy.

If you write on (a) or (b), choose as your audience some person or group, real or imaginary, that you picture taking a position contrary to your own. Try to persuade that person to accept your views. If you write on (c), choose as your reader anyone who would be interested in the issues contained in the dialogue.

As you can easily observe, none of the quotations will allow you merely to trot out facts, studies, or statistics in support of your position. You will have to argue in the same way that all of us have to argue about important issues every day: by developing your opinions and supporting them with the best arguments you can find. Be sure your essay can answer all seven questions before you hand in your final draft.

1. Knowledge is capable of being its own end. Such is the constitution of the human mind, that any kind of knowledge, if it be really such, is its own reward. [John Henry Cardinal Newman]
2. Who often reads, will sometimes wish to write. [George Crabbe]
3. The pleasure of learning and knowing, though not the keenest, is yet the least perishable of all pleasures. [A. E. Housman]
4. There is today a clearly visible trend toward making it the aim of education to defeat the Russians. That would be a sure way to defeat education. Genuine education is possible only when people realize that it has to do with persons, not with movements. [Edith Hamilton]
5. The mentality of mankind and the language of mankind created each other. If we like to assume the rise of language as a given fact, then it is not going too far to say that the souls of men are the gift from language to mankind. [Alfred North Whitehead]
6. A little learning is a dangerous thing. [Alexander Pope]
7. I have considerable admiration for scientists in general, and evolutionists and ethnologists in particular, and though I think they have sometimes gone astray, it has not been purely through prejudice. Partly it is due to sheer semantic accident—the fact that "man" is an ambiguous term. It means the species; it also means the male of the species. If you begin to write a book about man or conceive a theory about man you cannot avoid

using this word. You cannot avoid using a pronoun as a substitute for the word, and you will use the pronoun "he" as a simple matter of linguistic convenience. But before you are halfway through the first chapter a mental image of this evolving creature begins to form in your mind. It will be a male image, and he will be the hero of the story: everything and everyone else in the story will relate to him. [Elaine Morgan]

8. We here begin to discern one of the reasons for the prevailing anti-intellectualism in this country. People who think do not fit in easily. The trouble with thinking is that it leads to criticism. A person who thinks is one who dislikes falsehood. And since it is impossible to dislike it and never say anything about it, it is impossible to think and never say anything controversial. [Robert Maynard Hutchins]

9. It is language . . . that really reveals to man that world which is closer to him than any world of natural objects and touches his weal and woe more directly than physical nature. For it is language that makes his existence in a community possible; and only in society, in relation to a "Thee," can his subjectivity assert itself as a "Me." [Ernst Cassirer]

10. Prejudice apart, the game of push-pin [a trivial game like Pac-man or pin the tail on the donkey] is of equal value with the arts and sciences of music and poetry. . . . Between poetry and truth there is a natural opposition: false morals, fictitious nature. The poet always stands in need of something false. When he pretends to lay his foundations in truth, the ornaments of his superstructure are fictions; his business consists in stimulating our passions, and exciting our prejudices. Truth, exactitude of every kind, is fatal to poetry. The poet must see everything through colored media, and strive to make everyone else do the same. . . . If poetry and music deserve to be preferred before a game of push-pin, it must be because they are calculated to gratify those individuals who are most difficult to be pleased. [Jeremy Bentham]

11. The consistency of human behavior, such as it is, is due entirely to the fact that men have formulated their desires, and subsequently rationalized them, in terms of words. The verbal formulation of a desire will cause a

man to go on pressing forward towards his goal, even when the desire itself lies dormant. [Aldous Huxley]

12. The great enemy of clear language is insincerity. When there is a gap between one's real and one's declared aims, one turns as it were instinctively to long words and exhausted idioms, like a cuttlefish squirting out ink. In our age there is no such thing as "keeping out of politics." All issues are political issues, and politics itself is a mass of lies, evasions, folly, hatred, and schizophrenia. When the general atmosphere is bad, language must suffer. [George Orwell]

13. The first sign that a baby is going to be a human being . . . comes when he begins naming the world and demanding the stories that connect its parts. . . . Nothing passes but the mind grabs it and looks for a way to fit it into a story. [Kathryn Morton]

14. I resent it when I hear some professors and administrators say that students are getting away with murder and that it's time to crack down. . . . If any of my professors crack down I'll crack up. I cannot work incessantly—a lot, perhaps, but not always. People mean as much to me as the biochemical structure of lipids. When I'm old and gray, the thing I'll probably remember best about Yale is not all the literature papers I've written but rather all the beautiful afternoons I sat outside the library talking to my friends. It would be nice if all sorts of exigencies did not compel me to think about the future, but they do. . . . At 3 A.M., I'm most scared about the future—then, when the thought of living becomes as scary as the thought of dying and being nineteen feels no different than being seven and a half. Thank heaven it's not 3 A.M. all day long. I'd never get any work done. [Edna Goldsmith]

3

Purpose: Finding something to say and a reason for saying it

Why write an "essay"?

In the past you may have heard writing assignments called papers or assigned topics or merely reports. We will call them **essays**, to suggest that writing is always an "attempt" or a "trying out." The original sense of "to essay" meant to weigh or to "assay," as the related word still means when we evaluate the gold or silver content of ore. In an essay, writers appraise ideas or problems, trying out solutions but seldom, if ever, resolving them once and for all. We think of everything we write in this book as an essay in this sense, the best we can do but always subject to a later attempt, a further *re-*vision. We hope that you will think of your own writing in the same way.

Of course some attempts are better than others, and sometimes, after many revisions, a writer will even produce a final draft that feels perfect—at least for awhile. But more often a writer's "attempt" is finally published—in your case handed in—because deadlines approach or fatigue sets in, and not because the work is considered perfect. The poet Paul Verlaine once said that he never was able to finish his poems; he only abandoned them. All of your essays will be like that—the due date will arrive and you will have to abandon them to your teacher and fellow students, almost always wishing you had more time.

Essay writing is thus like other actions in life, never quite perfected, always subject to improvement. Often you will have a later chance to revise essays that you once thought of as already finished, and you will then find that revision teaches you more about how to write than you could ever learn by just moving quickly from one essay to another, or by trusting your first impulses.

Re-vising (which means re-*view*ing), "essaying," "trying out" (as metallurgists "try out" or "extract" refined metal by heating) —all these terms suggest that to write an essay is to pursue some **purpose**. Writers never actually set out simply to write an essay as an abstract exercise—or if they do they get into trouble. No one can even begin to write without settling on some *direction* worth pursuing, some *point* worth making, some *change* in the world worth working for. You will find that the harder you think about your purpose, *both before you begin and while you write,* the more effective you will be, both in writing first drafts and in making them better by revising.

Whom do we write for?

Usually such revising works best when the purpose is directed to some likely reader, some person or persons who you hope will respond in a particular way. You want them to accept some information as true, to feel some emotion that you feel, to change their minds about an important belief, or to take some action that you care about. If you don't know what you want your essay to lead your readers to know, feel, believe, or do—something they would not have known, felt, believed, or done *before* reading it— then you are not yet clear about your purpose. As we suggested in Chapter 2, purpose is not just an abstract word; it refers to the job that the essay does in moving a reader from *here* to *there.*

Whenever we think of our purposes as not just our own motives but as changes in our readers—changes that readers come to as a consequence of reading our words—we call them "rhetorical." Of course it is possible to think of yourself as writing only *for* yourself. The free writing we have recommended is often for your eyes only. But most writing—and certainly most of the writing you will do in college or on the job—will be governed by rhetorical, not private, purposes.

A few professional writers do claim to reject all rhetoric and to write only for themselves, to express feelings or ideas only *to* themselves. But when they agree to publish such statements they involve themselves in an amusing contradiction that can't easily be explained away: Why publish? You may find it useful at times to think of some of your writing as private in that way, especially if you keep a diary or journal recording your most intimate thoughts and experiences. But your public writing—what you hand in or show to fellow students—will be directed to readers, real or imagined.

From generally desirable qualities to specific purposes

If purposes to be realized in our readers really determine what we do in our essays, then obviously there are as many different kinds of essays as there are different kinds of possible effects. Many guides to writing try to simplify the writer's life by providing a neat list of purposes, often reduced to categories like "definition," "narration," "exposition" (or "description"), and "argument." Each of these "modes of discourse" is as a matter of course employed by every writer when needed. But as categories of *purpose,* they are sadly misleading. No one ever writes merely for the sake of defining, describing or narrating; rather, writers define or narrate and describe or argue because these techniques seem useful in achieving some purpose. Every kind of description, narration, exposition, or argumentation can be used for some purposes, and all might be used for any one purpose.

If we had to give a speech to convince the editorial board to elect our friend as editor for the coming year, we might use some *description* (of the newspaper's situation at the present time), some *narration* (a story about how our friend behaved in a crisis last spring), some *exposition* (of the standards that any editor ought to meet), and some *argumentation* (about how the precise qualities of our friend meet the standards and the situation as we have laid them out). But even when we have decided which of these writing methods we want to use, we still face many choices that we can only make on the basis of purpose, not technique:

- In what order shall we present our arguments?
- How can we make that order clear and forceful for our readers?
- What style should we employ—flowery and colorful or flat and plain?
- What tone of voice should we adopt—angry or dispassionate, superior and distant, or intimate and friendly?
- Shall we talk about our own qualifications or not?
- Shall we use special devices like metaphor, irony, or humor?

Some guides suggest even more general notions of purpose: Writers, they say, should strive to be "clear," or "unified," or "forceful"—as if these general qualities were sufficient to guide the creation of an essay. Not long ago most textbooks urged every writer to achieve "unity, coherence, and emphasis." These, like "clarity" and "forcefulness," are all-important general qualities and can be found in much good writing. Most good essays, once they are completed, will seem clear, unified, coherent, emphatic, and concise. But these are not purposes in our sense because they do not provide, on any *specific* writing occasion, guidance about what is to be done. They don't, for example, tell us how much clarity and concision versus how much emphasis—or profundity, or playfulness, or what not. To be emphatic, for example, to hit your reader hard, will often require lots of repetition—the opposite of concision. To strive too obviously for coherence and unity can be boring ("Now I turn to the next part of my essay to deal with my third point of the five points I have promised"). Should a writer ever sacrifice *interest* to these other general qualities? If so, when and how much?

What is even more troublesome is that when general qualities are treated as purposes rather than as means useful for some specific purposes, they can mislead us. The quest for clarity at all costs, for example, can be disastrous for the diplomat who must write a treaty that both sides can sign. If the American Constitution had been crystal clear, spelling out with great precision just who was to do what, it would never have survived as a useful document. Its ambiguity has allowed for flexible reinterpretations for over two centuries. Indeed, the one point on which it was most specific—spelling out that, for voting purposes, a slave should count as exactly three-fifths of a human being—turned out to be perhaps the weakest part of the document; it could even be said to have been one of the causes of our Civil War. In short, the true purposes of *some* kinds of writing—by diplomats, negotiators, constitution builders, and, we might add, writers of letters of condolence and petitions to the Dean—can sometimes require more tact than emphasis, more elaboration and repetition than economy, and more ambiguity than clarity. (Can you think of occasions when intentional vagueness has solved problems in your life?)

And how desirable is humor? Does a joke add clarity? Rarely. Is it economical? It may be the best way to reduce tension in essays dealing with highly controversial subjects—yet "reducing tension" is not *always* what is wanted.

Thus we find too many competing, generally desirable qualities to accept them as purposes. The only truly helpful goal in writing is success in a *particular* task. If you want to achieve a specific purpose, you must always abandon some qualities that are "generally" desirable.

Why rules won't work

It is no wonder—considering these complications—that nobody learns the principles of good writing quickly. Even experienced writers find that each new writing purpose presents new difficulties. No guidebook, no matter how grand its promises, can offer rules that will guarantee success. Some would-be guides have tried to cut through the complexities by divorcing writing from thinking. They seem to say, "If we just give students well-defined tasks, telling them in effect *what* to say, then they can concentrate on *how* to say it. But if we ask them to think through a problem while learning to write, they are sure to write badly." They have a nasty half-truth on their side: Sometimes when we think hard about a new problem to write about, it becomes more difficult. Thinking destroys our ability to rely on easy simplicities. But who will want to read your flawless essay describing something that everybody knows about already? And who will want to read an essay that has followed someone's rules so closely that the ending can be predicted after the first sentence?

It is true that if you simply borrow structures and rules and purposes from a guide and then apply them to your assignments, as you might follow a manufacturer's instructions for assembling a toy, you will learn *something,* and you may even get by with a decent grade. But you will not learn to write well.

In short, *the practice that we all need is practice in how to connect our purposes to the appropriate means for achieving them.* As we search for such connections, we find ourselves refining (or even discarding) our old purposes and turning to new ones in the light of what we have discovered. Despite what we said earlier about writers practicing like athletes and musicians, the kind of practice that writers need is in fact even more complicated than that. It *includes* the kind of routine that builds successful athletes and musicians but goes beyond it. The success of any piece of writing depends to some degree on how it *departs* from the kind of routine repetition that many other skills depend upon. A swimming or running star tries to perfect a repeatable style that will produce a victory in every race; nobody cares if a football punter exactly duplicates his previous form every time he punts, so long as he punts well. But if a writer duplicates an essay that earned an A last term, it may receive an F—and possibly a conference about plagiarism.

What a strange business this is! If you were able to "write well" last term, why shouldn't you be able to repeat yourself and have it accepted? But remember that you are not just learning a simple skill called "correct writing." You are learning to *think in writing,* or to use writing as a road to becoming educated. As you change your writing, you change your "self" into a person who can think on your own—and that kind of change never comes merely by repeating yourself.

The most important part of each week's assignment, then, will be thinking about your purpose, and that thinking is done not just as a step at the beginning; it, in fact, controls everything you do at every stage of composition.

NOTEBOOK ENTRY

Think now of some purposes that you would like to achieve—if only you could talk someone into seeing things your way. Avoid unrealistic or impossible goals, like becoming President by age thirty, and instead think of changes that might actually happen. Use complete sentences—that will be good practice in itself.

Examples:

> I wish I could persuade my parents to give me a larger monthly allowance.
> I would like to persuade Professor Henderson to let me into her class, even though it is already listed as full.
> I wish I could persuade my son or daughter to read more books and watch less TV.
> I would like to persuade the Dean to excuse me from the Phys. Ed. requirement.
> I wish I could persuade my boss to give me a raise.
> I wish I could convince _____ (a boyfriend or girlfriend) that I am a more interesting person than I have so far seemed to be.
> I wish I could find arguments that would convince my husband (or wife) that I'm not wasting my time in returning to college.
> I wish I could convince my younger brother that college is a good idea.
> I would like to persuade my roommate to believe in _____ (some idea you care about).

When you have listed two or three purposes (realistic wishes), choose one and then list any obstacles you can think of. Include what you take to be the *other person's* beliefs about the world or attitudes toward you.

Examples:

> "Professor Henderson won't let me in because she never allows an exception; and because she thinks I'm a poor student; and because she doesn't like to be

bothered with requests; and because she is afraid of appearing weak."

"My parents really don't have much extra cash; and they think I am wasteful; and I already asked for more last month; and Dad is mad at me because of my grades last quarter; and Mom is worried about whether they'll have enough money for retirement."

"My boss thinks women are inherently less valuable to his business than men."

"My husband had a miserable experience in college for the one term before he dropped out. Besides, he thinks that my place is at home."

Don't take longer than about ten or fifteen minutes at this, and don't worry about whether your writing is good or bad. Just think about the purposes and obstacles.

The range of rhetorical effects

No one will ever construct a complete list of all the possible rhetorical effects—that is, of all the possible purposes—that you might pursue. But there are several traditional classifications that remind us of the range from which we can choose. When stuck for something to write about, you might run through any of the following effects that seem to you worth pursuing.

One ancient tradition says that a speaker's or writer's rhetoric can:

1. move us or stir us to action, as when it changes our vote or leads us to join a demonstration.

2. teach us what to believe, or how to think about a given topic.

3. delight us or entertain us, as when we read a beautiful poem or funny story.

Another useful list, borrowed from Aristotle, says that rhetoric can:

1. change our views about the *past* and about who was responsible for past events (*forensic rhetoric,* the kind practiced by lawyers—and by all of us when we want, for example, to decide who is responsible for something that has happened).

2. change our decisions about how to act for a desired *future* (*deliberative rhetoric,* the kind practiced by members of Congress— or by our families when deciding where to go for a vacation).

3. raise our opinion of some person or institution in the *present* (*epideictic, display,* or *demonstrative rhetoric,* the kind used by college commencement speakers, orators at funerals—and birthday party toastmasters).

Another tradition classifies rhetoric according to whether it aims at an intellectual effect (addressed to the intellect), an emotional effect (addressed to passions and emotions), or ethical and moral effects (addressed to the judgment).

Instead of merely writing to "get the essay off my back," make a habit of running through questions like these (a kind of combination and elaboration of the three lists) until you find one you care about:

1. Am I trying to change the beliefs of my readers? If so, do I want:

- to persuade them to believe something about a subject they already care about?
- to persuade them to consider seriously some question they have previously ignored?
- to persuade them to open their minds to a possibility they had ruled out?

OR

2. Am I trying to think something through for myself (and consequently for a reader who will be in a sense listening in)? If so, I should decide, as I must with Question 1, whether my topic will allow me to present some sort of decisive proof or only tentative probabilities.

OR

3. Am I trying to provide thoughtful companionship or stimulation for my readers—not trying to come to conclusions at all but simply to explore issues in my reader's company?

OR

4. Am I simply trying to entertain or amuse (by no means a contemptible task for an essayist)?

OR (to be more precise)

5. Am I trying

- to explain a process, law, or rule?
- to clarify a common confusion?
- to console someone for a loss or grief?
- to warn of a danger?
- to praise something or someone, perhaps until now underrated?
- to blame or expose something or someone who has been overpraised?
- to lead someone to worship or to support some cause?
- to shake someone's naive faith or credulity about some cause?
- to complain about an injustice?
- to show a relationship between things that people have commonly separated (that is, to build a new *synthesis*)?
- to separate things that people have previously mushed together (that is, to perform a new *analysis*)?
- to proclaim my love?
- to get revenge?
- to gain employment?
- to correct an error?
- to induce an attitude of peaceful meditation?
- to move readers from passive belief to action?

Focusing on some one such purpose will not automatically enable you to write your essay, but it can get you started and keep you on track—or give you a clear reason for changing tracks.

A student looks for a purpose in narrative

Let's see how all this can be applied to improve a student essay. The assignment was to write an essay about "a personal experience, one of the worst (or best) things that ever happened to you." The teacher had not discussed the *point* of writing such an account, and neither she nor the student had thought hard enough about potential readers. The essay came out like this.

HOW I BECAME A VICTIM OF AN ARMED ROBBERY

Last summer when I was working downtown in the Center City districk, I had to go each afternoon from the ofice where I worked to the Main Post Ofice so the mail would go out that night and not wait for the next morning. I was trying to make enough money so that this fall I wouldn't have to work so many hours. I didn't like the job much, anyway, because I was just a glorrified erand boy, doing anything and everything that nobody else wanted to do. Sometimes I would have to just empty waistbaskets, sometimes sit at a desk and answer the phone while somebody or other was in the john. All kinds of stuff like that. Lots of times I could just sit around not doing anything at all, or I'd go out with somebody else for a cup of coffee.

But I sort of liked the trip each day to the PO, because things were sort of quite on the street, and I could then catch the west bound bus on Jefferson and be home by 7. And by doing that late afternoon job, I got to come into the ofice late each morning, about 10. I always did like to sleep late, and this job had that one advantage.

Nothing really happened all summer until this one night. But I did manage to save up quite a lot of money, because my long hours didn't give me much time for spending much. Anyway, it was usually about 6:30 by the time I would get to the PO, not dark yet of course but not many people left on the streets. Somehow I felt uneasy tho I hadn't ever felt uneasy before. The robbery I'm telling about took place at about 6:20 p.m., about five or ten minutes after I left our ofice and I was walking west along Jefferson. Just as I got to the old train tracks, on First Street, by the Wearhouse, I saw a couple of guys coming across the street toward me, sort of fast. Before I knew it one of them, he was white, the other one black, poaked a paper sack toward me and said, "I gotta gun in here. Gimme your money."

I dont have any money, I said, all I got is mail.

Dont gimme none of that shit, the guy said, and poaked the sack at me closer. I reached into my right pocket and took out a $10 dollar bill I had there, and held it out to him. He jerked it out of my hand and said, where's your wallet. So then I gave him my wallet, too, and they ran off down First, and I went to a phone and called the police. It took them a long time to answer. Then I told them what had happened, and they came, and they took a long written report, but you know, I couldn't remember much of what they wanted me to remember, like what each guy looked like, how tall they were, any marks, things like that.

I didn't start shaking until about an hour later when I thought again about that gun. Was it really there or not? I guessed that it was. Anyway, I'm glad I didn't do anything to find out.

How do you feel about this story, this piece of "narration"? You might at first be tempted to say only that it's pretty lively— okay except for lots of spelling errors and some rather sloppy sentences. But will simply "cleaning it up" turn it into a good *essay* that accomplishes its purpose? Suppose we try it. Here is a version that gets rid of the more obvious errors, most of which the author would have caught in a careful revision.

HOW I BECAME A VICTIM OF AN ARMED ROBBERY

Last summer when I was working downtown in the Center City District, each afternoon I had to go from the office where I worked to the Main Post Office, so that the mail would go out that night and not wait for the next morning. I was trying to make enough money so that this fall I wouldn't have to work so many hours. I didn't like the job much, anyway, because I was just a glorified errand boy, doing anything and everything that nobody else wanted to do. Sometimes I would just empty wastebaskets, and sometimes I would just sit at a desk and answer the phone while somebody or other went to the restroom, all kinds of stuff like that. Lots of times I could just sit around not doing anything at all, or I'd go out with somebody else for a cup of coffee.

But I sort of liked the trip each day to the Post Office, because the streets were sort of quiet, and I could then catch the west-bound bus on Jefferson and be home by 7:00. By doing that late afternoon job, I was permitted to come into the office late each morning, at about 10:00. I always did like to sleep late, and this job had that one advantage.

Nothing really happened all summer until one night in mid-August. But I did manage to save up quite a lot of money, because my long hours didn't give me much time for spending it. Anyway, it was usually about 6:30 by the time I would get to the Post Office. The streets were not yet dark, of course, but there were not many people left on the streets. Somehow I felt uneasy on this night, though I had not felt uneasy ever before. The robbery I'm telling about took place at about 6:20 P.M., about five or ten minutes after I left our office. I was walking west along Jefferson, and just as I got to the old train tracks, on First Street, by the warehouse, I saw a couple of guys coming across the street toward me, walking fast. Before I knew it, one of them, a white man (the other man was black), poked a paper sack toward me and said, "I gotta gun in here. Gimme your money."

"I don't have any money," I said. "All I have is mail."

"Don't gimme none of that shit," the guy said, and poked the sack at me closer. I reached into my right pocket, took out a ten dollar bill, and handed it to him. He jerked it out of my hand and said, "Where's your wallet?" So then I gave him my wallet, too, and the two of them ran off down First.

I went to a phone and called the police, but they took a long time to answer. I told them what had happened, and pretty soon they came and took down a long written report. Unfortunately I couldn't remember very much of what they wanted me to remember, such as what each man looked like, or how tall they were, or whether they had any identifying marks.

I didn't start shaking until about an hour later when I thought again about that gun. Was it really there or not? I guessed that it was. Anyway, I'm glad I didn't do anything to find out.

Notice that removing the obvious errors helps us to pay more attention to what is said. The paper would almost certainly get a better grade if handed in in this form. But is it yet a really good *essay*—an *attempt* to focus on a *single* purpose?

Despite the lively subject matter and some promising details here and there, the overall impression for us is a sense of rambling, as if the student had said to himself, "OK, Prof, you asked for an account, I'll give you an account. But don't expect it to be really interesting or powerful." Only an occasional bit, like the final paragraph, seems to have engaged the student's full attention.

What might he do to make it *work*? The obvious answer is: Find a purpose, make a point, and try to *do* something with the account. The material itself offers many possibilities. We'll now pursue only three of them. (You may want to try your hand at another one or two.) Notice that in each case we are asking a question in the form, "If I want to achieve such-and-such an effect, what must I do?"

Our first possible revision turns it into a brief anti-climactic adventure story, cutting out everything that distracts from the adventure of the failed hero.

HOW NOT TO CARRY THE MAIL

I've never been scared much about walking in the streets at night. I've always thought I could probably handle myself pretty well if any trouble came my way. I'm a big man— 6'3", 210 pounds—and I've had some training in karate.

So when I got a job last summer in what I like to call downtown Muggers' Haven, a job that required me to do some walking in the streets after most of the people had gone home, I didn't worry about it at all. I was sort of a general messenger boy for a company that had to have mail delivered to the Post Office in the early evening, so that it would reach other offices around the state by the following morning. I sort of enjoyed the city streets, empty of traffic and pedestrians, all peaceful and quiet instead of the hectic feeling in the daytime.

Well, one night I suddenly felt that something was different; I didn't know quite what. My path lay along Jefferson Street, just where the huge broken-down warehouse makes everything get darker than it does anywhere else in town. By the time I got to Second Street I was feeling a bit creepy, but

I said to myself, "Just let anybody try anything with me, and I'm going to use that blow to the throat that I've practiced so many times."

Sure enough, just as I got almost to First, a couple of dangerous-looking men, travelling east, angled across Jefferson toward me. Just when I was trying to pass them, one of them, the white one, looking about seven feet tall, poked a paper sack at me and said, "I gotta gun in here. Gimme your money."

Standing as tall as I could and trying not to look scared, I attempted the only lie I could think of.

"I don't have any money. All I have here is mail for the Post Office."

"Don't gimme none of that shit," he said, and poked what felt like a gun into my ribs. Suddenly what little courage I had left evaporated, and I pulled out the ten dollar bill I had in my right pocket and handed it to him.

"That ain't enough. Let's have your wallet." So I meekly gave him that, too, and they turned and ran up First.

I called the police as soon as I could find a phone, but it took a while because my hands were shaking so bad. When the police came—it took them longer than I hoped—I was embarrassed to discover that in my fright I had failed even to notice any identifying marks on those hoods. I couldn't remember a single useful detail. All my training and all my fantasies about being tough had gone up in smoke: one moment of sheer terror was all it took.

But I didn't start the real shaking until about an hour later when I thought again about that gun. Was it really there or not? I guessed that it was. Anyway, I'm glad I didn't do anything to find out.

This is still no masterpiece, but by cutting out the details that are irrelevant to his specific purpose, the writer has made an account that sounds as if he cared about it—one that might eventually become a first-class essay.

But of course he could have turned to other purposes. Suppose, for example, he had decided to work not primarily for anti-climactic suspense, but rather for humor. The story might have gone like this:

HOW BRAVE BOB CONQUERED THE HOODS

If there's one thing I've always prided myself on, it's guts. One of my first memories, in fact, was of my gutsy father saying to me, after I'd cut my knee falling out of someplace I wasn't supposed to be, "You shouldna been up there, kid," and then, turning to my mother, "but you gotta admit it, that kid's got *guts.*"

You see, I wasn't crying, so that meant I was the brave one —not like my older brother, the "cry-baby." By then I had learned that I had guts, and gutsy kids don't cry.

And they're not afraid of anything. I grew up thinking that that was true of me. If somebody threatened a fight, I was in there, ready to start swinging. And I swung a lot. Though I often got clobbered, it didn't seem to matter, because my father was always there to say, "You shouldna *done* that. But you gotta admit it, that kid's got *guts.*" I think he liked the sight of *my* blood.

So when I got this job downtown it didn't bother me a bit that it required me to walk each night into a "rough neighborhood." I heard a lot of people say that you wouldn't catch them on Anderson Street, between "I" and "J," any time of day, let alone at night. But I hardly noticed. Being gutsy— and now weighing in at 220, 6 foot 3, and with a real built body—why should I worry?

All right, we admit that it's not very funny *yet.* But would you agree that even a beginning writer could move from an opening of this kind toward a climax, in which Bob will turn chicken and play up the humor of his embarrassing downfall, which might go like this:

> *They* ran down First Street. *I* ran down First Street—the other way. They ran silently; I ran yelling. I also ran trembling. I didn't suffer any of those other embarrassing physiological disasters that afflict a lot of people when they have been scared—ah—spitless. But I came close.

(And then the essay might conclude with that lively paragraph from the original essay.)

Finally, instead of attempting a "humorous downfall," the student might turn the essay into an "instructive warning." Every detail would then serve *that* purpose. If any humor was included, it would then work toward the end of teaching something.

DON'T GO IN THERE ALONE, OR: LEARNING IT THE HARD WAY

Most people, when they talk about "crime in the streets," talk as if the problem is simply that there are criminals "out there." If society could just catch all of the criminals, crime would go away. Well, maybe that's so, but it's not going to happen. Every country in all ages has been plagued by at least a *few* criminals, so we're always going to have some danger in the streets. Meanwhile we ought to recognize that every crime requires a victim, and the victim often asks for it by carelessness or even by providing an open invitation to crime.

I learned this lesson the hard way—by offering myself as a victim for an ordinary street crime. There I was, walking along, in fading daylight, straight into a "high risk area," and *carrying an attaché case* that almost seemed to announce *MONEY INSIDE.* It didn't have money inside; it had mail. But I realized later, thinking about it, that if *I'd* been a criminal, seeing somebody like me walk down the street toward the Main Post Office, carrying that case, I'd have thought "Money!" I should at least have known enough to . . .

You can see how this new purpose is again shaping everything right from the beginning. Obviously every experience we have, every situation in life, contains a great many different possible stories or essays. Just which details you choose to rule out and which facts you include will always depend on what you want to accomplish.

It is true that in one sense Bob's robbery is a single event, but as a narrative *to be read* it is now four different possible essays, only one of them "just an entertaining story" (number 3, the narrative that attempts to be humorous). The rest are essays that use narrative and commentary to underscore a point.

Notice how in each case purpose controls choices:

- Each of them, when completed, will play up different details, and each will add some new details.
- Each of them will arrange the details in a different *design.*
- Each of them will adopt different stylistic devices, producing a different *tone,* different *voice* for the speaker, and thus a different set of expectations and attitudes in the reader.
- Each of them will use different connections between paragraphs and sentences to heighten different kinds of *cohesion.*
- Each of them will handle *evidence* and *argument* differently.

In all these ways (the list partially summarizes the chapters of this book) your purpose, your desire to make some kind of point, will determine what you do even when your material seems merely a plain report on something that actually happened.

NOTEBOOK ENTRY

Take ten or fifteen minutes now to think about possible purposes in your own writing. Do you write to please the teacher or some other reader? To get a good grade? To learn how to do it? For many of us the answer would be "Yes" to all three questions, but these *motives* are so vague that they don't generate specific ideas or lead in particular directions.

We come slightly closer to a generating purpose if we think about some situation we know first hand: "Life in the dorm," say, or "My hateful job," or "A day in my high school," or "The chaos of my tax return." But these suggest mere descriptions; they promise to do little for any reader. We come closer to what we need if we remember some event that occurred in that situation: "My grandmother's death and funeral"; "My automobile accident"; "My fight with my supervisor"; "My fight with the IRS."

But to write on any of these topics without being more specific about the purpose would probably still produce an essay like Bob's first one—loose, disorganized, and full of incoherent details. For practice in avoiding that kind of fumble, try now to take some such general subject and turn it into a subject-with-a-purpose. You can do that by writing a sentence or two about what you might *do* with your subject-with-a-purpose, like these:

"Using my memories of my grandmother's funeral, I'm going to attack the hypocrisy that everybody shows when death strikes."

OR

"Using the same experience, I'm going to show how, in spite of superficial hypocrisy, some people rise to acts of real generosity when they are faced with genuine suffering."

OR

"Using descriptions of what I see happening in my dormitory every day, I'm going to write an appeal to the dean of students to let me live off-campus."

OR

"Using that same material, I intend to denounce the dorm system in an article for the student paper."

OR

"Using that same material, I intend to show why it is wrong to say that human beings are either good or evil: they are always a mixture!"

OR

"Using that same material, I intend to write an amusing letter to my younger brother about the craziness of dorm life."

OR

"As a returning student, many years older, I intend to show the administration why their procedures, designed for eighteen-year-olds who live on campus, are hopelessly inadequate for someone who commutes and supports a family."

OR

"Using an account of my fight with the IRS, I'm going to show why the whole tax code is unfair to the little guy."

Don't worry about whether you could actually write such an essay. Just let yourself think freely about possibilities for molding general material into serious purposes.

A student looks for a purpose in description

We have seen how a promising but unfocused story can be sharpened and narrowed by a relatively specific purpose. We turn now from Bob's kind of material—a narrative adventure—to the kind of subject that insists on an argument, or that provides an argument in the form of description. Narratives have the great advantage for the inexperienced writer of being, or at least seeming, spontaneously interesting to most readers. Fewer readers are likely to be as spontaneously interested in my arguments for a fairer tax code than in my *story* of how I socked the tax man on the nose. Thus if we expect to engage our readers in our arguments fully, we must think even harder about purpose as it controls what must be said.

The first move if we are handling loose descriptive material —potentially pointless stuff—is to discover a thesis worth supporting. That means narrowing down and sharpening our purpose to allow for a coherent treatment in our allotted space. For the kind of papers you will generally be writing, this means very sharp focusing indeed.

Not: The US tax code should be revised.

But: The US tax code should be revised to provide rebates for families supporting college students.

Or better: For students like me, some federal tax relief is indispensable, if we are to stay in college.

Not: American literature has generally downgraded women.

Nor: Ernest Hemingway's works generally downgrade women.

But: Careful analysis reveals that Hemingway's novel, *A Farewell to Arms,* downgrades its main female character, Catherine.

Or, even better: Hemingway's short story, "The Short
Happy Life of Francis Macomber" is in part a disguised
attack on a revengeful, bitchy woman-as-killer, Margot.

The obvious drawback in the effort to narrow down a topic
is that readers are often more interested, in advance, in larger
rather than smaller claims. At each narrowing, we are likely to lose
some potential readers, since a thesis about "all American literature" covers the interests of more people than a thesis about, say,
one particular short story. Sometimes we can take care of this
problem by showing how the smaller thesis represents larger issues: "My thesis is that Hemingway's short story is not only sexist
but that it is typical of much American literature written by men."
Often, however, that is impossible.

We will now illustrate this first and most important step of
narrowing your thesis in some detail. Suppose we imagine the
process that Sam, an intelligent and hard-working student, might
go through after deciding that he wants to pursue the purpose "of
writing something about my anger and disappointment in my first
term in college." Sam knows that he has to get to something more
definite than that, and he rightly struggles first with purpose and
thesis.

Here is how Sam's first notes look—done in a kind of free
writing that is often called "pre-writing":

disappointments at this College   poor sports teams

bad food

          stuck up girls

     no liquor in dorms, crowded rooms, no lights for reading

poor teaching in Soc I—that crazy day when the professor forgot
his notes and just babbled

          way the dean treated me

     Too many disappointments to get them all into one paper?
Maybe just the dorms?

The *catalog*—how it lied about the dorms! That's it!

At this point in his doodling, Sam suddenly sees a possible *purpose* and *thesis* emerging—to write more about the dorm than the other disappointments—and he decides to make a brief outline:

HOW DORMITORY LIFE DISAPPOINTED ME HERE

I. What I found when I got here
    A. General
    B. Losing sports teams
    C. Crowded classes
    D. Lousy dormitories
        1. overcrowded rooms
        2. bad food
        3. unpleasant roommates
        4. no "college-type" conversation
    E. Unfriendly administrators
II. My expectations: What people told me and what I saw in the catalog
    A. General
    B. Winning sports teams
    C. Exciting classes
    D. Dormitories
        1. Gourmet food
        2. Spacious rooms
        3. Good conversation
    C. Friendly administration
III. Conclusion: So just about everything was a lie

After looking at that outline for a few minutes, Sam sees that he has too many examples of disappointments for one 700–1000 word essay. If he discussed adequately all six of the items listed under "I," with persuasive arguments supporting each claim, he'd have something more like ten to fifteen pages. Having already decided that he has more points to make about the dormitory than about the other items, and further realizing as he thinks about it that the teacher probably knows very little about present-day dorm life, he decides that maybe that would be an easier subject to treat—more limited, at least—than the whole range of disappointments.

So now Sam scribbles down another outline:

THE TRUTH ABOUT THE DORMS AT QUINCY

I. The way dorm life at Quincy really works
   A. The rooms
      1. The beds
      2. The lamps
      3. The toilets
      4. Studying
   B. The food
   C. The conversation
   D. The water fights and vandalism
II. My expectations about Quincy
   A. General stuff about everything being wonderful
   B. Especially the dormitories
      1. The rooms
      2. The beds
      3. The lamps
      4. Studying
      5. The food
      6. The conversation

Sam now sees that at least he has plenty to write about. But before he begins his first draft, he decides to think some more about his organization; he is troubled because the points under "I" and "II" are not parallel. Has he got the best organization for what he intends to accomplish?

Asking that question leads him to see that he hasn't really decided yet exactly what his purpose is—what he wants to accomplish, what he wants his account to do *to* or *for* its readers. He is beginning to sense that he wants to express indignation about having been cheated, but he also wants to be amusing. Without knowing any more than that for the time being, he decides (as you probably long ago decided for him) that he should reverse "I" and "II," so that his expectations of a glorious college can be followed by an amused account of the awful reality. Instead of retyping the whole outline, he just cuts it in two with scissors and reverses the order of "I" and "II."

As he has been thinking about some of the funny stuff in the dorm, he finds himself writing, on another sheet, a paragraph about what it's like when four students try to study in their shared dorm room (he plans to fit this in somewhere later):

Have you ever tried to study with three other people in a room 8' by 14', a room containing four single beds (stacked two and two, of course), two desks, two chairs, and only two lamps? There *is*—let's be fair—a hundred-watt bulb in the ceiling, so the room is not really dark. But if you happen to have the lower bunk, as this reporter did for fourteen solid weeks, you find yourself—when it's not your turn to have a desk spot—either working in shadow or leaning far out in order to catch the light from the ceiling. In my third week I had to check in at Student Health because of back problems. It took four visits before we figured out that my only problem was studying a couple of hours each night with my body shaped like a pretzel.

Sam puts that paragraph aside, maybe to be used later, and goes back to the questions about how to strengthen his case.

1. Have I thought of all the arguments that will make my strongest case?

2. Have I put them into the best order?

After thinking for a few minutes, Sam, writing now in warm weather, suddenly remembers how cold the dormitory was in the dead of winter. So he adds "temperature" to his list of topics and scribbles a sentence about how the college's economy program led to the barbaric decision to keep the rooms and dining hall at 64°.

After thinking some more, Sam now does a "final" outline. (Remember that different people quite legitimately start writing at different points in this process; many writers prefer to attempt a first draft before writing any outline, allowing the outline to emerge as they get warmed up. Sam is a fairly systematic type.)

DORMITORY LIFE AT QUINCY COLLEGE

  I.   INTRODUCTION: Getting the catalogue
 II.   WHY IT WAS ATTRACTIVE
       A. The pictures
             Esp. the dormitory

        1. The rooms
        2. The cafeteria
    B. The text and captions (joke)
III. THE REALITY
    A. The real students vs. the pictures
    B. The dorms
        1. The rooms
        2. The halls
        3. The food
        4. The conversation
    C. The administration
    D. The classes

Now Sam feels ready to write a draft. With the "final" outline beside the typewriter, and not worrying much on the first draft about spelling, grammar, or punctuation, he fairly quickly writes the following:

DORMITORY LIFE AT QUINCY COLLEGE

In my last year in high school, the postman began to mysteriously deliver about three college catalogs to my door each week, with letters explaining why each college thought I was their dream student. Most of them didn't interest me because they were either too expensive or too far away. But finally the one for Quincy College really caught my eye. I'd never even heard about it, though it's only about 200 miles from my home, but its catalog made me realize that it must be really quite a place. I found myself reading it cover to cover, in one evening. I had never seen such a beautiful catalogue, describing such a nice college. All of the pictures were of course *very* beautiful. The reader could see that throughout the year the campus was always beautiful. And every face of all the students shown looked like somebody you'd like to know. The indoor shots were even more impressive. I was simply bolled over by the shear bliss promised at Quincy— and the letter they sent with that catalogue as good as promised full tuition scholarship to anyone with a good grade record in high school. That catalogue was what brought me here.

What impressed me most about it was the description of dormitory life at Quincy. The photos of the rooms showed them as singles, with lots of closet space, handsome big desks and bookcases, and pretty reading lamps and comfortable-looking chairs. The shots of the lounges showed beautiful girls and guys all in the kind of clothes I wanted to wear, and they were all talking and smiling as if life was at last wonderful. One couldn't tell of course whether they were talking about sex or about ideas, but you could tell that they were having a good time.

Then there were the shots of the cafeteria. You wouldn't believe the shots of happy faces dining in comfort and with a kind of style that, compared with my high school cafeteria, looked like an expensive restaurant. The food was shown in multicolors, just like in Gourmet Magazine, and the glasses on the table appeared to be filled with white wine.

Well, you can see why that catalog caught my attention and brought me to Quincy.

But the photos were really mild compared with the rich juicy prose. Since I've been here I've tried to track down the Madison Avenue advertising type who wrote all that stuff, but so far I've not been able to get anybody to confess to it. Anyway, I'm the one who has to do the confessing—I'm the one who bought that stuff as a description more or less of the real thing. Oh, yes, I knew the old joke about why a college catalog and the college grounds are alike—they both "lie about" the campus. But I didn't *think* hard enough about it, and I didn't take what now looks like the rather elementary precaution of visiting this place before deciding.

Only if you've ever lived in a Quincy dorm can you guess at just how bad I was fooled, when I went to live in that "house." First of all, the students. I suppose they must have lined up the three best looking students in the college, for those shots of the animated conversation over the dinner table. I've been looking hard for three months now, and I've found only *two* who look like those three. And even them you shouldn't look at in daylight. The rest look about like me. The fresh*men* are mostly a bit underdeveloped physically (I guess all the real jocks decided to go down to the state school), skinny, pimply, trying too hard to look grownup;

the fresh*women* looking maybe a bit more mature, I'll admit
that, but not at all like those Hollywood stars in the catalog.
They wear nothing but dirty jeans and lumpy sweatshirts
with "Harvard University" on the front. In other words, they
look about the way I ought to have expected—about like the
girls in my high school, some not bad and some not bad at
all, but . . . well, none of them matching the fantasies I had
built up based on that catalog.

It's really the dormitory life that I'm writing about, and it
was the dormitory life that most disappointed me. You remember those spacious rooms with the high ceilings and
comfortable chairs? I was assigned not to a single, as the
catalog sort of promised, but to a "suite." That meant four
to a room, four rooms in a kind of quadrangle with a tiny
kitchenette in the center. Sixteen of us sharing a hotplate, 64
of us sharing a bathroom (when you could get in; Quincy has
developed some of my powers of retention)—that's about
what it amounted to! In my room, the four of us had a total
of two chairs, two lamps, and two desks. You can imagine
how much studying we managed to get done.

[Here Sam inserts the paragraph he wrote, an hour or so ago, about
his wrenched back.]

Going to the library should have worked. Isn't that what it's
for? The rules forbid talking there. But if people weren't
talking, they were sure thinking out loud to each other; the
noise was so great that I couldn't even sleep, let alone study.

That room was largely to blame for the terrible showing
I made the first semester here. In the second semester enough
kids had washed out—another thing the catalog didn't mention; Quincy has the highest drop-out rate of any college in
the state—to allow us to have only two to a room, and things
got a little better. Or I would say so if I didn't still have to
mention the food.

At this point Sam suddenly realizes that his paper is going
to be much too long. It's already about a thousand words, and
many points remain in the outline (and even more in his head
about those points). He has a lot more to say than he had thought,

so he's got to cut down his thesis one more time. Looking over what he has written, he sees that the disappointment about the *room* itself has plenty of material for his 700–1000 word job—and he realizes, too, that his strongest feelings of disappointment and anger center around that room. He sees that he wants more than anything else—more even than to be amusing—to get his teacher to share his indignation about what that room did to his first semester. So now, without bothering to write another outline, fired up at last, Sam sits down (he's been pacing the floor while making this last decision) and starts to write the real "first draft" of his actual essay:

A MOST ABOMINABLE ROOM

In my last year in high school, the postman began to mysteriously deliver about three college catalogues to my door each week, with letters explaining why each college thought I was their dream student. Most of them didn't interest me because they were either too expensive or too far away. But finally the one for Quincy College really caught my eye. I'd never even heard about it, though it's only about 200 miles from my home, but its catalogue made me realize that it must be really quite a place. I found myself reading it cover to cover, in one evening. I had never seen such a beautiful catalogue, describing such a nice college. All of the pictures were of course *very* beautiful. The reader could see that throughout the year the campus was always beautiful. And every student shown in a photograph looked like somebody you'd like to know.

But what impressed me most were the indoor shots, especially the ones of the dormitory rooms. Since I've always had to share a room with my brother, the description of how each student lived in a "single" really captured my soul: a room of my own at last.

The two photos of a "typical dormitory room" showed it as clearly a single with lots of closet space, a high ceiling, a handsome big desk and bookcase, and a neat reading lamp and a comfortable-looking overstuffed chair. The student shown sitting in the chair at the desk, studying, was about as attractive a brunette as I'd ever seen, and like all the other students shown in that catalogue she was dressed with real style. She just looked as if life was wonderful for her, in that beautiful room, and I naturally assumed that life would be wonderful for me, in a room like that, perhaps talking with a girl like that. But the photos were really fairly honest, compared with the rich juicy prose. Since I've been here I've tried to track down the Madison Avenue advertising type (liar?) who wrote all that stuff about the "well-designed dining halls," and the "private singles and spacious suites" and the "handsome decor." But so far I've not been able to get anybody to confess to it. Anyway, I'm the one who has to do the confessing—to stupidity. I'm the one who *bought* that stuff as a description more or less of the real thing. Oh, yes, I knew the old joke about why a college catalogue and the college grounds are alike—they both "lie about" the campus. But I didn't *think* hard enough about it, and I didn't take what now looks like the rather elementary precaution of visiting this place before deciding.

Only if you've ever lived in a Quincy dorm can you guess at just how badly I was fooled, when I went to live in that "house." First of all the roommates. Instead of living by myself with a beautiful brunette in a room across the hall, I found myself living with three other guys—four men to a room!

You remember those spacious rooms with the high ceilings and comfortable chairs? I was assigned not to a single, as the catalogue sort of promised, but to a "suite." It turned out there were in fact 25 singles—for an entering class of 1200! That meant for most of us four to a room, four rooms in a kind of quadrangle with a tiny kitchenette in the center. Sixteen of us sharing a hotplate, 64 of us sharing a bathroom (when you could get in; Quincy has developed some of my powers of retention)—that's what it amounted to! In my room, the four of us had a total of two chairs, two lamps, and two desks. You can imagine how much studying we managed to get done.

Have you ever tried to study with three other people in a room 8 feet by 14 feet, a room containing four single beds (stacked two and two, of course), two desks, two chairs, and only two lamps? Each room does contain—I want to be honest—a single hundred watt bulb screwed into the low ceiling, so the room is not quite as dark as I imagine the brainy (malicious? fiendish?) architect hoped it would be. But if you happen to have one of the lower bunks, as this reporter did for fourteen solid weeks, you find yourself—when it's not your turn to have a chair at one of the desks—either taking notes in shadow or leaning far out in order to catch the light from the ceiling. In my third week I had to check in at Student Health because of back problems. It took four visits before we figured out that my only problem was studying a couple of hours each night with my body shaped like a pretzel.

Of course we soon learned to do most of our studying in the library, but the conversational din there is shut out every weekend night at 10:30, and on Saturdays and Sundays— would you believe it?—they close at 6! Then it's back to that room-of-rooms, those "well-designed quarters where life-long friendships are cemented in bull sessions that last into the wee hours." Oh, we've had the bull sessions, all right, some of them not bad. But nobody wants to shoot the bull with the same three people day in and day out, especially when two of them turn out to be better at snoring than at conversation.

Oh, did I mention the temperature? It so happened that there was an energy conservation drive on throughout the college last winter. They kept the temperature in our room at 64 degrees—which "scientists have determined is most conducive to alert study." That meant that we lived under blankets most of the time. There was no room to exercise without stepping on somebody, so we just lay there, or sat in the straight-backed chairs when it was our turn not to be lying down—covered with a blanket and cursing the day we chose Quincy.

That abominable room was largely to blame for the terrible showing I made the first semester here. In the second semester enough kids had washed out—another thing the catalogue didn't mention; Quincy has the highest drop-out rate of any college in the state—to allow us to have only two to a room, and things got a little better.

I know it may seem unreasonable of me, but I have been

wondering whether the faculty members at this place care enough about students' welfare—and about the unnecessarily high drop-out rate—to protest to *somebody* about those abominable rooms?

Sam estimates that he now has about 1200–1300 words, and his teacher has made an absolute rule that the essays must not be shorter than 700 or longer than 1000. But he now has a draft that promises something pretty good. His next steps are not simply to cut but to *improve while cutting.* He is now ready to go back through the essay, looking to strengthen each sentence and paragraph.

Bringing in the voice of the opposition

Before turning in Chapter 4 to the ways in which Sam might improve his paragraphs and sentences, consider one last important point about discovering your thesis: As you think about your purpose try to state explicitly the arguments that might be offered *against* it. This move was not particularly useful to Sam, because he already had plenty to say about the abominable dorm, and what he had to say has a sharp (and therefore potentially interesting) controversial edge to it. But most thesis statements can be made more vital by recognizing from the beginning what the best opponents to your thesis might say.

Not just: For students like me, some federal tax relief is indispensable, if we are to stay in college.

But: *In spite of all that is said these days about the need to cut federal spending,* one kind of cut is disastrous: for students like me, some federal tax relief is indispensable to our remaining in college.

Not just: Hemingway's short story is in part a disguised attack on Margot.

But: *Although "feminist criticism" may be misleading when it oversimplifies stories and treats them like simple statements from their authors,* I am forced to agree with feminist arguments that Hemingway has used his short story as a vehicle for attacking a certain kind of woman . . .

As soon as the "although" or "in spite of" clauses get into your thesis, the resulting conflict will itself begin to suggest ideas for developing your points. The general form of this kind of thinking about your thesis runs like this:

Although such-and-such can be said against my case, *I still conclude* thus-and-so.

Conclusion

When we take the "although" clauses as seriously as our original notions, we are practicing a particular version of what we should always be doing as we write: *thinking* about our purposes in the context of complications and objections, not just trying to impose them dogmatically on the world.

In seeking for the purpose we really want to achieve, and in pursuing a thesis that we have discovered is really defensible, we are steadily increasing our understanding of the world, which necessarily includes not just our picture of how things are but also the rival pictures constructed by our possible readers.

Genuine thinking of this kind can lead to a curious effect that will sometimes feel like trouble: The objections you can think of may begin to make better and better sense, until finally they outshine your original thesis. Such moments can seem minor tragedies when they occur at 3:00 A.M. on a morning when the essay is due by 9:00 A.M. But when our "enemies" speak with so much power that we are shaken into thought or changed belief, we come out of the encounter with our minds stretched far beyond where they were when we went in. At that point, learning how to think productively and critically about our rhetorical purposes becomes learning how to educate ourselves.

ESSAY ASSIGNMENT

In this essay assignment, we suggest that you think of somebody who does not know something you know, or who disbelieves something that you know well or believe strongly, or who is acting in a way that you think is wrong. Write an essay, perhaps in the form of a letter or memo, in which you attempt to instruct that person, or change his or her beliefs or actions. You may choose one of the purposes you described in the Notebook Entry asked for on pp. 69–71. Or you may think of some other purpose that now interests you more. If you know of a whole group of people who are ignorant of something important, or who have the wrong belief about something, or who are acting badly, address them as a group.

Examples

> Teach a friend how to assemble or repair a piece of equipment you both care about.
>
> Write a letter to the student newspaper attacking some abuse on campus, or recommending some change in procedures.
>
> Write a review of a book or movie or TV program you admire, persuading your reader(s) to read it or view it.
>
> Write a letter to your fellow workers explaining to them why their attitudes about the boss (or management in general) are either justified or unjustified.
>
> Attack or defend the use of alcohol, tobacco, or other drugs.
>
> Debate the validity of an argument found in any essay you have recently read, or in a section of this book.

Warning: Be careful not to take on too large a topic ("drugs" or "Chapter 3" may be much too large). It is probably a mistake at this stage to try to change someone's mind about such complex issues as arms control or abortion.

Think hard about your purpose before you start writing. (Many people find it useful, in this planning stage, to follow Sam's practice and scribble some disorganized notes on a few sheets of scrap paper—any ideas that come to mind. These notes are often quite chaotic, but they make it possible to think for awhile, more or less irresponsibly, about how they relate—or don't relate—to each other.)

After playing with your disorganized possibilities, and deciding which ones really contribute strongly to your purpose, throw the others away or save them for another essay.

Next, spend some time trying out different patterns for the strongest sub-points you have selected. List your main points. Which point should come first, which last? (Usually your strongest point should be promised at the beginning and then fully delivered at the end.) Sometimes a written outline is useful at this stage, though often for a short paper you may be able to keep your points clear in your head without one.

Once you start writing a draft, be sure to let the words and sentences flow as freely as possible, without worrying about grammar and spelling. Leave space between the lines, so that later you can write in corrections and improvements. Most writers can do a better version by working in this way—making a fairly quick first draft followed by painstaking revision—than by trying to get it all right the first time.

Keep your final draft as short as seems reasonable, but don't worry about length as an objective in itself. Thinking about purposes means trying to do the job *right,* not just producing a pile of words. If as you write you think of a more challenging or interesting purpose, follow *it* wherever it leads.

4

Pursuing purposes with paragraphs and sentences

Paragraphs

The point of paragraphing

So far we have stressed the importance of finding a central purpose for each essay—a purpose that helps to control all of the other decisions you make. And we have shown some of the thinking that helps us discover and shape our purposes. The same kind of thinking applies to every paragraph and sentence of any essay. Paragraphs are organized to make points that allow the essay to work as a completed whole. Sentences are organized to make points that allow for the success of paragraphs. And words? Well, in a sense words too are organized—or at least chosen—to achieve the purpose of the sentence.

Actually you already know a good deal about how paragraphs are made, because you *experience* paragraphs in everything you read. It is not just that we see the indentations that signify paragraphs. Paragraphs existed long before writers decided to use indentation. To some degree we all tend to think in the blocks or middle-sized units that visible paragraphing was invented to dramatize.

Here is the beginning of the book *Thomas Jefferson,* by Gene Lisitsky (1933). (Gene was the pen name for Genevieve.) We print it without the paragraphing that Lisitsky actually employed.

TWO DIFFERENT WORLDS

To say that Thomas Jefferson, third President of the United States, was born in 1743 in what was then the British Colony of Virginia would mean very little. For in those days the people who lived in the eastern and western halves of Virginia were so different in their attitude and way of life that it could be said that although they spoke the same language and were ruled by the same Government they lived on two different continents, or even in two different worlds. The families who lived in the eastern half of the colony, along the Atlantic coast, still thought and talked about England as "home." They were determined to remain as English as those who had never left England. Most of them could not have gone on living in this strange New World, to which they had come to seek their fortunes, without the latest books and newspapers from England, the latest clothes and small talk from London, the newest comforts and inventions from Liverpool. If for some reason they had been cut off from all these things most of them would probably have gone back, rather than do without them. On the other hand the families who lived inland, in the western half of the colony, were people who thought of themselves not as Englishmen but as Americans. To them "home" was not the British Isles but the thirteen colonies on the Atlantic seacoast. They were not greatly interested in what was happening in England except as it affected their own interest; they looked west, toward the great unknown areas which seemed so full of promise of a full and free life, rather than east toward the Old World, with its injustices, cruelties, and quarrels which had been in existence for so long that it seemed nothing could ever bring them to an end. To which of these two worlds did Thomas Jefferson belong? The answer—and perhaps it is this which

made his life so valuable and the story of it so interesting—
is that he belonged to neither, and yet in a way to both. For,
born as he was on the borderline between the two, he grew
up to look both east and west, to get what was best from
both, and in a sense to help bring them together.

NOTEBOOK ENTRY

Now read through the passage again and mark the places (in
pencil, so that you can erase later if you want to) where you
think the author would have begun each new paragraph. (Use
the printer's mark ¶.)

    Remember: Each paragraph should make a single unified
point or exhibit a single *purpose.* You may find some one sentence
that states that point directly. Such a sentence, when it occurs,
is called a *thesis sentence,* but though all good paragraphs support
a thesis, not all good paragraphs contain an explicit thesis
sentence. If you have any trouble marking the breaks, think
carefully about the title and then read the passage again.

    After you have paragraphed the introduction, take a few
more minutes to explain why you put the marks where you did.
Part of your way of explaining might be to underline the
sentence in each paragraph that seems to you to summarize best
the single point that the paragraph adds.

Now let's see how well you and Lisitsky agree about paragraph breaks. Her own occur at these spots:

2. For in those days . . .

3. The families who lived in the eastern half . . .

4. On the other hand the families who lived inland . . .

5. To which of these two worlds did Thomas Jefferson belong?

How did you do? The only surprises we found in Lisitsky's
paragraphing came at Number 2. Ordinarily we would not use a
one-sentence paragraph as the beginning of an essay, chapter, or

book. Do you see any good reason for her using one here? We suspect she wanted to emphasize this sentence most strongly because it states the thesis for the whole chapter.

The other choices are unmistakable. Paragraph 2 makes the point that East and West Virginians "lived on two different continents, or even in two different worlds." Such a statement implies a promised explanation, since everyone knows that Virginia was not in fact on two different continents.

Paragraph 3 then describes the first "continent," with the first sentence serving as a clear topic sentence. Paragraph 4 describes the second "continent," the first two sentences together constituting the thesis statement. These descriptions set up Paragraph 5, which gives us the point of the whole section: Jefferson straddled the two "continents."

Note that since Lisitsky offers no evidence for the surprising claim that Jefferson belongs to two such different worlds, the section as a whole seems to promise that it will produce such evidence later on: documentation or argument to show just how Jefferson belonged to both eastern and western Virginia. The purpose of the chapter (and for all we can know so far, perhaps of the whole book) is thus made emphatically clear: By arranging her paragraphs as a sequence of clear points leading to her main initial point, Lisitsky ensures that no careful reader is likely to go astray, and that readers careful and careless will have good reasons for reading on—to find whether or not the initial points are supported. As you have probably noticed in your reading, some kinds of writing depend less heavily on paragraphing than Lisitsky's; some journalism indents almost every sentence, and some fiction offers paragraphs several pages long. Clearly, then, the content and size of paragraphs may vary widely, but their functions remain largely the same: to mark off blocks of thought.

NOTEBOOK ENTRY

It is always profitable to experiment with different arrangements of the same points. Try now for a few moments to read the paragraphs in a different order: 32451, say, or 54123. Can you find any other orders that work as well as Lisitsky's? The progress of her sentences is so clear that even if she had not used "On the other hand," to introduce Paragraph 4, we would still have no difficulty figuring out that we are moving from the East, in 3, to the West, in 4. Why, then, do you suppose that Lisitsky chose to underline the point of the transition, by adding the words, "On the other hand"?

Write a sentence or two as a possible answer.

Reorganizing paragraphs

Here is a paper by a beginning college student. Read it carefully, asking whether it seems all devoted to a single purpose. Does Rebekah include any useless details?

THE ADVANTAGES OF WRITING ON A WORD PROCESSOR

(a) More and more writers are now discovering the advan- (1) tages of writing on word processors. (b) Many colleges now provide access to computer terminals for all students. (c) I think that the advantages of computers far outweigh the disadvantages, and that the college should start working on this problem *now.* (d) One of the biggest weaknesses of this college is that we don't have computer access for students yet. (e) Every year more and more people are buying personal processors for use at their desks. (f) The old-fashioned ways of writing by hand or on a typewriter seem less and less satisfactory as the advantages of word processors become evident.

(a) The first one is the most obvious: speed in composing. (2) (b) Anybody can type faster on a word processor, because the electronic letters, which require no mechanical force, can be formed faster than by the fastest electric typewriter.

(a) Even more important, corrections can be made instan- (3) taneously, without retyping anything but the word or phrase to be corrected. (b) My teacher in Intro. to Lit. always makes fun of word processors. (c) He says he still writes everything by hand, because he can choose the words more carefully that way. (d) I'd like to tell him that I think he'd write a lot faster if he learned to use a word processor. (e) The second advantage is that you can get clean copies so easily that you do more revision, so your writing improves. (f) When I used to write by hand, the notion of having to copy the whole thing over was just horrifying, so I wouldn't make any changes unless I absolutely had to. (g) Now I make changes freely and don't worry about it at all.

(a) I write on an Acme 22 using the Word Easy program. (4) (b) It lacks some of the features of the more sophisticated programs, but it's OK. (c) Some of my friends who are computer buffs spend a lot of time shopping around for which are the best writing programs. (d) That probably wastes some time, so it isn't true that computers always speed things up.

(a) The third advantage is that you don't get as tired as (5) soon. (b) I used to find it easier to read than write, so when I had some spare moments I would sit down with a book. (c) Now I find it easier to write than read, so in my spare moments I just sit down and enjoy turning out words on my machine. (d) I own one of these special kneeling-chairs so I am really comfortable. (e) I can sit—or kneel—writing much longer at a stretch than I could before.

(a) In the "old days," I can remember once writing a final (6) draft, in ink, and just as I wrote the final word, I noticed that I had left out a whole paragraph, so the paper didn't make good sense. (b) I had only five minutes until class time, so I just had to hand in the paper in the garbled form. (c) Sometimes though you can have troubles with a word processor, too. (d) It can get pretty funny, sometimes, when you think you have lost your text—the program has crashed, or something, and you may have lost a whole night's work. (e) But usually if you play around a while, or ask for some advice, you can find out what happened and get your lost stuff back. (f) One time though that didn't work, and I had a hard time convincing the teacher next day that not having a paper was the computer's fault.

(a) I think that the students here should all organize a (7) protest about our not having computer access. (b) Everybody's work would improve if we could write on word processors. (c) It is not fair for some students, like me, to be able to afford their own computers and other students still have to write by hand or on a typewriter. (d) I read in a computer magazine that several manufacturers are willing to subsidize colleges for arranging college-wide deals, with up to 50% knock-down for individual buyers. (e) It would be ridiculous not to take advantage of a deal like that.

It's easy to see that Rebekah has not yet organized things very well. Both the essay as a whole and her individual paragraphs read about the way our first drafts almost always read—more like notes toward an essay than like a coherent engagement with a clear purpose.

NOTEBOOK ENTRY

What steps might Rebekah take to make the essay work? Use your notebook now to take those steps for her; then compare your results with ours.

Decide which of Rebekah's several purposes is going to rule over the others. What seems to you the most prominent purpose in the piece as it stands? Write a sentence or two now summarizing that purpose.

Did you choose something like "She wants to get the college to install computers (or perhaps even to organize and *force* the college to do it)"? That seems to us the point that most of her material now supports, and it serves to organize most of her first paragraph. But you might also decide that she is more interested in writing about, "My amusing struggle with word processors," or, "Writing disasters, old and new." Perhaps least inviting is the purpose that she slides toward in several sentences: "How word processing works"—a simple step-by-step description.

Let's assume that she chooses to revise in order to strengthen *the appeal to the college,* and that after thinking about it a bit she rejects the idea of a protest demonstration and elects instead to find the strongest arguments she can think of, organized as well as possible. Can you determine what material would then have to be cut?

Write your answers out like this—numbering the sentences within each paragraph: "Sentence 1-e must go because—at least as it stands—it has nothing to do with the case made about the college."

Did you cut the following?

- Paragraph 3, sentences c, d, and e, Rebekah's remarks to her professor
- All of Paragraph 4, the reference to shopping around for programs
- Everything after "c" in Paragraph 6 (though *maybe* these descriptions of problems could be recast to help Rebekah's case)

Now let's reorganize the first paragraph, to make it a more forceful introduction to "the case for computers."

In what order do you think the sentences work best? Try out different sequences until you find one that seems right. You may want to add a phrase or sentence here and there.

Now write out your new paragraph.

When we do this exercise, we find the opening paragraph going like this (words that we have added to Rebekah's are in brackets):

(d) One of the biggest weaknesses of this college is that we don't have general computer access for students yet. (b) [In this we are falling behind the] Many colleges [that] now provide access to computer terminals for all students. (f) [Administrators at those colleges have discovered that] The old-fashioned ways of writing by hand or on a typewriter seem less and less satisfactory as the advantages of word processors become evident. (a) Indeed, more and more writers are now discovering the advantages of writing on word processors. (c) I [too] think that the advantages of computers far outweigh the disadvantages, and I am convinced that because of these advantages this college should initiate a program next year.

Now that the paragraph is reorganized, Rebekah can see that it is extremely repetitive, and needs some trimming. But she can also see what direction to take—for example, now that she has the most important "promise" at the end, she can sharpen its effect by changing it from a flat announcement to an inviting question: "What are these advantages?"

She can also now see that some other paragraphs are extremely thin. While working in the original draft to dramatize her personal experiences, she neglected to make the various *advantages* vivid and forceful. So now she can go through the advantages and work up a good paragraph on each one. If she can think of ways to make her personal experience count for her case, fine. If not, she may have to refer to other people's experience.

If we were to work further on Rebekah's paper, we would want to develop the paragraphs like this:

Paragraphs 2 and 3 should be joined, and then developed with some evidence or examples. Do you see why?

"The second advantage" needs more illustration. Might Rebekah actually describe how she revises her prose using a word processor?

"The third advantage" needs to be thought about some more. Will it really seem like an advantage to anyone planning for the college? Should it perhaps be brought up as a possible objection ("students may read less")—and then turned to an advantage, because in the long run we can predict (she might say) that those who write more will want to read more?

Paragraph 6, now that it is shorn of the irrelevant stuff about troubles with processors, looks skinny. Can the troubles with processors still be used, as another possible objection? ("Of course processors can make trouble too, *for beginners.* But that's all the more reason for having them available. Computers are here to stay; our graduates are going to have to know how to use them. We'll be much better off making our mistakes in college, where we are supposed to be learning, than later on when the consequences of mistakes may be much more serious.")

Paragraph 7, now that Rebekah is clear about the nature of her argument with college officials, needs some reworking. It raises an issue that she has not addressed sufficiently in her essay (unfairness to students who lack money). If she gives this point a separate paragraph in the body of the essay, then the final paragraph could conclude that "for all these reasons the college should seriously consider providing increased access to computers for student writers, especially since the cost will not be as great as might appear."

Sentences

We'll be doing more work with paragraph organization later, especially in Chapter 5. For now, the important point is that what we have said about paragraphs applies to sentences as well. Though a sentence usually has fewer and of course smaller "parts," it also, for most purposes, needs to be organized carefully to make a single point. In fact, that's what a sentence is defined as: "the smallest unit of discourse that makes a single point." This definition should not be confused with what we've already said about the "single" points made by paragraphs, sections, and whole essays. Sentences are the smallest units that make an intelligible point. Note that some "sentences" are thus very small indeed: single words or phrases that imply unspoken parts:

"Absolutely."
"Right on!"
"Not on your life!"
"Oh, yeah!"
"Are you finished?" "Not quite."

These phrases have no spoken subjects or verbs, so they can hardly be called conventional sentences. But they can easily be translated into fully articulated sentences by providing both the unspoken subject and the unspoken verb: "No, I am not quite finished."

Making points with sentences

The slightest change of wording can sometimes make an immense difference in the emphasis of a sentence:

While the general idea of this essay is sound, the details, sentence by sentence, are badly in need of revision!

OR

While the details of this essay are badly in need of revision, the general idea is sound!

Though the term is half over, we still have seven weeks.

OR

Though we still have seven weeks in the term, it is half over.

Both sentences in each pair convey exactly the same literal information, but the emphasis is shifted radically by the reversal of clauses. And this is just one of many kinds of changes that you can achieve as you practice revising sentences with specific purposes in mind.

If you are having trouble with sentences—either their structure or their punctuation—remember that you learned the basic rules for making English sentences by the time you were three—without the benefit of schooling! A character in Molière's play, *The Bourgeois Gentleman,* is proud to learn from a grammarian that he has been speaking *prose* all his life without knowing it. Well, you have been making good sentences all your life, and you have a lot of experience in recognizing when sentences do not make a point, or when they make the wrong point at the wrong time. If you doubt our word, pause now and do the following exercise.

NOTEBOOK ENTRY

Here is the sixth paragraph of Lisitsky's book on Jefferson, printed without her punctuation (just as the earliest books had no paragraph markings, they also had no punctuation; every reader had to do what you are now asked to do). We've added a sentence that makes the wrong point for this paragraph. Now put in the periods wherever you think they belong. Do it in pencil, so that you can make changes on second thought. Then put parentheses around the one unit, the one "point," that does not belong in this paragraph. You can fill in commas too, if you want, but they are not our business here.

The differences between these two worlds are based on the division of Virginia into east and west halves divided by a long range of mountains called the Appalachians from these mountains Virginia's rivers start on their journey to the Atlantic Jefferson always loved geography and architectural design and filled notebooks with maps and plans for half the distance to that ocean the rivers are just ordinary streams not very wide with little waterfalls here and there the country they flow through is somewhat hilly and is called the Piedmont which means simply "foothills."

You probably had no difficulty putting periods after "Appalachians," "Atlantic," "plans," and "there." If you placed any elsewhere, or missed any of these, go back to the paragraph and think about it again. After all, we authors may have missed something.

No doubt you also noticed that the sentence beginning with "Jefferson" just does not belong in this context. The point of the paragraph is Virginia's geography, not Jefferson's interest in it. The sentence about him makes a point that might well belong at some other place in the book (though we made it up); but it certainly does not belong here.

Losing the point

The point of a sentence can be blunted or twisted if the sentence is badly organized. A sentence should make its point with the reader like a firm handshake, not like a limp wave of the hand in passing. In thinking further about how sentences make their effects or contribute to meaning, the most important general rule is that each sentence should lead the reader from the one before to the one after, with the greatest possible force—force of the kind appropriate to those surrounding points. To carry their proper force, or weight, sentences must be organized so that they do, in fact, lead from *before* to *after* without diminishing the reader's engagement.

Lisitsky might have written her third paragraph like this (compare this paragraph with Lisitsky's on page 87):

The families who lived in the eastern half of the colony, along the Atlantic Coast, still thought and talked about England as "home." Just as those who had never left England still thought of England as home, so did those who had come to Virginia. The latest books and newspapers from England, the latest clothes and small talk from London, the newest comforts and inventions from Liverpool—all these were thought to be necessary by those who had come to seek their fortunes in Virginia; they could not have gone on living without them, in this strange New World. In my opinion, judging from the documents of the time, it seems likely that the inhabitants of the eastern part would have preferred to go back to England, if for some reason they had been cut off from the good things that still all seemed to come from "back home."

This new paragraph has no grammatical or spelling errors. Each sentence in itself is not badly formed, and they are all in the same order as before. But because the sentences are not shaped to lead from *before* to *after*, they lose much of their force (They lack **cohesion**, the quality we will study in Chapter 7.) For now it will be useful simply to ask yourself which version, Lisitsky's or ours, gives the reader more help in both reading *and* grasping what is being said.

NOTEBOOK ENTRY

We should take a few moments now to dramatize the difference between the original third paragraph and the one we have just written. A good way to do that is to draw pencil lines between the units in each sentence that lead the reader's attention forward or backward. (If you need an example of how to do this, see pages 405–406 in Chapter 13.) Generally speaking, the more such lines you can draw, and the shorter those lines are, the better the writing will seem to the reader. Another way is to underline those words and phrases that make it possible for you to draw the lines: all the "thises" and "thuses," the "therefores" and "howevers." (You may want to consult our list of "connections," on pages 202–208 of Chapter 7.)

Do you find a strong difference between your "drawings" of the two paragraphs?

Another way to see how sentence structure can bind or lose a reader's attention is to imagine yourself cutting up the paragraphs into strips of paper, one sentence per strip, and then throwing them into a fan. Would a reader who picked up those strips find it easy to reassemble the paragraph? Which paragraph would give greater problems? A paragraph that any attentive reader can reassemble correctly can be said to have passed "the fan test." No paragraph will pass it easily unless each sentence is designed to lead clearly from the sentence before it to the sentence that follows. In general, effective sentences lead off with a reference backward, explicit or implied, and end with a promise or hint leading forward.

ESSAY ASSIGNMENTS:

1. Copy out Lisitsky's paragraph on 3×5 index cards, one sentence per card, each card numbered on the back in its correct order. Then scramble the cards and number them in their scrambled order on the front of the card.

Next, solicit the help of a few people who are not using this text. Give the cards in the same scrambled order to these friends, and ask them to arrange the sentences in the best order for a good paragraph. (Do not define "best order" or "good paragraph" for them.) Keep a record of each person's final order.

Now write an essay to your classmates describing and interpreting your results. If several people made the same mistake in ordering, for example, you might question whether Lisitsky's order is as clear as it should have been. And so on.

2. *Alternative Essay:* We cannot predict what this little game will yield. If you learn anything interesting about paragraphing or sentence structure from it, or if the game doesn't work, we'd like to hear about it. Write an essay addressed to us at Harper & Row Publishers, College English Division, 10 E. 53rd St., New York, NY 10022, describing what you have learned and making suggestions about how we might revise this part of our chapter for the second edition.

Revising sentences

No sentence is good for all occasions. When we meet a sentence sitting by itself we can tell whether it is ungrammatical or redundant or full of **solecisms** (expressions considered absurd or non-idiomatic in English). What we cannot tell is whether a wider context might call for bad grammar or redundancy. Purpose ultimately dominates sentences just as it dominates design, tone, use of evidence, and other matters. A sentence that is perfect in an essay called "Why I hate politics" might be jarring or nonsensical in an essay called "Six reasons every American should be politically active." It might even seem ironically pompous in a piece of satire directed at politicians. Whether a sentence is good, then, must be determined by how well it performs its assigned job in furthering the aims of a specific essay.

This means that there are many kinds of good sentences. It does not mean that there is no such thing as a bad sentence. No matter how much readers may like our purposes, they will be annoyed whenever we offer them carelessly constructed sentences. They will rightly take sloppy sentences as a sign of sloppy thinking and lack of consideration. Even on those occasions, rare for most of us, when our purposes dictate a violation of normal **syntax** (sentence structure) or grammatical rules, we will find a real difference between "perfected" sentences that do their job and the misshapen monsters that we often toss off in our first drafts, when our attention must often be on other matters.

We suggest now a few guidelines that may help you improve your sentences from one draft to the next. We all need what we might call "general-purpose sentences," even if we cannot use them for *all* purposes. Our guidelines should not be confused with strict rules, but if used as a kind of checklist, they can help you avoid the most common problems: sentences that are flabby, unclear, awkward, or absurd.

Wordiness and excessive length. By and large your sentences should strive for the kind of tautness that athletes and dancers call having "thin skin": no fat underneath the skin, no excess body weight. They should be in racing trim: taut enough to leave the starting block without stumbling, to move without sagging by the middle of the race, and to finish without trailing off in exhaustion.

This statement, despite the flashy metaphor, is at least half false. All such generalizations can be confronted with many exceptions. Looking to the history of English writing, one finds that none of the great writers of the past wrote in the thin-skinned style generally admired in our time (although some of them were "thin skinned" in the sense of hypersensitive). Shakespeare, John Milton, Thomas Browne, Samuel Johnson, Cardinal Newman— most authors considered great stylists—created sentences that would not escape the red pencil of editors who passionately distrust "redundancy," "pleonism," "deadwood" or "excess baggage." These authors practiced a kind of "copiousness" or eloquence that the rhetoric texts of their time recommended; they felt that much good writing results from saying the same thing in many different and colorful ways. To remove all excess, they would have said, is to remove all color and passion. There was a time earlier in this century when many writers—Ernest Hemingway perhaps most notably—took the opposite position. To them, good style meant prose shorn of all visible adornment: "Down with all adjectives and adverbs." Even today one often reads unthinking claims that economy is all we need.

Here are a few typical sentences written in the more ornate style praised by past generations of readers and still admired by many today. (Do not worry if these sentences fail to make good sense to you. Out of context they are relatively flat, probably even puzzling. Look at them simply as examples of a kind of elaboration or ornateness that an overly rigorous application of our first guideline would ban.)

And after all, if men differ in their opinions concerning such matters, their difference is not attended with the same important consequences, else I make no doubt that the logic of Taste, if I may be allowed the expression, might very possibly be as well digested, and we might come to discuss matters of this nature with as much certainty, as those which seem more immediately within the province of mere reason. [Edmund Burke, "Introduction on Taste." In *Of the Sublime* (1768).]

Some authors, indeed, do far more than this, and indulge themselves in such confidential depths of revelation as could fittingly be addressed, only and exclusively, to the one heart and mind of perfect sympathy; as if the printed book, thrown at large in the wide world, were certain to find out the divided segment of the writer's own nature, and complete his circle of existence by bringing him into communion with it. [Nathaniel Hawthorne, "The Custom House." In the introduction to *The Scarlet Letter* (1850).]

I conceive him to indicate that the realistic method of a conscientious transcription of all the visible, and a repetition of all the audible, is mainly accountable for our present branfulness, and for that prolongation of the hasty and the noisy out of which, as from an undrained fen, steams the malady of sameness, our modern malady. [George Meredith, "Prelude." In *The Egoist* (1879).]

It filled her with exasperation to think that he should be necessary to the happiness of his victims (she had learned that whatever they might talk about with her, it was of him and him only that they discoursed among themselves), and one of the main recommendations of the evening club for her fatigued, underpaid sisters, which it had long been her dream to establish, was that it would in some degree undermine his position—distinct as her prevision might be that he would be in waiting at the door. [Henry James, *The Bostonians* (1886)].

Obviously athletic tautness is not a universal ideal of sentence construction. On the other hand, if our guideline is half false, it is also half true. Unless you are already an experienced writer with a fairly well-developed voice of your own, you probably need to think about "cutting down," "shearing off," "weeding out," or "cutting deadwood" before you worry about being cramped or inhibited by concision. Most beginning writers are plagued with the problem of wordiness. You should do some thinking about where you fall on the continuum from "using too many words that are drones, doing no work," to "using too few words to achieve the desired effect." You may find, as we do, that some occasions call for more effective cutting down (simplification), and some for more building up (amplification).

For now, we are working on the side of simplification. One of the main reasons for mastering tight, trim sentences is that most of your college and work writing will be expository prose, not the prose of fiction or drama. Usually the greatest possible *clarity* is essential in such prose because its main job is to expound ideas and commitments. You only defeat yourself if your readers cannot clearly understand your positions and arguments. We all need to make our sentences clearer, more emphatic, even more elegant. But few writers ever turn out perfectly formed sentences on the first stroke. They learn how to shape their sentences as they perform a kind of spiral activity, moving back and forth from one version to another, each one a revision of the former, and each one coming closer and closer to a polished finish.

If you will go back and take a look now at the opening paragraph of this book, the one that turned out *not* to be the way to begin a book, you will see that we loaded it with the kind of wordiness we are talking about. The purpose of that paragraph is clear enough, but the sentences are bloated. That paragraph's wordiness—wordiness without any justification in style or substance—is the kind that almost all writers fall into, especially early in a writing project when their minds are focused not on sentence structure but on the many other problems that plague beginnings. Each of us must then "turn against" those flabby sentences (as Gregory turned against Booth), and work off the fat.

When we speak to each other we tend to be relaxed, even careless, about using more words than we need. In fact we often use certain all-purpose phrases as filler, even though they carry little or no meaning in themselves. We may very well say, "In the case of the students . . ." when there has been no "case" at all and we only mean something like, "As for students . . ." or, "Students, in contrast . . ." We may say, "So far as the significance of space flight is concerned . . ." when all we need is, "About space flight we may say . . ." or just, "The significance of space flight is . . .".

All of us use a long list of such fillers when we want to hold the floor and haven't quite got hold of our next sentence: fillers such as "with regard to" (rather than "about"), "at this point in time" (rather than "today" or "now" or "these days"), "in this connection I would like to say" (rather than "I think this" or "About that I can only say"). We throw in "factors" and "aspects" and "areas" and "levels" whether they say anything or not. We pad our speech with empty phrases like "in terms of," "in relation to," "as regards the aforementioned," and "with reference to."

The trouble is that this kind of "educated jargon" is so widespread among administrators, bureaucrats, and other people who want to sound educated that our ears have become deaf to it. It ceases to jar us and then we become infected ourselves. Once we start using these words and phrases in our formal writing, they function as dead weight and drag our sentences to a halt. A literary critic writes in *The New York Times*, "As far as this reader was concerned, 'A Corner of a Foreign Field' remains the finest story in the collection." The opening phrase might be partially justified if the critic had just been talking about *other* people's opinion and needed a strong connection. But all he means is, "I thought 'A Corner . . .' the finest story . . ."—eight words saved and not a sliver of meaning lost.

Given the growth of such mealy-mouthed language in the prose of business, government, and institutions (even educational institutions), and given the universal tendency of all inexperienced writers to use such verbiage without realizing it, the half-truth about striving for a thin-skinned sentence style should be taken seriously by every learning writer—and should continue to be taken seriously until enough mastery is achieved that it can be ignored safely. You will always find occasions for continuing to work on that other half-truth, learning how to amplify, complicate, and vary your sentences for special effects. But reaching too early for complications would be like trying to do a backwards no-hands flip before you know how to do a forward roll.

SENTENCE PRACTICE

Wordiness

Here is a paragraph from a letter written by James Thurber to E. B. White, listed as a series of consecutive sentences. We have inserted additional, unnecessary words into each sentence, not straining to cram in as many words as possible, but choosing the kinds that spoil many a sentence. (The number of words added is noted in brackets at the end of each sentence.) After reading the whole paragraph, revise each sentence, pruning words that make the sentences fat or that muffle and blunt their effect.

1. It is impossible to have any faith at all in the full-grown adult male in these days: he continues in typical manner to boggle everything as he always has boggled it. [5 added words]
2. But because he is doing this I see no good or sound reason why I should go to pieces personally. [6 added words]

3. I see every reason in the world not to. [3 added words]

4. I don't think that manning the barricades is an answer to the issue, nor giving up appreciation of and interest in such fine, pleasant, and funny things as may still be around. [5 added words]

5. A couple of Englishmen have written books recently saying that the better minds, the finer souls, the nobler spirits, should kind of go into a monastary, form a group on the old pattern of the isolated, hermit-like monks, and see if that wouldn't help things out any. [6 added words]

6. Everybody wants to do something strange, and as far as I am concerned, is doing it. [8 added words]

7. It remains for a few people to stand and watch them and make a report to the rest of us about what it all looks and sounds like. [8 added words]

8. Among such persons who can do this there isn't anybody more soundly or better qualified for the job of doing this than you are. [10 added words]

9. If you will quit sending pieces to that weekly magazine, *The Saturday Evening Post.* [3 added words]

10. I have pondered and pondered all day long about you sending your piece the Memoirs of a Master there. [5 added words]

11. What was the matter with that excellent weekly magazine called *The New Yorker* by its publishers? [4 added words]

12. It is important to everyone concerned that things like Memoirs of a Master be printed for public consumption and perusal and continue to be printed. [8 added words]

13. I wish you would explain to me in so many words what all this *Post* business is really about, anyway. [6 added words]

14. That's not your audience who will like your stuff. [5 added words]

15. Of course, it does no good at all to try to reason with you in a rational way in these matters, but still I keep on trying. [9 added words]

16. I not only feel, but I also know as an accepted fact, that anyone who can write the way you do has to keep on writing. [3 added words]

17. I don't mean to refer at all to any crap about the Urge or anything like that. [5 added words]

18. I mean to say that it is a point of solid moral necessity. [4 added words]

19. It seems to be easy for you to rationalize, deprecate, and dismiss this, but I don't think that in my considered opinion it will really work for you to do it. [10 added words]
20. Like tucking sex in the back of your mind and saying well, I guess, everything considered, that's *that* . . . [4 added words]

How did you do? Adding all these extra words is like stuffing insulation around the words that really work, making dead-air spots where all movement seems to cease.

Here is the Thurber passage restored to its original trim shape. Compare his sentences with your revisions. You might discuss in class whether Thurber's own versions could have been made even livelier with a little pruning, as in the phrase "kind of" in sentence 5. But remember, he was writing a letter, not a piece to be published, and his lean prose was probably a first draft.

(1) It is impossible to have any faith at all in the adult male in these days: he continues to boggle everything as he always has boggled it. (2) But because he is doing this I see no reason to go to pieces personally. (3) I see every reason not to. (4) I don't think the barricades is an answer, nor giving up appreciation of and interest in such fine, pleasant, and funny things as may still be around. (5) A couple of Englishmen have written books recently saying that the better minds, the finer souls, the nobler spirits, should kind of go into a monastery, form a group on the old pattern of the monks, and see if that wouldn't help. (6) Everybody wants to do something strange, and is.

(7) It remains for a few people to stand and watch them and report what it all looks like and sounds like. (8) Among such persons there isn't anybody better qualified for the job than you. (9) If you will quit sending pieces to *The Saturday Evening Post.* (10) I have pondered all day about you sending the Memoirs of a Master there. (11) What was the matter with that excellent weekly called *The New Yorker*? (12) It is important that things like Memoirs of a Master be printed and continue to be printed . . . (13) I wish you would explain

to me what all this *Post* business is, anyway. (14) That's not your audience.

(15) Of course, it does no good to reason with you in these matters, but still I keep trying. (16) I not only feel, but know as a fact, that anyone who can write the way you do has to keep on writing. (17) I don't mean any crap about the Urge or anything like that. (18) I mean it is a point of moral necessity. (19) It seems to be easy for you to rationalize, deprecate, and dismiss this, but I don't think it will really work. (20) Like tucking sex in the back of your mind and saying well, that's *that.* . . .

Excessive passive voice. The most basic form of English sentence—what linguists call a "kernel sentence"—runs in the order of subject + verb + direct object: Jane hit the ball; John dusted the furniture; the General ordered the troops; the freshman wrote the essay. Sentences written with verbs that take direct objects in this way are said to be written in the **active voice:** The subjects act with the verbs directly on the objects.

As a native speaker, you are aware that any kernel sentence can be worded in a way that shows the subject acting less directly on the object: The ball *was* hit *by* Jane; the furniture *was* dusted *by* John; the troops *were* ordered *by* the General; the essay *was* written *by* the freshman; and so on. As you can see, this way of wording each sentence combines the active verb of the former versions with some form of the verb "to be":* "*was* hit" replaces "hit"; "*was* dusted" replaces "dusted"; "*were* ordered" replaces "ordered"; and "*was* written" replaces "written." Sentences in which forms of the verb "to be" are used in this way are said to be written in the **passive voice:** These sentences emphasize the

---

*For those of you who may be unsure what we mean by a "form" of the verb "to be," we mean those different versions of the verb "to be" that vary depending on the tense and number of the subject.

I	am	was	will be	will have been
he, she, it	is	was	will be	will have been
you	are	were	will be	will have been
we	are	were	will be	will have been
they	are	were	will be	will have been

objects and show the subjects in a much more passive light than in active voice sentences. "The ball was hit by Jane" seems almost to make Jane incidental to the act that the sentence describes. Except in certain contexts, the important thing in this version of the sentence is that the ball "was hit," not that Jane was doing the hitting.

Although there are many instances in which the passive voice is not only unavoidable but desirable, sentences written in it are usually less emphatic and vigorous than sentences written with active verbs. To rely excessively on "to be" verbs will weaken your voice. The passive voice often makes the writer seem hesitant or evasive.

If you write, for example, "It is generally known that . . ." instead of "Most people know . . . ," you can not only see but hear a distinct difference. The first version of the sentence names no specific subject, leaving the question of who generally knows what up in the air. The second version of the sentence is both more clear and vigorous. "It was determined in six months of investigation that the accused judge was innocent." Here the passive is considerably more evasive. We do not learn who did the determining. The writer may not want us to know who did the deed—the passive makes a good disguise for those who prefer anonymity. But as prose the sentence is strengthened by turning it around: "The special commission determined, after six months of investigation, that the accused judge was innocent."

The passive voice almost always takes more words than the active voice. When you use it unnecessarily or excessively, therefore, you add wordiness to weakness. We can state our guideline here, then, as *Check all verbs for unnecessary use of the passive voice.*

SENTENCE PRACTICE

In the following sentences change each passive verb to an active one.

1. Your beautiful flowers were appreciated by us.
2. My proposition is that we settle the matter now.
3. The instructor said that the papers would be graded by him in two or three days.

4. A great deal of originality was shown by some of the Indian artists.

5. Two weeks in Hawaii would be enjoyed by all of us.

6. A great deal of practical wisdom is contained in his writings.

7. The loneliness of pioneer life could not be endured by his mother.

8. The game was not won by Charles alone.

9. It was always amazing to us that the horse was ridden by the jockey so well so consistently.

10. Although I cannot truthfully say that I was acclaimed during my high school career as a prodigy, being what is generally known as an average student, I was able to survive the rigors of four years of academic pursuits and to achieve graduation without ever having received a single failing grade in any subject.

In order to give you practice at revising in context, we offer here some consecutive sentences from the opening paragraph of an essay by Richard A. Lanham* on the way that shifts in America's student population may affect the teaching of English. We have changed most of the verbs in this passage from active to passive, keeping the passive where Lanham used it. We invite you now to test the effect of changing the verbs back to active voice.

1. "Bombs are known to educate vigorously," Henry Adams is known to have maintained.

2. Population bombs, apparently, are not seen to have the same effect.

3. Although several have been known to hit English studies in the past twenty years, we can be seen to have learned very little.

4. First, the baby boom that is known to have followed the Second World War is also known to have prompted us to assume that enrollments that were seen to go up would never be seen to come down again.

5. After that bubble was seen to have burst, a series of social and demographic changes is known to have brought more black and Hispanic and, in California, Asian-American students into our teaching lives, but no fresh thinking was prompted by this fundamental change that I can be said to have detected.

6. And now may be seen the current waves of coming immigration that are bringing more first-generation Asian

*As printed in *Composition and Literature: Bridging the Gap,* ed. Winifred Bryan Horner. Chicago: University of Chicago Press, 1983.

immigrants who are known to speak a dozen different languages, more Middle Eastern students, and so on.

7. While these chasms may be seen to grow ever wider, and partly because of them, the American system of public education is known to have broken down completely and the void has been filled by the fifty-hour television week.

8. To gift wrap such alarms and excursions, the world during these twenty years has become, through revolutions in trade, energy, and communications, a genuinely global society. . . .

9. During these years we were sneaked up on by what promises to be the biggest bomb of all—the computer revolution.

10. The written and the read word may be said to have suffered, in their whole manner of existence, a radical electronic transmogrification.

Now compare the increase in vigor and the decrease in wordiness when Lanham's active verbs are restored.

"Bombs educate vigorously," Henry Adams maintained. Population bombs, apparently, do not have the same effect. Although several have hit English studies in the past twenty years, we seem to have learned very little. First, the baby boom that followed the Second World War prompted us to assume that enrollments that go up will never go down. After that bubble burst, a series of social and demographic changes brought more black and Hispanic and, in California, Asian-American students into our teaching lives, but this fundamental change has prompted no fresh thinking that I can detect. And now have come the current waves of immigration that are bringing more first-generation Spanish-speaking students, more first-generation Asian immigrants speaking a dozen languages, more Middle Eastern students, and so on. While these chasms grow ever wider, and partly because of them, the American system of public education has broken down completely and the fifty-hour television week has stepped in to fill the void. To gift wrap such alarms and excursions, the world during these twenty years has become, through revolutions in trade, energy, and communications, a genuinely global society. . . . Finally, during these years what promises to be the biggest bomb of all has sneaked up on us—the computer revolution. The written and the read word have suffered, in their whole manner of existence, a radical electronic transmogrification.

Faulty parallelism. Parallelism is symmetry of sentence construction: balancing different parts of a sentence against each other, making the structure of each part mirror the structure of other parts. "On our vacation we went to Boston, to Philadelphia, and to Williamsburg." In this sentence each of the prepositional phrases introduced by "to" parallels the others. Compare "On our vacation we went to Boston, also to Philadelphia, and then Williamsburg was our goal." Here no part matches any of the others. "I propose this year to improve my grades, widen my social life, and enter the adult world." Here, the structure is parallel because the verbs are all in the same form. Compare "I am eager this year to improve my grades, and for finding a wider social life, so that in general the adult world is my goal." Without the parallel structure, the sentence limps.

Many famous sayings depend largely on parallelism: Julius Caesar's "I came, I saw, I conquered"; Abraham Lincoln's "government of the people, by the people, and for the people"; John F. Kennedy's "Ask not what your country can do for you; ask what you can do for your country." The most memorable song lyrics are likely to show parallelisms, like the lyrics of an Elvis Presley tune:

> "One for the money,
> Two for the show,
> Three to get ready,
> Now go cat go!"

In each case to destroy the parallelism would destroy the force of the saying or the lyric. "Don't ask what your country can give you, but instead think about what kinds of service your country needs from you" is weaker and more difficult to follow than the original.

Parallel elements in a sentence create both smooth rhythm and clarity. When a writer breaks or ignores a potential parallelism, the effect is frequently confusing. "He has a quick mind, personal integrity, and I hear he has a good sense of fun too." Compare: "He has a quick mind, personal integrity, and a lively sense of fun." The corrected parallelism of the final phrase improves the sentence's rhythm and clarity.

Parallelism may be employed with units larger than mere phrases. One of the most famous examples of a fairly complex parallelism is Thomas Jefferson's use of "that" to introduce a series of parallel clauses in the second paragraph of the Declaration of Independence:

> We hold these truths to be self evident: *that* all men are created equal; *that* they are endowed by their Creator with certain inalienable rights; *that* among these are life, liberty, and the pursuit of happiness; *that* to secure these rights, governments are instituted among men, deriving their just powers from the consent of the governed; *that* whenever governments . . . [and so on].

Participles ("-ing" verbs) are almost as common as "thats" in introducing parallel clauses, as in this example from "Aes Triplex," an essay by Robert Louis Stevenson.* He is talking about different attitudes toward life and death (by "tearing divines" he means "ranting preachers"):

> There is a great deal of very vile nonsense talked upon both sides of the matter: tearing divines *reducing* life to the dimensions of a mere funeral procession, so short as to be hardly decent; and melancholy unbelievers *yearning* for the tomb as if it were a world too far away.

Shakespeare gives a wonderfully vivid example of parallelisms within parallelisms, all kept straight by the symmetry of form. The whole passage is composed of four parallel units, each unit composed of two compound clauses:

> I cannot hide what I am: I *must be sad when* I have cause *and smile* at no man's jests, *eat when* I have stomach *and wait* for no man's leisure, *sleep when* I am drowsy *and tend* on no man's business, *laugh when* I am merry *and claw* no man in his humor. [*Much Ado About Nothing* (1598), speech by Don John.]

A final example comes from Virginia Woolf's opening chapter of *A Room of One's Own* (1928) in which, responding to a request to speak on the subject of "women and fiction," she retraces her first thoughts about how to proceed:

*In *Virginibus Pueresque,* 1881.

The title women and fiction might mean, and you may have meant it to mean, women and what they are like; or it might mean women and the fiction they write; or it might mean women and the fiction that is written about them; or it might mean that somehow all three are inextricably mixed together. . . .

SENTENCE PRACTICE

In the following sentences either create parallelisms that will make the series more effective, or improve existing parallelisms. (Does our instruction sentence use parallelism?)

1. The new sales manager is young, personable, and has an aggressive manner.
2. Government of the people, for the people, and government available to the general populace.
3. Give me liberty or I will welcome death.
4. We shall fight on the land, in the air, and will, unless I'm mistaken, probably face intense struggle on the beaches also.
5. Many a young artist just starting out has faced debts and poverty, neglect and criticism, and self-doubt and she has sometimes been discouraged.
6. The higher they rise, they sometimes tumble all the harder.
7. If you look into this matter as I did; if you find what I found; and if you wish the same thing I find desirable, then you will be sure to discover what to do.
8. I aspire to be a man of action, truth, and I would like a reputation for these two things.
9. Brought up in a stern land, tested by harsh trial, and proving himself by facing the kinds of experiences that could be called grim, the general knew how to confront danger without flinching.
10. "There is a gusto in the coloring of Titian. Not only do his heads seem to think—the quality of feeling seems to be expressed by his bodies." (Hazlitt, "On Gusto")

Of all the principles of sentence construction, the three we have discussed so far—avoiding wordiness, emphasizing active verbs, and maintaining parallelism—are the most important. Attending to these three features as you work through your various drafts will increase the vigor, elegance, and clarity of your sentences. But these by no means exhaust the principles of good sentence revision. Here are a few others you may find helpful.

Flabby sentence endings. In general, sentences that end with independent clauses are more emphatic than those ending with dependent clauses or dangling participial phrases. "The robber fled on foot, according to the witnesses." In this sentence the phrase "according to the witnesses," not an independent clause, dangles weakly at the end, whereas, "According to the witnesses, the robber fled on foot" places the independent clause in the final spot and gives the whole sentence a more commanding tone. Don't forget, however, that this suggestion can be overridden by particular rhetorical needs. For example, if we wanted to cast some doubt about the testimony, the sentence might be more useful in its original form. "We have a mystery here about just how the robber got away. He fled on foot, according to the witnesses. But the blood in the sedan suggests . . ."

"Not . . . but" construction. When you are referring to two things that contradict each other, especially when the second "takes away" what the first offers, the "not . . . but" construction (called "antithesis") offers an efficient and powerful way of gaining emphasis. "*Not* that I loved Caesar less, *but* that I loved Rome more" (Shakespeare). "Death serves to make us think, *not* of itself, *but* of what is about us" (Leigh Hunt). "It's *not* that I don't want to, *but* that I can't." Sometimes the "but" is merely understood, not actually stated, as in President Kennedy's statement that we already quoted: "Ask not what your country can do for you; [*but*] ask what you can do for your country."

Illogical order. When you refer to things in series, place them in some kind of reasonable or logical order. Go from least to most important (or vice versa), from smallest to largest (or vice versa), from earliest to latest (or vice versa), and so on. In "The news spread from country to city to nation to state," the progression of size is broken twice. "He was an arsonist, a murderer, and a jay walker" reverses the obvious importance of the crimes. (Remember, however, that this reversal of what seems the natural order may sometimes be useful for comic effect.)

Empty subjects. In general, "it" subjects tend to be unclear and wordy. "It will always remain a mystery how they escaped," gets the reader less quickly into the meat of the sentence than, "Their escape will always remain a mystery." "It" subjects also tend to invite passive verbs. "It hasn't been made clear to me what you mean," is both less clear and vigorous than, "I don't understand you." Similarly, "There is . . ." sentences tend toward flabbiness. They are useful whenever we need to back into a topic, but they always postpone the main course:

Not "There are many cases in which students have cheated."
But "Many students have cheated."

Not "There were many doubts in my mind."
But "I had many doubts."

Inadequate or misplaced references. "Fried in butter fresh from the dairy, the guests thoroughly enjoyed the oysters." Fried guests are here created by an inadequate and ambiguous reference of the kind that makes a writer look and feel foolish. Many weak effects and misunderstandings can be avoided simply by looking closely to see if the parts of your sentences relate to each other as you intend. Though there are many fancy grammatical terms for inadequate relations, you can usually recognize when something is wrong if you just read each sentence aloud slowly, and think about what it says. Most **dangling modifiers**, for example, give themselves away when you look them in the eye.

Here are two of them recently committed by professors of English in memoranda to their colleagues:

1. "Instead of being apathetic, the times call for a new surge of enthusiasm."

2. "In the fall the English Department will initiate a new course in Advanced Composition for undergraduates with large enrollment."

If the author of (1) had read it aloud, he probably would have noticed something wrong about suggesting that the *times* might be apathetic when he means that his *colleagues* might. What he meant to write was something like, "Instead of apathy, the times call for a new surge of enthusiasm"; or better, "Instead of being apathetic, we should invest these times with a new enthusiasm."

If the author of (2) had not been in a hurry, he would surely have recognized that he didn't mean to talk about *undergraduates* with large enrollment (whatever that might be—several professors from across campus made some amusing suggestions), but meant rather to talk about *classes* with large undergraduate enrollment.

Similarly, **misplaced adverbs** and other **modifiers** will usually reveal faulty positioning once we take a close look: "He said on Tuesday to send him the check." Does this mean that he said what he said on Tuesday, or does it mean that he wanted the check mailed on Tuesday? The misplacement of "on Tuesday" leaves the matter unclear. Does "Sadly the fugue ended" mean that the ending was sad or that the listener was sad? As in the former example, the misplacement of a modifier—in this case the adverb "sadly" —creates the confusion. "The fugue ended sadly" clarifies matters at once.

Most of these problems are readily correctable. You just don't want to get caught saying anything like, "Bouncing full of spit and vinegar, the jug was hoisted by the hot-headed, belligerent young man." It is one thing to *be* bouncing full of spit and vinegar, but quite another to drink from a jug of it.

Conclusion

Throughout this chapter we have been discussing both how to find your purposes *within* paragraphs and sentences, and how to let your purposes dictate the *shape* of paragraphs and sentences. We hope our examples have made clear that the gift of gab is not much help in learning this skill, and may in fact be a hindrance. The writer who has been rewarded for sheer fluency, and has thus not learned how to develop a clear point from sentence to sentence and paragraph to paragraph, may easily mistake the feeling of motion for a sense of direction. Such writers may clip right along, but the reader soon loses sight of the destination.

Learning how to revise paragraphs and sentences effectively offers the writer a genuine pleasure—the pleasure of being in control. Many inexperienced writers feel that whether sentences come out right or not is a mysterious matter beyond control or comprehension: "If you're lucky, sentences come out right; if you're not lucky, they come out flawed." This view is simply wrong. All good writers spend much time revising their paragraphs and sentences, and they do not rely on luck or mysterious and inscrutable intuitions. Good writers know about the principles of revision we have described: concision, parallelism, and so on. They systematically tinker with their sentences, using these principles as guides.

Such labor in the workshop never precludes inspiration. If you hammer out a good sentence on a first try, fine; don't ruin it with secondary blows. But while waiting for such delightful moments, you are not helplessly bound to your first tries, most of which will, like everyone else's, be improvable.

What would you now want to do with this one?

writing well

It has been brought to our attention that writing well is time-consuming and takes a lot of energy and is labor-intensive, as well as you can say that it is one of the most important and elevating forms of communicating whatever you might have to say about most matters that concern the resolution of human affairs.

For example, if you have matters   something to say about   writing is one concerning the resolution of human affairs, anything you might have to say can be said through writing.

Invention and discovery: Finding something to say

*The friends that have it I do wrong
When ever I remake a song,
Should know what issue is at stake:
It is myself that I remake.*

—WILLIAM BUTLER YEATS

Exploring the world for topics

Most writers say that their biggest single problem is finding what they want to say. They often make claims like, "Once I got my idea, the book almost wrote itself, but it took me years to get to that point." Our students often report to us, "Well, now that I see what I want to say I know how to revise this paper, but my main point came to me only as I wrote my final paragraph—and now I don't have time to rewrite it."

As you have already discovered, you seldom—maybe never —find what you want to say all at once. Most of the time, we all begin to work from faint glimmerings of a purpose, search through the world and our own minds for ideas, facts, or examples that might support that purpose, and try out various points to be made and lines of argument that might also help. Exploring these, we discover that our original purpose has shifted under our eyes—or even that we have to abandon it because it no longer makes sense. In time we arrive at a purpose that we really care about, and a thesis that we adopt because it seems believable and likely to accomplish that purpose. We all discover that until we find something that we *want* to say, writing can be a boring and painful chore.

In working on purposes in Chapter 4, you have already begun to think about how to find something to say. Whenever you explore changes that you want to produce in your circumstances —in the wide world or in your immediate life—or try to think through any problem that comes your way, you are exercising your mind on what can become the "stuff" of writing. Since all your life you have been trying to figure out how the world works and how to get it to go your way, you already have a great deal of experience in this kind of exploration.

> "Dad, I really think it's about time that you treated me like a grown-up [your purpose]. I'm eighteen years old, you know [your thesis, self-proving because it's a plain fact]."
>
> "Mr. Samuelson, I really wish you would stop coming into my department and telling the secretaries what to do without checking with me first [your purpose]. I've run this department efficiently for three years, but ever since you came here six months ago you have been undercutting my authority and messing up my system [your thesis]. Just yesterday we missed a deadline because one of my typists was working on a sideline task that you had assigned to her [first piece of evidence]."

Probably you do not think of such everyday requests, even when you work up your reasons for them, as "finding something to write about." But they provide a base to build on as you begin systematic work on your writing.

Thus you may think of every goal that you would like to achieve, and every past success or failure in achieving a goal by talking or writing, as a kind of location or storehouse where writing ideas can be found. Some theorists have called such finding **discovery,** and some have called it **invention.** Both terms are useful, because in one sense writers discover their arguments in the materials they work with, and in another sense they invent the arguments themselves. Arguments and the **topics** (locations where arguments can be found) certainly do not emerge in human affairs until some inventor discovers their usefulness on a given occasion.

Purposes, theses, arguments, and topics

In the last paragraph you may have noticed that we used "topics" in an unusual way. We are basing our use on the old meaning of the word, which originally meant "place" or "location." In older theories of rhetoric, "topics" referred to the innumerable "locations" in our mental worlds where we can "go" to find good arguments to support what we want to say. When we "go" to our memories, our personal experiences, or other people's arguments to find support for our arguments, then all three of these—memories, experiences, and other people's views—are "topics" in our sense of the word. Notice that this sense differs from the most common modern usage, which employs "topic" as a synonym for "subject": "I'm writing on the 'topic' of abortion," you might say. But for us, 'topics" are all the places you can "go," usually without getting up from your desk, as you search for interesting or powerful reasons to make readers accept your *thesis* and thus accomplish your *purpose.*

NOTEBOOK ENTRY

Since the four terms, *purpose, thesis, topic,* and *argument* (or *reasoning*) will continue to be useful in your work, take some time now to think about them. Without worrying about style or correctness, write in your notebook two complete sentences, describing what you take to be our purpose and our thesis in Chapter 1.

Now do the same thing for Chapter 2.

When we perform this exercise ourselves, we discover that our purpose was about the same in both chapters. In fact, the same overall purpose will govern what we say to you throughout the whole book—something like: "to engage you in the process of improving your writing." Everything we do, every thesis we develop, and every topic we explore, will be in pursuit of that same purpose.

But our theses will vary from chapter to chapter, from section to section within each chapter, and from paragraph to paragraph within each section. The thesis of Chapter 3 is something like this: "If you want to improve your writing, you must learn to make every step contribute toward some purpose, some effect you want to achieve in a reader." The thesis of Chapter 4 (except perhaps for some parts of the final section) runs something like this: "The same notion of purpose that governs whole essays should govern paragraphs and sentences." The thesis, or point, of this present chapter is something like this: "Good writers do not just wait for 'something to say.' They develop a repertory of topics that can be explored in the search for arguments that will support a given thesis."

The range of topics that might be usefully explored in supporting a given thesis can never be limited in advance of hard thinking about purposes. Even a single sentence might employ arguments derived from several topics: "Every student who wants an education today is faced with many obstacles, including shamefully low salaries for teachers, poor textbooks, inadequate funding, and distractions such as TV and dating." At least four topics are visited (or we might say "explored," or "raided") here: (a) financial remuneration; (b) quality of educational materials; (c) adequacy of support for public enterprises; (d) ways of spending time in the world. (The last one might be split into two. Can you see how?) These highly general topics (members of a larger group sometimes called "*common* topics," because they are useful in most discussions) are available to everyone, since in themselves they are neutral and could yield arguments in opposing directions. The topic "financial remuneration" could, for example, yield both the argument that "teachers are in fact overpaid" as well as the argument "teachers are underpaid," since judgments about what is overpaid and what is underpaid will depend on what arguments we can invent (or discover) about these comparisons. Topics are thus no more than places where we can look for persuasive arguments.

Arguments make assertions in support of theses and then, if necessary, support those assertions with further arguments. Only the development of the arguments themselves—and in our example they are still entirely undeveloped—could lead us to decide whether or not rival arguments are sound, and whether or not to explore other topics for further arguments. (In Chapters 11 through 13 we discuss ways of distinguishing good arguments from bad, and in the process hope to expand the range of topics available to your thinking.)

NOTEBOOK ENTRY

Make a short list of some of the topics we have used in pursuing our theses in the two previous chapters. Where did we go for arguments that might support our theses? Don't expect to find the one right answer. Just glance back through the book (or through your memory) and list a few "places" that we have turned to and explored, such as "the student's previous experience," "what the authorities say about good writing," "the authors' experience with students," and so on.

You can see that we have explored dozens of topics to find arguments to support a smaller number of theses all serving a single purpose. If we were writing a short essay of the kind you are usually asked to write, we would usually have only one purpose and one main thesis, supported by a small number of arguments derived from however many topics we needed. An initial set of notes for such an essay might look like this:

I want to persuade my reader to believe [purpose] that participation in sports need not interfere with education [thesis] by referring to my own experience [topic 1, where I find the argument: "I myself have been able to combine scholarship and athletic success"]; to the records of athletes at this college [topic 2, where I luckily find that the varsity athletes here have a GPA of 3.1]; and to theories about the relation of bodily health to mental health [topic 3, where I had time to find only a few tried-and-true quotations in *Bartlett's Familiar Quotations*—like "a sound mind in a sound body"]. I also tried to explore the topic of the authority of "common opinion," by surveying about 25 students. But most of them said that they believe athletics *does* interfere with studies, so I decided not to include that topic. (Or, if I want to be *really* honest, and thus persuasive even to the toughest skeptic, I'll deal with their views and try to show why they are wrong, using some other line of argument. Or, finally, I may discover, in exploring this contrary evidence, that my views have changed.)

Six generally useful topics

Perhaps you can see now why learning to explore the world of useful topics is at least as important for a writer as developing a large, flexible vocabulary. (In fact the chief value in building your vocabulary is that new words often bring with them possible new topics.) But where should the explorer go? In this chapter we'll talk about six large locations (or storage bins) where you can find arguments (or things to say): (1) your readers' qualities, prejudices, and emotional responses; (2) your "self" or character, both as it is (in your view of it) and as it might be projected to readers; (3) your memory and your readers' memories of past experience; (4) your first-hand observations of the world around you; (5) your conversation with friends and acquaintances, especially as they give you observations, arguments, and criticism; and (6) your reading and research—in the assigned material and in related sources.

Notice that some of these seem to be located outside you, in what we call the world, and some are already inside your head. But as you work, you can gradually appropriate them all—you can take them in. Notice also that as you "take in" topics from the world around you, you cannot remain unchanged. Whenever you internalize topics you have never internalized before—as Yeats says in the epigraph to this chapter—you are actually changing not just your writing but your own self. And notice, finally, that learning how to explore topics is one way of giving yourself an education. When we say that someone is educated in a given field or profession, we mean that he or she has taken in a large number of worthwhile things to say about a subject and can say them well.

In college we finally choose a major field in order to master the arguments found in the *special* topics of that field. In this course you are learning to write for all those occasions when writing will be required of you. And a good way to define "being educated in general" is to say that those who are *generally* educated know, first, how to discover (invent) worthwhile things to say about any important subject, even if they are not specialists, and second, that they can say them well.

Now let's see how this might work in practice. Suppose that you have received the following assignment: "Read Carol Bly's 'Enemy Evenings' and write an essay (500–600 words) agreeing or disagreeing with the author's thesis."

*   *   *   *   *

Enemy Evenings

In Minnesota towns one sometimes has the feelng of moving (1) among ghosts, because we don't meet and talk to our local opponents on any question. We know, for example, that somewhere in our town of 2,242, there live people who believe that the preservatives sodium nitrite, sodium nitrate, and BHA variously threaten future health, and also in town live the local staff of the Agricultural Extension Division, who have just published an essay saying the advantages of these preservatives outweigh the disadvantages. Yet these two sets of people don't meet each other on open panels, and scarcely at all even privately, thus providing another major American issue which small-town people are left out of.

The case is always made that to keep a town from flying (2) apart you must discuss only matters in which there is little conflict. That means that whenever a woman physician enters a room in which a few people are urging, intriguingly enough, that the man should be head of the woman (St. Paul), the topic must automatically be changed to whether or not we are getting that hard winter they kept talking about last fall.

There is nothing much wrong with weather talk except that (3) far from preventing people from feeling "threatened" it is in fact the living proof that you don't care about those people: you haven't any interest in their thoughts; you don't want to hear them out.

There is little lonelier than small-town life when small talk (4) is the principal means of peace. Sherwood Anderson illustrated it long ago, but people who still read Anderson seem to do so in a mist of nostalgia rather than for any revelation we can put to use. Also, I'm not content with the usual explanations for small-town citizens' being so uneasy around intense feelings. The question is: why are thousands and thousands of lively and feeling people who live in the countryside willing to give up, for their whole lives, the kind of friendship people enjoy who deliberately, curiously, and civilly draw out one another's views on serious subjects?

The reason generally offered, of course, is that airing last (5) night's hassle at the church council will curtail this morning's sale of advertising space in the paper. This reason presupposes that serious exchange is a *hassle*, and must be the result of gaucherie. I don't believe it. Another commonly offered explanation is that less-informed or less-intelligent people will feel unequal to frank self-expression in the presence of more-informed or more-intelligent people. That is abundantly untrue. I have heard extremely strong opinions plentifully and bravely offered by people including myself who could hardly have been less informed or less gifted about the subject.

We simply need experience in taking an interest in the other (6) side and doing so with the proponents of the other side present. If we could get this habit going I think we could reduce one of the most dismal characteristics of small-town life—the loneliness. Of course human loneliness is general, but this particular source of it, exercised in hypocrisy, could be ended.

Therefore, I propose that small community groups develop (7) panels for Enemy Evenings. Obviously some much better word has to be used, but I like the pure madness of this one: it reminds me of that fantastic creation of Nixon, Ehrlichman, and Haldeman —the enemies list. Enemy Evenings would definitely need two things: a firm master of ceremonies in whom general affection for human beings would be paramount, not a chill manner or a childish desire to get the fur flying; second, it would need very just panel representation. An example of unjust panel representation would be a four-person panel to discuss the defense budget made up of a leader of American Writers vs. the Vietnam War; a director of Episcopal Community Services, Minneapolis; Senator Mondale; and (the chump) an American Party spokesman. It would be helpful too, if controversial panels were conducted with humor, but that isn't essential.

In discussing this notion at a Cultural Affairs Committee (8) meeting in my town, we observed with interest the 1974–75 policy of the Minnesota Humanities Commission, emphasizing the relation between private concerns and public policies. Also, the National Endowment for the Humanities (through the Upper Midwest Council) has supported a series of television dialogues this winter, covering controversial subjects. All that is interesting, but for the common viewer what is seen on television is irrevocably "something they had on television." Seeing one's own neighbor speak out passionately (and having the chance to respond) is immediately engaging.

Here is a suggested rough list of seldom-discussed subjects (9) with strongly opposed participants:

1. Additives in commercial food products and the relationship of 4-H instruction materials to the Wheat Institute.
   Suggested participants:
   > Home Extension personnel
   > Local members, the International Academy for Preventive Medicine

2. Fertilizing methods
   Suggested participants:
   > County agent
   > Anhydrous ammonia dealers
   > Bag fertilizer dealers
   > Soil Conservation Service Experiment station personnel
   > Members of the Soil Improvement Association
   > Local subscribers to Department of Natural Resources publicatons and *Organic Gardening,* and readers of U.S. Agricultural yearbooks

3. Fall plowing vs. spring plowing
   Suggested participants:

County agent (The official Ag. stand now is that fall plowing is detrimental, but by far the largest number of farmers still do it when they have time.)

Farmers committed to both plowing practices

4. Defense Department budget of the United States
Suggested participants:
VFW or Legion Auxiliary officers
VFW or Legion Post officers
Local members, Women's League for Peace and Freedom
Local members, Common Cause
National Guard unit officers

5. St. Paul's stand on man as the head of woman
Suggested participants:
Fundamentalist church representatives
Local Charismatic Christians—who tend to be nicely divided on this, providing an interesting confusion
Local members of Business and Professional Women's Clubs
Local officers of American Federation of Women's Clubs
Grain elevator managers

6. The growth of shopping malls *around* small towns
Suggested participants:
Local promoters of comprehensive plans
Main Street businessmen
Members of senior citizens' clubs
High School Ecology Club members
The mayor or council members

7. The emphasis on technical training at the high school level
Suggested participants:
Local painters, writers, and musicians
Vocational center director and staff
Visiting college humanities division members
Visiting Vo-Tech schools' faculty members

8. Drainage ditches
Suggested participants:
County commissioners and engineers holding contracts for ditches
Soil Improvement Association members
DNR staff members on loan
SCS personnel on loan

9. Competition vs. cooperation, as taught in U.S. elementary schools
Suggested participants:
Angry parents on both sides
School counselor
Fifth- or sixth-grade faculty members
Psychology faculty from neighboring community colleges

10. The lives of men and women in rural towns
Suggested participants:
President of the Jaycees
President of the Mrs. Jaycees
Larry Batson or Robert T. Smith of the *Minneapolis Tribune* or anyone half so lively
Very conservative pastors or priests
Personnel from West Central Mental Health Center

A painful fact of American life is that people from small (10) towns are afraid of directness. Small-town kids, unlike suburban kids, can't take much from the shoulder. Example: A suburban Minneapolis child with a first-rate music instructor goes off to her piano lesson. She is working up a small piece of Mozart, she hasn't done her homework, and she smears the counting. The music instructor tells her it's an irresponsible job, sloppy phrasing, whatever she tells her—in any case, it won't do. The child returns home and works the piece up much more conscientiously next time, having learned that music is a disciplined pleasure.

A rural piano student cannot be spoken to so plainly. It is (11) hard for her to be stirred into being responsible to the music at hand because the instant a teacher tries to correct her directly her soul sags into mere self-condemnation. Our style, in the countryside, is not to criticize children at all: we very seldom tell them the plane model was glued carelessly and the sleeve set in without enough easing. (The counterpart of this is that we seldom praise them much for anything either. "You played a real good game against Dawson"; "You did a real good job of that speech contest" —not "I knew you'd do well at the speech thing; I didn't know that I would cry—in fact, I'm *still* moved by what you said!") So the children develop neither stamina about criticism nor the imagination to picture to themselves gigantic praise if they excel. They live lightly handed into a middle world of little comment, and therefore little incitement to devotion. Should a music teacher try to explain Mozart's involvement in the music—what *he* had in mind for this or that phrase—the student wouldn't hear over the ground noise of dismay in her own feelings. "I'm being attacked! I'm being attacked!" is all her inexperienced soul can take in. Piranhas when you're out swimming, mean music teachers when you're taking piano—it's all the same to her. On a psychological ladder, she is rungs below being able to move from self to Mozart.

What we need in rural life is more Serious Occasion. By the (12) time a child is ten, he or she should have heard, at least a few hundreds of times, "I loved that dying cowboy routine. Do it again. Do be quiet, Uncle Malcolm. Noah's going to do his dying cowboy routine." And adults would have shut up, listened, and praised. That moment would have been a Serious Occasion. Then a child is caught lying. It is horrible to lie—the notice of it should be serious and major. Then lying—whether or not one did it—is the subject of a Serious Occasion. Then, after some hundreds of such occasions, one can take in a conversation about music—what does Mozart want out of this piece? Remember: we are not now talking about you or yourself. We are talking about someone *other* —a musician long dead—and he is making a demand on us, and we are going to meet that demand! We are not going to scream and flee, because discipline is not the same thing as piranhas in the river.

I think we will surge into twice as much life through Serious (13) Occasion.

At the same time, Minnesota rural life gives comfort and (14) sweetness. Our young people are always returning home on their college weekends. When they drop out of college they tend to wander back here instead of prowling the streets of San Francisco or St. Paul. Apparently they garner genuine comfort from the old familiarity, the low-intensity social life, and with it a pretty good guarantee of not being challenged. Their ease has been bought, however, at the expense of the others who live here year round. To preserve our low-key manners, they have had to bottle up social indignation, psychological curiosity, and intellectual doubt. Their banter and their observations about the weather are carapace developed over decades of inconsequential talk.

The problem isn't like the major psychological phenomena (15) in the United States—the increasing competitiveness and cheating in Ivy League and other top colleges, the multiplication of spies and counterspies in private corporations, the daily revelations of crookedness and irresponsibility on the part of major corporations, the ominous pursuance of the Law of the Sea conventions regardless of Cousteau's warnings, the overriding of public opinion about strip mining in the West. These are the horrible things that depress everybody. Remembering them, I think we can skip toward solving small-town dilemmas rather cheerfully. I commend frank panel evenings with opponents taking part: let's try that for a change of air, after years of chill and evasive tact.

*   *   *   *

Now let's assume that you have read this piece a couple of times—enough to decide in a general way whether you like Bly's thesis or not. You then sit down at your desk—and nothing comes. You get up and sharpen pencils, sort books, listen to a record, stare out of the window—and still nothing comes. (If the "you" we imagine here seems to *you* a bit slow on the uptake, please forgive us. To be clear we must explain steps that you may actually take in a flash.)

What's wrong? And how can you fix it? You know that you lack a purpose (except that of "writing an essay," which is no help). Where are you going to go to find a real purpose?

There are no rules about how to proceed. Energizing purposes sometimes come to us uninvited while we are showering, walking to class, dancing, or daydreaming. Sometimes they refuse to come at all, no matter what delicious bait we offer. But usually we can manage to make a catch by fishing in one or another of the locations (topics) that we'll now run through. In doing so, we'll assume that you have read and reread the essay two or three times, doing your best at the beginning to make use of what is usually your most important resource, the one we'll save for discussion at the end: the assigned reading. You have read the essay, and read it again, and you still feel threatened by that blank page. Our point here is that even though you may feel that your mind is as blank as that page, you will in fact find it richly stocked, once you look in the right places.

Your audience as a resource

Who will be the reader of your as-yet-unwritten, as-yet -*unconceived* essay? The wording of the assignment is not helpful (look at it again). It requires you to choose your own audience. Will you write straight to your teacher? If you decide to try that one, you might think like this:

> Let's see now: What does my teacher already believe about this subject? I know he's from New York City, or at least he said so, so he may agree with Carol Bly that conversation in small towns is bad. So what is there to say to somebody like him? Nothing that I can see. Being a teacher, he is sure to like all the kinds of talk Bly does—politics, the arts, that kind of stuff, and he already knows everything the essay says. So what's to be said? Everything I can think of he has already thought of.

So far so bad; nothing has come. This is a typical moment in writing, the moment when you think that no matter how gloomy things looked at first they look much worse—maybe even hopeless —now. To stop here is of course fatal, like refusing to take medicine when you're sick because you think you'll never get well anyway. The truth is that while writing is always hard it is never hopeless. A "desperate" student might go on, for example, to discover things to say in this manner:

> But is it really true that my teacher has thought of everything? One thing he does not know is where *I* come from, either geographically or mentally. He doesn't even know whether I'm from a small town or not. In fact he doesn't know *anything* about me or my opinions. And he probably

thinks I am one of those mice who would never raise a controversial point. What would happen if I just flatly disagreed with Bly? Or—here comes something! I could argue that education at this college produces the very kind of non-talk that Bly attacks. Most of our professors do not encourage us to think for ourselves. We just parrot back what they lay out for us. Even in this class—I've got to move cautiously here—even in this class we somehow never disagree with the teacher. Why? Because it would seem impolite? Because we fear he wouldn't like it? Because the students attending this school are lazy? Maybe he'd be interested if I tried to answer this question.

What you are trying to find, at this stage, is some *entry point* into your reader's mind, some angle that will motivate him beyond his duty as a teacher to read the paper. Sometimes such probing will turn up a beautiful idea for an essay with a clear purpose and thesis—perhaps "How to get some 'enemy evenings' into our class discussions." And sometimes, of course, it will fail.

If you're still stuck you might try this line:

My teacher will surely agree with Bly; in fact he probably assigned her essay to stir us up a bit. But what he *doesn't* know is that *she* ignores most of the really good talk that goes on in small towns. For her—and probably for him—"good talk" has to be *intellectual,* dealing with BIG issues. Well, I'm going to show him that in my small town we have good talk about each other and about the past, even though we don't discuss the Great Books or quarrel about nuclear armament on every street corner. He might be interested in the way my grandparents talk with my aunts and uncles about their childhood, and in my next-door neighbor's talk about the "old country," or in my mother's way of distinguishing good and bad neighbors . . .

Notice that thinking about the reader has led you here to another location, your own memory (see the section on "Your Memory as a Resource").

Sometimes, no matter how hard you probe, you find nothing that will interest this first possible audience—the teacher. Then it is always a good idea to invent a new audience—perhaps Carol Bly herself, to whom you might write your essay as a letter, either giving her additional ammunition for her claims or showing what she has left out. Or you might choose to address your classmates, defending or attacking Bly's charges. Or, if your class has discussed the essay, you may remember how particular students responded, and then address them as your primary audience, discussing what they have overlooked or misunderstood. A brief note at the beginning of the paper can explain your choice of audience: "I have chosen to address my essay to those in the class who were angry about Bly's claims." Or: "My paper is in the form of a letter to my parents; I try to explain Bly's case in a way that they could understand and accept."

In thinking about audiences, try to expand the list of qualities that you think different readers possess. If you are writing to your teacher (we have imagined a young man from a large city, but we urge you to think about your actual teacher), don't think only about small towns, suburbs, and cities. Ask yourself in addition whether males and females would respond differently to Bly's essay—and thus to yours. Think about the effects of age: An older teacher might be interested in conversations different from those that might interest younger people, and older people are almost always interested in discovering the ideas of younger people. Think about circumstances: Does the teacher have a family? If he does, I'll bet he's tolerant of friendly conversation about sentimental, non-controversial matters. What subjects does he refer to when telling anecdotes or illustrating a point? Sports? Shakespeare? Current movies? Politics? His children? Books? What kind of books? And so on. When any of these questions leaves your mind blank, just move on to another one.

If you decide to write to classmates or the folks back home, you can pursue the same kinds of questions. Folks from home make an audience that you are likely to know better than any other. You can predict their responses to "Enemy Evenings" with some confidence, and any differences between their responses and yours will give you a lot to write about.

In general, then, you are asking, "At what points does my encounter with Bly intersect with the likely interests of my readers?" If you can't find some point of intersection, look for some other audience and purpose. You might, for example, address the

whole campus through a letter to the student newspaper, com-
plaining about the lack of "enemy evenings" on campus: "Where
are we to go for good talk about controversial issues? Nobody here
seems to care about anything except sex and sports . . ."

Your "self" as a resource

In thinking about your audience, you already have had occasion to probe your picture of yourself a bit. But once you have
chosen a specific kind of reader, it is always useful to think more
concretely about who they will think *you* are, before they read, and
who you will *want to be,* in their eyes, when they have finished.
Thinking about how your audience is likely to view you may
reveal certain problems that you otherwise would not see. Writing
to your parents may be difficult, for example, because they may
think of you only as their child, not as someone whose words carry
any authority. Writing to your boss may be difficult if he or she
is intolerant, defensive, or stupid. Writing to the student paper,
you know that many fellow students may say, "Why should I pay
attention to *you*? You don't know any more about this than I do."
And in writing to your teacher, you may fear that your work will
be found deficient no matter what you say. On the other hand,
writing a letter to your younger sister in high school, recommending Bly's essay, may present you with the problem of sounding too
superior.

The point is that once you think about all of these difficulties, they can become opportunities. In every case, you can discover in yourself useful qualities to play up, and other qualities to
play down. We'll talk more about this when we discuss *voice* and
tone in Chapters 9 and 10, but for now let's return to those readers
whom you most frequently address: your teachers. What resources can you find, in your "self" as a topic, that may win their
attention and respect?

First, there is no substitute for giving evidence that you have
worked on the assignment thoughtfully, energetically, and carefully. Your teacher has to read many papers, and some of them will
betray in every line that the student is simply filling an assignment, trudging dully through the work, avoiding thought at all
costs. If you can find some *personal* edge to the assignment, some

point that grabs you and demands to be played up, you will move toward solving the first problem of every writer: getting the reader's attention. Readers sit up and take notice when they hear a voice that sounds committed because it meets a challenging problem or claim head on.

Of course this means working hard on the reading, as we'll see in a moment. (See also Chapter 14, "Research Papers," pages 445–452.) But there is a second kind of attention that more directly refers to your "self," to your character and to how other people are likely to view it. Do you think of yourself as a passive, non-controversial person? Have you done little in class to stimulate "enemy evenings"? If so, your teacher may have reason to expect from you a quiet, passive, or bland essay. But you can make capital out of what may seem like a fault by taking it up as a problem in the essay itself.

> It's all very well for Carol Bly to wish that small towns were full of stimulating and colorful types like herself. But what about those of us who were born to listen? What about those who *like* peaceful small talk? Why is she sure that stirring us up is always good? Why does she try to make us feel inferior because we don't like to argue?

On the other hand, if you see yourself as perhaps overly talkative, overly given to controversy—if you have perhaps dominated class discussion in the past—you might contemplate exploring another possible self, one that would be reflective, quiet, inclined to think before you speak.

> I see some danger that Carol Bly's argument will offer too much encouragement to those of us who already love to take part in *enemy* evenings. I am often accused of having a conversational hair-trigger. I love to combat everything anybody says, just for the sheer fun of controversy. But I am beginning to learn that my combativeness sometimes shuts off my own learning before it even begins.
>
> Somehow Bly's "enemy evenings" seem to invite people like me to argue just for the sake of arguing. She says almost nothing about how her evenings of combat are going to produce any *progress* in the discussion. Instead, she seems to

suggest that the ideal person goes into combat for the love of combat itself.

That may be good advice for some people in some small towns; I wouldn't know about that, since I come from a family that butted horns in mortal combat over the weather report and cake recipes. But I suspect that people like me need another message entirely, a plea for something more like *"friendly* evenings," in which the goal is not controversy but conversational progress.

Thinking about your "self" in this way need not lead to much talking about that self directly in the essay. Some purposes will be served by openly referring to yourself and some will be harmed by it. But when an assignment asks us, as this one does, to think about what kinds of behavior we admire, we are free to make direct personal references. (By the way, don't fall for that phony old rule that forbids the use of "I" in an essay. Only in extremely rare kinds of writing is the first-person pronoun banned. In most of your writing, you can write as personally as your audience, purpose, and thesis dictate.)

Even if you make no direct reference to your qualities, you cannot avoid projecting a picture of yourself. And you can work at projecting a person whom your teacher and other readers will respect. What this means, at a minimum, is that your manuscript or typescript must be as error-free as you can manage. Nothing so undermines the authority of a paper as the misspelling of names or other signs that you as author do not really take much pride in your results. Though incorrect grammar and spelling usually do not affect clarity, they can be fatal when they imply that you simply couldn't be bothered to give the assignment your close attention.

But what you say will obviously be much more important than clean pages in creating a trustworthy character for yourself. Since everything you say will imply who you are, it is especially important to think here about how to express your feelings without falling into embarrassing self-consciousness or sentimentality. Whether you liked "Enemy Evenings" or not, you must have had *some* emotional responses to it. Use those responses as one resource. Try to get them into your paper, not necessarily as assertions ("I was really excited by the ideas here") but by the *way* you write. If you feel anger or contempt, don't say "Reading Bly made me angry." Rather, look for ways to show what made you angry, and then attack *that* specifically, letting the anger show in your way of describing it. If you admired the piece don't say "I just loved it." If you do, your teacher may suspect insincerity. *Show* your admiration by the way you make your points.

This advice is so general that you may just have to put it to one side for now. We'll return in Chapters 9 and 10 to ways in which you can make your "writing personality"—what students of rhetoric call your *ethos*—work for you.

Your memory as a resource

In talking of your hunches about readers and your insights into your "self," we have already said a good deal about your memory as a topic. Every human being commands a memory-bank richer than that of even the most elaborate computer. It can "call up" not only those literal memories that computers recall so rapidly, but a seemingly unlimited number of actions and responses, experiences and feelings, hopes and disappointments, relations and ruptures—all embedded in contexts, complete with nuances and judgments that no one would know how to store into a computer's memory. We can "remember," even while thinking about something else, the extremely complex controls that enable us to reach for, grasp, and take a cup precisely to our lips, without spilling its contents, take in liquid without choking, return the cup to the table without breaking it, and release our hold without tipping it over. We can all remember an impressive variety of routes between our homes and our school, our bank, our church, our friends' houses. I (Booth) can remember details of the newspaper delivery route that I followed hundreds of times about 50 years ago, with the names of the streets and of some of the companions who also had what we called "rowts." I (Gregory) can remember the precise feeling of jubilation in the air when I was 5—horns blowing and people rushing out into the streets—on the day that World War II ended in Europe.

But people not only remember things as they *did* happen (or as we think they happened—our memories are highly fallible); we also remember imaginings, wishes, hoped-for events that we know did *not* happen. We all carry different versions of events in our minds as we *wish* they had occurred, not as they did occur. Sometimes we carry the memory of these "never-happened" versions with us all our lives. "If only my cousin had stayed and talked with us five more minutes, he wouldn't have been going through the intersection when that truck ran the red light . . ." "Why do I always criticize my daughter's outfit when she dresses for a date? That's what my mother always did to me and I hated it." The memory of every event that has ever happened to us exists within a matrix of imagined versions of how the event might have occurred differently. These alternative versions are as much a part of our memory—and consequently of our stock of writing material —as events that did happen.

Our memory is also stocked with the ideas, feelings, and experiences of other people, people whose lives we have taken in at second hand: stories about our parents' youth, stories about our friends' experiences, and, of course, stories by the thousands from movies, TV, comic books, literature, song lyrics, and historical accounts. We remember fictional characters' feelings and thoughts much as we remember our own. Sometimes, in fact, these memories lead to spontaneous comparisons with fictional characters who live in our heads. "You know, I'm sounding just like Archie Bunker these days. I guess I've really had it with being picked on by teachers and bosses." "When he proposed I felt just the way Elizabeth Bennet feels in *Pride and Prejudice* when Darcy proposes the second time."

You may or may not turn up a memory that connects specifically with Bly's piece, though most of us will have at least a few experiences that do: memories of lively and dull conversations, big cities and small towns, successful and unsuccessful efforts to get good talk going. When we find nothing coming to mind we simply pass on to another of the inexhaustible sources of ideas, feelings, and examples that reside in our memories. On any given writing occasion only a few of these memories will be useful, but every piece of writing can be filled out or deepened to some extent by memories. (Note how Bly herself uses memories.) Most often, perhaps, we use memory simply to provide vivid details or images in support of points found in other topics. But often enough memory can provide just what we need—if we only learn how to tap it.

FREE WRITING EXERCISE

We hope that you have been following our advice to practice free writing for ten minutes or so every day. No doubt a great share of what you have written in those carefree moments has been based on memory. Now we suggest that you take off from one or two of the following topics that bring up specific memories and write for about 15–30 minutes:

> a boring conversation
> an exciting argument
> a quarrel
> a fight
> a victory or defeat
> an embarrassing moment
> a triumph
> a moment of despair
> a clever reply
> a stupid comment
> a classmate—detestable or admirable
> the way people talk (my father, my mother, my
>   roommate, my grandparents)
> relatives, favorite and awful
> teachers: good, average, lousy; dour, spacey, funny
> jokes, good and bad
> dinner conversations (at home, in the dorm, on a date)
> unmentionable topics (at home, in class, in the dorm)
> fashionable topics
> how I talked _____ into doing _____
> a big mistake I once made in agreeing uncritically with a
>   clever talker
> a big mistake I once made in not listening

These suggestions all were called up from our memories by thinking about "Enemy Evenings." No doubt many of them, like many of your memories, would not be useful in a written response to Bly, but some of them clearly would. And if you look through what YOU have written, you will see that you too have experience that relates to her claims; you do have *something* to say.

ESSAY ASSIGNMENT

Now run through what you have just written and pick one point that seems closely connected to any part of Bly's plea for open controversy. First write a paragraph (perhaps 100–150 words) using something like one or the other of these beginnings:

My personal experience suggests that Carol Bly is right in at least one of her claims.

My personal experience suggests that Carol Bly is wrong in at least one of her claims.

Next develop your paragraph into a full essay, by exploring one or more of the resources we have described so far. You might want to think of all the evidence you can find *against* your thesis, and then systematically answer an imaginary critic, perhaps Bly, who would use that evidence as an attack on your case. Or you might just systematically probe your memory—of yesterday, of five years ago—for details that will clarify, reinforce, or even clinch your case.

In discussing memory as a topic, we have written so far as if it would yield personal experiences only. But in your academic writing it will prove to be equally important as a resource for ideas and arguments. Having now read Bly carefully, your memory has been enriched with points about conversations in city and country, and with claims about the value of controversy. When you encounter the next discussion of what makes good conversation, or the next comparison of village and city life, your memory is likely to offer spontaneous associations with Bly's essay.

Such associations will occur, of course, only if what we have read has made *some* kind of sense in the first place. We simply cannot take in any event or concept that is totally unrelated to our past experience. Perhaps you have noticed that you remember very little about subjects that you do not understand. Some people can remember hundreds of baseball percentages from last season yet not a single line of poetry, while others can memorize a poem on one reading and will forget baseball statistics in five seconds. It's as if intense experiences open up pigeonholes in the mind where new experiences *of related kinds* may enter to roost.

One reason education sometimes threatens us is that we are not sure what points to hang on to; new concepts seem to get lost or jumbled almost as fast as we learn them. When we have trouble in a calculus or literature class, we may feel that we just don't have open pigeonholes for *that kind of stuff,* though we can remember other things quite well. Everybody faces this difficulty when learning new subjects. Booth can forget an article about economics within a day, even when he *tries* to remember; his "economic pigeonholes" are just not there, though he always *intends* to do some studying and open up some space for economics. Gregory has trouble remembering things visually. His wife can recall the basic layout of a house they have been in only once, while he may be unable to recall the color of the wallpaper in a house where he has spent several evenings.

You can in fact train your memory in any area that you want to. If you want to begin opening up pigeonholes for knowledge about how to read and write, each new reading and writing experience will make the next task easier. And the more you have in your memory, the freer you will feel to be creative in deciding on any given occasion which elements to use and how to work on them.

Before printed books became available in great numbers, speakers and writers had to develop their memories much more extensively than we do today. Can you imagine what it must have been like to write before there were dictionaries, encyclopedias, or any other alphabetized reference works? In those days, memory specialists devised elaborate systems for connecting physical images with concepts. Scholars developed imaginative mental buildings so that students could place each different subject in a memorable part of the building and then, when speaking or writing, "walk" to the appropriate topic (still in the mind) and find there the concepts useful for making a speech delivered without notes. You may have played games using similar devices of association. When we associate an idea with the image of some tangible thing, most of us seem to retain a more durable memory of it than if we tried to remember the idea abstractly—which is one good reason to make our writing as "concrete" or as tied-to-the-senses as possible. The concept "bigotry," for example, may be associated in your mind with some character from a movie, or with some face that you once saw in a newspaper, or some event that you remember from a class. The useful word "supercilious" carries more weight if it calls to mind, as its roots suggest, a picture of a face with a condescendingly lifted eyebrow.

We do not suggest that you memorize any elaborate chart of physical places organized according to different topics, though at one time that kind of chart was an essential part of everyone's education. (You might enjoy reading in *The Art of Memory*, by Frances Yates, to discover just how productive such storehouses once were.) The metaphor of a store of topics could be dangerous if it suggests that ideas are like pieces of meat or potatoes, lying inert and waiting to be picked up. But we have organized this book to follow the key topics about any piece of writing that every good writer must consciously or unconsciously explore at some stage in each writing project. Since these topics, organized in this way, help us think about how to write, we suggest that you "lift" them off the table of contents, and store them in your memory. If you check through them, before doing your final drafts, to see whether you have covered each topic, you will gradually develop habits that will to some degree combat the empty feeling of having nothing to say.

We have now considered three "storage bins" from which past experiences can be drawn: what you know about other people who may be your readers; what you know about yourself; and what you have accumulated in the way of memories.

But of course we are not limited to past experience. In the next three sections we'll talk about how you can move in on the world around you and make it yield *new* stuff for your writing. In *observation* (looking and listening), in *conversation,* and in *reading* and *research* (that more systematic conversation with experts that we learn to conduct in college), you will discover immense reservoirs filled with riches free for the taking.

Your everyday experiences and observations as resources

Already today, no matter how uneventful the day has been, a great deal has happened to you. As you read here, more is happening in you and around you. Many of these happenings you have hardly noticed, and many of them you have not noticed at all. (Some you could not have noticed even if you tried: all the inner workings of your body and subconscious mental processes.)

Despite this great quantity of happenings, you may feel that nothing *dramatic* has happened, nothing worth writing about. You might want to say:

> Surely you don't expect me to write something like this: "I woke up after a bad dream, blew my nose, went to the toilet, brushed my teeth, showered, combed my hair, ate cornflakes for breakfast, hurried to class, five minutes late, and had a hard time keeping awake. Now I am sitting here, my head aches . . ." What happens to me most of the time is like that, just boring routine stuff.

Quite right. No one routine moment, *if* it is viewed in a routine way, will provide material for writing. But one person's routine is another person's original observation. Any one of those moments, from the dream to the boredom in class, could provide original material for writing, if you learned to *look* at it, *study* it, and *think* about it intensely.

NOTEBOOK ENTRY

Take a comfortable position for writing, close your eyes, and concentrate for a few moments on what you can hear. Now list the sounds, leaving three or four lines between each sound, like this (the following list is what Gregory "receives," writing the first draft of this paragraph on his word processor, in Chicago, Sunday, March 3, 1985, 8:53 A.M.):

> Foghorn, Lake Michigan, every 12 seconds or so
> A truck backfires
> A plane in the distance
> A speeding car in the distance
> Ringing in my ears
> Hum of my computer printer
> Another car, nearer
> Rattle of my computer keys as I type

> Squeak of my chair as I rock a bit
> My teeth tapping out a nervous rhythm from *My Fair Lady*

Now do the same exercise on what you can *see*, again leaving space for comments later. What Booth sees when he does that is this:

> Lots of plastic—my Apple computer set-up. All beige
>   plastic
> A multicolored apple with a bite out of it, the bite made
>   by the A in Apple
> Scattered papers, more than I realized
> A roll of toilet paper for nose-blowing
> Books scattered all over the scene, disorganized
> A flowered coffee cup
> An overflowing wastebasket
> Two huge old Chicago telephone directories
> A tan dial telephone
> Seven reference works
> My reflection in the monitor screen (absolutely startling—I
>   had never noticed that before!)

So far these lists seem to bear out the claim that everything around me is routine, boring—except maybe that reflection in the screen. Perhaps your list seems the same. But now, as a second step, either in the "hearing" list or the "seeing" list, run through quickly, filling in the first thought about it that comes to mind. Here's Gregory's for the hearing list:

> *Foghorn:* Strange that there's a foghorn on this sunshiny
>   morning. Somebody forgot to turn it off?
> *Truck backfiring:* Or was it a shot? The *Tribune* delivery
>   truck? Too late for that. Too many shots these days.
> *Plane:* Who's flying where, at this time on a Sunday
>   morning? People hurrying home from conferences
>   after news of disaster? Grandparents flying to see
>   newborn grandchildren?
> *Speeding car:* Drag racers at this time of day? Police chase?
> *Ringing in ears:* My cold is not really cured. Better take it
>   easy. Shouldn't I just stop writing here. This writing
>   is too hard, in my weakened condition!
> *Hum of computer:* I am surrounded by electronic gadgetry.
>   Am using more machinery in this one room than my
>   grandparents *saw* in a lifetime. Could I manage to

> live their kind of life? What would they make of
> mine?
>
> *Second car:* Why isn't everyone at home, where one ought
> to be on a Sunday morning?
>
> *Rattle of keyboard:* I hadn't noticed that sound for weeks, yet
> it accompanies me many hours of each week.
> Whatta racket!
>
> *Squeak of chair:* Too many things around here need oiling.
>
> *Teeth tapping:* This nervousness—does it mean that I have
> no confidence at all in this part of this chapter? I'm
> *sure* I should stop. This is too hard!

As you fill in your associations, remember that it doesn't matter at all whether they are good or bad, bright or stupid. They are what they are.

As the third step, read over your whole list, thinking about what it would tell some observer from another planet (or any other culture) about who you are and how you live. If someone from an earlier century looked at ours, for example, he or she would be surprised, even shocked, by how weird, how exotic, how unintelligible everything is. What feels like routine to us— trucks, planes, fear of shooting, computer hums—all would seem like a fascinating mystery to anyone from any other time and place. About the only sounds that would be familiar would be the ringing ears and perhaps the foghorn—though even the absolute regularity of that has become possible only in our century, with electric timing devices.

And how *much* of our lives are spent performing what machines require us to perform! Are we the boss or are they? More than a century ago, Samuel Butler, in a great satirical novel, *Erewhon,* speculated about the danger that we will all become simply servants of machines—"affectionate machine-tickling aphids." Have we become that?

In this way, spend a few more moments *thinking* about what your two lists say about you and the life you lead. Then go through your visual list again and pick out what seems to you the most puzzling or complex or interesting single item—and now really *look* at that object for at least five minutes. If you spend five minutes really *attending* to something you ordinarily just "see," you will make yourself an expert in that thing— you'll know it better than just about anybody else except the person who made it. And you will be surprised at what you find.

Booth writes:

I'm going to choose something I've only glanced at until this morning—the multicolored apple used as the logo for the Apple company—the one with the bite out of it. Soon I am seeing details that I had never noticed before: the apple is embossed, raised from the beige background. The silver letters, "apple II," are highly polished, reflecting patterns—suddenly I see that they are really quite beautiful patterns—I had never before noticed just how well-designed the letters are, how carefully styled, all lower case. How lovely the patterns of light on the burnished letters! I wonder why the "a" in "apple" is not capitalized? Is it only to allow for that slick bite out of the apple? Or did it seem to the designer more stylish, more modern to avoid the capital, as in some modern poetry?

And why the bite out of the apple? I had not thought much before about the association with Adam and Eve. What do I make of *that?* Is this supposed to be a machine for use when innocence has been lost? Are the makers suggesting the way the ultra-sophisticated new man and woman emerges into the computer age? Suddenly I think of something that may have been obvious to most computer users: the relation of the bite in the apple to the computer jargon terms, "bytes" and "bits." It may have nothing to do with Adam and Eve. How typical of someone like me, trained in the humanities, to think of literary associations before mechanical or technical ones.

Finally, what of the colors? Of course the stem of the apple must be green, and the dominant tone must be red. But why not *all* red, with a green stem? Oh, I see: the rainbow suggests the multiple possibilities that this machine will open for my life —the "pluses" my "Apple II-plus" will offer me.

None of what we have been doing here constitutes writing that one would call ready for reading (except that ours gets used as an example in a textbook). It's warm-up stuff, designed to reveal just how much you can discover in your world simply by opening your eyes and ears.

PARAGRAPH PRACTICE

Continue the warm-up now by writing a paragraph or so on one or more of the following observations—suggestions that might, sooner or later, tempt you toward a developed essay.

My life as it would appear to my grandfather
The best-designed object in my room—Why I consider it
    well-designed

My life as an "affectionate, machine-tickling aphid" (me
    and my gadgets)
Why my desk is more (less) visually interesting than
    Booth's
Sounds (smells, sights) I most like to remember, and why

We have only scratched the surface of the riches that will turn up whenever you open your eyes and ears—and then use your mind on what you find. Most of what you see and hear will not in itself make an essay. But it will stock your mind (and perhaps your notebook) with material that may prove useful in many essays. Remember that you are learning to write just as much when you are sitting in the dining hall scribbling notes on the way students talk "when nobody is listening" as you are when you write at your desk.

Your conversations as a resource

Merely to listen to conversations is often worthwhile, but taking part in them is more likely to enrich our stock of opinions and our ways of improving them. Learning to hold good conversations can be one of the best ways to find something to say worth saying.

If we had to rely only on our private thoughts, we would never acquire much of an education, or much of anything else. As the great philosopher of science, Karl Popper, puts it, "We owe most of our knowledge to others." We all must learn from other people, and we do that best when we carry on conversations with those who can talk to us best and thus teach us best.

Such conversationalists need not be living. We meet them in books and articles, in poems and stories, movies and on TV. In the conclusion of this chapter we'll consider those mysterious friendships that we find in our reading, the authors who are perhaps the friends most important to our writing. But important as book-friends are, they can never replace actual conversation with living people. Conversing in class, in the dormitory, at work, at home, we

learn not only what other people believe—and thus learn something about how to make our writing appeal to different readers—
but what we ourselves believe. Going somewhat beyond Bly's own
point, we could say that *only* when views clash or differ do they
become clarified and then modified; only when I say something that
stirs you to disagree am I likely to grow into a new position—
perhaps one that can accommodate both of our original views.

Here is a possible conversation about Bly's argument:

SANDRA: I didn't like that "Enemy Evenings" piece.

JACK: Why not? I liked it a lot.

SANDRA: I don't know—it sort of made me feel uncomfortable.
I felt she was attacking *me.*

JACK: Oh, so you're from a small town?

SANDRA: No, I'm from New York City. Are you accusing me
of being a hick?

JACK: Oh, no, that's not what I meant. I just thought that
maybe you thought Bly was attacking small towns,
and you . . .

SANDRA: I don't think she's really attacking small towns. What
she's attacking is people who don't say what they
think.

JACK: And you don't say what you think?

SANDRA: Not often. I don't know quite why—maybe because
I'm the third child in our family, and I learned to
keep out of trouble by watching the mistakes of my
two older brothers and keeping quiet. Yeah, I think
that's probably why; in our family saying what you
thought meant trouble.

JACK: Your parents didn't allow disagreement? Mine didn't
allow us *not* to disagree. It was wild. Did you just
have to keep quiet?

SANDRA: You know, I'm not at all sure that I *had* to. Maybe it
was just that my brothers were always so smart-assed
—*they* were maybe the ones that didn't want
discussion . . . Anyway, I don't like to read stuff that
makes me feel under attack.

JACK: Well, I liked Bly's essay because it made me more
determined to give my honest opinion in discussions.
I think if I hadn't just read it I would have responded

to your dislike by just saying something like "yeah, I didn't like it either." And then we wouldn't be talking.

SANDRA: You know, I'm glad we're kicking it around, because now I think I know *why* I didn't like Carol Bly's piece.

Notice that a conversation of this kind does not lead the participants to conclude that their differences don't matter because they are all "mere opinion." One widespread belief these days is that there are only two kinds of statement: *opinions* about matters that cannot be proved and that are therefore merely personal or subjective; and *facts* that can be shown to be either true or false. The views that you develop in good conversations will not fit either of these extremes. Dealing with the issues that matter to us most in life, we cannot hope for certainty, but we are not thus condemned to mere unsupported opinion. We can learn to weigh opinions in conversation and discover those that, though uncertain, still carry the most weight.

What people call "mere opinion" is thus the necessary starting point in all conversation. As we converse, we discover that we must modify some opinions because they clash with other beliefs, while we strengthen others as we formulate good reasons for holding on to them. Though opinions untested are often dangerous, they are the stuff out of which our thinking is made. Many opinions are not just "mere." We all learn early in life that some opinions are in fact better than others, deserving perhaps a better name. Some are indeed simply off-the-cuff, undeveloped hunches that will not stand up long under thoughtful investigation. But others stand the test of experience. We all say things like, "I once thought the Rolling Stones were the best rock group going, but now that I've heard a lot more rock, I know better"—meaning "my *informed* opinion has some right to replace the *uninformed* opinion."

We arrive at informed opinions in many ways, of course, but perhaps the most frequent correction of hasty judgment is provided in conversation, when someone gives us information we didn't know about, or ideas we hadn't thought of, or says, "Why do you say that?" or, "That's crazy," or, "You must be kidding!" At such moments, ideas that had seemed perhaps obvious and unquestionable receive the questioning that they deserve—and thinking begins.

Such challenges, often quite accidental, can take place almost anywhere, in or out of class. They may occur more often in the "college of hard knocks" than in an established college. In fact, too many students manage to pass through a college and pick up the diploma without ever being touched by the kind of genuine education that occurs when uninformed opinion clashes with informed opinion and gets worked out in genuine conversation.

In short, the kind of education you earn for yourself will depend more on whether or not you find and develop conversation partners than on anything else (except *possibly* working seriously on your assignments). Discussion classes in which everyone tries to listen to the reasons supporting different positions will be useful to you. Even more useful will be regular small-group seminars or tutorials in which you and other students can hammer out your opinions about the readings and about your writing problems. If you have not yet discovered how much you can learn from such a group, the suggestion may seem strange to you. But if you make it work, it can be one of the most important steps in your educational experience. (If you're lucky, late-night rap sessions in the dorm can be even more valuable!)

Short of such regular sessions, you can learn a great deal by practicing one simple device. Whenever anyone says something that you do not understand or do not agree with, speak up. Ask for clarification. Though some people will be annoyed, either because they don't *know* why they believe something or because they have secret reasons, most people will enjoy entering into a conversation, especially if you seem to have asked the question not to put them on the spot but to find where the discussion leads.

Finally, don't forget your teachers as primary conversational partners. Teachers may sometimes tire of students who camp in their offices to butter them up for good grades rather than to solve problems. But teachers are never annoyed when someone has got stuck on a question or problem and then comes in for genuine discussion. You may of course encounter exceptions. Booth once went to a teacher's office and found only one chair in it, the teacher's, an arrangement so awkward that no student would spend longer than thirty seconds with him. But such people should not discourage you. Try again with another teacher, and yet another, until you find one who will be grateful to exchange *good* talk.

The "subject itself" as a resource

We turn at last to the reservoir of topics that is sometimes treated as if it were the only one: the assigned reading—in this case Bly's article—and other possible reading. The obvious place to look for ideas about "Enemy Evenings" is in the article itself.

Good essays on such an assignment will *always* show evidence of serious digging in. Even when you find the other resources indispensable, you will use them best when you have a detailed acquaintance with the assigned subject. Such mastery will in fact play an essential role in your use of the other resources. The best evidence, for example, of your authority, as you make use of your "self" (see "Your 'Self' as a Resource" section) will be the quality of your engagement with an author's ideas.

How can I ensure that my reading of Bly yields the greatest assistance toward writing well on the assignment? Notice that this question is really identical with the question, "How should I read *any* essay that I really want to understand?"

A good answer, though highly general, is, "Read actively, not passively. Ask questions as you go." Anyone who reads passively, simply accepting what is said, without *putting questions to the text,* will not find anything interesting to say about it. The most that such passive reading can produce is a summary of what the essay seems to say—and probably an inaccurate one at that. If you have read "Enemy Evenings" passively, you have discovered what you think every other reader has also discovered in it, and of course you will be bored as you think of telling your teacher what he or she probably knows already.

Active reading is not like that. The active reader asks questions at every point—questions that *interpret* what the author is saying. Interpretation can be thought of as taking place in two stages (though they will always overlap): a stage where you *analyze* the author's text, and then a stage where you appraise or *evaluate* it. It is sometimes useful to think of the first stage as one of **understanding,** allowing the author to be master for awhile, and the second as one of ***overstanding*** (a word not in your dictionary), the point where you take charge and ask questions that the author might not even have thought about and might even reject as irrelevant or unfair.

Understanding. In the first stage, it is usually useful to look for ways in which the text responds to questions that we have been asking you to put to your own writing: What is the author's purpose? What theses develop the purpose? What topics are explored, yielding what kinds of support for the theses? What is the organization of the piece? And so on. The text itself will to some degree dictate what questions are most appropriate at each stage of your reading, but you will at least want to touch the following bases.

Purpose. Always pay close attention to the structure of the essay, in order to come as close as possible to reconstructing the author's purpose—not just as a vague summary but as what controls everything else she does. A reader can become increasingly confident about understanding an author's purpose by formulating what *seems* to be the purpose and then asking whether the details of the essay make good sense as an effort to support that purpose.

The testing can be best done in the form of "Why?" questions put to the author. Why do your paragraphs move in their present order? Why do you, Bly, begin with the particular descriptions of Paragraphs 1 and 2 rather than, say, with the anecdotes of Paragraphs 10 and 11? Why do you put your long list of suggested topics in the middle instead of at the end? Why do you have a one-sentence paragraph (13)? Do you find that the answers to such questions confirm or undermine your initial notion of her purpose?

When we put these questions to every paragraph in sequence, we produce for ourselves an outline of topics, and theses about the topics. Often the outline will itself reveal a tight argumentative design, as seen in our analysis of the letter to *The New York Times* about Governor Cuomo (p. 41). But often enough we find that even admired essays produce no clear sequence of tightly connected points in their outlines. Instead they produce more or less interesting puzzles. The "thuses" and "therefores" don't quite follow, or, as in Bly's piece, they don't occur frequently enough to give complete clues to her plan. For example, at the beginning of Paragraph 6 she leaves it to us to provide the unspoken "The real reason is that . . . ," and at the beginning of Paragraph 10 she makes a sudden leap backwards, as if starting over with fresh anecdotes about the contrast between urban and rural practice.

When an author makes such moves you can often discover a good reason by again asking, "Why?" Why does Bly do this? What *purpose* do these moves serve? If you find no answers to such questions, it may well be that you are looking at a poor essay.

Another example: When Bly says, "At the same time . . ." (beginning Paragraph 14), what does she mean? Same time as what? How does the phrase relate to the "however" in the fifth sentence of the paragraph? "Oh, I see now! 'At the same time' signals a momentary acknowledgment of a qualification about the whole essay: She is turning to a 'possible objection' before moving to her concluding, witty climax about her relatively cheerful kind of controversy."

After continuing this kind of close re-reading of the text for awhile, asking questions all the way, you may feel confident about both the author's purpose and her detailed moves in carrying it out. Reading Bly, we find that we can do the first of these but not the second, though we did not finally give up on making a confident and clear outline until we had read the essay a third or fourth time.

What we did come up with was not a clear outline but a disconcertingly fluid summary, secure only in the knowledge of her thesis, which is given in her final sentence. In spite of her loose organization and avoidance of explicit statements like, "What I am trying to prove is . . .," we know what she wants us to accept, not just because authors generally conclude with their most important point but because everything else in the essay is subordinate. Our confidence is increased when we notice that the only strong *logical* claim in the piece, the only "thus" or "therefore," precedes another statement of the same thesis: *therefore, I propose* (Paragraph 7).

Design. Having done our best to understand her purposes by attending to her organization, we are ready to ask further questions about Bly's reasons for an unclear surface design. We can ask: What does she gain, if anything, from *not* laying out her main points as "One . . . ," "Two . . . ," "Three . . . ," "Therefore . . . ," "Conclusion . . ."? Asking that question, we see something that no superficial reader of the essay is likely to have thought of: If she is to make her "enemy evenings" inviting, she must not sound like someone who would play *her* part in any such evening by hammering everybody else into submission. The evenings she suggests must sound like fun; they must not be heavy battles marked by real enmity, but delightful explorations of highly diverse material—like her essay itself. The reader must feel that she would be a fine companion in an evening's discussion. (Note how this subordinate purpose—to establish a particular *ethos* for herself—complicates the simpler purpose of urging us to engage in controversial conversation.)

Reasoning. Once we feel reasonably secure about what the author is up to, we are ready to raise questions about her supporting details. (Whether or not this support is the best possible we save for the stage of evaluation.)

It is usually useful at this point to distinguish the claims that the author tries to support, from those that are merely asserted as self-evident. Every author relies on some beliefs—called *assumptions*—that are not explicitly supported; often these beliefs are not even stated. Such assumptions, once uncovered, reveal a great deal about the text we are reading. ("This author thinks that such-and-such an assertion requires no support. Yet to me it *does* need support—so I've learned something about her.")

As for the kinds of statement that *are* given support, we can ask just *how* the reasons are handled. Does the author offer any tight logic or rigorous statistical proofs? Obviously Bly does not. She presents reasons mainly through personal anecdotes and appeals to common experience. She expects us to know, even before we read her essay, what kinds of experiences will validate her claims. Rather than putting arguments in a precisely ordered sequence, she has selected examples that she apparently thinks will ring true, primarily because we know of other examples that hers will call to mind.

Obviously Bly is not doing the kind of writing that relies on logical "clinchers," but rather the kind that relies on free speculation. She is imitating in her essay the precise kind of conversation that the essay recommends. When, for example, she says "therefore," at the beginning of Paragraph 7, it does not and need not carry strong logical force; it is a kind of conversational "therefore," followed by proposals that do not follow from any strict logical preparation. Notice that none of her other paragraphs begins with strong logical claims either. The movement throughout is anecdotal, casual, chatty—like a friend talking to friends.

At some points, it is true, we can reconstruct a fairly rigorous logical path. At the beginning of Paragraph 2, for example, "The case is always made that . . ." must really mean something like, "Against what I have just said, the case is always made that . . .," and what follows could be preceded with, "to which I answer that . . ." Indeed, we can usually find *some* sort of progression that could, with a little effort, be translated into logical terms, although her instincts as a writer lead her to be colloquial and casual, not tight and rigorous. Strong "therefores" and "thuses" would be inconsistent with her overall tone.

Overstanding. Just how long we dwell at the stage of reconstruction will depend on many variables. But sooner or later— often even on the first reading—we move to the evaluative level of questioning the validity both of the author's general enterprise and her way of carrying it out. Even at the stage of *under*standing we will have inevitably moved toward many evaluative comments; at the stage of *over*standing we make them explicit. As we do so, we of course move increasingly away from the author's interests and closer to our own. We ask questions such as: "Is Bly's example of the suburban piano teacher convincing, to *me*? Is it not possible that she's just frustrated at having to live in a small town? How well established is her claim that 'enemy evenings' will produce the advantages she claims for them? Will they in fact help 'reduce loneliness'? Will they provide 'a change of air,' a release of 'social indignation,' of 'psychological curiosity,' and of 'intellectual doubt'? Will they increase our capacity to feel deeply? Can she really believe that *suburbs* are characterized by critical thinking? (*Suburbs?* Who's she kidding?) Does Bly give me any good reason to think that people can engage in open disagreement about politics and religion without getting mad at each other? What real evidence does she offer that her methods will produce these results?" The answer to this last question is perhaps puzzling: hardly any. She relies on our readiness to believe that debates about drainage ditches or "competition vs. cooperation" will produce people who are able to offer praise and blame to each other without disaster.

As we said earlier, you can always—not just sometimes but always—find some claims for which the author gives no evidence or argument: the *assumptions* or fundamental beliefs that she expects you to share without proof. Since all arguments, including valid ones, rely on some principles that are accepted but not proved, finding that Bly too relies on assumptions hardly discredits her case. But the nature of those assumptions helps to reveal the kind of person we are "conversing" with, and it thus provides material worth discussing in an essay. When you discover, for example, that Bly gives no argument whatever for her claim that, "It is bad for people to live out their lives without having their ideas challenged," you have found something worth writing about because not all writers would think that *that* assumption needs no support, and because not all readers will have noticed it. Is it *really* worse for people to live relatively unchallenged lives in small towns than to live under the steady and often hectic challenges of big city life? Now *there's* a point worth discussing.

On the other hand, if you find that you accept her assumptions without argument, and if you find the line of argument from those assumptions to the conclusions solid, then you have good reason to accept those conclusions and to argue that other readers should do the same; your essay can be an expansion or development of her ideas.

When a free-wheeling procedure like Bly's works, it can be highly persuasive. When it doesn't work, it risks seeming paltry or opinionated. Do you think Bly's essay succeeds? Whatever your answer, you should have no trouble now in finding something to say, something that would not be obvious to casual readers. You have been discovering openings for both agreement and disagreement. At every point where an author relies on a loose connection, you can in effect squeeze through it and argue for another view. Bly says, "There is little lonelier than small-town life when small talk is the principal means of peace." "What's the evidence?" you ask, politely. The essay responds by simply referring to a piece about loneliness by Sherwood Anderson. Since this is not tight evidence but mere illustration, you are free to look closely at the words and to pick a quarrel: "I can think of lonelier places and times: being a bag-lady in the big city is lonelier; attending a cocktail party where hypersophisticates use abstractions to avoid looking closely at anyone other than themselves—that can surely rival small-town loneliness." And so on.

When this kind of careful reading is extended over several books or articles on a single question, we call it "research." You may be asked to do a research paper later in this course (Chapter 14), and we'll have some advice then about how to carry on a conversation among several friends, choosing from their ideas those most useful to you. But for now, the point is that even the shortest essay provides an endless supply of material— for the reader who knows how to ask the right questions.

Exploring objections to your own theses

Throughout our discussion of the six resources, we have had implicitly in mind a resource for invention that we discussed briefly toward the end of Chapter 3 (pp. 82–85): bringing opposing voices to life in your own prose. In each of the resource domains we have described, one of the most fruitful moves you can make is to ask yourself persistently, "What can I say to *oppose* the point I am making now? What could my most intelligent opponent say *against* my case?" Even when consulting your memory or observation, you can ask, "What would be revealed by someone else's memory of those events? What would someone with a radically different point of view probably see here?"

Becoming educated is in part learning to take in the contrasting perspectives of other lives. If you work at learning, this broadening will to some degree just happen. But if you carefully seal yourself off from any new and potentially threatening viewpoints, it will not occur. You can dismiss an opposing viewpoint without having to think very hard: it's crazy, nonsensical, radical, stupid, ignorant. But simply by asking questions of such opinions— "What evidence can you offer for yourself?" or, "Is that opinion *really* stupid?" or, "Can that opinion be as silly as I have thought, when people who seem otherwise intelligent hold to it?"—you can often drive yourself into some hard thinking and solid learning. Whenever that happens, you'll find plenty to write about.

Conclusion

As you move through college, the chief instrument of progress will be learning how to ask an ever-expanding repertory of
questions. The kinds we have been illustrating can turn up useful
theses for your essays, because pushing hard on any one of them
will teach you something not obvious to the passive or hasty
reader. And whenever you *learn* something you will have something to write about. Even your teacher will not have discovered
everything you might discover, *if* you concentrate on some one
question for an hour or so, using not only the essay but the other
resources we have described. No teacher can predict what you will
find if you think about your reader, your "self," your memories,
your observations, your conversations, and your reading as resources in thinking about the essay.

Usually you will find your richest source of answers in whatever essay or book you have in hand. The reason your teachers ask
you to read these works rather than others is that they have been
found to raise the most interesting questions. But you will find
additional help in the other five resources. As you become more
sensitive to differences among audiences, as your self is enriched
and your knowledge of it deepens, as your memory is stored with
questions and answers, and as you develop the art of conversation,
you will find that every article and every book are full of suggestions for your essays. Indeed, you may soon reach the point where
your chief difficulty is not finding something to say but choosing
from too many good possibilities.

It is said of Socrates that he could never read through even
one book. Starting on page one, so many questions would come
to mind that he could scarcely get to page two. You needn't go that
far in your questioning, but you can take him as a model whenever
you think you have nothing to say.

6

Design: Making a shape

Finding the right organization

Design is everywhere

Once you have found something to say, you may sometimes see the best order for saying it at once. Some purposes and theses seem to dictate only one possible order of presentation. But more often a major problem remains: Not only must you decide which topics are important enough to be included, but—even more important—how to order them, how to give the whole essay an effective design. You will recall from Chapter 2 that "design" refers here to the organization of parts into the best possible order (see pp. 36–37). The "best" design of an engine or a kitchen, for example, is the one that allows all of the parts to fit together properly and make the whole thing work. **Design** in writing, then, emphasizes the writer's active role in achieving *interrelatedness* and *proportion* among parts.

When designing something we discover that some parts are simply more important than others. The parts of any object can be listed in a *hierarchy* of descending importance. If you owned a car that ran smoothly, got good gas mileage, handled well on the road, and started in the winter, you would probably not consider its ugly taillights to be a major design flaw. The shape of the lights is simply less important than a reliable engine. But bad brakes *would* count as a serious design flaw. Since our lives depend on good brakes, we place them higher on our hierarchy than either the taillights *or* the engine.

Whether an object works well depends more on how its parts are arranged than on whether each part itself is a "good" one, as judged by some general standard. The best carburetor for a Mercedes-Benz would stall most other cars. The best sentence for a scientific report might seem dull and weak in a humorous essay. The same concept applies to everything we make: movies, wedding ceremonies, buildings, poems, essays, and so on. The parts of these "made things" do not arrange themselves spontaneously into the right order. The parts of made things must be arranged *by* someone into a design. And the "goodness" of the parts cannot be assessed without considering the whole, or the organization that makes the whole.

We can see everyday consequences of bad design all around us. The world is full of shoddy, annoying, illogically made objects: garden trowels that bend, adult scissors with child-sized handles, paper towels that won't tear straight, repetitive and dull music, knobs and off/on switches that snap in your fingers, ill-fitting clothes, rambling speeches, wind-up toys that break, appliances that can't be repaired, mattresses that give sleepers a backache, running shoes that fall apart—and essays that get nowhere and say nothing worth saying. Even expensive and presumably high-quality machines such as automobiles and computers are frequently recalled for design failures—not just for careless assembly-line mistakes, but for mistakes made on the drawing board. Writing an essay is like making any other object in at least this one respect: Whatever makes for bad design in any object or procedure— inconsistency, disorder, poor proportions, incompleteness—will also make for bad design in writing.

You may encounter people who say that design in writing is unimportant: "Just say what you think, spontaneously, and it will be more interesting than if you make elaborate plans." There are occasions when that may be true—when inspiration strikes and our quick first drafts are better than our most carefully designed revisions. But in such cases we can always discover, analyzing after the event, that we have intuitively hit upon a design even if we did not consciously plan it. To rely on our intuitions alone, however, is too unpredictable. For every good design that comes in a flash, we are likely to find ten that need to be improved by hard critical thinking.

Conventional arrangement of parts

At this point you might want to say, "All right, I'm willing to think about my overall design—if I only knew what it was. I can see that the parts of a pair of scissors are basically two blades and a handle, but what are the 'parts' of an essay?"

As implied in the example about defective brakes and ugly taillights, some of an essay's parts are necessary, others are optional. In an essay, necessary parts include an **opening,** in which you engage the reader's attention and introduce your purpose and thesis; a follow-up to the opening, the **development,** in which you arrange the arguments, reasons, facts, evidence, explanations, statistics, examples, analogies, or appeals to general knowledge that provide logic or underscore your assertions; and a **conclusion,** in which you wrap up your case, make final appeals to the reader, and create a sense of closure.

The simplest and most conventional arrangement of these parts is as follows:

Beginning: Getting Readers To Bite
   Opening gambit (optional): anecdotes, personal references, etc.
   Introduction: stating the thesis, raising questions, or posing the problem
Middle, or Development: Keeping Readers Hooked
   Factual evidence (Inductive argument):
      analogies
      examples
      statistics
      anecdotes
   Logical proof (Deductive argument):
      axioms or general rules
      authority
      analogies
Ending: Landing Readers
   <u>Conclusion</u> (depending on purpose and thesis, may be simply

Most important - its the last thing the readers remember sums up the whole essay

a summary, but may be open-ended, suggesting further questions)

Our metaphor from fishing should not suggest that you set out to make fools of your readers. But it is true that, like fish, readers don't *have* to swallow our line; however, we must give them a decent reward for doing so. The reward may be nothing more than good company—we don't have to be deceitful or self-serving—but we need bait of some kind.

Note that few actual essays will follow the preceding outline precisely. Sometimes the entire middle may be taken up with a persuasive anecdote, or with one decisive logical proof. The style, tone, and length of the parts will vary enormously among different authors and different writings. But the conventional design we have just illustrated is still the most commonly observed arrangement and you can see why: It makes sense; it carries readers toward a completed statement. Just as "John hit the ball" is what many linguists think of as a the most simple and basic sentence form in English, the "kernel sentence," so *"introduction* leading to *development* leading to *conclusion"* is the "kernel arrangement" of all the parts of an essay.

NOTEBOOK ENTRY

Turn now to examine some object that has recently failed you or proved otherwise annoying because of bad design. Write a paragraph of about 200 words in your notebook criticizing the design of the object and suggesting how it could have been improved.

Then turn to one of your recent essays and write another paragraph of the same kind of criticism. Consider whether the promises you make in your opening (promises about what will follow) are really fulfilled, whether your arrangement of reasons or evidence makes sense, whether your conclusion really concludes anything, and so on. Without rewriting the essay now, suggest ways in which the design, or arrangement of parts, could be improved.

You may use this second paragraph as the basis for rewriting the essay at some future time.

Design variations

A few patterns of design are so useful and familiar that speakers and writers fall back on them again and again. We use many of them every day without giving them much thought. Others depend on conscious decision and sustained attention to revising. There are no rules about which design will prove best, but you should ask, at some point in every writing task, whether your design—perhaps one of the following—is the best choice for achieving your purpose.

Chronological order. This design entails observing an appropriate sequence in time. When you are writing about events in the past, especially about personal experiences, chronological order will usually seem best, and it will often come about almost automatically. Of course you may choose to violate chronology for special effects or purposes, but as a general rule, sticking to the most straightforward sequence will prove least confusing for your readers. For example:

> My rotten day began with the phone ringing at 5:00 A.M.: wrong number. I knew right then that things did not look promising, and I was unfortunately right. At breakfast I discovered that I was out of coffee; at lunch I accidentally left a five dollar bill instead of a one on the table; at afternoon break I dripped the stuffing from a pineapple danish onto my new skirt, and I missed my bus on the way home. The way things have gone today I'll consider myself lucky if I can get through the rest of the evening without falling down the stairs and breaking a leg. I'm not even angry any longer; I just want to make it to tomorrow.

A common variation on chronological order is to describe the ending first and then "flash back" to the events that led up to it. Ralph Ellison does this in his much-admired novel, *Invisible Man* (1952). His Prologue presents the final event of his story. He begins his account of all the events that lead up to the Prologue later, in Chapter 1. One may even begin in the middle of things, as George Eliot does in *Daniel Deronda* (1876), flash back to the beginning, catch up to the present, and then follow simple chronological order from that point on. Essayists often use these variations, but they may also follow patterns like that of the standard newspaper account, which goes something like this: Give the whole story in the headline, then in the first paragraph give the whole story again, but with more detail, and then give the whole story again in greater detail; finally perhaps offer some interpretation or commentary. Note that this design, like all the others, is chosen because of its service to a certain range of possible readers: Some will want to skim only headlines, some will take time to read only the first paragraph, and some will want to catch every detail. In most essay writing, we try to "outsmart" readers who are looking only for headlines. Good design will not only capture readers' interest but provide good reasons for continuing to read, from paragraph to paragraph.

Causal order. In this arrangement, the writer traces known consequences back to their probable origins, or predicts consequences from known causes. This design often overlaps with chronology, for causes and their effects occur in time, and explanations of them often become explanations of chronological sequence as well. But even though chronology and causes overlap, a writer may clearly emphasize one more than the other. Most historians, for example, take care to keep the chronology of events clear, but they often place a stronger emphasis on *why* things happened rather than *when*. Often you may strengthen an account by giving the consequences first and then telling why they occurred. Many arguments about policy—about what we should do today to ensure a good tomorrow—are based on claims that such-and-such causes will produce such-and-such effects. For example:

> Tuition increases are a great source of concern to students (and their parents), but few students or parents have any detailed knowledge of their underlying causes. A primary cause, one that few students think about, is their own demand for specialized programs that require expensive, sophisticated equipment (and the facilities to house them), plus the services of highly trained specialists. A hundred years ago when getting an education meant mainly learning to read the classics, all a school had to finance was a square box (only moderately heated and lighted) where teachers and students could read together. A second big cause of cost increases has

been rising utility bills. Heating costs alone have quintupled in the last decade, and the increased cost of heating huge buildings, many of them built without regard to energy conservation, has been a terrible drain on college budgets. A third important cause is the need to raise faculty salaries. During the double-digit inflation of the mid-1970s, faculty salaries fell far below increases in the cost of living, which means that most faculty actually lost salary for a six or seven year period. To make up for those losses now is a necessity, but extremely expensive. Other causes also contribute to tuition increases, but these three contribute the most.

Climactic order. Essays designed to reach a climax arrange every detail so that the most emphatic or dramatic point comes at the end. If, for example, you were a waiter describing various categories of customers, you might want to progress from the least unexpected or least objectionable type to the most unexpected or most objectionable type. If you were describing an experience that had changed your mind or feelings about something important, you might want to build up to the moment of change, thus ending with the most dramatic part last.

Climactic order points to the importance of endings: The final impression is usually the one we remember longest. Endings provide a sense of closure and finality—like the "Amen" at the end of a hymn—and signal that the thing is now complete. When an ending is illogical, inappropriate, or simply missing, we are likely to feel that the whole thing—the movie, the book, the game, the essay—has been ruined. The effect (or lack thereof) of the ending, in other words, reflects back over the entire object or event.

We used our opening in Chapter 1 to show that beginnings are hard. Effective endings are at least as hard to write, and often they are even more important. For example:

My wife and I had taken childbirth classes at the local hospital, and had seen films of other births, so I had slipped into thinking that the real event would be just that easy, as devoid of drama as a TV replay. And if you know what to expect, the initial stages don't seem very exciting. After labor begins and you arrive at the hospital, the mother-to-be receives an enema and gets dressed in one of those goofy gowns that make the wearer look like something on its way to the laundry.

But it's not long before things get more intense. The contractions come closer and closer, stronger and stronger. The woman becomes totally engrossed in fighting off the pain, maintaining control. The drama increases as the baby moves down the birth canal. Tension builds as the woman is impelled into the pushing stage.

And then, at last, the miracle occurs: a blueish purple aquatic creature emerges all in a rush. For a moment it wears a disgruntled, pained expression—looking human only by a charitable act of the imagination—and then, as the special valve opens and blood rushes into the lungs, the baby turns pink from the head on down, a transformation that conjures up the image of God breathing life into Adam's dust.

Hierarchical order. This arrangement involves going from least to most important or valuable. Sometimes going from lower to higher importance can be identical with climactic order—going from least to most dramatic—but not always. Two different essays on the beginnings of the American Revolution, for example, could discuss either the colonists' growing feelings of indignation and outrage (climactic order), or England's least to most-important political blunders (hierarchical order).

Hierarchical order becomes extremely important when a writer is trying to decide in what order to discuss reasons and evidence. What we said earlier about endings applies here also. Because arguments unfold in time, you may want to order your reasons from least to most important, in order to place your most important points in the reader's mind last (although this principle of order is not a rule, even in argumentative essays). For example:

> Recent research suggests that three factors correlate in ascending order of significance with the writing abilities of high school and college students. The first factor is predictably important: the student's motivation. How much time and energy students devote to writing correlates highly with how much progress they make. The second factor, which seems to correlate even more highly, is more surprising: how many hours per week students and their families spend together in conversation. Students from families that talk to-

gether at meal times tend to be better writers than students from families that watch TV during meal times. But the third and most important factor seems to be students' reading experience. Students who are avid readers consistently score better on writing assignments than students who read little. And the correlation follows the reading curve closely: Students who "read some" score better than those who "don't read at all," while those who "read a lot" score better than those who "read some." Researchers also find that students who are readers are the same students whose parents consistently read them bedside stories when they were little.

Deductive order. Here we progress from a general statement to particular examples. While it is often important and useful to cite the particular cases that illustrate your general claims *as you go,* a complicated subject that requires a theoretical introduction may in fact be covered more efficiently if the general principles are laid out first, and the examples developed last. To avoid the charge that you relied on sensational or lurid examples instead of argument, for instance, you might want to begin an essay for or against "abortion on demand" by articulating the case in abstract moral terms *before* you cite particulars. (See Chapter 13 for a fuller treatment of deduction.) For example:

> As teachers, we do not think that the most powerful arguments in support of writing and literature courses should be based on predictions about how "communication skills" will increase one's future income. Income is important, of course, but we think the most powerful arguments are made by linking the development of one's language skills to the development of thinking, character, and citizenship. If people need to be able to think well in order to make sound moral judgments and to be good citizens, then they must achieve some sophistication in their use of language. Otherwise they wind up like those who want to be good athletes, but who never develop any muscular strength or coordination. For example . . .

Inductive order. Such an arrangement progresses from particular examples to general statements. Any essay that begins with a citation of "the facts of the case" and leads up to a general proposition—"Corruption is rife at County Hospital," or, "Corrupt politicians dominate public institutions in the state"—is designed inductively. An essay on campus racism might begin by citing such specifics as the low percentage of minorities in the Greek houses, or the absence of minorities among officeholders on the Student Council, or the prevalence of bigoted graffiti in the washrooms, or the scarcity of pictures of minority students in the recruiting brochures, and so on. The essay might pause to discuss each of these particulars, building up to the generalization, "Racism on this campus is thus more widespread than most people realize." (See Chapter 12 for a fuller treatment of induction.) For example:

> Dear Sir,
>
> As head of the Department of Transportation, you should know that the city desperately needs a traffic light at the corner of 6th and Broadway. This intersection has seen an average of one accident a month for the past year, involving several injuries and one death. In addition, Broadway's curves make it hard for the drivers crossing Broadway on 6th Street to see without edging dangerously close to cross-flowing traffic. What's more, a lot of people trying to avoid this intersection cut through Roseland Hills on Sanders Drive. But Sanders Drive was not designed for heavy traffic flow, so the drivers avoiding 6th and Broadway are only bringing congestion and danger to a residential neighborhood. Everyone I know who uses that intersection is convinced that a light is needed. May I hope that you will agree?

Procedural order. As its name suggests, this arrangement follows the order of a process or a procedure. This may sound like the simplest of all designs: "Just write up the lab procedure to accord exactly with each step of the experiment." As you know if you have ever tried to do it, fulfilling such an assignment accurately and clearly can be devilishly hard. Many of the activities that go into any procedure or process depend on sight or touch and are difficult to put into words. How do you tell someone in words exactly how a batch of bread dough should feel when you have kneaded it long enough? How do you describe how it feels when

Spacial - how things apper in a space; discriptive.

you *haven't* kneaded it long enough? How do you tell someone in words how to roll out noodle dough so that the sheets all have uniform thickness? How do you describe the way to tune a car engine? How to play a piano piece? How to write a good essay? (We have tried to design this whole book as an account of the procedures that go into essay writing: a cookbook on writing.)

Just how hard it is to describe a process or procedure well is nowhere better illustrated than in those maddeningly ambiguous and sometimes impossible sets of directions that come with such items as disassembled toys, furniture, and bicycles. It is obvious that even though writers are being paid to write these accounts, and even though they have no reason to be unclear or to drive you insane, they often almost manage to do both. For some of us the most maddening procedural accounts these days are found in the manuals that come with computers. Since they ought to be intelligible to raw beginners, they should ideally cover every conceivable step in systematic order. But in our experience the user quickly becomes completely baffled, because the writer has not thought hard enough about the reader's needs.

To illustrate how much might be required in a fully useful procedural account, we offer here "Greg's Favorite Health Bread Recipe." As you read it, you might ask yourself what kind of reader Gregory had in mind as he wrote:

Step One

Put ¾ cup of milk and 3 tablespoons of sunflower seed oil in separate pots and place them on very low heat to warm. While the milk and oil are warming, measure out ¼ cup of honey for adding to the milk (later), measure 1½ cups of lukewarm water into a measuring cup, and measure out the dry ingredients into a large mixing bowl:

> 6 cups unbleached flour
> ¼ cup bran
> ¼ cup wheat germ
> 1 tablespoon salt
> ⅓ cup dried milk

Mix the dry ingredients together with a big spoon. Add the honey to the warmed milk, mixing the honey and milk until they are blended. Turn off the oil so it doesn't get too hot. (You only want it to be warm to the touch, not hot enough to burn your finger.) Add 2 packets of dry yeast (2 tablespoons if you are using bulk yeast) to the cup and a half of water, and mix until the yeast is dissolved.

Step Two

Pour the milk and honey mixture into the dry ingredients and mix until the flour forms soft little balls about the size of marbles. Make sure that the mixture is balled up uniformly throughout. Then pour in the yeast and water, mixing with a large spoon until the dough begins to form one large ball. Pour the warm oil over the sticky ball and work it in with your hands, pulling the dough away from the sides of the bowl and greasing the bowl at the same time with the oil. At this point the dough becomes too hard to stir with a spoon any longer and it is time to knead.

Kneading is important. It releases the gluten in the flour and makes the sticky ball elastic and cohesive. The dough should be kneaded for at least ten minutes by spreading a little bit of flour on the counter top and dumping the dough on it, then pushing against it with the heels of both hands, using your fingers to grab the part of the dough that you just pushed forward, and folding it back over toward you. You need to get a rhythm going or kneading will cramp your muscles. The movement is push/fold, push/fold, push/fold. You'll have to find your own rhythm and speed, but when the dough is well kneaded it will spring back when you push your finger into it, and it will have a satiny sheen on its surface. Keep putting a little flour under the dough if it sticks to the counter top as you are kneading.

Step Three

When the dough is kneaded, place it back in the mixing bowl with the oiled sides and cover with a damp cloth. Put the bowl in a warm, draft-free place: The inside of an oven heated only by a pilot light is a good place. Let the dough rise for one hour or longer until it has doubled in size. Then punch it down, pushing the gas out of it, and form it into a smooth ball. You may have to knead it a little more to make it smooth. Cut it in two equal halves with a knife. Turn each ball so that the smooth surface is on the counter top and the cut surface is up. Pinch the cut surface together into a seam, pushing down on the dough and shaping it with your hands into a rough imitation of a small football. Placing the pinched seam on the bottom, put each loaf into a greased loaf pan, and let the loaves rise again about 30 minutes—not in the oven this time—until the dough puffs up 1 inch above the top of the loaf pan.

Step Four

After the loaves have started rising in the pans for about 15 minutes, turn your oven to 400°. When the dough is ready, put the pans in the middle of the oven and let them bake for 10 minutes at 400°. Then turn the oven down to 350° and continue to bake for an additional 20 minutes. When the bread is done it will be medium brown and sound hollow if tapped on the top with your finger nail. Turn the loaves upside down onto a cooling rack, letting the bread fall out. Place them on their sides and let them cool or slice a loaf while it's hot. It's great with butter and honey.

Even with these detailed directions you may still have questions about how to follow this procedure unless you have seen some of these things done. We don't tell you, for example, how to grease a loaf pan (or even what a loaf pan is, for that matter), nor do we describe a cooling rack, nor do we define precisely what we mean by lukewarm or medium brown, nor do we explain why there is gas in the dough after it rises. (And what is "rising" anyway?) Yet the description is already getting lengthy—and making bread is not nearly as complicated as, say, writing an essay. Remember, then, that there may be times when a procedural design is what you need, but if you need to make it comprehensive and unambiguous—so that even someone who had never seen the procedure could follow your directions and get it right—you are tackling a job harder than it may look.

As we have already indicated, these design patterns are not mutually exclusive; they sometimes overlap. A chronological order may overlap a causal account; an inductive account may overlap both. The important thing in choosing a design is not to strain for one that has never been used before, but to be consistent.

Design doesn't depend on the gift of gab or knowing what the teacher wants, but on a clear sense of purpose.

There is no one moment in the process of writing when all good writers will choose a design. Some writers like to make early outlines. Others do not make outlines on paper at all. Whether or not you actually work from an outline, one way to test the soundness of your design is to see if you can outline your essay *after* you think it is completed. If you cannot find a consistently developed ordering of parts at that point, then it may be time to rethink your design.

NOTEBOOK ENTRY

Here is a poem by William Wordsworth, "The World Is Too Much With Us" (1807), in which he attacks his fellow citizens' money-grubbing materialism ("getting and spending"). After you have read the sonnet, we will consider one possible way of organizing an essay in response to it.

> The world is too much with us; late and soon,
> Getting and spending, we lay waste our powers:
> Little we see in Nature that is ours;
> We have given our hearts away, a sordid boon!
> The Sea that bares her bosom to the moon;
> The winds that will be howling at all hours,
> And are up-gathered now like sleeping flowers;
> For this, for everything, we are out of tune;
> It moves us not! Great God! I'd rather be
> A Pagan suckled in a creed outworn,
> So might I, standing on this pleasant lea
> Have glimpses that would make me less forlorn;
> Have sight of Proteus rising from the sea;
> Or hear old Triton blow his wreathed horn.

Suppose now that you had to write an essay in response to this poem and that the general purpose had been given you by the teacher: "Analyze the theme of the poem and give your reasons for believing that the theme is either trivial or important." Suppose that your readers are the other students in the class who have also read the poem but whose opinions about it you do not know. Suppose, finally, that you have already decided on the thesis, "I would like my reader to agree with me that Wordsworth's disgust with the materialism of his countrymen applies as easily to Americans today as it did to his own audience over a hundred years ago."

Inductive Order

I.   Opening: Quick sketches to hook the reader.
    A.   A brief view of what it's like at the shopping mall almost any hour of the day or night.
    B.   A quick description of my Aunt Mary's suburban acquisitiveness, her uncritical acceptance of "getting ahead," as the main goal in life, and her unembarrassed tendency to measure the value of everything by how much it costs.

II.   Middle (Development): A systematic look at some major influences in American culture—to show the reader that I've really looked around me and thought about this subject.
    A.   The Media: Television, radio, newspapers, and magazines are dominated by advertisements which generally portray happiness as buying and owning commercial products.
    B.   Sports: Sports have become big business, giving grossly inflated salaries to players, and becoming inseparably tied to the money-making power of television.
    C.   Education: Too many college students' interest in an education today is economic advancement, not personal growth, expansion of knowledge, or acquisition of wisdom.
    D.   Religion: Even churches have adapted commercial practices and become big businesses on TV. The preachers don't know their parishioners (if "parishioners" applies to TV church-goers) yet they make millions endorsing and selling trinkets, records, and books to their "flock."

III. Closing: The generalizations drawn from my examples.
    A.   American culture is deeply materialistic and acquisitive.
    B.   What Wordsworth implies about the people of his time, that they were once *not* so materialistic, is also true about Americans today, and this narrowing of the value of everything to its price represents a loss of spiritual values and sensitivity.
    C.   Our own barbaric indulgence in "getting and

spending" and "laying waste our powers" is worthy
of the same kind of scorn that Wordsworth heaped on
his contemporaries.

Work out in your notebook at least one other outline
revealing another design, one that you might actually use if you
were to write an essay on this poem.

An example from professional writing

Your ability to make appropriate designs of your own can be
sharpened by studying the designs that other writers have used.
You may never want to use anyone else's design as a precise model
for your own, but if you think about why any one design works,
you can learn something about how to improve your own.

As an example of how a skilful author works, here is an essay
by William Golding, the British novelist who recently was
awarded the Nobel Prize for literature. We suggest that you read
the essay at least twice: the first time fairly rapidly and the second
time flagging with your pencil the clues to his design.

*   *   *   *   *

Thinking as a Hobby *

While I was still a boy, I came to the conclusion that there were (1)
three grades of thinking; and since I was later to claim thinking as
my hobby, I came to an even stranger conclusion—namely, that
I myself could not think at all.

I must have been an unsatisfactory child for grownups to (2)
deal with. I remember how incomprehensible they appeared to me
at first, but not, of course, how I appeared to them. It was the
headmaster of my grammar school who first brought the subject
of thinking before me—though neither in the way, nor with the
result he intended. He had some statuettes in his study. They
stood on a high cupboard behind his desk. One was a lady wearing
nothing but a bath towel. She seemed frozen in an eternal panic

*From *Holiday,* August 1961.

lest the bath towel slip down any farther; and since she had no arms, she was in an unfortunate position to pull the towel up again. Next to her crouched the statuette of a leopard, ready to spring down at the top drawer of a filing cabinet labeled A-AH. My innocence interpreted this as the victim's last, despairing cry. Beyond the leopard was a naked, muscular gentleman, who sat, looking down, with his chin on his fist and his elbow on his knee. He seemed utterly miserable.

Some time later, I learned about these statuettes. The head- (3) master had placed them where they would face delinquent children, because they symbolized to him the whole of life. The naked lady was the Venus of Milo. She was Love. She was not worried about the towel. She was just busy being beautiful. The leopard was Nature, and he was being natural. The naked, muscular gentleman was not miserable. He was Rodin's Thinker, an image of pure thought. It is easy to buy small plaster models of what you think life is like.

I had better explain that I was a frequent visitor to the head- (4) master's study, because of the latest thing I had done or left undone. As we now say, I was not integrated. I was, if anything, disintegrated; and I was puzzled. Grownups never made sense. Whenever I found myself in a penal position before the headmaster's desk, with the statuettes glimmering whitely above him, I would sink my head, clasp my hands behind my back and writhe one shoe over the other.

The headmaster would look opaquely at me, through flash- (5) ing spectacles.

"What are we going to do with you?"

Well, what *were* they going to do with me? I would writhe my shoe some more and stare down at the worn rug.

"Look up, boy! Can't you look up?"

Then I would look up at the cupboard, where the naked lady (6) was frozen in her panic and the muscular gentleman contemplated the hindquarters of the leopard in endless gloom. I had nothing to say to the headmaster. His spectacles caught the light so that you could see nothing human behind them. There was no possibility of communication.

"Don't you ever think at all?"

No, I didn't think, wasn't thinking, couldn't think—I was (7) simply waiting in anguish for the interview to stop.

"Then you'd better learn—hadn't you?"

On one occasion the headmaster leaped to his feet, reached up and plonked Rodin's masterpiece on the desk before me.

"That's what a man looks like when he's really thinking."

I surveyed the gentleman without interest or comprehension.

"Go back to your class."

Clearly there was something missing in me. Nature had en- (8) dowed the rest of the human race with a sixth sense and left me out. This must be so, I mused, on my way back to the class, since whether I had broken a window, or failed to remember Boyle's Law, or been late for school, my teachers produced me one, adult answer: "Why can't you think?"

As I saw the case, I had broken the window because I had (9) tried to hit Jack Arney with a cricket ball and missed him; I could not remember Boyle's Law because I had never bothered to learn it; and I was late for school because I preferred looking over the bridge into the river. In fact, I was wicked. Were my teachers, perhaps, so good that they could not understand the depths of my depravity? Were they clear, untormented people who could direct their every action by this mysterious business of thinking? The whole thing was incomprehensible. In my earlier years, I found even the statuette of the Thinker confusing. I did not believe any of my teachers were naked, ever. Like someone born deaf, but bitterly determined to find out about sound, I watched my teachers to find out about thought.

There was Mr. Houghton. He was always telling me to think. (10) With a modest satisfaction, he would tell me that he had thought a bit himself. Then why did he spend so much time drinking? Or was there more sense in drinking than there appeared to be? But if not, and if drinking were in fact ruinous to health—and Mr. Houghton was ruined, there was no doubt about that—why was he always talking about the clean life and the virtues of fresh air? He would spread his arms wide with the action of a man who habitually spent his time striding along mountain ridges.

"Open air does me good, boys—I know it!"   (11)

Sometimes, exalted by his own oratory, he would leap from his desk and hustle us outside into a hideous wind.

"Now, boys! Deep breaths! Feel it right down inside you— huge draughts of God's good air!"

He would stand before us, rejoicing in his perfect health, an (12) open-air man. He would put his hands on his waist and take a tremendous breath. You could hear the wind, trapped in the cavern of his chest and struggling with all the unnatural impediments. His body would reel with shock and his ruined face go white at the unaccustomed visitation. He would stagger back to his desk and collapse there, useless for the rest of the morning.

Mr. Houghton was given to high-minded monologues about (13) the good life, sexless and full of duty. Yet in the middle of one of these monologues, if a girl passed the window, tapping along on her neat little feet, he would interrupt his discourse, his neck would turn of itself and he would watch her out of sight. In this instance, he seemed to me ruled not by thought but by an invisible and irresistible spring in his nape.

His neck was an object of great interest to me. Normally it (14) bulged a bit over his collar. But Mr. Houghton had fought in the First World War alongside both Americans and French, and had come—by who knows what illogic?—to a settled detestation of both countries. If either country happened to be prominent in current affairs, no argument could make Mr. Houghton think well of it. He would bang the desk, his neck would bulge still further and go red. "You can say what you like," he would cry, "but I've thought about this—and I know what I think!"

Mr. Houghton thought with his neck.

There was Miss Parsons. She assured us that her dearest wish (15) was our welfare, but I knew even then, with the mysterious clairvoyance of childhood, that what she wanted most was the husband she never got. There was Mr. Hands—and so on.

I have dealt at length with my teachers because this was my (16) introduction to the nature of what is commonly called thought. Through them I discovered that thought is often full of unconscious prejudice, ignorance and hypocrisy. It will lecture on disinterested purity while its neck is being remorselessly twisted toward a skirt. Technically, it is about as proficient as most businessmen's golf, as honest as most politicians' intentions, or— to come near my own preoccupation—as coherent as most books that get written. It is what I came to call grade-three thinking, though more properly, it is feeling, rather than thought.

True, often there is a kind of innocence in prejudices, but in (17) those days I viewed grade-three thinking with an intolerant contempt and an incautious mockery. I delighted to confront a pious lady who hated the Germans with the proposition that we should love our enemies. She taught me a great truth in dealing with grade-three thinkers; because of her, I no longer dismiss lightly a

mental process which for nine-tenths of the population is the
nearest they will ever get to thought. They have immense solidar-
ity. We had better respect them, for we are outnumbered and
surrounded. A crowd of grade-three thinkers, all shouting the
same thing, all warming their hands at the fire of their own prejudices, will not thank you for pointing out the contradictions in
their beliefs. Man is a gregarious animal, and enjoys agreement as
cows will graze all the same way on the side of a hill.

Grade-two thinking is the detection of contradictions. I (18)
reached grade two when I trapped the poor, pious lady. Grade-two
thinkers do not stampede easily, though often they fall into the
other fault and lag behind. Grade-two thinking is a withdrawal,
with eyes and ears open. It became my hobby and brought satisfaction and loneliness in either hand. For grade-two thinking destroys without having the power to create. It set me watching the
crowds cheering His Majesty the King and asking myself what all
the fuss was about, without giving me anything positive to put in
the place of that heady patriotism. But there were compensations.
To hear people justify their habit of hunting foxes and tearing
them to pieces by claiming that the foxes liked it. To hear our
Prime Minister talk about the great benefit we conferred on India
by jailing people like Pandit Nehru and Gandhi. To hear American
politicians talk about peace in one sentence and refuse to join the
League of Nations in the next. Yes, there were moments of delight.

But I was growing toward adolescence and had to admit that (19)
Mr. Houghton was not the only one with an irresistible spring in
his neck. I, too, felt the compulsive hand of nature and began to
find that pointing out contradiction could be costly as well as fun.
There was Ruth, for example, a serious and attractive girl. I was
an atheist at the time. Grade-two thinking is a menace to religion
and knocks down sects like skittles. I put myself in a position to
be converted by her with an hypocrisy worthy of grade three. She
was a Methodist—or at least, her parents were, and Ruth had to
follow suit. But, alas, instead of relying on the Holy Spirit to
convert me, Ruth was foolish enough to open her pretty mouth in
argument. She claimed that the Bible (King James Version) was
literally inspired. I countered by saying that the Catholics believed
in the literal inspiration of Saint Jerome's *Vulgate,* and the two
books were different. Argument flagged.

At last she remarked that there were an awful lot of Metho- (20)

dists, and they couldn't be wrong, could they—not all those millions? That was too easy, said I restively (for the nearer you were to Ruth, the nicer she was to be near to) since there were more Roman Catholics than Methodists anyway; and they couldn't be wrong, could they—not all those hundreds of millions? An awful flicker of doubt appeared in her eyes. I slid my arm round her waist and murmured breathlessly that if we were counting heads, the Buddhists were the boys for my money. But Ruth had *really* wanted to do me good, because I was so nice. She fled. The combination of my arm and those countless Buddhists was too much for her.

That night her father visited my father and left, red-cheeked (21) and indignant. I was given the third degree to find out what had happened. It was lucky we were both of us only fourteen. I lost Ruth and gained an undeserved reputation as a potential libertine.

So grade-two thinking could be dangerous. It was in this (22) knowledge, at the age of fifteen, that I remember making a comment from the heights of grade two, on the limitations of grade three. One evening I found myself alone in the school hall, preparing it for a party. The door of the headmaster's study was open. I went in. The headmaster had ceased to thump Rodin's Thinker down on the desk as an example to the young. Perhaps he had not found any more candidates, but the statuettes were still there, glimmering and gathering dust on top of the cupboard. I stood on a chair and rearranged them. I stood Venus in her bath towel on the filing cabinet, so that now the top drawer caught its breath in a gasp of sexy excitement. "A-ah!" The portentous Thinker I placed on the edge of the cupboard so that he looked down at the bath towel and waited for it to slip.

Grade-two thinking, though it filled life with fun and excite- (23) ment, did not make for content. To find out the deficiencies of our elders bolsters the young ego but does not make for personal security. I found that grade two was not only the power to point out contradictions. It took the swimmer some distance from the shore and left him there, out of his depth. I decided that Pontius Pilate was a typical grade-two thinker. "What is truth?" he said, a very common grade-two thought, but one that is used always as the end of an argument instead of the beginning. There is a still higher grade of thought which says, "What is truth?" and sets out to find it.

But these grade-one thinkers were few and far between. (24) They did not visit my grammar school in the flesh though they were there in books. I aspired to them, partly because I was ambitious and partly because I now saw my hobby as an unsatisfactory thing if it went no further. If you set out to climb a mountain, however high you climb, you have failed if you cannot reach the top.

I *did* meet an undeniably grade-one thinker in my first year (25) at Oxford. I was looking over a small bridge in Magdalen Deer Park, and a tiny mustached and hatted figure came and stood by my side. He was a German who had just fled from the Nazis to Oxford as a temporary refuge. His name was Einstein.

But Professor Einstein knew no English at that time and I (26) knew only two words of German. I beamed at him, trying wordlessly to convey by my bearing all the affection and respect that the English felt for him. It is possible—and I have to make the admission—that I felt here were two grade-one thinkers standing side by side; yet I doubt if my face conveyed more than a formless awe. I would have given my Greek and Latin and French and a good slice of my English for enough German to communicate. But we were divided; he was as inscrutable as my headmaster. For perhaps five minutes we stood together on the bridge, undeniable grade-one thinker and breathless aspirant. With true greatness, Professor Einstein realized that any contact was better than none. He pointed to a trout wavering in midstream.

He spoke: *"Fisch."* (27)

My brain reeled. Here I was, mingling with the great, and yet helpless as the veriest grade-three thinker. Desperately I sought for some sign by which I might convey that I, too, revered pure reason. I nodded vehemently. In a brilliant flash I used up half my German vocabulary.

"Fisch. Ja. Ja."

For perhaps another five minutes we stood side by side. Then Professor Einstein, his whole figure still conveying good will and amiability, drifted away out of sight.

I, too, would be a grade-one thinker. I was irreverent at the (28) best of times. Political and religious systems, social customs, loyalties and traditions, they all came tumbling down like so many rotten apples off a tree. This was a fine hobby and a sensible substitute for cricket, since you could play it all the year round. I came up in the end with what must always remain the justification for grade-one thinking, its sign, seal and charter. I devised a coherent system for living. It was a moral system, which was wholly logical. Of course, as I readily admitted, conversion of the world to my way of thinking might be difficult, since my system did away with a number of trifles, such as big business, centralized government, armies, marriage . . .

It was Ruth all over again. I had some very good friends who (29) stood by me, and still do. But my acquaintances vanished, taking the girls with them. Young women seemed oddly contented with the world as it was. They valued the meaningless ceremony with a ring. Young men, while willing to concede the chaining sordidness of marriage, were hesitant about abandoning the organizations which they hoped would give them a career. A young man on the first rung of the Royal Navy, while perfectly agreeable to doing away with big business and marriage, got as red-necked as Mr. Houghton when I proposed a world without any battleships in it.

Had the game gone too far? Was it a game any longer? In (30) those prewar days, I stood to lose a great deal, for the sake of a hobby.

Now you are expecting me to describe how I saw the folly (31) of my ways and came back to the warm nest, where prejudices are so often called loyalties, where pointless actions are hallowed into custom by repetition, where we are content to say we think when all we do is feel.

But you would be wrong. I dropped my hobby and turned (32) professional.

If I were to go back to the headmaster's study and find the dusty statuettes still there, I would arrange them differently. I (33) would dust Venus and put her aside, for I have come to love her and know her for the fair thing she is. But I would put the Thinker, sunk in his desperate thought, where there were shadows before him—and at his back, I would put the leopard, crouched and ready to spring.

*   *   *   *   *

Can you now fill in the paragraph numbers that correspond to what we take to be Golding's main sections?

I. Introduction (Paragraphs   ).
II. Development (Paragraphs   ).

       A.   Grade III thinkers (Paragraphs   ).
       B.   Grade II thinkers (Paragraphs   ).
       C.   Grade I thinkers (Paragraphs   ).
III.   Conclusion (Paragraphs   ).

If you designated Paragraphs 1–9 as the Introduction, you rightly saw that in these paragraphs Golding sets his tone and introduces his subject: thinking. But Golding can no more write an essay on thinking in general than you could write one "in general" on astronomy, love, or warfare. He needs some angle on the subject, a way of marking off a limited piece of it: a thesis. The first nine paragraphs map out the territory: He is going to write about thinking, starting with the confusing references to thinking that he heard his elders make when he was a child. You don't yet know what his thesis is (does it damage his essay that he doesn't clearly announce his thesis in Paragraph 1?), but the fact that he makes all of his elders sound pompous and self-righteous suggests that he might be writing a satire, and this in turn suggests something about his purpose even before we come to his thesis. If this *is* a satire, then he is writing it to make fun of something. Since his own thoughts, even those that describe his earlier poor thinking, are in themselves clear, he can't be making fun of himself as he is now. The thinking of his elders, however, is so unclear, and so phony, that the object of his ridicule may be seen at once. He intends to make fun of the adult world's smug inconsistencies and hypocrisies about thinking.

The next 20 paragraphs constitute the *development*, or the middle part, of the essay. Within this section of his text, Golding creates three sub-categories of thinking which he arranges in ascending order of importance. Paragraphs 10–17 define Grade III thinkers, those who dignify their self-indulgent or self-contradictory prejudices with the term "thought," yet have not the slightest idea of what real thinking entails. Paradoxically, their complete inability to think allows them to feel complete confidence in their thinking ability. Grade III thinkers are not hypocrites, for they don't possess enough thinking power to deceive themselves. Since they call all of their feelings thoughts, and since their lives are full of feeling, they just assume that they are full of thought.

Observe that although Golding does not bestow the name "Grade III" on these thinkers until near the end of this sub-section (Paragraph 16), his way of handling examples prevents our becoming confused. By the time he has given you his extended example of Mr. Houghton (Paragraphs 10–14), and has referred to Miss Parsons, Mr. Hands, and "my teachers" in general as Houghton's counterparts, you are quite prepared to hear that his main interest is neither Mr. Houghton nor his teachers, but in some larger quality: a human failing that they all share. When he finally calls them "Grade III thinkers" he is only naming a category that he has already taught us to recognize.

Paragraphs 18–22 define Grade II thinkers, those juvenile critics (of any age) who gleefully scorn the Grade III thinkers' foolish inconsistencies and self-indulgences, but who fail to see that their own debunking is not in itself first-class thinking. By now we are quite sure that Golding *is* writing a satire. By the end of Paragraph 22, four-fifths of the way through the essay, it is clear that he is scoffing at the tendency of human beings to dignify most of their *non*thinking as first-rate mental activity.

If we were doing a complete analysis of this essay—guided by our seven questions from Chapter 2—we would here want to ask questions about character and tone. Since Golding is criticizing his fellow creatures for vanity and shallowness, for example, how does he avoid coming off as a snob? If self-indulgence about one's own prejudices and vanity is as universal as he says it is, what makes *him* a competent critic of these vices? The answer, clearly, is that he does not exempt himself from the scorn he heaps on others. He implies that he has earned the right to criticize others because he sees how much he has been like them. Where they have been vain and self-indulgent, so has he. He thus gives himself the character of the kind of critic we most readily believe: the one with first-hand knowledge of the sin he condemns. We are likely to think that any other critic speaks mere pious humbug.

These effects are not obviously the result of design, since they permeate the whole essay. But can you see how they would be reduced or destroyed by careless design? We see here again how the parts of an essay, like our terms for analyzing essays, intertwine. Golding's character is finally found everywhere, not just at those points where he refers to it explicitly; his design is finally everywhere, not just in the grand outline. Similarly, his purpose, his topics, and his thesis are all finally detectable wherever we look. Only when we analyze do we deal with them one by one.

Turning back to the larger design, we see that Paragraphs 23–30 define Grade I thinkers, those few who do not assume that their feelings are thoughts, who do not assume that to scorn others' failings is to be intellectual, and who focus on the pursuit of truths outside of themselves. They do not bluster like Mr. Houghton, nor do they criticize unconstructively like the youthful Golding. They serve other masters than their own passions and vanity. Here Golding's design shows itself to be a crucial component of his meaning. He could have concluded his essay, after showing himself to have matured enough to see the difference at last between Grade II and Grade I thinkers, with the Einstein anecdote. This ordering would have been logical and clear. But Golding's real point is that even when we mature enough (and some never do) to see what is right, we don't always do it. Thus, before he relates the concluding episode, he shows himself still subject to the pull of nature. Having decided to be Grade I-lofty instead of Grade II-snide, he commits the sin of vanity all over again. He refers to his youthful naiveté and egocentrism in a tone of devastating sarcasm as he observes, "I devised a coherent system for living. It was a moral system, which was wholly logical. Of course, as I readily admitted, conversion of the world to my way of thinking might be difficult . . ." If Golding had not injected this part—this further exposure of his youthful vanity—much of his overall effect would be lost.

Golding's realization of his own foolishness precipitates the Conclusion (Paragraphs 30–33), in which he ends these spiraling descents into vanity, and thus resolves the essay, by ceasing to treat thinking as a hobby. He turns professional instead and makes thinking a lifelong activity. The final image in the essay is one of humility: The professional—that is, dedicated—thinker knows that nothing will ever save him from the potential attacks of human nature. As we have moved toward this conclusion, we have slowly discovered that his many satirical thrusts have not been made simply for the fun of mocking human error. Behind the mockery there is a celebration of genuine thinking—and an effort to demonstrate just how difficult and rare a thing it is.

Although Golding's ideas and feelings make a complicated weave, his design is thoroughly simple, thoroughly unoriginal as a general plan, and thoroughly effective: *introduction* leading to three-part *development* leading to brief *conclusion.* The test of a good design is not how fancy or subtle it is but how well it works. Imagine how Golding's essay would suffer if he had reversed his treatment of the different grades of thinkers. Think what he would have lost if he had left out the charming details of his Introduction, and had begun with a three-sentence, abstract lead-in such as this: "While I was still a boy, the various scrapes I got into, usually followed by irritated put-downs from adults about my thoughtlessness, convinced me that I didn't know how to think at all. The whole thing was incomprehensible. Like someone born deaf, but bitterly determined to find out about sound, I watched my teachers to find out about thought." Think what he would have lost if he had skipped the picture of himself turning Grade I thinking into the same kind of silly, vain activity that he had been doing as a Grade II thinker (Paragraphs 28–29). We can neither rearrange nor omit any of the parts of Golding's essay without damaging it. That's good design.

Finally, note that it would be possible to describe the design of Golding's essay as either chronological or hierarchical or climactic. The various stages of thinking Golding passes through as he matures correspond to the passage of time, and thus give the essay a chronological framework. However, since the sort of maturity he describes does not always occur as people get older (else Mr. Houghton would have been a better thinker himself), chronology seems less important than hierarchy. The heart of the essay is the distinction he draws between the three kinds of mental activities —regardless of chronological age or the passing of time.

PARAGRAPH PRACTICE

1. In a paragraph of about 150–175 words, discuss what the effect would be if Golding had eliminated Paragraph 9.
2. In another paragraph of about the same length, discuss the likely effect if he had omitted all of Paragraph 2 past the dash in the middle of the fourth sentence of the essay, and all of Paragraph 3.
3. In a third paragraph, discuss the effect if he had reversed Paragraphs 8 and 9.

NOTEBOOK ENTRY

Part of the problem of achieving effective design is maintaining paragraph-by-paragraph cohesion (the subject of Chapter 7). You have already performed some exercise in paragraph tracking

in Chapter 3 but it is useful to think about this issue while you
are thinking about overall organization.

Here are five paragraphs in scrambled order from the
beginning of Northrop Frye's *The Educated Imagination* (1962). Each
paragraph contains clear clues to its proper position among the
others. Study those clues carefully until you can decide on
the proper order. Then record in your notebook the evidence
you used and the interpretation you placed on it. Does your
order agree with the order chosen by other students in your
class?

That complicating factor is the contrast between "I like this"
and "I don't like this." In this Robinson Crusoe life I've
assigned you, you may have moods of complete peacefulness
and joy, moods when you accept your island and everything
around you. You wouldn't have such moods very often, and
when you had them, they'd be moods of identification, when
you felt that the island was a part of you and you a part of it.
That is not the feeling of consciousness or awareness, where
you feel split off from everything that's not your perceiving self.
Your habitual state of mind is the feeling of separation which
goes with being conscious, and the feeling "this is not a part of
me" soon becomes "this is not what I want." Notice the word
"want": we'll be coming back to it.

The language you use on this level of the mind [i.e., while
one is "simply looking at the world"] is the language of
consciousness or awareness. It's largely a language of nouns
and adjectives. You have to have names for things, and you
need qualities like "wet" or "green" or "beautiful" to describe
how things seem to you. This is the speculative or
contemplative position of the mind, the position in which the
arts and sciences begin, although they don't stay there very
long. The sciences begin by accepting the facts and the
evidence about an outside world without trying to alter them.
Science proceeds by accurate measurement and description,
and follows the demands of the reason rather than the
emotions. What it deals with is there, whether we like it or not.
The emotions are unreasonable: for them it's what they like and
don't like that comes first. We'd be naturally inclined to think
that the arts follow the path of emotion, in contrast to the sciences.
Up to a point they do, but there's a complicating factor.

In the second place, you find that looking at the world, as
something set over against you, splits your mind in two. You
have an intellect that feels curious about it and wants to study
it, and you have feelings or emotions that see it as beautiful or
austere or terrible. You know that both these attitudes have
some reality, at least for you. If the ship you were wrecked in

was a Western ship, you'd probably feel that your intellect tells
you more about what's really there in the outer world, and that
your emotions tell you more about what's going on inside of
you. If your background were Oriental, you'd be more likely to
reverse this and say that the beauty or terror was what was
really there, and that your instinct to count and classify and
measure and pull to pieces was what was inside your mind. But
whether your point of view is Western or Eastern, intellect and
emotion never get together in your mind as long as you're
simply looking at the world. They alternate, and keep you
divided between them.

So you soon realize that there's a difference between the
world you're living in and the world you want to live in. The
world you want to live in is a human world, not an objective
one: it's not an environment but a home; it's not the world you
see but the world you build out of what you see. You go to
work to build a shelter or plant a garden, and as soon as you
start to work you've moved into a different level of human life.
You're not separating only yourself from nature now, but
constructing a human world and separating it from the rest of
the world. Your intellect and emotions are now both engaged
in the same activity, so there's no longer any real distinction
between them. As soon as you plant a garden or a crop, you
develop the conception of a "weed," the plant you don't want
in there. But you can't say that "weed" is either an intellectual
or an emotional conception, because it's both at once. Further,
you go to work because you feel you have to, and because you
want something at the end of the work. That means that the
important categories of your life are no longer the subject and
the object, the watcher and the things being watched: the
important categories are what you have to do and what you
want to do—in other words, necessity and freedom.

Suppose you're shipwrecked on an uninhabited island in the
South Seas. The first thing you do is to take a long look at the
world around you, a world of sky and sea and earth and stars
and trees and hills. You see this world as objective, as
something set over against you and not yourself or related to
you in any way. And you notice two things about this objective
world. In the first place, it doesn't have any conversation. It's
full of animals and plants and insects going on with their own
business, but there's nothing that responds to you: it has no
morals and no intelligence, or at least none that you can grasp.
It may have a shape and a meaning, but it doesn't seem to be
a human shape or a human meaning. Even if there's enough to
eat and no dangerous animals, you feel lonely and frightened
and unwanted in such a world.

An example from student writing

The following essay was written by a first-year student in response to the following assignment: "Write an autobiographical essay in which you describe as precisely as you can how you developed your picture of what it means to be male or female. Don't try to describe any present hang-ups. Your task is to dramatize how you first learned that, 'what a *man* does (or is like) is so-and-so, while what a *woman* does (or is like) is such-and-such.' (Note: Do not try to develop a general thesis about sex or sexual relations in American society. Limit yourself to remembering those experiences that teach men and women how to view themselves from any early age.)"

HOW I LEARNED MY PLACE

In an essay called "The Human Continuum," Betty Roszak (1) mentions the conditioning that convinces females of their second-class status. My own experiences made it clear to me that first, my brothers were more important than I, and second, that men in general are more important than women. My childhood treatment, my teenage privileges, my literary background, and my educational experience have made clear this distinction.

I have no recollection of being fussed over as the youngest (2) child. I was born "baby sister" to a 3-year-old boy, and, at one day short of 18 months, became "big sister" to another brother. With the advent of a new baby, my older brother got his own room, and I moved in with the baby. Four years later I again moved in with the baby; a sister, this time.

As soon as Kevin, my older brother, grew big enough to (3) help with the dishes, I stretched over the counter to wash them while he did something more important. When Kevin was deemed mature enough to watch his brother and sisters, I sat with my younger siblings while he ran off to do something more important. Once I got old enough, Kevin escaped entirely. All domestic chores fell to me in the absence of my mother. Now that I live at school, the responsibility lies with Megan, the next girl; not with Brian, the next child.

When my brothers and I reached the age when the car (4)

became an issue, my secondary status was again made plain. For my first year of driving privileges, my curfew was 10:30, with occasional exceptions made for special events. At the same age, Kevin was teased when his first date kept him out until 4:00 A.M. Later, when I complained that Brian was given until 11:00 on his first night with the car, I was dismissed with the assurance that his party was important. Both my brothers have since had trouble with drunk driving. I never touch a drop, but I need special permission to have the car later than 12:30. My consistently better behavior and judgment are not issues in curfew disputes—my sex is, so I always lose.

The books I read subtly back up my feelings of inferiority. (5) I read a great deal of the science-fiction Ursula Le Guin denounces as full of male elitism. I adore Regency romances which usually depict meek women falling in love with rakish men. These are the same books my mother reads and in which I began to take an interest at age nine. I have now steeped myself in the sexist British literary tradition for almost ten years.

School offered the first real proof of my inferiority. In (6) kindergarten, I lost my best friend, Guido, to a group of boys. In elementary school, we had separate bathrooms, separate lines, separate toys; we were made aware of our differences. In junior high, only girls were scolded for cussing. In high school, the dress code applied primarily to girls. Even at Brandon University, Schwitzer Hall [the woman's dorm] is locked to ensure observance of the visitation hours. Ross Hall [the men's dorm] is never locked.

Everywhere, males, whether men or boys, enjoy more (7) freedom and more consequence than their sisters. Betty Roszak observes that "from the moment of his birth a higher value is placed . . . on the male infant," and this seems to be true. In every instance, from my relations with my brothers to my relations with men in general, I have been shown my subordinate stature. Employers, fathers, brothers, lovers; all men, gently or otherwise, point out female inferiority. And in so doing, they warp the female sense of self-esteem and further feed male domination.

DIERDRE MAHAN

After reading the essay once quickly, read it again looking for the "joints" in the design, just as you did for the Golding essay. In our view, this is a strong essay. The purpose is clear—to convince readers that our society values men more than women. The thesis, stated in Paragraph 1, is also clear: "My own experience made it clear to me that first, my brothers were more important than I, and second, that men in general are more important than women." The sentences are also well-shaped, vigorous, and appropriately plain: no serious awkwardness, no flabby reliance on unnecessary passive verbs, no excessive indulgence in sentimentality or lush adjectives.

What about the design, the organization? Here too the writing seems strong. The last sentence of Paragraph 1 makes it clear that four areas—topics—will be explored: childhood, teenage years, reading matter, and schooling. As we progress through the essay it becomes obvious that the first three of these are arranged chronologically. Paragraphs 2 and 3 treat childhood; Paragraph 4 treats the teenage years; Paragraph 5 treats reading matter, with a strong chronological arrangement that brings the author into the present: "I have now steeped myself in the sexist British literary tradition for almost ten years" (between ages 9 and 19, the author's age at the time of writing). Paragraph 6 continues the chronological ordering: elementary school, junior high, high school, and college (the present).

This essay could also be seen as organized inductively, with an Introduction (Paragraph 1), a series of particular examples in the Middle (Paragraphs 2 through 6), and a generalization based on those examples in the Conclusion (Paragraph 7). This student has obviously taken care with her design, and has thought hard about which examples from her own experience will appropriately illustrate her thesis.

ESSAY ASSIGNMENT

Choose one of the following:
   1. Try now to write two one-page accounts of the same event organized according to two different principles of order. For instance, you could write two accounts of your first month at college, giving first a chronological account of the adjustments you

had to make, and then a hierarchical account of the dominant emotions of that month.

Or you could try inductive or deductive versions of the same essay. For example, you could discuss some issue on campus that you feel needs changing (city/college antagonism, prejudice against musicians, racism, sexism, rudeness at dramatic productions or concerts, and so on). In the inductive argument, begin with several examples that lead up to a generalization about the problem. In the deductive version you will have to begin with some general proposition which you discuss and then support with particular examples.

A deductive essay might begin this way: "The basic goal of any good college program should be to help its students mature intellectually and ethically. All lesser goals, such as getting a job immediately upon graduation, pale in importance. Yet these goals are seldom mentioned to students by recruiters or teachers here. Instead, they hear endless recitations of how much money college grads make, and they are never tested for real thinking or ownership of ideas. If this is true, then this college is failing miserably at meeting the basic goals of any good college." And so on. Sentences 1 and 2 state a general proposition; sentences 3 and 4 begin to support them with particular examples; sentence 5 anticipates a conclusion.

2. Taking your subject from another college course, select some event or phenomenon that you can write about according to any of the organizational schemes discussed in this chapter. An event from history, for example, might be discussed causally, chronologically, or hierarchically. A theory in sociology might be discussed hierarchically. The case study of a particular neurosis in psychology might be discussed causally, hierarchically, or climactically. A problem in philosophy, ethics, religion, or literature could be discussed either inductively or deductively.

Even if you seldom work with an outline in advance of your composing, we suggest that you make one for this essay, at least toward the end of your work. The outline will reveal the skeleton of your design. If you are following an inductive design, for example, your essay should begin with a discussion, citation, or account of particulars and move finally toward generalization(s). Hand in the outline with your essay.

3. Look over some editorials in any newspaper and outline two or three to reveal the design, and then, in an essay directed to your teacher, discuss the effectiveness of the authors' designs. Are they consistent? Are they complete? Finally, discuss which other organizational schemes might have been used to present the same arguments. Would any of them have been *better* for the author's purposes?

6. If choosing a pattern and then writing an essay that illustrates it turns out to be too frustrating, work the other way round: Write on some issue or problem that you care deeply about or that seems most inviting to you. Revise the essay as carefully as possible, trying to ensure that your purpose is realized. *Then* make an outline of its design, and discuss in a paragraph or two whether that design is the best possible for your purpose. Would any other design work nearly as well? What would the alternatives lose or gain? Has thinking about design explicitly helped you see how you might improve the essay further with another draft? Attach your commentary to the essay when you hand it in.

Conclusion

All successful essays will reveal good design to the careful reader; in a sense the very notion of success is identical with the notion of effective design. But just how and when a writer should take conscious thought about the best possible plan will vary from writer to writer and essay to essay. Some writers find it difficult to begin with any sort of conscious plan; they like to concentrate on ideas, or insights, or purposes—and let the design "follow naturally." In fact for some writers, worrying about organization *before* writing is worse than not thinking about it at all. Worrying about it too early can prevent the kind of open exploration that leads to original ideas. Other writers (far fewer, probably) claim in contrast that they never write a word until their general outline is clear, either in their heads or on paper.

You should experiment until you find the profitable stage for you to introduce design worries. The main point is to make sure that your final draft can stand up under close attention. That will almost certainly require that you take a close hard look, after a draft or two, at the emerging design, in order either to sharpen it, or to scrap it and reach for a better one.

In the end, you should be able to look even your most critical reader in the eye and say, "If it looks disorganized to you, that's your fault, not mine."

7

Connecting for cohesion: Keeping your reader hooked

Coherence and cohesion

You have been learning how to find something to say, and how to build the best design for saying it effectively. Shouldn't that be enough? Surely the main problem in learning to write ought to be solved when we have settled on our purpose, found (or "invented") the best topics, turned them into the best theses and supporting arguments, and put each one into its right place. Why should not purpose, invention, and design be enough?

The truth is that a plain statement of what we mean does not in itself ensure success with our readers. Our design and arguments may not be recognized for what they are unless we provide the clues needed to show *how* everything is connected. Even when we talk directly with people and can observe their reactions, and even when we think we have been completely clear, we are often misunderstood. When we write, we are unable to watch or question our readers. If they misunderstand us, we have no way of finding out until it is too late. This means that when writing we must work carefully to ensure that our readers can follow us step by step through every transition to our conclusion.

We often overlook this immense difference between writing and speaking, probably because we seem to do them both in the "same language." But they are not really the same; the languages of everyday talk and of most writing differ greatly. Writing is words strung out in a line and uses only verbal signals. The conclusion of a *written* conversation, for example, must usually offer explicit clues like "In conclusion . . .," "In short . . .," "Therefore . . .," "Thus . . .," or "Finally, . . ."—relatively formal devices that might seem absurdly heavy in conversation: "We see, therefore, that . . .," "We can surely conclude, then, that . . ."

That's not how we usually end our talks with friends. We're more likely just to break off with a "See you!" or to say things like, "Gotta go now," or, at the most explicit, "Well, I'll think about it," or, "So that's it, then," or, "Let's talk it out again sometime."

In short, writing must have not only **coherence,** an effective design, but **cohesion,** an explicit set of "hooks" and "ties" that ensure a reader's interest and comprehension. Coherence is the kind of "holding together" that a good design will give any discourse, whether written or spoken. Cohesion is the result of giving readers the right kind of explicit help in *figuring out the design.* Cohesion gives readers the clues for discovering coherence.

When we talk with someone face to face, we have literally thousands of ways to keep each other on track, to make sure that we are really talking *together.* Although our talk may jump from point to unrelated point, and thus lacks formal coherence, we both can keep together, "in sync," as we say, by using a whole range of visible and tangible devices that accompany our words: we can grab an elbow, punch or pat a shoulder, wink, smile, frown, scowl, or squint; we can shake our heads, point a finger, pound a fist, or throw up our arms in mock horror. If my talk bores you, you give me nonverbal clues to that effect—yawns, wandering eyes, tapping of fingers—and these clues may contradict the explicit assurances of interest that you politely offer. When we as speakers receive such clues, we can change our tactics. If we are misunderstood, we can often pick up clues about the misunderstanding: a quizzical look, a furrowed brow. And we have many resources for correcting boredom and misunderstanding.

But this rich collection of physical devices—our "body language"—is totally denied to writers. If our writing is to hook and land our readers, it must provide written equivalents for those devices.

Cohesion in writing thus results when the reader is aided not only in discovering quickly and effectively how an essay or talk is put together but in realizing whatever interest is potentially in the design. Of course an essay with a bad design will inevitably lack coherence no matter how many "thuses" and "therefores" the author sprinkles in it. It is true that a skillful writer can sometimes disguise incoherence, at least from careless readers, and even keep them reading because of faked connections that say little except, "Keep with me and you'll not be sorry." Such connections are like the cliff-hangers that the poorest TV serials put at the end of each episode to make us tune in to the next episode. They read like this: "My most exciting discovery, which I'll come to in a moment . . .," or, "Little did I realize, as I started out on this project . . ." Careful readers will notice the flabbiness of such faked teasers—and simply stop reading. Or they may even laugh at you behind your back. None of us ever goes so far with clumsily faked connections as the comic character Dogberry, in Shakespeare's *Much Ado About Nothing.* The absurdly pompous night watchman has captured the villain of the play, and his superior, Don Pedro, tries to get a coherent report from him:

DON PEDRO: Officers, what offense have these men done?
DOGBERRY: Marry, sir, they have committed false report;
moreover, they have spoken untruths;
secondarily, they are slanders; sixth and lastly,
they have belied a lady; thirdly, they have
verified unjust things; and, to conclude, they are
lying knaves.
DON PEDRO: First, I ask thee what they have done; thirdly, I
ask thee what's their offense; sixth and lastly, why
they are committed; and, to conclude, what you
lay to their charge.

Though our connections are never that obviously irrelevant, they will seem absurd to careful readers if they fail, like Dogberry's, to perform a *necessary* task of *tying together.*

Keeping readers hooked

You may be tempted to assume that when you write an essay in a college class, you have been granted the floor for the full time. After all, isn't your teacher required to read through to the end? Well, yes, but the truth is that teachers get bored just like other readers. Though they may feel duty-bound to read every word you write, their responsibility does not release you from *your* duty to provide the "tracking" clues that will keep them with you. No teacher is duty-bound to consider a disjointed essay interesting. To interest the teacher—or some other reader— is *your* job.

Why does anyone ever go on reading what other people have said? To put the question another way, "How can we as writers keep our readers hooked, once they have bit?"

An obvious answer is that usually we can't. Readers on the whole do not stay hooked. More often than not, most people do not finish what they have started to read. There are always other good things to do, other good—perhaps better—pieces of writing to read. As readers we may throw away what we have begun, cursing it; we may shuffle it to the bottom of some pile, promising dutifully that we'll return to it later; or we may just drop the stuff to the floor as we fall asleep. But unless we are addicted to reading and have nothing else to do, we only rarely say to all potential distractions, "Go away and stop bothering me; I simply must read this through to the end."

Why does this *ever* happen? The answer may seem easy if the work is a flashy adventure story, full of exciting problems or puzzles that grip us until the author offers a solution. But authors of essays about ideas can use the devices of adventure and puzzles only sparingly, if at all. How do they manage—when they do—to hold us to the page? The most important answer— to repeat—is having something worthwhile to say. Even the most interesting subject, however, can get lost if its parts are not clearly connected.

Many of those clues you have already used many times, both in writing and speaking; nobody entirely avoids clues like "Firstly," "secondly," "and," "but," and "however." On the other hand, many are probably not yet readily available in your workshop when needed. It is time, then, to think systematically about the available ways to tighten any essay's cohesion.

NOTEBOOK ENTRY

Underline the "connections" in the previous two paragraphs, every word or phrase that *refers back* to something said previously, or *refers forward* as a promise of something to be said. Include the pronouns—those words that stand in the place of, or refer back to, people or names or ideas that have been named (as nouns) or suggested earlier. In your notebook try to identify how each connection works.

Don't worry if your list doesn't exactly match that of other students. Many words and phrases are borderline—they can be considered either as connections or as what is connected. What is important here is practice in noticing how authors try to tie everything together as they move from point to point.

A principle of cohesion

The rule to remember is this: *In most good writing, readers should never be left without some clue to where they have been and where they are going.* The kind of writing you will be asked to do is always better when "before" and "after" are tightly bound.

This rule means first that every paragraph should begin with an echo of what has gone before, as this paragraph begins with "this rule." Secondly, every paragraph should quickly provide some clear clue about *why* the next part comes where it does. Similarly, every sentence should provide, *as early as possible,* some direct or implied reference to what has been said immediately before, and the last part of the sentence should lead forward to what will follow. In general, the tighter the reference, the better the writing. (We'll meet exceptions—as always!—

later on. Every "rule" of writing is at best a principle or guideline.)

NOTEBOOK ENTRY

Again make a list of the connections in the preceding paragraph,
beginning with, "This rule means . . ." Develop the habit now
of noticing connections in everything you read. When you take
notes on your reading, an author's connections are your best
guides to what is important. Underlining them can be your best
aid in later review.

Now compare your list with ours:

> This rule—a precise reference to previous paragraph
> echo—reference to "clues"
> secondly—obvious clue to design of paragraph
> clue—another repetition
> next—obvious sequence
> it—reference to "part"
> similarly—guidance about a relation
> every sentence—similar phrasing recalls "every paragraph"
> in first sentence.
> sentence—repetition
> reference—useful repetition
> exception—reference to rule
> in general—promise of summary
> reference—useful repetition of term
> exceptions—"to the rule" understood

Whenever we look at writing that grabs us, we find evidence
for our rule. And when we look at writing that seems flabby or
loose-jointed, we find the rule violated. "Loose" writing reads like
this:

> Socrates was killed by the Greeks. The judges said the youth
> of Athens had been corrupted. It was Socrates' false teach-
> ings that were objected to.

"Tight" writing reads like this:

Socrates was killed by his fellow Greek citizens, because they believed that he had corrupted their children with his false teachings.

You can dramatize the difference by drawing lines between the elements that are connected—all the terms that refer backward or forward as those did on your lists just now.

How many lines do you find for the loose version? We find only two explicit, direct connections—the repetition of the word "Socrates" and the word "that." How many do you find in the tight version? We find eight stated connections: his, fellow, because, they, that, he, their, and his.

You might at first think that the tighter version is better just because everything has been packed into one long sentence. But something like the same tightness can be obtained with a series of short sentences:

Socrates was killed by the Greeks. *The Greek* judges said that *he* had corrupted the youth of Athens. *They* objected to *his* false teachings.

Though this version is not as graceful as the longer sentence, it is at least clearly *cohesive.* Note also that a careless writer can easily write a long combined sentence that is incoherent:

Socrates was killed by the Greeks, and the judges said that the youth of Athens had been corrupted because it was Socrates' false teachings that were objected to.

In this sentence, the "and" does no useful work, and the "because" is worse than useless; it misleads the reader. Can you explain why? The only other genuine connection is the repetition of "Socrates." If you try to draw connecting lines in this one, there's no place to put them.

We can summarize our rule, then, like this: Wherever possible, sentences and paragraphs should begin with an economical, clear reference to what has been said before, and the endings of sentences and paragraphs should in some way lead to what comes next, implying that something *new* is coming—some new idea or some further development. Faked connections, connections that go back and forth between ideas that simply repeat themselves, no matter how clearly, are worthless because what is connected adds nothing.

PARAGRAPH PRACTICE
The fan test once again

We have scrambled the order of the sentences in the following paragraph about argument, as if they had been thrown into a fan. (For discussions of the fan test, see Chapter 1, p. 45, and Chapter 4, pp. 98–99). Try reading it first as you would ordinarily read any paragraph.

(1) Maybe George was a pushover. (2) We could then just learn a set of neat tests, like using a circuit-tester to check for live wires, and then easily check out the relative strength of Jeanne's and George's arguments. (3) Maybe Jeanne was just very clever at concealing the flaws in her argument. (4) A good argument, in the sense of a good *case* must stand up under close *analysis*. (5) Who are the experts who test our arguments, and how many of them are needed to decide that an argument is sound? (6) Not necessarily. (7) If there were simple answers to such questions, a college education would not require four years. (8) What makes a good argument—a good case? (9) If George and Jeanne have an argument (in the other sense of the word), and if Jeanne convinces George that she is right, doesn't that show that she presented the best argument—the best case? (10) We might think that it would be whatever convinced one party to accept the other's presented case. (11) If all the experts in the study of argument could agree on what makes a good or bad one, our lives would be simple. (12) You may want to ask here a question that will come up again and again throughout your work in college: Stand up under *whose* analysis?

Why is the paragraph unreadable? The answer is obvious but its lesson is crucial: The clues to design don't *fit.*

Now copy the messed-up paragraph onto a separate sheet of paper, using double spacing, with each sentence beginning a new line, like this:

(1) Maybe George was a pushover.
(2) We could then just learn . . .

Better still, copy each sentence on a 3 × 5 card.

Next try to tie together (either in your mind or on paper) those elements that you are sure are closely connected—for example, between Jeanne and Jeanne, between "analysis" and "analysis," between "case" and "case," between "such questions" and the questions that are actually asked.

Now try to put the sentences into a clear order. Don't worry about whether your order is the only possible one, but be prepared to defend your choices. If you work with student teams of two or three, the exercise will probably teach you more than if you work alone.

Are there any sentences that you cannot place in a likely position? Are there any that do not contain tight visible connections with preceding and following sentences? Discuss in class any differences in the order that you and others have reproduced.

As a final step, look back through what you have written so far this year and choose one of your own paragraphs that seems to you well organized. Cut it into strips, sentence by sentence, or type each sentence on a card, and then scramble them. Give them to a classmate or friend and ask for reassembling. Was the reassembling easy, hard, or impossible? If you were using your connections properly, the task should be at least possible, though not necessarily easy. If you were careless with them, the task will be difficult, if not impossible.

The point of this "fan test" is to dramatize just how carefully writers must work if they are to lead their readers quickly and clearly along each step. To write clearly requires that we not only provide a good many handles, but handles of the right kind.

Perhaps you have noticed by now the curious way in which connections both cue readers and clarify the writer's own thinking. In a final draft, it is often impossible to say whether a given connection is just the natural way of joining two elements in the writer's thought or is designed to help the reader grasp the thought. Paying attention to this double focus of connections, *inward* toward the subject and *outward* toward the reader, is one of the best ways to test our thinking. When the connections work well, without strain, without a faked "thus" or "we see, then," all is well, at least for the moment. When they feel forced, when a *genuine* connection escapes us, we know that something is wrong.

The arsenal of connections

Writers have invented so many different ways to join one point to another—so many ways to lead from point to point—that authorities have never fully agreed on how to classify them. We offer here our own classification of the steps you can ask your readers to take with you, together with examples of each kind. We suggest that you first read through the list quickly, to get a rough sense of the immense variety of available resources for tasks that most of us carry out with a pitifully limited set of tools: a "but" and "however," perhaps, and an "although" and a "furthermore" or two.

Don't worry, on this first reading, about whether you can ever find a *use* for all of these—though other writers have used them often.

A. Duplication. We can simply repeat what has come before. Some manuals still repeat the old warning, "Never repeat a key word within a sentence, and try to avoid repetition of nouns even within paragraphs." The warning (note *our* repetition) can sometimes be useful, for writers who rely too heavily on choppy duplication that sounds like a reading primer: "President Reagan was once a movie actor. President Reagan was not a really famous movie actor. President Reagan was an actor who was often given the part of the hero's best friend. As an actor, President Reagan was . . ." Obviously too much repetition is too much. But in an essay on President Reagan, your reader will expect to meet his name many times, and you can spoil your writing with trying for fancy variations: "The tall, handsome son of Illinois was not a really famous movie actor. The great communicator was often given . . ." In short, feel free to use simple repetition whenever it is helpful. We can duplicate:

1. By repeating a key word:

    "Beauty is nothing. *Beauty* is everything. *Beauty* is anything the critic cares to call it."

2. By using a pronoun for a noun:

    "Jones struck out. In fact, *he* went down swinging and fell flat on *his* face. *He* never played professional ball again."

3. By using a demonstrative adjective:

    "Some people say that good writing should be colorful. *This* claim is . . ."

B. Addition. We can *add* to what has gone before.

1. We can add the next word or sentence or paragraph to the last one, as meaning exactly (or roughly) the same thing. All writing guides warn against "redundancy" or "pleonasm," but few go on to point out that without repetition no writing would carry any force. It is true, again, that "too much" repetition, of the "wrong kind," can spoil writing: If you write of a "bibliography of books," of "needed prerequisites," of "the up-to-date world of today," or of a gift that is "free gratis," you may justly be accused of using "deadwood" or "redundancy." But few points worth making can be made without some repetition. If a thesis is at all controversial—and we must ourselves repeat the point that most interesting theses *are* controversial—it will require more than one blow to hammer it home. Often this kind of addition requires no explicit connection:

    "Go away. Clear out. I want you out of my life."

    "He's a complete idiot, an airhead, a bubblebrain. I think he's stupid."

    But often some explicit term is needed or useful:

    "*In other words,* he's stupid."
    "*In short,* we're in trouble."
    "*To put it differently,* we could say . . ."
    "*That is to say,* no. Flatly, finally no!"

2. We can add something new:

    "Go away. *And* don't come back."
    "I love her. *What's more,* I want to marry her."
    "She's the best student in the college. *Even more impressive,* she's on the varsity tennis squad."

3. We can add a series of similar but not identical points:

    "First . . .; second . . .; third . . ."

    Other Adding Terms:
    again, further, in addition, furthermore, moreover, also, too, additionally, add to this, to cap this, as if that were not

enough, likewise, besides, to boot, etc., and so on, into the bargain, not to mention, let alone, along with, coupled with, in conjunction with, *a fortiori* (Note: Avoid "plus" in formal writing, as in "Plus, I then went and broke my ankle." "Etc." is usually avoided in formal writing, just as "*a fortiori*" won't be useful in street talk.)

C. **Subtraction.** We can subtract, diminish, or undermine what has gone before.

1. We can subtract the next word or sentence or paragraph from the last one, as a partial qualification:

   "She's the best student in the college, *but* she failed her music course." "My English teacher is tough *but* fair."

2. We can subtract the next element as a full cancellation of the last one:

   "He talks like a saint, *but* he acts like a devil."
   "When I came to America I fell in love with it. After a few months, *however*, my love turned to fear."
   "Our organization would like very much to respond to your request. *Nevertheless*, we find that . . ."
   "All of these arguments make sense, so long as we are thinking only of the welfare of faculty members. We reach a different conclusion, *though*, when we turn to students."

3. We can concede the partial validity of a point before or after subtracting from it:

   "*Although* I would never deny the force of these arguments, I must confess that my final view is . . ."
   "I *admit* that much of what Smith says here makes sense. *But* when we turn to look at further evidence, we find that . . ."
   "*While it is true* that he failed, he tried again."
   "*We must grant, of course,* that . . . *but* . . ."
   "I must admit, *though*, that . . ."

   Learning to make genuine concessions—openly admitting the strengths in views that oppose or seem to oppose your own conclusions—can be one of the most important steps not only in your efforts to persuade others but in your efforts to think through what you really want to say. Real thinking occurs at the moment when you find yourself pausing to ask, "Do I really want to say 'Although X, really Y,' or doesn't it now make more sense to say 'Although Y, really X.' "

Other Subtracting Terms:

yet, on the contrary, conversely, except, with the exception of, barring, save, exclusive of, in contrast, on the other hand, *au contraire* (used these days in English only playfully), "To our surprise, the opposite turned out to be the case," "While granting most of this claim, we must insist . . .," "Smith's views to the contrary notwithstanding, I would claim . . .," "not x . . . but y"

D. Causal Connections. We can trace causes and effects (see our sections on causal design in Chapter 6 and causal reasoning in Chapters 11–13.

1. We can show how a cause produces an effect:

    "She left him not *because* she hates him but *because* she loves him."
    "*Not* that I loved Caesar less, *but that* I loved Rome more." [The reason Brutus gave for killing Caesar.]
    "Why have our sales gone down? It's all *due to* the recession."
    "These figures must be right, *because* our accountant has never yet made a mistake."

2. We can show how an effect must have come from a given cause (the staple diet of detective stories):

    "*Since* the traces of blood began only three feet within the room, the corpse could not have been dragged in."
    "The dean wishes to report that Professor Jaworski must be grading too harshly; nobody in his honors class received a higher grade than D." (The semicolon here implies a "since" or other causal term.)

Other Causal Terms:

hence, as a result, resulting from, accordingly, owing to, thanks to, the next step was inevitable, so that, so (used informally)

E. Logical Inferences. We can infer or deduce logical connections (which may in some cases overlap with tracing causes):

"Seventy-five percent of all respondents admitted that they had cheated. We *can only conclude, then,* that our monitoring practices have been lax."

"We have agreed that there are only three possibilities here. And we have seen that the first two are utterly unlikely. *Therefore . . .*"

"*Thus* we see that . . ."

"We see, *then,* that . . ."

Other Terms for Logical Connection:
hence, accordingly, it follows that, *ergo* (for formal deduction or, more often, for humorous deduction), we can deduce from this, what this proves is, we can infer from this, what this shows is that

F. Comparison and Contrast. We can compare or contrast (this is not quite the same as, though related to, adding and subtracting):

"*In the same way,* the king's troops were forced . . ."

"In *contrast,* the juniors did very well indeed."

"*The differences* are striking. Note how . . ."

"*On the other hand . . .*"

Other Comparison and Contrast Terms:
relatively, comparatively, ratio, in terms of percentages, as compared with, similarly

G. Exemplification. We can give examples and illustration:

"We see, *for example,* that . . ."

"*For instance . . .*"

"*To illustrate,* let's consider . . ."

Other Terms of Exemplification:
in substantiation, a recent case will show, I can show this best with a story, namely, e.g. (avoid in formal writing), 24 recent cases tell the tale, cite

H. Summing Up. We can recapitulate:

"*In conclusion,* then . . .

"*In sum . . .*"

"Surely we are justified, *then,* in saying that . . ."

"*All in all,* we are forced to conclude that . . ."

"*What all this amounts to* is that . . ."

Other Recapitulation Terms:
to summarize, in short, where then does this lead? what can
we say about all this? what can we make of this?

I. **Dramatizing Limited Choice.** We can clarify an alternative:

   "On the one hand . . . On the other hand . . ."
   "Either we attack *or* defeat is ours."
   "Neither flattery *nor* bribery can change my mind."
   "Not selfishness *but* altruism is . . ."

J. **Modal qualification.** We can modulate our claims, as less cer-
    tain, more certain; broad or narrow in range; dependent on
    future contingency or chance:

   "Up to a point, this claim . . ."
   "Occasionally, this will lead to . . ."
   "Under extreme circumstances, this will yield . . ."
   "Part of the trouble, then . . ."
   "While this is *often* the case, we find sometimes that . . ."
   "If this were the case, *then* . . ."
   "If only it were so, *but* . . ."

Other Modulation Terms:
probably, usually, sometimes, approximately, relatively,
conditionally, on the remote chance that, even if this were
granted (all subjunctives and conditionals belong here)

K. **Adjustment of Perspective.** We can adjust the point of view:

   "To some readers, this may seem strange; *to me* it . . ."
   "As *all Faulkner enthusiasts* know . . ."
   "From a philosophical point of view, the case looks rather differ-
   ent."
   "From the standpoint of Freudian psychology it appears . . .
   while to a Marxist . . ."

L. **Emphasis.** Finally, we can simply insist, dramatize, or empha-
    size:

   "In fact, they know nothing about it."
   "Even more revealing, she . . ."
   "Indeed, we can go further and say . . ."
   "Let me *repeat:* I did not . . ."
   "Yes, that is exactly what he did."

"Mark the significance of this: . . ."
"Note that . . ." *

Almost every term on the entire list can work for emphasis on some occasions. *Remember,* however, that although we *can* get emphasis with italics and caps, it is *usually* more *emphatic* to *avoid* such *easy* devices and *instead* to construct our sentences so that they *really* ARE emphatic! (The temptation to *easy emphasis* like *this* can be especially strong in textbooks, as you may have noticed here.) Usually, if you work hard enough on a sentence, you can make it emphatic without such visual aids as boldface, italics, capitalization, and exclamation points.

Subtle differences of meaning can be achieved by slight shifts of terms for the same type of connection. In these examples from the "subtractions" group, you can see that the differences can be striking:

> *"Although* you are very bright, you are so absent-minded that you do stupid things."
> "You are so absent-minded that you do stupid things, *but* you are very bright."
> "You are so absent-minded that you do stupid things. *I must admit, though,* that you are very bright."
> "For someone who is very bright, you do awfully stupid things."

Much of the force of your writing will depend on finding the connections that convey the precise connotations you intend. Practicing regularly with a few terms in each group can increase your command of nuance, your control over subtle shades of meaning. It can also help prevent over-reliance on any one term of each kind.

SENTENCE PRACTICE

From any one of our twelve groups, choose two or three terms that you can use with confidence. For each term, make up two

---

*In constructing our lists, we have done some borrowing from Joseph Williams, Frederick Crews, and Maxine Hairston.

sentences that require joining (or one sentence with two clauses), using the term as the main connection. For example, under the category "Causal Connections":

> "He missed three classes, *with the result that* the teacher gave him an 'F.' "
> "You know why you were fired. It was *because* you goofed off too much."

Now choose another term or two from the same group, and rewrite your sentences substituting the new terms. For example:

> "*Although* he missed only three classes, the teacher gave him an 'F.'
> "He missed three classes. *Accordingly,* the teacher gave him an 'F.'
> "Your firing *resulted from* your goofing off too much."
> "You goofed off too much, *so* you were fired."

Not quantity but quality:
Two examples from student writing

If you practice what we have suggested so far, if you work steadily to increase your repertoire of connections, and if you think hard about them, your readers will inevitably find your essays clearer and easier to read—perhaps even more interesting. But the nasty truth is that tight cohesion is never enough. Indeed, devices of cohesion laid on too thick actually reduce our readers' interest. Too many clues about organization can weigh your writing down or just seem absurd. "Furthermore, I would like to add, on the other hand, that in addition we should . . ."

Decisions about how many connections to use are always complicated by the varying levels of reading skill among different readers. A heavy application of explicit connections necessary for inexperienced readers might seem annoying to experienced readers. "What's all this numbering for? I can see for myself that we have three parallel points here."

Obviously nobody can lay down any easy rules that will tell you when a reader will find an explicit "for example" helpful or intrusive. Should we, *for example,* call your attention to the fact that this sentence, needed for no other reason, is added to illustrate again the point, made in the previous sentences, that excessive explicit reference to how sentences connect, reference of the kind that it contains too much of, can destroy good writing? Such a sentence would be ridiculously overloaded for *any* reader, but how do we decide in less extreme instances?

Here we must turn to the principles that underlie our concern with connections in the first place. Our goal is not just to be clear but to be persuasive, forceful, finally effective. It is not enough merely to enable our readers to follow our thinking step by step; we want them to follow us to the end, with mounting interest and conviction. And at the end, they not only should know what the essay says, but they should be moved to say (or think), "This argument is terrific," or, "I'd like all my friends to read this," or, "I'd like to meet the author," or, "I must read this again and think some more about it." Obviously clear connections alone will not accomplish that kind of effect.

Consider now the following opening paragraphs from two papers written by freshmen. Read them through rapidly, then ask yourself which interests you more. The writers assume that their readers—their fellow students—have just read the two philosophical works that they discuss. If you have not read these works, or have not read them recently, you may feel handicapped as a reader, but you can still form an opinion about which writer more effectively invites you to read on.

#1.

Is Socrates guilty or innocent? This is the question that the judges, judges of the court and the readers, must decide. Obviously the jury in Plato's *Apology,* by declaring Socrates to be condemned to death, did not find his actions free from guilt. But what about his character? Can a man charged with guilt have an innocent character? Socrates believes so.

Socrates tries to present himself as innocent and clean of guilt. In attempting this feat, he contradicts himself frequently, throughout his weak defense. He also tries to appeal to the sentiments of the listener. Both the readers and the jury acknowledge these flaws.

Socrates is worried for his life and tries desperately to put together a plausible defense. This effort fails. Socrates grasps for any possible evidence regardless of its significance.

#2

In his *Meditations,* Descartes tries to prove the existence of God by first doubting everything and then systematically removing that doubt. But in doing so, Descartes creates a monstrous problem for modern philosophy: his skepticism is far more convincing than his counter arguments, and he leaves us able only to doubt everything and to know nothing. His "proof" of God's existence is nothing more than a series of circular definitions, based upon some rather dubious assumptions.

Let us put Descartes' philosophy to his own test, subject it to rigorous doubt, and unravel it from the ends all the way back to its foundations. Let us discover if indeed anything in this world is certain and beyond doubt. Descartes tells us that there is, but we will analyze it for ourselves. We will start by doubting his very conclusion, namely that God exists. On what grounds does this conclusion rest? . . .

Both of these students had been rather poor in their use of connections when the course started in the fall. Each received the same instruction about their importance. Both essays now seem to pass the fan test pretty well. But though both provide lots of visible hooks, #1 is obviously much less interesting than #2. (If there is disagreement in class about this judgment, discuss it.)

What does #2 have that #1 lacks? One could draw about as many lines between connected parts in the one as in the other. But in #2, the lines lead us forward, promising us something interesting to come—an unraveling that will solve a "monstrous problem." In #1 each sentence seems to sit passively. The cohesion it exhibits seems to be only in the paper, not in any possible reader; even the connections seem to promise little more than boredom ahead.

We see why this is so if we look at crucial differences between its connections and those in #2. First, they show less precision, and the author thus inspires no confidence that he is a careful guide. (Look at the "also" in the middle of paragraph two.)

Second, although the student has learned to use connections that "lean backward," he has not learned how to make a sentence "lean forward." "This effort fails." The statement gives little forward promise (except for the vague suggestion, not fulfilled, that the writer will provide evidence of how the effort failed). "The readers and jury realize this." The same point applies. Notice in contrast the other author's "monstrous problem" in the second sentence. It leads us forward to find out how she will solve that problem.

This contrast seems obvious, once we think about it, and it provides us with a simple but important principle: The best connections—especially when used early in an essay—will create a kind of suspense, leaning heavily forward and promising the reader something to be learned. Usually it is a rhetorical error to give away, in your early sections, everything you have to say. Instead, work at rousing the reader's interest in thinking a problem through with you.

NOTEBOOK ENTRY

Here are some sample efforts at connection. Identify in your notebook those that lead you to read forward. Compare your judgments with those of your classmates.

1. "Having made my first point as clear as possible, I now move to my second. It is that . . ."
2. "I have now said perhaps enough about the complexities of the troublesome problem of cohesion, and it is time to turn to the more specific matter of how to handle explicit connections."
3. "But having 'something to say,' even if that something is well-organized in your head and in your outline, will never be enough. Even the solidest organization can be quite lost on your reader if it is not dramatized, underlined, and clarified by providing *visible* transitions."
4. "Having discussed some of the essential requirements for cohesion, it should be worth our while now to turn to some specific instances of how . . ."
5. "It will be useful now to move on to . . ."
6. "It should be mentioned in this regard that . . ."
7. "What we have said about cohesion so far makes sense—up to a point. But it may produce disaster if it is applied mechanically. To see why this is so, consider . . ."
8. "The two points I have made so far seem to make sense, but what happens when we put them together? Does this not push me toward a nasty paradox?"

Now choose a paragraph from your last essay and examine its connections. Do they lean forward, promising something to come, or simply tie things together? Revise the paragraph now, in a way that will invite your readers to read on.

What we are suggesting about connections, then, is the same point we previously made about whole essays. Good essays are neither inert objects, to be viewed as products, nor simple reports of a process that has been profitable to the writer. They are perhaps best viewed as invitations to a dialogue, a conversation. Or we might think of an essay as a script for a little drama—with only the writer's words to cue the readers in their parts.

First you play your role as writer, acting out your own conversation, revision after revision, with the many critical voices inside you. You then offer what you think is true or sound about your subject, thus inviting the reader to perform in your play. The word "play" here has two senses: It is a drama, and it is also, at its best, a kind of playing, a playfulness, an enjoyable game that feels in some sense free, like golf or tennis, even though like all games played well it requires discipline and close attention.

An example of "suspense" in professional writing

The best examples of creating an appropriate intellectual "suspense" extend over many pages—too long for quotation here. But consider how, in the following paragraph, the movie critic Pauline Kael playfully keeps us wondering for five sentences, without using overt connections to tell us that she is doing so.

John Boorman is an intoxicated moviemaker, with a wonderful kind of zeal—a greed to encompass more and more and more in his pictures. His action scenes are rarely comprehensible. He can't get any suspense going. He doesn't seem to understand the first thing about melodrama. He has no particular affection for humor. And his skills are eccentric and his ideas ponderously woozy. But I don't know of any other director who puts such a burnish on his obsessions. [*The New Yorker,* April 20, 1981, p. 146]

Here the one word "wonderful" seems to promise explicit praise for certain superior qualities. Instead we come immediately to "rarely comprehensible"—*dis*praise rather than praise. We have been given a problem: The promise seems to be broken as soon as given. We can either quit reading (if we think the author is merely clumsy) or move forward to find the grounds for praise (if the author has hooked us). Hooked, we find ourselves moving on through the critic's list of remaining faults, our suspense growing. What *good* quality will Kael find that can possibly outweigh all of these faults—outweigh them sufficiently to justify that early promise in the word "wonderful"?

Notice that none of this would work as well if Kael had not provided visible connections; the "he" in each sentence keeps us absolutely clear about where we are. But the real interest of the passage comes from the tension between "wonderful" and the list of faults—leading to the precisely right word, "burnish."

Coherence found by pursuing cohesion

You can see now that our thinking about cohesion has led us back to the subject of design. Kael's cohesion is produced by her coherence—by her careful invention of contrasting points that produce an interesting problem. You will find that in the best writing you can seldom distinguish clearly between the essential design of parts and the elements that explicitly work for cohesion. The reader is carried forward by combinations of the two that are never easily broken apart.

We can now see more clearly why it is misleading to say that a writer first decides what to say and then finds ways of making it clear and enticing for a reader. The need to seek the right connections, in an effort to make a piece as interesting and accessible as possible, reveals faults in its coherence. Discovering flaws in how our arguments track, we seek new arguments, and sometimes even a new writing purpose, or at least a new round of invention. What you really believe about your subject will not be clear until you can tie it all together with genuine connections. (Remember what faked transitions are: They simply assert that a next step is coming, without stating why. "While I'm on the subject, I should just mention . . .," "It might be well to include here . . ." Well, *why* should one mention? *Why* would it be well? "I might just emphasize here that . . ." And then again, you *might* not. Does it matter? If so, why?)

Any transition that attempts to fit two mismatched pieces together, or that disguises my failure to think hard enough about how they match or don't match, can clue me that all is not well with my thinking. The faked transitions will accuse me of faked thinking. If I write a "therefore" that connects a seeming conclusion to unrelated reasons, if I attempt so much as a "but" that does not really reverse my direction, I can know that in failing to get my clauses together I have failed to put my thoughts together.

We can see how this difficult but important point works by looking more closely at the kind of sentence combining we practiced on pages 208–209. Consider this simple sentence:

My English teacher is tough but fair.

The "but" declares to the world that toughness and fairness somehow are not *expected* to go together, but that I am justified in saying that sometimes they do. But what if I say, "My English teacher is *both* tough *and* fair," or, "tough *and thus* fair," or, "tough—and *what's more*, fair, *my expectations to the contrary notwithstanding,*" or, "tough *and* fair, *as few people in this corrupt world of ours ever manage to be,*" or, "tough, with a toughness *that leads to* fairness, *much as God's fierce implacability is indistinguishable from his justice*"? When I put any one of these connections in place, I make a quite different thing of my subject. Each joining implies a different world made of different values, because a world in which toughness and fairness are expected to go together is quite different from one in which they clash. Each version will offer my readers a different world, and it will thus ask them to respond with slightly different kinds of responses if they want to join me in conversation.

Unsatisfactory connections can thus betray not only our carelessness or our ignorance but our need for further thought. And just as our finished essays are in one sense dramatic dialogues with friends—their proper readers—who are not present, so our work in revising connections is in a sense a dialogue among the various selves, or voices, that speak to each other in our own heads. I learn to write better by learning to put better questions to myself.

An example of sloppy cohesion in professional writing

We should now dramatize that point one last time. Suppose my "first-draft self" has got excited about the discovery that much human communication takes place not with words but with gestures and body position—the point we made at the beginning of this chapter. "Why not write an essay about body language?" the excited self asks. "All right," says the critical self. "I authorize you to turn yourself loose and see what comes out." The first draft of my first paragraph may go like this:

> Within the last few years a new and exciting science has been discovered and explored. It is called body language. Both its written form and the scientific study of it have been labeled kinesics. Body language and kinesics are based on the behavioral patterns of nonverbal communication.*

I—meaning my first-draft self—may feel pretty good about this; it sounds OK for a start. But then the "critical I" takes over. I look at my first solid connection, that first pronoun, "it": "It is called body language." Is "it" a good connection? What does "it" refer to? Obviously "science." So the science is *called* "body language"? But that's obviously not what I want to say; the new science is not *called* body language; it *studies* body language; it is *called* "kinesics." I must revise.

"Both its written form . . ." Now my "it" has reversed itself and refers, as it should do, to the science. Or has it? "Both its written form and the scientific study of *it* have been labeled kinesics." Now the "it" is the body language again.

*This is the first paragraph of *Body Language,* a book that tries to talk about how we persuade with our posture and gestures, quite independently from our verbal cues. The author must have failed to conduct the kind of conversation with himself that we are recommending.

"Body language and kinesics are based on the behavioral patterns . . ." Is that quite right? Is "body language" *based on* behavioral patterns? No, not exactly. Body language *consists of* the behavioral patterns; that's what the language *is.*

Nagging at myself in this way I might manage to revise the paragraph into something that will stand up under my own criticism:

> Within the last few years scientists have discovered a new and exciting subject, the kind of nonverbal and often unconscious communication that we all perform with our gestures and changes of posture. They call such communication "body language" and the science that studies it "kinesics."

I still may not be satisfied—the paragraph is colorless and stiff. But at least it is now clear, reflecting a "self" who has thought about what the words mean.

ESSAY ASSIGNMENT

From the essays you have written so far, choose the one that seems to you to be the most interesting, or the one that at least deals with the most promising thesis. (Think of this essay as #1.) First underline all of the obvious connections. Then mark with a "?" all points where a connection is needed but none is supplied, or where the connection seems weak or unclear.

Now write a new draft, improving as many connections as you can. (Think of this essay as #2.) Think hard about every connection and try to make it as clear and helpful as possible. This draft should have no inconsistencies or gaps in logic. Your reader should be able to reassemble it if given the sentences in scrambled order.

If you have done this exercise seriously, you are probably dissatisfied both with what you originally tried to say and with how you said it. Now write a new essay (#3) on the same subject, one that makes the better case that you have discovered while "playing" with your connections.

Nobody can predict how different #2 and #3 will be, but they may be so different that a reader would think they were entirely separate essays. You will have to decide what you now think about your original subject.

Submit all three versions to your teacher, clearly labeled as 1, 2, and 3.

Conclusion

In conclusion, it might be well at this final point, considering all of the ground we have covered, to summarize this chapter by rounding out a little survey of our results, in the form of an overview or encapsulation of the main points covered, both about coherence and cohesion, respectively, and in the proper order.

(You might have fun, in free-writing time, trying your own hand at this kind of parody of excessive use of connections.)

All good writers think hard about how to make solid connections among the points of their essays. Doing so will always be a service both to your readers and to yourself. In trying to show more clearly how your arguments interrelate, you can often discover gaps and inconsistencies hidden in your earlier drafts, as well as new connections more interesting than those you began with. When that happens, your struggle with connections can reshape your whole enterprise—the thesis and purpose of your essay. And when *that* happens, learning how to write becomes learning how to learn.

8

The power of words

Isolated words—words in context

If writers picked the words that embody their ambitions and insights at random, they could never achieve concentrated, focused effects. Not all words nor just any words will do: The words we pick must be the *best* ones. But to pick the best words for our purposes, we must of course have enough words in our possession to allow for rich choices. And how many is enough? Unabridged dictionaries of English contain nearly half a million words. It is said that Shakespeare had a larger vocabulary than any other author—but even so, he used less than one-tenth of the words available in the language. Most of us know and use only about one-tenth to one-fifth of the number used by Shakespeare. In short, we are all exceedingly limited in our "lexical range."

Yet in casual conversation most of us seldom feel that we lack words, or that we have difficulty picking the right ones. We get by. But if we think of language as a reservoir with half a million words swimming past us, we recognize only about one in 50. Thus we make do by simply grabbing at the same small number over and over: the words for foods, parts of the body, weather, physical sensations, the simpler emotions, and common household items.

When we write, however, we often find that the same words that serve us in everyday conversation are suddenly not sufficiently, powerful, suggestive, or colorful. We find ourselves peering into the murkier regions of the language reservoir for less familiar words that we *think* we recognize but really don't. When we use them in our writing, we find that we know them, at best, only approximately or, at worst, not at all.

Part of the problem is that all words have multiple layers of meanings—so many potential meanings, in fact, that they possess little meaning outside of specific contexts that highlight one meaning and temporarily obscure others. The problem is not that words have too few meanings to serve our purposes. Rather, they have more meanings than we know how to assess. What, for instance, is *the right* meaning of such words as "light" or "strong"? "Light" can refer to the absence of darkness, to a particular shade of almost any color (light brown), to a particular mood (light hearted), to a particular kind of literature (light reading), theatrical production (light comedy), soup (light broth), beer (light beer), or it can mean the opposite of heavy in many senses (a light load, light feeling)—and these possibilities just scratch the surface. "Strong" can refer to an odor, a taste, muscular strength, chemical concentration, brightness of light, intense feeling, swearing (strong language), booze (strong drink), and so on. Clearly, all of these meanings are *right* meanings, but none of them is *the* meaning, and only *one* of them will be right for specific purposes in specific contexts.

Our understanding of any given written or spoken utterance is not achieved by simply adding up the meanings of the individual words and thus arriving at a sum that equals the meaning of the sentence. In, "The hands had trouble manning the old tub," simply adding definitions would confuse things immediately. To most of us "hand" would first refer to that part of our body at the end of our arm, but in this sentence the word clearly means "sailor," just as "manning" means "operating" and "tub" means "ship." We cannot know what the individual words really mean, then, until we have heard or read the whole utterance, until we have seen the words *in context*. Other kinds of words present even more difficulties. Some articles such as "a" and "the," and all-purpose verbs like "to be" and "to have," are enormously difficult to define. They perform important functions, but they have little specific content of their own.

Single words have meaning only in social contexts that are simplified by special circumstances such as a crisis or an emergency. If you see someone struggling in the middle of a river crying "Help!" you need no more than that single word to know what the speaker means. But even in such situations, single words may be deceptive. A young man in a large city once responded to a female voice crying, "Help!" He ran down the alley in the direction of the cries where he found a large dog, a burly man, and a young woman all struggling furiously on the ground. The young man immediately jumped into the fray, attacking the burly man—incorrectly. The young woman was being attacked not by the man, but by the vicious dog. The burly man, a passing truck driver, was trying to help her. The young man was responding to a clear social context —a young woman walking her dog and apparently being mugged or raped by a criminal in the alley—but he was wrong. The word "help" was not enough help. If there had been time for more words, he might have been saved from drawing his false conclusions.

But to be aware of ambiguity of words in isolation does not mean that we cannot hope to be precise. Meaning is produced by contexts, and effective writers create *precise* contexts. Although adding the literal definitions of its words does not yield the full meaning of our sample sentence, the fact remains that it does have a relatively unambiguous meaning. Meanings produced by whole utterances can be precise even if the individual words are ambiguous in isolation.

How, then, may we as writers increase our ability to create informative and precise contexts? The answer is complicated: Any kind of serious effort to use language for particular tasks not only educates us about the task but about language itself. But this answer is so general as to provide little help in identifying the next useful step. A less complete answer, but one that points in a particular direction, is to enlarge one's vocabulary by every means available. The more words we have—with all of their potential meanings ready to serve us—the more accurately we will listen and read, speak and write.

Using the dictionary

In expanding our word supply, good dictionaries are essential—as long as we remember that sheer quantity can be dangerous. (Booth once received a letter signed "Vehemently yours" by a young man who had memorized that "vehemently" means "strongly.") Dictionaries may be hazardous to your lexical health unless you use them always in relation to your reading and writing tasks.

A special dictionary that offers help of a kind not achieved by any other is the *Oxford English Dictionary*. The *"OED"* does not only give current definitions, but the history of a word's definitions, along with examples. Often a word's current connotations derive from its semantic history (etymology), the centuries-long history of its changing and developing meanings. You will find in the *OED* that while some words have lost meanings through time and others have gained new meanings, some have even reversed meanings, and almost all have added many overtones in their journey through society and history. The more connotative overtones you hear in a given word's history, the more richness it will hold for you. "Explode," for example, originally referred to the sound of clapping hands, which was an audience's way (in the eighteenth century) of expressing its displeasure with an actor's performance (although nowadays clapping for actors is a reward, not a punishment). In the word "explode," then, the knowledgeable and attentive listener can "hear" not only the explosion of shells, bombs, and dynamite to which the word refers today, but also the noise which "exploded" (clapped) an actor off the stage. If you know that "lord" (as in "lord" of the manor) comes from an Old English compound *hlafwearde,* and if you know that *hlaf* means "loaf" and *wearde* means "warden" (as in guardian)—information available in most desk dictionaries—then you can see that *hlafwearde* expresses in microcosm the whole structure of medieval society, in which the lord of the castle was literally "the guardian of the loaf" for all of his dependents from his children right down through his serfs. His wife, the lady of the castle, was called *hlafdige,* the "kneader" *(dige)* of the loaf. Thus many words in English carry in the history of their meanings little miniature stories or insights into past society: methods of agriculture, for example, or beliefs about medicine, the influence of the stars, and the relationships between men and women.

NOTEBOOK ENTRY

Here are six words with interesting etymologies. Look up each one in the *OED*, and record in your notebook any past meanings that create connotative overtones you would not otherwise have heard. Date the occurrences of major shifts in meaning.

1. hussy	**3.** lewd	**5.** curfew
2. quick	**4.** leech	**6.** nice

The historical view is always illuminating, but not always necessary for understanding many words. Here is a list of 16 words that you might find in the writings of any contemporary novelist or essayist. These words are neither esoteric nor arcane, yet they are often misused. They are also words that can help you to achieve flexibility, economy, and accuracy—if you use them correctly. Look up the definitions of those you are unsure of, and for every word on the list write two sentences, each using the word in a different sense. Put your definitions and sentences in your notebook for future reference.

1. esoteric	**7.** affinity	**12.** sycophant
2. arcane	**8.** trenchant	**13.** jocular
3. obsequious	**9.** ubiquitous	**14.** replicable
4. unctuous	**10.** inherent	**15.** expiate
5. invidious	**11.** indolence	**16.** unequivocal
6. contentious		

We all use dictionaries, but most of us use them only in the way we use nutcrackers: to extract the meat as quickly as possible and throw everything else away. A careful look at a common word quickly shows how much information dictionaries provide, and how complex definitions can be.

Consider again the word *light.* Here is the entry for *light* in the 1955 edition of Webster's *New World Dictionary*. The range and diversity of this word's meanings make it a one-word kaleidoscope: Every turn reveals a new pattern of possible meanings.

light (līt), *n.* [ME. *liht;* AS. *leoht;* akin to G. *licht;* IE. base **leuq-*, to shine, bright, seen also in L. *lucere,* to shine, *lux, lumen,* light (cf. LUCID, LUMINOUS), *luna,* moon (cf. LUNAR), etc.], 1. *a*) that which makes it possible to see: opposed to *darkness;* form of radiant energy that acts upon the retina of the eye, optic nerve, etc., making sight possible: this energy is transmitted at a velocity of about 186,000 miles per second by wavelike or vibrational motion. *b*) a form of radiant energy similar to this, but not acting on the normal retina, as ultraviolet and infrared radiation. 2. the rate of flow of light radiation with respect to the sense of sight; it is measured in *lumens.* 3. the sensation that light stimulates in the organs of sight. 4. brightness; illumination: usually with reference to a particular case. 5. the thing from which light comes; source of light, as a lamp, the sun, etc. 6. the light from the sun; daylight or dawn. 7. a thing by means of which something can be started burning; as, a *light* for a cigarette. 8. the means by which light is let in; window or windowpane. 9. knowledge; enlightenment; mental illumination: as, early writings shed *light* on our past. 10. public knowledge or view: as, every day new facts are brought to *light.* 11. the way in which something is seen; appearance due to what is presented to view; aspect: as, he put the matter in an unfavorable *light.* 12. facial expression showing a mental or emotional state: as, a *light* of recognition came into his eyes. 13. a person whose brilliant record makes him an example for others; outstanding figure: as, a shining *light.* 14. in the *fine arts, a*) the quality suggestive of light. *b*) the part of a picture upon which light is represented as falling. **adj.** [ME. *liht;* AS. *leoht*], 1. having light; not dark; bright. 2. pale in color; whitish; fair. **adv.** [< the *adj.*], palely: as, the ribbon is *light* blue. **v.t.** [LIGHTED (-id) or LIT (lit), LIGHTING], 1. to set on fire; ignite: as, let's *light* a bonfire. 2. to cause to give off light: as, she *lit* the lamp. 3. to give light to; furnish with light: as, lamps *light* the streets. 4. to brighten; animate. 5. to show the way to by or as by giving light: as, the beacon *lighted* the planes safely to the airport. ***v.i.*** 1. to catch fire: as, the fuse *lighted* at once. 2. to be lighted; brighten (usually with *up*).

according to one's lights, as one's opinions, information, or abilities may direct.
bring to light, to reveal; disclose.
come to light, to be revealed or disclosed.
in the light of, with knowledge of; considering.
light up, 1. to make or become light. 2. to make or become bright, cheerful, etc. 3. [Colloq.], to begin smoking (a cigar, etc.).
see the light (of day), 1. to come into existence. 2. to come to public view. 3. to understand.
shed (or **throw**) **light on,** to give facts about; clarify.
stand in one's own light, to harm oneself or one's reputation by acting foolishly, thoughtlessly, or unwisely.
strike a light, to make a flame, as with a match.

In addition to the 14 definitions of *light* as a noun (n.), there is one definition of it as an adverb (adv.), five as a transitive verb (v.t.), two as an intransitive verb (v.i.), and there are nine examples of the word's appearance in idioms—and all of this in clarification of only *one* of the word's senses, the sense having to do with light as brightness or radiation. The other main sense of the word ("not heavy," a tactile rather than a visual sense) requires another entry as long as this one.

NOTEBOOK ENTRY

Can you identify and translate all the different kinds of information contained in this entry? Identify the following and enter the definitions in your notebook for future reference:

1. ME.	**5.** L.	**9.** Colloq.
2. AS.	**6.** *liht*	**10.** IE.
3. <	**7.** *leoht*	**11.** cf.
4. G.	**8.** *licht*	**12.** *

(Use the chart given in the front of your dictionary to identify the abbreviations and symbols. Most of them are standard; you do not have to locate the particular dictionary we used. You should be able to figure out *liht, leoht,* and *licht* from the context of the entry itself.)

Notice the amount of information that is connected to an understanding of light, but that is not part of its definition: the speed of light, the fact that ultraviolet and infrared light cannot be seen by the human eye, the fact that light is a form of radiation, the term for measuring the rate at which the eye can absorb light, and so on. Careful dictionary work throws more light on a subject than one might think.

Moving beyond the dictionary— but carrying it along

Although the measurable, tangible benefits of possessing a flexible and wide-ranging vocabulary in today's world are clear to most people, some people feel uncomfortable or even threatened when they have to speak or write in formal situations: being interviewed, taking tests, speaking to the school board, or organizing reports. When such people face the ordeal of expressing the force of their thinking and character through words, they sometimes feel defeated before they start. Yet today's society requires verbal skills more than ever before. Police officers, social workers, educators, nurses, doctors, lawyers, media people, scientists, government workers—all must use words as the essential "matter" of their business. It takes little observation to see that the best writers usually earn the best grades, that the best speakers usually get elected to class office, that the most clever commercials sell the most products, that the smoothest talkers get the most dates, and that the most articulate interviewees get the best jobs. Those who can work with words better than others improve their odds for advancing.

The prestige that accompanies powerful word usage can be seen among successful politicians, who are almost always effective speakers and writers—not necessarily literary or elegant, but effective. They know how to put their constituents' feelings, disappointment, frustration, and longing into words that validate those feelings. Politicians who fail at this task do not survive long.

But those who use words solely to get ahead in the world—

regardless of how important they may be in this respect—ignore the most important justification for enlarging one's active vocabulary. As word creatures—the only species that we are certain possesses language—human beings have a natural delight in hearing words used with particular effectiveness, appropriateness, or cleverness. As children we show our affinity for language early; we all go through babbling stages, rhyming stages, riddle phases, pun phases, and so on. We never lose our susceptibility to a well-turned phrase or vivid description, as is shown by our life-long interest in jokes, commercials, advertisements, puns, innuendoes, double meanings, epigrammatic slogans, unexpected rhymes, and other forms of wordplay. This susceptibility also shows itself in more serious ways. There is a critical moment in almost every quarrel when the right word or sentence—if you can come up with it at the right moment—will go far to heal hurt feelings and soothe a painful situation. But if the moment goes by—if you can't find the right words—then chances are the hurt persists and the anger builds. The right word, at the right moment, turns the world into the kind of place you want to live in. As we become adults we learn to cut and tailor our different uses of language according to the social constraints of time and place, and we retain a permanent pleasure in the right word placed squarely in the right spot.

Given all these good reasons for improving our mastery of words, what can we do, beyond the limits of dictionary consultation, to enlarge our active vocabulary? On the TV program *Electric Company,* superhero Word Man typically crashes through a brick wall and delivers the right word to the innocent young thing tied up by gangsters. But college provides you with no superheroes. You learn mostly on your own; nobody does it for you. So what can you do to enlarge your vocabulary—on your own?

First, you can read more, and more widely. The best way to make a new word's acquaintance is to meet it face to face in the company of a writer who cares about a purpose. Literary contexts —stories, essays, poems, novels, and plays—are particularly helpful, for despite their enormous variety, most of them employ words with a full sense of their richness, their layered meanings, and their evocative power.

In the following sentence from the opening of George Eliot's novel, *Middlemarch,* the ordinary meaning of the word "relief" as "an easing of pain or discomfort" will not suffice to make sense of the narrator's statement: "Miss Brooke had that kind of beauty which seems to be thrown into relief by poor dress." Even if we know the more relevant meaning—"standing out from a background"—a little dictionary work can add to our understanding. "Relief" in both our everyday sense and in that of Eliot's passage goes back to the Latin *relevare,* meaning "to lift up again." In a literal sense, to lift something up is to contrast it with the thing on which it was lying. This meaning of the word entered the domains of architecture and sculpture, where "relief" came to mean "the projection of figures and forms from a flat surface." Sculptures "in relief" are figures that partially stand out from a flat surface, but the backs of which merge into that surface. Eliot is thus creating a richer metaphor than at first appears when she says that Miss Brooke's beauty is "thrown into relief"—meaning "is given contrast or emphasis"—by her poverty of dress.

When you do look up the meanings of unfamiliar words, jot them down in your notebook or—if you own the book where you found them—in its margins. This practice helps fix the words' meanings firmly in your mind. Although there may be times when you simply want to read for pleasure with no dictionary to nag you, most of the time—especially when preparing assignments— you should read with a dictionary close at hand. (The small, paperback dictionaries are handy for carrying, but you will need one of the larger desk dictionaries for your room.)

In addition, listen closely in class and ask questions. Jot down in your notebooks unfamiliar words that your teachers use; ask for definitions of new words. Such attentiveness will not only repay you by increasing your ability to remember facts and deal with ideas, but may lead to interesting discussions.

Finally, if your school offers a good course in Greek and Latin derivatives, try to take it. Better yet, take a course in Greek or Latin. We are aware that this is not conventional advice, but in such a class you will quickly learn hundreds of word stems and roots that will help you to recognize the meanings of thousands of English words, often without having to use a dictionary. (This is true, for example, of most of the 16 words we asked you to look up in the previous exercise.) If you can't take such a course, you might buy any one of several inexpensive paperbacks that list Greek and Latin roots and stems.

In all of these ways you will be going beyond superficial dictionary work and enlarging your usable vocabulary.

NOTEBOOK ENTRY

Can you distinguish between the meanings of the words in the
following sentences? Look up all the words that you are unsure
of.

1. Winston Churchill's "blood, sweat, and tears" speech was a
   (historic, historical) moment in Britain's resolve to resist the
   Nazi bombing of English cities.
2. His paragraph (implied, inferred) that English was a terrible
   course. As I read it, I (implied, inferred) that the author was
   an idiot.
3. The earth turns on its axis in a (continuous, continual)
   movement.
4. I am going to (except, exempt) you from the swimming test,
   if you will (accept, except) a written test instead.
5. No, I didn't (explicitly, implicitly) *say* you were right, but by
   not disagreeing with you, I surely showed my (implicit, implied
   explicit) agreement.
6. When you drink too much at parties you (aggravate, irritate)
   me to tears.
7. Your wound should (cure, heal) in a couple of weeks.
8. Your happy whistling suggests that you are in a very
   (sanguine, sanguinary) mood today.
9. That new set of Bulwer-Lytton's novels (compliments,
   complements) your nineteenth-century British fiction
   collection nicely.
10. The shop steward was (grieved, aggrieved) at management's   *distressed*
    violation of contract rules.
11. Human beings' capacity for language is (innate, instinctive).
12. The CIA has been accused of conducting (covert, overt)
    military operations in friendly countries.
13. Your attacks on my position (depreciate, diminish) my   *belittle*
    credibility with my colleagues, an effect I (deprecate,
    depreciate).
14. (Capitol, Capital) investments in the company will help us
    update plant facilities.
15. The quarrel over money created a (fracture, rupture) in their
    friendship.
16. Your (noisome, noisy) gathering produces (noisome, noisy)   *harmful*
    effects on my health.   *impartial*
17. As an arbiter, he will be a (disinterested, uninterested) judge
    of the (self-interested, disinterested) claims of the injured
    parties.

18. The dry underbrush was (brittle, fragile) and easily crushed.
19. His (precipitous, precipitate) arrival on foot shocked all of us who had concluded he would be late.
20. I am going to (effect, affect) a few changes around here.

Becoming more sensitive to connotations

Not only must your vocabulary be wide-ranging enough to capture the sometimes-elusive subjects you pursue, but it must be capable of expressing fine distinctions and subtleties. Otherwise you are left with the ability to make only crude generalities and gross distinctions. To express subtleties of thought, you must develop a sensitivity to words' connotations—the power of words to insinuate, to imply, to color, to suggest, to hint, to shape the reader's emotions without being noisy or obvious, to lead the reader's judgment without straining or being preachy.

A word's common dictionary definitions are those meanings that are explicit and direct, often called its **denotations,** while the word's "suggestions," those meanings that are implicit and indirect, are called its **connotations.** For example, "house" is defined as "a building for human beings to live in; a dwelling place"; "home" is defined as "the place where a person (or family) lives; one's dwelling place." But despite each word's nearly identical denotations, we all know that their connotations differ. "House" for most of us suggests a building; "home" suggests family. "I'm going to my house for Christmas vacation" means that you are not going to someone else's house; the inflectional emphasis would probably fall on *my*. "I'm going *home* for Christmas" means that you are going to be with family (in the familial house). Moreover, "home" carries many connotations of family life: shared memories, holiday rituals, gift-giving, birthday parties, relatives visiting, parental support, sibling rivalry, summer vacations, teenage rebellion, family-car borrowing, and so on. (If your family is unhappy, divided, or hostile, the connotations of "home" are of course different.) Several years ago the owner of a *house* of prostitution punned on the connotations of "home" in the title of her book, *A House Is Not A Home.*

NOTEBOOK ENTRY

In each of the sentences below appear two words, the
connotations of one of which are more appropriate to the
context than the connotations of the other. Choose the more
appropriate word, discussing in your notebook why it is more
appropriate. You may want to support your reasons with
dictionary evidence.

1. The young boy has a (manly, masculine) way of shouldering
   responsibility.
2. The President walked forward to greet the Queen with a
   (jaunty, bouncy) air.
3. The new Paris designs for women have a very (mannish,
   manly) cut this year.
4. He's so (modest, humble, compliant) that he'll do anything
   you say.
5. He showed a (preference, bias) for the taste of apple pie,
   which revealed itself as a real (preference, bias) in his
   advertising.
6. A cool swim on a hot day is (refreshing, refurbishing).
7. The dam broke, sending tons of water (rippling, cascading)
   down the valley.   communicate with the dead
8. He has a true interest in (spiritual, spiritualist) matters; he
   goes to a seance once a week.
9. One member of our department has a (notorious, famous)
   reputation for back stabbing.
10. The glutton (gorged, engorged) himself.
11. The chicken was (tasteful, tasty).
12. He has a (luxurious, luxuriant) villa in the south of France.
13. Her damaged olfactory nerve deprived her of an important
    (sensual, sensory, sensuous) capacity.
14. He took a (fateful, fatal) poison.
15. He is an extremely (contemptuous, contemptible) person; he
    seems to scorn everyone equally.

Connotations and social life

In social and personal relations, all of us are sensitive to a
wide range of connotations. Social life turns to a great extent on

our stroking or stiff-arming one another with appropriate connotations. If you wanted to question or challenge another person's
opinion, you would not say, "How could you be so stupid?" unless
you intended to be insulting. But political enemies sometimes call
each other stupid, and if you wanted to get rid of the fifth caller
of the day who was trying to sell you magazines or home improvements over the telephone, you might use a curt "Buzz off!" The
suggestion that telephone salespersons are troublesome insects is
precisely the connotation you want.

You probably have a clear sense of the difference in everyday
conversation between

thin *and* beanpole
cautious *and* cowardly
masculine *and* macho
unconventional *and* weird
pleasingly plump *and* obese
independent *and* uncooperative
proud *and* arrogant
emotional *and* sentimental
aggressive *and* intimidating

and so on.

As native speakers of English, we all recognize that contemporary American culture is likely to place a positive value on the
first term in each of these pairs, and a generally negative value on
the second term—yet both terms in each pair *denote* roughly the
same thing. "Emotional" and "sentimental" both refer to having
feelings; "pleasingly plump" and "obese" both refer to being over-
weight. But the connotations of each term are quite different. To
describe someone as "proud" when you mean "arrogant" is to say
something more approving than you mean; to describe someone
as "arrogant" when you mean "proud" is perhaps to insult someone unintentionally. In both cases insensitivity to connotations
would cloud your meaning.

Although everyday terms that describe personal feelings and
social relationships usually give us little trouble, the terms for
analyzing ideas and making moral judgments often do. Most of us
Americans have too few terms for these complex tasks. And the
terms we do have are sometimes ambiguous, crude, or simplistic:

terms that foster social antagonism rather than create community. The problem in political disputes is, of course, seldom entirely a matter of words and their connotations; people do hold profoundly different positions on many important issues, and clearing up their language may on occasion even deepen opposition. But public debate which might well lead people to air their differences and seek common ground sometimes degenerates unnecessarily into public name-calling and edges toward violence, not because name-calling and violence are inevitable, but because speakers and writers are either ignorant about the connotations of their words, or because they are simply self-indulgent enough, perhaps demagogic enough, deliberately to choose terms with antagonistic or insulting connotations.

NOTEBOOK ENTRY

Here is a list of ten words whose connotations extend far beyond their denotations. For each, enter into your notebook the word's two or three main dictionary definitions and then, below that, write three or four sentences (50–100 words total) discussing the word's connotations. If you are unsure about the connotations, you might consult your instructor, other students, a thesaurus, or a usage dictionary.

1. heart	**5.** faith	**8.** scum
2. freedom	**6.** royal	**9.** hearth
3. liberal	**7.** vision	**10.** passion
4. tight		

Emotionally charged language

Any discussion of connotation leads naturally into a consideration of emotionally charged language in general: language that soars or burns with passion and attempts to make the reader share the writer's full intensity. Emotionally charged language sometimes creates indelible experiences both for individuals and groups. It's the stuff of eloquence, and eloquence, though "only words," has a way of outlasting monuments, kings, and even civilizations. The eloquence of Homer was already ancient when Sophocles and others were inspired by it almost 2500 years ago. By now the worlds of Homer and Sophocles have both crumbled, but the charged language that each of them created still endures.

A culture quite alien to the Greeks has given us the eloquence of the Bible, and the much more recent Anglo-American culture has produced the eloquence of Shakespeare, Milton, Keats, Dickens, Pound, Joyce, and countless other literary figures whose language resonates richly throughout our culture.

But literary figures have no monopoly on emotionally charged language. Even in America's brief history, a potentially endless list of statesmen and public leaders has helped form our national character with stirring utterances. The passion embodied in Thomas Jefferson's assertion that "all men are created equal" has never ceased vibrating along the nerves of our national sensibility, even in the face of indisputable evidence that many "men" have not been treated equally.

A similarly powerful passion has continued to reverberate in the language of our most influential leaders: Patrick Henry's, "Give me liberty or give me death"; Abraham Lincoln's, "that government of the people, by the people, and for the people shall not perish from the earth"; Woodrow Wilson's, "The world must be made safe for democracy"; Franklin Roosevelt's "The only thing we have to fear is fear itself"; and Martin Luther King's, "I have a dream." Emotionally charged language of the right kind—true eloquence—turns disparate individuals into a community fused together by the passion of the speaker or writer.

Not all emotionally charged language, however, is lofty and eloquent. Intense emotion can be expressed without either depth of vision or profundity of thought. Consider two examples at two extremes: invective and fulsome praise. Invective is violent verbal attack and is emotionally charged without necessarily revealing much except the writer's agitation:

> You lying snake. I wouldn't believe you again even if you were standing on a stack of bibles and being cooed over by baby angels. You'd be faking it all with mirrors and pulleys, somehow. You promised you'd love me, you miserable cheater, and now I know you're nothing but a dreary, com-

mon, selfish pig. I hope you roast in hell over a fire fueled with the souls of other flim-flammers just like you!

If you ever do find yourself in a position to use invective, you may as well pull out all the stops. Lukewarm invective just doesn't work.

Fulsome praise, the opposite of invective, offers praise so exaggerated it can seem disgusting:

> Tonight, ladies and gentlemen, I have the proud honor of presenting to you the first lady of country and western music, every Adam's wished-for Eve, the wonderful warbler whose singing stills the nightingale. The queen of country music and the heartthrob of Nashville, she's also a God-fearing, humble woman. Hollywood wants her, folks, but her heart and hearth, family and friends, are here in Nashville. Let's all give a great big welcome to the most glamorous and dearest little lady this town has ever seen, Miss Eula Belle Truejingle!

NOTEBOOK ENTRY

Pause now to make a notebook entry—20 to 30 minutes of writing—discussing your personal response to some piece of eloquent writing. As you try to decide *how* this piece worked for you, translate it into ordinary business-letter prose. This will help you to see its true eloquence. "Fourscore and seven years ago our forefathers brought forth on this continent a new nation, conceived in liberty and dedicated to the proposition that all men are created equal" becomes "Eighty-seven years ago our predecessors established here a new socio-political entity based on a commitment to individual liberty. It also made the value judgment that all persons—regardless of race, color, or creed—are equal in the eyes of the law"—or something like that.

If you make that kind of translation of your favorite hymn, speech, poem, Bible selection, or essay, you will have plenty to say—at least for a notebook entry—about how the original achieves its emotional power. Contrast as many details as you can.

Note that with a little development and some additional thinking, this exercise could easily turn into an essay.

PARAGRAPH PRACTICE

Write two paragraphs, one of invective and one of fulsome praise, pulling out all the stops, and then write an additional paragraph discussing what you might do to turn either of the other two into an expression of *responsible* criticism or praise.

Slanted language

We have already seen that the emotional power of words tempts people to abuse them. Our natural response to skillfully charged language makes us potential prey to a more sinister kind yet to be examined: **slanted language.** Like eloquence, slanted language is intended to move passions, to stir longings, and to create a new sense of possibilities in the reader. But there is this crucial difference: Eloquence is not underhanded, while slanted language is. Eloquence makes its appeals openly; slanted language uses an air of innocence to disguise trickery. While eloquence is an open invitation to agreement, to assent, to community, slanted language manipulates agreement and assent in the interest of those who stand to gain from it. Slanted language attempts to fix our gaze on ideas and promises that are so alluring, distracting, or emotionally charged that we fail to see what the writer is really up to. And even when we do see the manipulative aim, we may find ourselves willing to be had in order to experience the pleasure of the words or images.

Advertisements and commercials provide many examples of slanted language. Designed to be provocative, to awaken expectations or desires (usually of a sort that no commercial product could really fulfill), advertisements frequently make readers feel that their own lives are dull, grey, bland, unglamorous, and unexciting—until, of course, they buy the car, perfume, wine, or jeans specifically created to make life wonderful.

Consider the graphics and the text of this perfume advertisement that we found in the *New Yorker* magazine: The top two-thirds of the page is a close-up photograph of the bottle of perfume with the company logo on it, a single hollyhock blossom on a stem surrounded by small leaves, the whole drawing filling the inside of a double-lined square and done in a stylized, vaguely medieval mode. Underneath the picture is the following text. Read it through once, and then underline the words that seem to you especially slanted.

Non-Conformist.

For good reasons, all of Elixir products are fragrance-free. Then why is a perfume sold at Elixir counters?

It started out as a service. For customers who wanted a fragrance that typified the unique qualities of the Elixir woman. Elixir was the answer. But for years the company let it be a private discovery, and didn't say much about it. Quietly left it on its own, to sink or swim.

Elixir was noticed. Asked about. Word spread that this blend of herbs and essences has remarkably magnetic effects. It performs. Attracts interest. Gets fascinating results.

Find it only at Elixir counters. Spray it on. See for yourself why it's like no other perfume.

Elixir never conformed. Needed no fanfare. It's the only self-made perfume success.

Now let's run through it again, looking closely at how the language tries to move us without our quite being aware it. The first word in very large type is

Non-Conformist.

The large type turns "non-conformist" into a printed shout: "Hey you, the independent, classy non-conformist who does things her own way, listen to me for a moment." Any woman reading the ad is being set up: Who wants to admit that she's a dull conformist, a crowd follower, with nothing distinctive to recommend her to men or to give her a competitive edge over other women? Of course some women may be invulnerable to this kind of manipulation—those who do not measure their success as women by the degree of their attractiveness to men or their competitiveness with other women. Even women who do not measure themselves by traditional standards might be taken in. A career woman, say, might want to consider herself *creatively* non-conformist, a trend setter. As long as she is convinced by this ad that Elixir is a measure of her non-conformity, she is a victim no less than any other woman. And for those uncritical women who have *not* thought their way past cultural stereotypes, the ad plucks every possible nerve ending. The ad's makers obviously think many women are vulnerable to this kind of manipulation.

> "For good reasons, all of Elixir products are fragrance-free. Then why is a perfume sold at Elixir counters?"

Apparently this company puts out unscented bath products because some women are allergic to perfumes, but it is now trying to break into the perfume market, and is suggesting that the company really has women's best interests at heart.

> "It started out as a service."

Notice the slant: The language suggests that the company isn't after a profit, but provides a "service" instead.

> "For customers who wanted a fragrance that typified the unique qualities of the Elixir woman."

By claiming that the Elixir woman is "unique," but by not specifying what the uniqueness consists of, every woman is invited to assume that her own qualities are the ones referred to—*if* she decides to be an Elixir woman.

> "Elixir was the answer. But for years the company let it be a private discovery, and didn't say much about it. Quietly left it on its own, to sink or swim."

The company pretends that it never really cared whether anyone bought Elixir; it only wanted to interest the woman discriminating and knowledgeable enough to find it on her own. The ad portrays the woman who buys Elixir as a member of an exclusive group, a "private" club. And notice the pseudo-nonchalance of the language—the way the deftly dropped incomplete sentences create a special kind of talk that enhances the illusion of exclusiveness. Such "sentences" imitate the effect they are designed to create. They almost whisper in their quiet softness. And they plant the suggestion that between the speaker and her special, non-conformist reader, an intimacy exists that allows many things to be left unsaid.

> "Elixir was noticed. Asked about. Word spread that this blend of herbs and essences has remarkably magnetic effects. It performs. Attracts interest. Gets fascinating results."

The classy women who knew enough to buy unadvertised Elixir in the first place are spreading the word, and the word is that this stuff "magnetizes" men, "attracts interest." Notice the sexual innuendo of "gets fascinating results," and notice the personification of "performs." The perfume is made into an active agent: It will draw men into the range of the wearer's charms all by itself. Women don't have to be sexually attractive in themselves; they can leave everything to Elixir.

> "Find it only at Elixir counters. Spray it on. See for yourself why it's like no other perfume."

Any woman not thinking critically is going to find it difficult at this point to admit that she *doesn't* perceive Elixir's uniqueness. It would be like admitting that she's a tasteless clod. And once the woman goes so far as to walk to the counter to prove that she's *not* a tasteless clod, the ad has done its work. The next sales stage is up to the women behind the counters, those women who look like living proof of the benefits that Elixir offers to feminine beauty. Again the exclusiveness of Elixir wearers is emphasized: The product is found "only" at Elixir counters. This is of course a fake exclusiveness—the kinds of counters referred to can be found in department stores all over America—but it does separate Elixir buyers from the people who might buy perfume at dime stores or discount houses. And since discount shoppers are probably less likely to be subscribers to the New Yorker, the company can insist on the exclusiveness of its customers without running a large risk of offending others and losing sales.

"Elixir never conformed. Needed no fanfare. It's the only self-made perfume success."

At this point, the end of the ad, the reader realizes that the "non-conformist" label, which seemed at the beginning to describe the kind of woman who would buy Elixir, now applies to the product itself, further reinforcing the independence and exclusiveness applied to the woman who would buy such an extraordinary perfume.

Deciding when language is slanted

The irony of the ad is that all of this insistence on the company's non-conformity, its fake, high-minded refusal to advertise, is itself "conformist"; it is part of the text of a conventional advertisement.

Clearly the copywriters count on the slanted language of the text to blind women to its inconsistencies and exaggerated claims, to entice them to want to be the kind of exclusive women who buy Elixir because it "performs," "gets fascinating results."

Slanted language of this kind is sleazy not because it aims at producing changes in the readers' attitudes, habits, or beliefs, but because it aims to produce those changes by undermining the readers' critical judgment. All writers, including the writers of this book, aim to produce real effects in their readers, and all writers attempt to present their views in the best light. At the moment we are trying, for example, to convince you of the virtues of examining the various uses of language critically. But most advertisements deal in innuendo, half-truth, and omission of relevant data; they associate products with riveting images or promises; they try to quiet readers' critical intelligence; and they invite them instead to yield submissively, to be swept along on the wings of "hype," to be carried away with desire for a particular kind of "life style."

PARAGRAPH PRACTICE

Find an advertisement that you think is particularly full of slanted language and, in two or three paragraphs, analyze the way the language is supposed to work—from the ad maker's point of view.

Follow this with your own criticisms of the underhanded manipulation. Be as specific as possible.

You should note that the line between slanted and non-slanted language is seldom sharp. How does eloquence become emotional manipulation? Surely not in one big obvious leap. It does so by degrees; there are always borderline cases: writers who *seem* to have both passion and substance but about whom you can never be quite sure. In any event, the kinds of issues that most of us deal with when we write do not admit of conclusive factual solutions. When nearly every case we want to support turns out to be supportable by good arguments *on the other side,* then it is easy to see how people on *both* sides might accuse their opponents of using slanted language. The desire to avoid this accusation, however, should never lead us to sanitize either our character or our passion. Our concern should be, rather, to avoid using passion to deceive, coerce, or manipulate. All writers want their messages to be both heard and believed, and many responsible writers want people to act on their ideas. If they are successful that does not necessarily mean that they have used language dishonestly. They are guilty only if they try to get readers to follow without *thinking* about the cost, the direction, or alternative paths.

Slanted language: A final example

We have tried to be as clear as possible about the direction we are leading you in this book: We have let you know that we are trying to convince you to work hard to improve your sensitivity to language and your writing ability. But instead of leading you like sheep, we keep inviting you to think critically about our claims and our arguments. Our purpose—to help you become critical and persuasive writers and thinkers—would be undermined if we turned you into uncritical readers of what *we* write and think. Suppose, however, we were not trying to help you become critical thinkers. Suppose we were writing this book under the assumptions, common ones these days, that writing doesn't have much to do with thinking, criticism, citizenship, or character: learning to write is simply a mechanical procedure like learning to change a tire or read a map, and its only importance rests in the advantages it will bring to you later on the job market. If we were working from this point of view we could sell writing to you as a kind of investment: "Throw a few seeds in the ground now; reap the harvest later." To do so, we would want to de-emphasize the work involved and we would try to keep your gaze riveted on the payoff down the road: better jobs, faster advancement, more money, or a more exciting and successful life. Here's how we might have begun our book with these aims in mind, writing in a kind of slanted language designed to make you buy our goods and not think about the real issues.

That you are reading this book probably means you are a freshman in college, one of those selected persons who likes to compete and looks to the future as a challenge. You don't want to mess around or waste time, but you do want the skills that will allow you to advance in the real world after graduation. You are undoubtedly wondering what a required course in writing has to offer you. Your attitude is, "Show me the goods before you ask me to buy."

Well, this is a spirited demand in the great American tradition of not taking any wooden nickles. The bottom line is this: Jobs that require brains, professional skills, and diplomas are the only ones that pay anything, and they frequently require that people know how to write good English.

Now don't panic: "Good English" is mostly grammatical correctness with a dash of active voice and a sprinkle of zippy expressions. If you haven't got this all down pat by now, don't worry. We will help make your dreams come true by bringing you the latest advancements in high-tech ingenuity as applied to writing instruction: a new computer software program called "Easy English."

You will no longer have to fight your way through dark forests of old-fashioned, heavy, boring reading. Nor will you have to waste valuable writing time learning about fancy-schmancy stuff like rhetoric, argumentation, and style. With our software program you can get right down to the real job at hand: communication.

You don't have to live in uncomfortable doubt anymore when writing. All you have to do is check your questions about grammar, style, and usage against the computerized lists that we have programmed for you, choose the "Easy English" option that you like the best, and sit back, secure in the knowledge that you are writing good English. Generations of students in English classes have had to sweat and suffer to write well. You can do them one better and not have to sweat at all. When you use "Easy English," the computer will *tell* you when you've committed a mistake, and it will provide you with a *correct* alternative. It's spectacular!

Do you occasionally use a cliché? Not to worry: "Easy English" will flag it for you and give you a substitute. Remember the rule about avoiding passive verbs? "Easy English" absolutely refuses to accept any passives—ever. Remember how you used to have to worry about proof and evidence? "Easy English" notes every claim for which you fail to provide quantitative evidence and suggests a reformulation that doesn't require evidence.

Never has learning to write been made so simple, so much fun. "Easy English" may even improve your love life. As you improve your communication skills, you may uncover that witty, well-spoken person inside you that could never be coaxed out before. But regardless of reactions from the opposite sex, you will certainly impress prospective employers with your sureness and efficiency at writing business letters and memos. Like flying *over* the Rockies instead of hiking *through* them, our "Easy English" program takes out all the sweat and lifts you over all your past troubles. The future is here today. Enjoy.

Slanted language and freedom

This last example makes clear that almost any piece of writing, if carefully considered, can lead to important issues. It is clear, for example, that all of the goals we have discussed so far in this chapter—expanding vocabulary, increasing sensitivity to connotations, and developing sensitivity to the distinction between eloquence and slanted language—will influence both your character and your world. Only someone who has *thought* about slanted language can resist its ceaseless appeals in our culture. It is sobering to think how many people are the victims of whichever huckster gets to them first. They buy the clothes, cars, food, and entertainment that the ad writers tell them to buy. It is even more sobering to realize that these people may be equally vulnerable to manipulation of their ideas—and their votes.

Thus it turns out that learning to think critically about the way powerful language is used in our culture is really the same as learning to think about the culture itself: about freedom and community. Neither you nor anyone else can be free without making choices, and the person who is seduced and "stimulated" into behavior by commercial ad makers is not making independent choices. In a society of such people community is not a matter, as it should be, of dreams shared in discussion. Instead, it gets replaced by groups who share spending and purchasing patterns: Our community becomes merely a sharing of taste in consumer goods as that taste is shaped by ad makers and hucksters. If such a world is not the kind of world we want to live in, vote in, and rear children in, then it is up to us, not anonymous officials, to acquire the critical skills and insights that can help us create another and better world.

ESSAY ASSIGNMENT

1. Based on your own thinking and what you have read in this book so far, write a letter to the purveyors of "Easy English" software, offering criticism or expressing approval of their views about writing and how it can be taught. In either case, give your reasons.

2. In two one-page essays, present two differently worded versions of the same argument. Avoid such topics as nuclear war and abortion; they require more argument and space than you have. A possible source of subjects might be campus, job, or family issues: dorm hours, family budgets, campus drinking, job problems, fraternity and sorority rushes, child rearing, driving privileges, going to school and holding a job at the same time, allowances, support for getting married, and so on.

   Choosing an appropriate audience for your subject—fellow students, administrators, job colleagues, a teacher, parents, children, siblings, etc.—present in one version an argument for your position in straight language, language that shows awareness of other people's views, and conscientiously avoids dishonest manipulation.

In the second version present the argument in slanted language, language that tries to gain your audience's favor by flattery, by disregarding legitimate objections, or by suggesting that the reader who accepts your position will gain exciting payoffs or other advantages.

Finally, write a one-page essay analyzing the difference between the two versions of your position.

Making things concrete: Figurative language and other vivid appeals

We have talked about enlarging vocabulary, about increasing (or controlling) the suggestiveness of our word choices, and about some of the benefits and problems of emotionally charged language. Now we must focus more narrowly on the heightened effects that we can achieve with metaphor and other **figures of speech.**

Metaphor

Metaphor is the verbal assertion, or discovery, of a likeness between two things that are ordinarily seen as dissimilar. "Richard the Lion-Hearted," for example, metaphorically asserts that "Richard" (A) is *like* a "lion" (B), even though the word "like" is not used. (A) and (B), originally separate and dissimilar pictures, now both form a new picture (C): not just Richard and not just a lion, but a new object, *Richard the Lion-Hearted.* Here is another example from a letter to the editor of *The New York Times:* "Your call for more judges in New York's Criminal Court as a way to solve the problems of overwhelming caseloads is like adding more musicians to an orchestra that plays out of tune—the volume goes up, but the music is not improved" "More judges in New York's Criminal Court" (A) is asserted to be *like* "more musicians in a bad orchestra" (B), thus making the world of (C): more volume (of both music and legal work) without any improvement in quality. The writer could have simply said that adding more judges was not going to solve the problem of overwhelming caseloads, but he would have lost all vividness and concreteness.

Three points should be clear from even these simple examples. First, such discoveries of likeness appeal powerfully to the reader's imagination and feelings. The comparison invites (or more accurately *forces*) the mind's eye to see Richard's bravery, nobility, and strength—and to see these qualities much more vividly than if the writer had simply said, "Richard is brave, noble, and strong." Second, discoveries of likeness all break down at some point. Richard may be lion-like in courage, nobility, and strength, but he certainly is not like a lion in many other respects. Overwhelming caseloads in New York's Criminal Court may be like an out-of-tune orchestra in some ways, but certainly not in others. Third, insofar as these metaphors are effective at grabbing attention and making a point, they reveal something true about all good metaphors: They are extremely powerful tools for turning insights into pictures and planting those pictures in the minds of readers or listeners.

When Robert Burns writes, "My love is like a red, red rose" (the explicit use of the word "like" creates a special kind of metaphor called **simile**), he expresses a powerful sense of his love's beauty, freshness, and fragility. If he had pushed the metaphor too far—"and she has to be periodically sprayed with insecticide and covered with a basket in the winter"—he would have crossed the line into absurdity. But in the meantime, having avoided absurdity, Burns has discovered an enduring way of saying what his love is *like.* As the absurd extension of Burns' metaphor suggests, however, metaphors, like all powerful tools, can be dangerous. The writer has to keep them under control in order to exploit their advantages without wandering into foolishness or falsehood.

We have frequently stressed, for example, that learning to write is *like* practicing a skill. But we need to be careful when we say what writing is "like," because in some important ways practicing writing is quite different from practicing tennis or piano. In some ways writing your essays will be more like *making* something than like practicing. When we are writing, we do not have anything like musical notes that we must hit: We must make, or compose, our own plan—our own score. It is easy to see that in some ways the writer is more like a builder or a sculptor than a performer. But *that* metaphor can in turn be misleading.

When metaphors are introduced into a discussion, either written or oral, they frequently have the power to compel assent until they are either discredited, abandoned, or replaced. Looking at reality through different metaphors is like looking at light through different colored filters. When one filter is changed for another of a different color, a new version of reality may suddenly come into view. This kind of power has in the past led people to say, "Well then, let's abandon metaphor—get rid of all filters— whenever we want to talk seriously and precisely. When we want to be objective, scientific, or straightforward, we'll just say what a thing *is* in itself, not what it is like."

This approach would seem to provide a simple alternative to metaphor—*if* we could assume a reality which we could really see and describe without using metaphor, and *if* we could hope to discover a literal version of language separate from metaphor. But increasingly in the contemporary world, even scientists and mathematicians have come to realize not only that they rely on metaphors in ways that they never before recognized, but that their basic scientific and mathematical concepts are themselves metaphorical. Does DNA really get "sliced"? Does gravity really "pull"? Does time really "flow"? Does space really "curve"? These metaphors are not only common in science, but essential; there are no literal terms with which to replace them. Some philosophers and linguists claim, in fact, that the whole notion of "literal language" is a fiction, and that all language, even the strictest mathematical equation, ultimately resolves itself into metaphor.

Without attempting to address this complicated issue here, we can observe that even common names for things are often disguised metaphors. The word "daisy," for example, comes from the Old English metaphor, "day's eye," based on a metaphorical comparison between the yellow "eye" of the flower's center and the yellow "eye" of the day, the sun. The word "money" is a metaphorical renaming of Juno *Moneta,* the wife of Zeus, in whose temples the Romans minted coins. When we "grasp" a point or "see" an idea we are using physical metaphors to describe mental operations that no one, not even a neurologist, has a literal language sufficient to explain.

Metaphors not only prove indispensable in science and lie

hidden in ordinary words—they shape the very concepts we think with. As George Lakoff and Mark Johnson have shown in *Metaphors We Live By* (1980), we often, perhaps always, *think* in metaphors, as when we use war metaphors to talk about arguments (He "shot down" his opponent and "exploded" his arguments), or money metaphors to talk about time (You're "wasting" my time; I'm "investing" my time, and so on). Such half-buried metaphors (sometimes called "dead metaphors") are unavoidable, and they don't do much to heighten our writing style. But metaphors that are fresh and vividly tied to the senses can throw new light on a subject, and we rely on them especially when we are dealing with difficult conjectures, trying to flesh out abstractions, or trying to enliven accounts of sensory experience. To say that "Patriotism is the love of country" is to make a metaphor, but a weak one; it substitutes one vague abstraction, "love," for another abstraction, "Patriotism." Saying that "Patriotism is the last refuge of the scoundrel" builds a sharper picture—of some crook hiding behind a protective screen, perhaps?—and carries some emotional punch. Going one step further—"Patriotism is that lump in your throat when you hear the national anthem" offers both a visual picture and an emotion-laden physical sensation.

For various reasons, political commentary is always loaded with metaphor. The day after the Iranians took over the American embassy in Teheran in 1978, Gregory overheard one student angrily asserting that the Iranians were "turkeys," and another asserting that they were "clowns." As long as the talk was governed by these metaphors, opinion ran strongly in favor of America's taking powerful military retaliation. But when another student suddenly suggested that "America should be careful, because the Iranians might just be *pawns in the hands of the Russians,*" the discussion immediately reorganized itself around this new metaphor— the way iron filings organize themselves around a magnet. The new metaphor "showed" how dangerous military retaliation could be. Changing metaphors may suddenly change old ways of viewing things, and simultaneously bestow authority on new ways.

As pervasive and necessary as metaphors are, however, they carry a price. Their power and concreteness is often purchased at the cost of generality and breadth. That is why discussions of any activity as complicated as writing often require more than one metaphor. The following Notebook Entry gives you the opportunity to create some appropriate metaphors of your own for what writing is.

NOTEBOOK ENTRY

Take a few minutes now to make a list of some metaphors for "what writing is" or "what a writer is," and jot down a sentence or two that explains the appropriateness of each entry. Feel free to use "like" or "as" if these words seem appropriate. Be prepared to use your list in contributing to a class discussion of different ways of thinking and talking about writing.

Examples:

> Writing is a nightmare for me.
> Writing is a way for me to get a better view of my own opinions.
> Writing is like having a tooth pulled.
> Writing unpacks issues for public discussion.
> Writing is like mining for gold in a vein that may be exhausted.
> Writing links minds.
> Writing is thinking.
> A writer is a gladiator battling beasts with many faces.
> A writer is a diplomat caught between extremists.

SENTENCE PRACTICE

For each of the abstract concepts listed below, write a one-sentence statement that creates a metaphor and gives the concept a concrete dimension.

Examples:

> freedom: Freedom is a flame in the heart of every human being.
>
> despair: Despair is a black bog sucking the soul into oblivion.
> "Despair in vain sits brooding over the putrid eggs of hope." [John Hookham Frere, quoted in *Bartlett's Familiar Quotations*—a good source for undeveloped suggestions about almost any topic.]

meditation: Meditation is the pool of thought in whose
depths we catch glimpses of wisdom as it
swims fleetingly by.

love   happiness
courage   determination
laughter   democracy
truth   integrity
cowardice   history

Metaphor and sensory experience. The power of metaphors to make abstractions concrete is rooted in their appeal to the physical senses. (Some metaphors do not: "Truth is beauty"; "God is love." But most do.) As we saw in the example from the Sentence Practice above, an abstract concept like freedom gives the reader nothing to see, feel, hear, smell, or taste. But when freedom is called a flame, two physical sensations are brought into play: The reader *sees* the fire as a visual image and *feels* its heat as a sensation of touch.

By long-standing convention, the word "image" refers to all the metaphors of physical sensation, not just the metaphors of sight. Critics thus talk about "images" of touch and smell as well as images of sight.

Metaphors of sight are called *visual* images.
Metaphors of touch are called *tactile* images.
Metaphors of hearing are called *auditory* images.
Metaphors of smell are called *olfactory* images.
Metaphors of taste are called *gustatory* images.

Thus, in the examples above, the "black bog" of despair is a visual image—it gives the reader the look of a thing—with some borderline suggestions of tactile sensation: coldness, wetness, suction. The "pool" of thought is also a visual image with tactile suggestions. Wilfred Owens's "hoot of gas shells," referring to the sound of mustard gas canisters being dropped in World War I, is strictly an auditory image (from "Dulce et Decorum Est" [1920]). Sometimes a cluster of related images can appeal to almost all of the physical sensations, as in the first three lines of Robert Herrick's "Upon Julia's Clothes" (1648):

> Whenas in silks my Julia goes,
> Then, then (me thinks) how sweetly flows
> The liquefaction of her clothes.

In this collection of delicately suggestive images, "sweetly" suggests both taste (a gustatory image) and innocence; "flows" and "liquefaction" are both visual and tactile images, capturing the sight and sound of Julia's rustling silks. The only physical sense not directly appealed to here is the sense of smell. Herrick's images thus appeal to almost all the senses simultaneously.

NOTEBOOK ENTRY

Take time now in your notebook to work up as many different kinds of the five images as you can for each of the following items. In other words, try to translate each experience into images appealing to as many of the five senses as possible.

> The excitement of a sports crowd (or the game itself)
> Being moved by a work of art (or drama, novel, or movie)
> Working hard to gain a prized objective
> Being disappointed over a failure or loss
> Growing up in your home town

You may not find a complete range of images for each of these items, but be as comprehensive as you can.

Example:
Images to describe an evil person:

1. Visual: John's a real rat. (This image may also carry tactile suggestions insofar as it introduces the physical sensations that go along with the filth and squalor of rats' holes.)
2. Tactile: John makes my flesh creep.
3. Auditory: John hisses his insinuations and lies into every conversation.
4. Olfactory: John's self-interest pollutes the air that decent folk have to breathe.

5. Gustatory: Talking with John always leaves a sour taste in my mouth.

Extended metaphors. Sometimes a metaphor involves more than simply discovering a likeness between (A) and (B) expressed as metaphor (C). Sometimes the (A)'s and (B)'s form a larger cluster of related likenesses that are logical extensions of the combining metaphor. Sometimes, in fact, the extended metaphor serves to illustrate a complex idea, or operates as the unifying concept of a whole essay. (See the discussion of this same point in the treatment of extended analogies, Chapter 12, pp. 384–391.) Biblical parables are among the best-known examples of extended metaphor in Western culture.

> That same day Jesus went out of the house and sat beside the sea. And great crowds gathered about him, so that he got into a boat and sat there; and the whole crowd stood on the beach. And he told them many things in parables, saying: "A sower went out to sow. And as he sowed, some seeds fell along the path, and the birds came and devoured them. Other seeds fell on rocky ground, where they had not much soil, and immediately they sprang up, since they had no depth of soil, but when the sun rose they were withered away. Other seeds fell upon thorns, and the thorns grew up and choked them. Other seeds fell on good soil and brought forth grain, some a hundredfold, some sixty, some thirty. He who has ears to hear, let him hear." [Matt. 13:1–9]

Observe the remarkable advantages conferred by the extended metaphor: vividness, action, repetition for emphasis, and concreteness. It would not be hard to translate this vivid passage into many different possible meanings, using abstract language. Here is one version of Jesus' parable. Observe the loss of effectiveness, power, and depth of meaning.

> One who tells the Truth went out to tell it, and as he did so some of his messages simply went unnoticed. Some people

of inadequate understanding responded eagerly and hurriedly to the Truth, but when living by the Truth meant that they had to oppose their inclinations they gave it up. Others heard the Truth but were so preoccupied with their worldly affairs that they did not heed it. But others heard the Truth and did live by it, bringing to themselves great blessings.

Nothing is plainly wrong with the second version—it is in one sense "good English"—but nothing is much right with it either. The abstract language turns the vigor of the original into vaporous generalities. Notice that not only the words but the whole conception of the parable now lacks concreteness. "Understanding" and "inclinations" are not only vague words; they are vague concepts. But the original gives us pictures of birds devouring the seeds, of shallow-rooted plants springing up but soon withering, and of deep-rooted plants bringing forth a great harvest. These are images that have the stir and movement of life to them. And, as innumerable sermons and commentaries on this passage testify, the overarching metaphor—seeds and growth—can be unpacked at great length. Each listener is invited to contemplate the metaphorical nuances in pursuit of more and more likenesses. Extended metaphor, then—if well-chosen for a particular task and appropriately developed—may turn impoverished abstract language into riches.

At the same time it sometimes can make difficulties for your readers. Although the image of birds devouring seeds is vividly concrete, and thus in one sense precise, it can allow for a wider range of interpretations than "saying it straight" might. To use extended metaphor is to take more risks than to use plain talk. But when it works, the rewards can be great.

ESSAY ASSIGMMENT

Select a piece of writing that is highly metaphorical—a short poem, perhaps, or a passage from an essay, or the lyrics to a song —and rewrite it as far as possible in literal language. Follow this with a discussion of the specific qualities that the metaphors impart to the passage. Finally, discuss whether any alternative metaphors of your own making might improve the passage, and why.

Other figures of speech

Complete books have been written cataloging and analyzing the various figures of speech. But most of the technical categories are useful only for analyzing and naming figurative devices that other writers have employed; they aren't much help in deciding which figures will be useful in your own writing. Since many of the conventional figures can be considered as versions of metaphor, we add here only a brief overview of a few of the many remaining figures—the ones you are most likely to use.

Antithesis. We have already discussed antithesis in Chapter 7 as the "not . . . but" construction (pp. 204–205). "I did it *not* for me alone, *but* for you as well."

Apostrophe. Apostrophe is breaking off what you are saying to address some person or thing directly. In speaking to his disciples, Jesus suddenly breaks off and turns to the city: "Jerusalem, Jerusalem, how oft would I have taken thee under my wings, but you would not." In writing a letter to the editor about white-collar crime, for example, you may suddenly turn and address white-collar criminals directly: "And don't you know, you selfish cheaters, that the rest of us have to pay for your crimes!"

Epistrophe. Epistrophe is the repeating of endings, as in "When I was a child, I spake as a child, I understood as a child, I thought as a child." This is not a figure anyone would use often, but in the conclusion of a passionate statement, either written or oral, such a repetition can create a build-up of emotional intensity: "I don't *want* to say goodbye, I don't *like* to say goodbye, I *won't* say goodbye."

Hyperbole. Hyperbole is deliberate, extravagant exaggeration: "His hands hung out of his sleeves a mile" (Washington

Irving). "Don't come near me; I'll scream my head off!" "If I don't graduate in May I'll die a thousand deaths." Like all other figures of speech, hyperbole can be effective but must be used judiciously. It is such a strong spice that a little of it goes a long way.

Metonymy. Metonymy is the substitution of a word for a related word, such as substituting the container for the thing contained ("The *kettle* is boiling"), the finished product for the raw material ("The foresters cut the *lumber*"), or a part for the whole ("The *hands* manned the ship"; "The flotilla had twenty-one *sails*"; "The cop *fingered* the enforcer"), or a whole for a part ("unlock the house").

Rhetorical question. A rhetorical question is a question you do not expect anyone to answer explicitly, only implicitly: "Are we going to behave like mice?" If not used in just the right spot, this figure can make the writer sound stilted, awkward, or pompous. But it is sometimes useful as a way to open up an issue at the beginning of an essay or to bring an essay to a climax. If you were writing a letter to fellow students about a campus issue like sexist attitudes toward women in student government, you might begin, "How many of my readers are aware that women in student government are under-represented by 80%, based on the percentage they comprise of the entire student population?" You obviously don't expect anyone to answer; you are simply asking the (rhetorical) question in order to open the issue for discussion. And you might close with, "How long must we wait before the men in charge wake up to what they do to women, and to themselves?"

Personification. Personification is the attribution of humanness or human attributes to animals, objects, or abstractions. "She's a great old ship." "My memory *skips out* on me when I need *her* most." "The Statue of Liberty *smiled* with promise on millions of immigrants during the first two decades of the 20th century." "My computer *gets tired and gives up* about once a week." Personification is an extremely useful figure. It helps the writer avoid abstraction by achieving animation: "The test stared up at me grimly from the desk, but I just stared back until its eyes shifted. Then I knew I was going to be OK."

Conclusion

Writers who are serious both about reaching their audiences and about achieving the strongest possible effects not only take the power of words seriously; they also take delight in language that is unusually graceful and evocative. As we have said before, the power to use words is a unique and precious human birthright. We cannot attempt to fulfill our potentialities as human beings unless we attempt to increase our power of words.

But words used powerfully are not just a personal achievement; they are a social achievement as well. As Loren Eiseley says, "Those monumental structures known as civilizations . . . are transmitted from one generation to another in invisible puffs of air known as words. . . . As the delicate printing on the mud at the water's edge retraces a visit of autumn birds long since departed, so the little scrabbed tablets in perished cities carry the seeds of human thought across the deserts of millenia" (from "The Hidden Teacher" in *The Star Thrower,* 1978).

Does this highly metaphorical passage, read out of its proper context, strike you as needlessly "highflown," or as an impressive underscoring of the points made in this chapter? Even to ask that question is to dramatize the wonderful but sometimes dangerous power we wield when we deliberately enrich our language. When we wield that power badly, when our readers see us as manipulative or pretentious, we fail more completely than if we had tried just to say things straight. When we wield that power well, we create an intense bond with our readers that goes far beyond the simple communication of language unadorned.

ESSAY ASSIGNMENT

At the beginning of Wright Morris's autobiography, *Will's Boy* (1981), the author addresses a small essay to the reader. It is only three paragraphs long, but complete within itself. It contains several discrete metaphors and an extended metaphor that is worked out in Paragraphs 1 and 2.

Underline each metaphor in the passage and record, perhaps in your notebook, the three elements of each one as we did for

Richard the Lion-Hearted: (A) the element that is being likened to
something else; (B) the something else that (A) is said to be like;
and (C) the new thing that results from the metaphorical union of
the two.

In an essay directed to your instructor, unpack the extended
analogy in Paragraphs 1 and 2, explaining what each element
stands for, and how the author links them together.

Then discuss what you take the passage to mean, evaluating
both the appropriateness of the metaphors in light of the author's
intentions, and the truthfulness or appropriateness of the passage
as a whole.

TO THE READER

Few things are so wondrous as our assurance that we are each
at the center of a cosmos. Nor does learning we are not long
disturb us. In the early thralldom of this feeling we accumulate
the indelible impressions we will ceaselessly ponder but never
question, pebbles that we fondle in the mind's secret pockets.
One center and one only lies within us, as clearly perceived in
a dream of Joseph, told by Thomas Mann.

> For lo, the world hath many centers,
> one for each created being, and about
> each one it lieth in its own circle.

Since first reading those words my mind has sought an
image that is commensurate with my wonder. One I find
congenial is that of a vast tranquil pond on which a light rain is
falling. Each drop that falls is the center of a circle that is soon
overlapped by other circles. The apparent obliteration of the
circle does not eliminate the radiating vibrations. This image of
endlessly renewed and expanding circles is my own ponderable
cosmos.

The first of my childhood impressions is that of lampglow
and shadows on a low ceiling. But under my steadfast gaze it
dissolves like tissue. It resists both fixing and enlargement. What
I am left with is the ache of a nameless longing. On my child's
soul lampglow and shadows have left radiating circles that a
lifetime drizzle, of lapping and overlapping, has not washed away.

(If thinking about the extended metaphor leaves you with
nothing to say, review the resources of invention in Chapter 5.)

9

Voice

Voice: The writer's presence

Here are two scholars introducing books addressed to students of language. Each author claims that his book is intended to fill a gap in scholarship. Which opening makes you more inclined to continue traveling in the company of its author, to discover how the gap is filled?

#1

I didn't really want to write this book, but I decided in 1974 that it would be easier for me to write it than to not write it, assuming, that is, that I was going to continue teaching courses on logic for linguists regularly. While there are many admirable logic textbooks, several of which I had used to considerable advantage in my courses . . . , none matched very well my conception of what a course of logic for linguists should provide: a survey of those areas of logic that are of real or potential use in the analysis of natural language (not just 'basic' areas of logic, but areas such as presuppositional logic and fuzzy logic that are usually ignored in elementary logic courses,) and rich in analyses of linguistically interesting natural language examples. . . . I was able to offer a course along these lines only by supplementing an assigned textbook with numerous extra readings and lectures aimed at filling in what from my point of view were major gaps in the textbook and correcting naive and superficial treatments of linguistic matters. I soon concluded that the only way I was likely to be able to offer a relatively exasperation-free course on logic for linguists would be to write a textbook that conformed to my list of desiderata. [James D. McCawley, *Everything That Linguists Have Always Wanted to Know about Logic, but Were Ashamed to Ask,* 1980]

#2

Professional linguists have long been aware that languages differ from each other in many patterned respects. Similarly, professional sociologists have long been aware that societies differ from each other in many patterned respects. However, for several reasons, there has thus far been too little realization in either camp that language and society reveal various kinds and degrees of patterned co-variation. The sociology of language represents one of several recent approaches to the study of the patterned co-variation of language and society. Under "language" one may be concerned with different *codes . . . , social class varieties* of a particular regional variant . . ., *stylistic varieties* related to levels of formality, etc. Each of these varieties may be studied. . . . [Joshua A. Fishman, *Readings in the Sociology of Language,* 1977]

While each of these beginnings tells us what the book is about, each one simultaneously portrays a radically different picture of the author who is speaking. The first brings himself on stage with the very first word, "I," and with a direct declaration of his engagement with the topic. And he keeps himself on stage throughout, speaking as one person to another. He is not just a scholar but a teacher, who cares about effective teaching. (He is even willing to attack the rule against split infinitives head on; by using the construction "to not write it," he shows us that as a linguist he detests arbitrary grammatical rules.)

We can't even be sure that the second author thinks of himself as speaking to someone at all. Perhaps quite unconsciously, he adopts what he would no doubt describe as a standard "scholarly voice." He tries to keep himself offstage, writing sentences that seem to be uttered by sociological truth itself, with no human intervention. He steadily and unself-consciously repeats his matter-of-fact descriptive terms, and he proceeds comfortably as "one," rather than as "I" or "we."

Which voice do you prefer? The answer may seem obvious —at least our own choice will be obvious from what we have just said about the two passages. But some people may consider McCawley's voice to be self-indulgent and distracting. (You'd better not risk anything like it in your next lab report!)

Whatever your preference, you can see that every piece of writing, even the kind that attempts to sound perfectly neutral, will imply a speaker whose tone of voice will partly determine whether the writing succeeds. Every essay is "spoken" in some particular "tone of voice"; but not every author chooses a tone of voice that can "speak" the message of the essay powerfully and appropriately.

The tone of voice you project, consciously or unconsciously, is so important that we now must treat each of its aspects separately, *voice* in this chapter and *tone* in the next.

Voice in writing is like "presence" on the stage. Poor actors have weak presence; they somehow lack the ability to make the characters they portray come alive. Successful actors, like successful writers, generate a level of energy and magnetism that compels attention, admiration, respect, and authority—we have many terms for this effect—regardless of whether their role is supposed to elicit love or hatred, admiration or contempt. When good performers come onstage—whether actors, dancers, singers, lecturers, or musicians—the stage suddenly comes alive. Sometimes the flow of energy is so intense that it fuses the audience into a single unit concentrated solely on the central performer.

The stages on which we writers perform are our essays, and we depend on voice as much as performers rely on presence. No essay will ever achieve its full effect, even if it is well-designed and logically sound, unless it is "spoken" in an appropriate voice.

But where does voice in writing come from and how do we achieve it? Oral speech is rooted in physical causes, and each spoken voice is as unique as a thumb print; we thus "sound like" ourselves even when our words are confused or disorganized or incoherent. But voice in writing is not rooted in physical causes; it is rooted in who we are—in our character, our *ethos*—and when we write in confused or incoherent ways we do *not* sound like ourselves—or at least not like "selves" worth listening to. When we are confused, disorganized, or incoherent in writing, our presence emerges weakly—like a radio voice coming through on a weak signal or garbled from static. Presence gets lost in confusion; energy gets dissipated in incoherence.

For voice to emerge in writing, you must present a self who knows what it wants to say. No one essay will express your total self, but your total self will be the soil out of which any single essay grows. And this means that, like all the other important elements in writing, the problem of voice cannot be solved by learning a few tricks or mechanical skills. Voice is rooted in character, and character is neither a trick nor a skill. It is who you are in the deepest sense.

On the other hand, by saying that voice is not a skill, we do not mean to suggest that you cannot work to acquire it. We do not simply have to wait for voice to descend on us like a mysterious mantle. There are steps we can take that will help us develop a natural and comfortable writing voice. They don't constitute a formula or a guarantee, but they will help. If you both work *and* play at writing long enough; if you practice the suggestions we now offer; and if in your later drafts you ask whether your words sound like someone you yourself might want to talk with, your own voice will gradually emerge without your having to strain for it. Your "self" may even become more confident and developed as you write, for as you make decisions about how to speak, you make decisions about who you are.

Ten principles of voice

1. *When possible, write only about subjects you really care about.* The student who writes on a topic for the same reason that the mountain climber in the old joke climbs the mountain, "simply because it's there," is headed for a fall. The freshman who writes an essay with the title "Leprosy as a Social Problem" (one of Gregory's first freshman papers) is probably writing on a topic chosen at the last minute in desperation. Professional writers do sometimes write about things that don't interest them, simply for the money. They are like baseball players who play equally well for any team that hires them. But inexperienced writers who deal with topics distant from their feelings and know-how cannot help showing their lack of confidence. Writing about subjects that don't warm your voice will usually leave the reader cold.

2. *When possible, write only to readers you really want to reach, and always address them with respect.* Note: Wanting to reach readers doesn't mean that you have to like them. You may dislike some of your prospective readers intensely, but they should still constitute an audience you really want to talk to.

If you feel that you cannot address your readers with respect, you are probably better off not addressing them at all. This is *not* the motherly admonition, "If you can't say anything nice, don't say anything at all." You do not have to limit yourself to saying nice nothings. Your readers' opinions and positions are fair game for attack, sometimes even for ridicule, but stick to opinions and issues, not personalities. Except on rare occasions, the writer who slashes at personalities comes off sounding worse than the intended victim.

Imagine this surly beginning to a letter in the campus newspaper: "If the fools who support dorm hours get what they want, this campus will be turned into a day-care center. Chaperones on dates will be next. How could anyone be so stupid!" By speaking to readers as if they had no right to their own opinions, the writer has probably done his cause more harm than good. But there is more at stake here than simply not getting what you want. Your readers deserve respect for the same reasons you do, and they deserve it even if every last one of them opposes your favorite cause. Your favorite cause is not automatically meritorious because it is yours, nor is it going to win support from people you have insulted with your words or to whom you have denied the right of independent thought. (It will not surprise you by this time to learn that speaking with respect, like every other piece of advice we have offered you about writing, has been successfully turned upside down by some fine writers. See the selection from John Ruskin, below, pp. 314–316.)

3. *Don't indulge in shocking or outrageous statements just to create an effect.* The world is full of so much variety that what you see as outrageous and shocking may strike others as only commonplace. If you sound to readers like the kind of person who makes big deals out of small things, they may write you off as immature, obnoxious, or silly. And if you make shocking statements guaran-

teed to offend *everyone,* even those with standards widely different from your own, then you will probably wind up with no readers at all.

Writers who smugly say shocking things to show up their readers' inferiority—whether their target is, say, those who hate the middle class or those who love it—often sound like naughty children who say nasty things just to see the shock on mother's face.

4. *Never say things you don't believe merely to flatter your audience.* Even if the flattery works, as it sometimes will, you will have built up layers of falseness through which it will be hard for you to discover your own opinions. And your hypocrisy is almost certain to be spotted by all discerning readers—the very ones you would most like to please.

5. *Avoid unnecessary euphemism.* Euphemism is nicey-nice talk: the kind of talk you use when you've got company rather than the kind of talk you use when your family has the house to itself. As we all know, different social contexts sometimes demand widely different vocabularies, but choosing words and expressions that avoid naming things directly, that try to pretty things up, creates a voice for you that is prim, sickeningly sweet, or immature.

Consider this beginning for an essay: "The last symbol of my childhood remaining in my parents' house disappeared today. Mom finally pulled my old broken-down rocking horse out of the attic, and I watched with mingled feelings as the sanitary engineers threw it into the truck with all the other waste products." This could possibly become an interesting essay, but the effect has been undermined by referring to garbage collectors as "sanitary engineers" and to garbage as "waste products."

The impulse to euphemism leads one to say "john," "potty," or "little girl's (boy's) room" rather than "toilet" (which was once itself a euphemism), "pass away" rather than "die," "growth" rather than "tumor" or "cancer," "interment" rather than "burial," "mortuary science" rather than "embalming," "go to the bathroom" rather than "defecate," and "sleep with" rather than "copulate." Euphemisms are not always wrong, of course—we all use them *in certain social circumstances* in order to avoid being considered crude. But in writing, their use should be kept to a minimum, or you will sound like someone who can't face reality straight on. (On the other hand, don't forget suggestion #3; don't say "copulate" when you really mean "make love." *'Dys*logism"—choosing worse terms than normal usage or accuracy requires—is as much a fault as *eu*phemism.)

Americans apply euphemisms especially to five areas of life: death and dying, poverty and low social status, sex, bodily functions, and war. Americans place their dead in "memorial gardens" rather than "burying grounds," and have fellow citizens who are "low income" or "underclass" rather than "poor." In some circles people say "private parts" rather than "penises" or "vaginas" (which, like defecate and copulate, were Latin imports to replace cruder terms still used in slang and vulgar talk); and they "have a friend" rather than "menstruate."

In the workplace euphemisms are invented to bestow a kind of phony dignity on low-paying or low-status jobs. According to the *Quarterly Review of Doublespeak* (published by the National Council of Teachers of English), 1985 saw the emergence of the "part time career associate scanning professional" as the new "title" for part-time grocery store checkers. Secretaries are being turned into "office automation specialists"; manicurists are becoming known as "nail technicians"; spoiled fruits and vegetables are now being called "distressed fruit"; and greeting cards at Hallmark are being elevated to "social expression" products.

"Public relations officers" for the military have always relied on euphemisms to cloak the horrific realities of war and weaponry. The *Quarterly Review of Doublespeak* reports that three American servicemen killed while unloading a Pershing missile were not (according to the Pentagon) killed by an explosion but by "an unplanned rapid ignition of solid fuel," and that the six marines who died in a helicopter crash were victims only of a "hard landing." When the Soviets had to destroy one of their own missiles that got away from them during testing, the American Secretary of Defense refused to admit that the missile had been shot down; he insisted instead that, "It had ceased to fly." Notice that the Department of Defense is not called, as it used to be, the Department of War, and that war dead are "casualties," not "corpses." Warriors we support in foreign countries are "freedom fighters"; warriors we oppose are "insurgents." The Korean War was

called a "police action"; our vast chemical spraying in Vietnam
was "defoliation." And so on.

As you can see, we often cannot tell whether someone uses
a euphemism in order to deceive us or in order to save us pain or
embarrassment. In writing as in speaking, some euphemisms will
be useful and necessary; others will be superfluous, mawkish, or
dishonest. Your use of them will depend on your purposes, on
your readers, and on your integrity.

6. *Say what you have to say as simply as possible.* Of course some
points cannot be made simply because the subjects are not simple.
Complex subjects sometimes require complex wording or technical vocabulary. But before you jump to use this excuse as a justification for muddy prose, remember the number of writers (like
Plato, Samuel Johnson, and Cardinal Newman) who succeeded in
explaining profound or complex ideas in lively prose readable by
any educated person. In any event, what you say should never be
more complex or technical than the subject and the audience require. Whether writing letters (even to officials), position papers,
memos and reports to fellow employees, or term papers, a plain,
simple voice will usually serve you best.

Warning! Do not imitate the stuffy, pedantic, bland voice of
too many textbooks. Textbooks are often written as if their authors had set out to avoid simplicity. The following paragraph
comes from a textbook about the development of fiction in English
literature between 1660 and 1700. It is entirely free of errors, and
the style is neither grotesque nor absurd, but the writing is much
more complicated than simple ideas require.

> Not until halfway through the Restoration period did that
> new impetus so badly needed come to revive English fiction
> and to take it out of the doldrums. The new animating spirit
> when it arrived came from France; under the influence of
> translations and imitations of French short fiction English
> fiction found itself transformed. The chief agent in the
> change was the concept of verisimilitude (called *vraisemblance*
> in France) which insisted that the elements of a story bear
> some recognizable resemblance to corresponding elements in
> contemporary life. The first appearances of this incipient

realism are, to be sure, weak and sporadic, but they are there, and with their appearance we are on the way to the full sweep of the English novel as we know it.

The author uses 125 words to say what can be said in 51—with no loss of meaning.

Around 1680 English writers imported from France the concept of *vraisemblance*—"verisimilitude," "life-likeness," or "realism." It not only revived but eventually transformed English fiction. The first attempts at realism were both weak and inconsistent, but under its influence the character of the English novel as we know it began to appear.

Textbooks are of course not the only source of such pretentiousness. We see it everywhere. In 1985 a highly-paid consultant to the President of the University of the District of Columbia advised him as follows:

The administrative behavioral dimension directiveness (initiated structure) has been found to have a positive correlation with the performance of employees who are engaged in ambiguous tasks. The clarity with which employees perceive their functions impacts the level of performance, motivation, enterprise, and morale on the part of the worker.

Can you figure out what the consultant meant? We *suspect* it was nothing more than this:

Administrators can improve the performance of employees by clearly defining their assigned tasks.

Thirteen words here do the work of 49.

7. *As you write, try to concentrate on your subject and audience more than on yourself.* Whenever we feel unsure about an activity, we are likely to show symptoms of embarrassment and self-consciousness. First-time tennis players tend to giggle, stumble, and talk constantly about how badly they play; once they start thinking about tennis instead of their appearance, they begin to improve.

The same holds true in writing. Students who get into a sweat about the commas in their first draft defeat themselves. Including little parenthetical remarks in your essays like "I can't get this right, but you know what I mean," or "sp?" (in the margin), or, "Well, this is quite a difficult assignment but to get started . . .," make matters worse—much worse. Verbal fidgeting indicates that writers are not concentrating on the work to be done, but on whether they will be liked.

You can't know how good you might be at anything until you have given it your best try, and there is no point in torturing yourself with self-doubt. In the words of Martha Graham, the famous dancer and choreographer, "It is not your business to determine how good [your ideas and inspirations are], nor how valuable, nor how [they] compare with other expressions. It is your business to keep [them] yours, clearly and directly, to keep the channel open." In other words, think about the work, not about your image or your reward. The channel from which true voice ultimately emerges will open most freely when the writer begins to care more about the work than about the ego.

You might think that there is a contradiction between this advice and what we said just now about projecting a strong voice. But there is a great difference between taking pains with the voice that you project and proclaiming self-conscious doubts about the state of your soul. For the most part, save your writing designed to "get you in touch with your feelings" for diary and free-writing times. In itself it can be good practice and a valuable step toward self-discovery. But in writing to be read by others, except in rare kinds of fiction, it is usually disastrous.

8. *Don't be afraid to experiment.* Artists' sketchbooks and writers' journals show them often playing around. They juggle new techniques, approaches, points of view, ideas, and problems. If we always attempt the same thing, we invite drudgery for ourselves and boredom for our readers. Your notebooks and free writing give you perfect opportunities for cost-free experimentation. Don't be afraid to transfer experiments from these efforts into your essays. Workshop sessions in class give you no reason *not* to experiment. Try doing sentences in different voices just to see if you can get the feel of the language. Try your hand at a paragraph each of street talk, jock talk, professor talk, interview talk, formal talk, casual conversation, and so on. You can't make any progress without stretching, and you can't stretch unless you try new moves now and then.

9. *Don't approach your writing with grim seriousness.* We keep saying that writing can produce significant and wide-ranging effects in the real world, and this is true, but this does not mean that you will do it best by approaching your tasks grimly. Most serious activities are done best by people who know how to play. All of us have underground veins of creativity buried somewhere beneath our fears and self-consciousness. The best tool for finding the gold is a sense of fun, a sense of playfulness in the task itself. William Stafford, the poet, illustrates this point: "If you let your thoughts play, turn things this way and that, be ready for liveliness, alternatives, new views, the possibility of another world— you are in the area of poetry. A poem is a serious joke—a truth that has learned jujitsu." Some of your essays might read better if you treated them as serious jokes. If looking at things in new ways does not make you a poet, it can at least move you toward creativity.

Having fun is infectious. Consider this example from E. B. White, commonly regarded as one of America's best essayists, who has fun describing a potential disaster as if it were a congenial social event.

HOME-COMING

On the day before Thanksgiving, toward the end of the afternoon, having motored all day, I arrived home and lit a fire in the living room. The birch logs took hold briskly. About three minutes later, not to be outdone, the chimney itself caught fire. I became aware of this development rather slowly. Rocking contentedly in my chair, enjoying the stupor that follows a day on the road, I thought I heard the dull, fluttering roar of a chimney swift, a sound we who live in this house are thoroughly accustomed to. Then I realized that there would be no bird in residence in my chimney at this season of the year, and a glance up the flue made it perfectly plain that, after twenty-two years of my tenure, the place was at last afire.

The fact that my chimney was on fire did not greatly surprise or depress me, as I have been dogged by small and large misadventures for the past ten years, the blows falling around my head day and night, and I have learned to be ready for anything at any hour. I phoned the Fire Department as a matter of routine, dialing a number I had once forehandedly printed in large figures on the edge of the shelf in the telephone closet, so that I would be able to read it without my glasses. . . .

My call was answered promptly, but I had no sooner hung up than I observed that the fire appeared to be out, having exhausted itself, so I called back to cancel the run, and was told that the department would like to come anyway. In the country, one excuse is as good as another for a bit of fun, and just because a fire has grown cold is no reason for a fireman's spirits to sag. In a very short time, the loud, cheerful apparatus, its red signal light blinking rapturously, careened into the driveway, and the living room filled rapidly with my fire-fighting friends. My fire chief is also my barber, so I was naturally glad to see him. And he had with him a robust accomplice who had recently been up on my roof installing a new wooden gutter, dry and ready to receive the first sparks from a chimney fire, so I was glad to see *him*. And there was still a third fire-eater, and everyone was glad to see everyone else, as near as I could make out, and we all poked about learnedly in the chimney for a while, and then the department left. I have had dozens and dozens of homecomings at the end of an all-day ride on U.S. 1, but strangely enough this was one of the pleasantest. [*Essays of E. B. White,* Harper & Row, 1977]

Not only are human beings the only creatures who use fully developed language, they are also the only creatures who laugh. Shared laughter creates bonds between people more quickly than almost any other behavior. E. B. White is clearly having a good time in these paragraphs, and so we have a good time too, even as we discover that he is beginning to make a quite serious point.

10. *View writing as a craft,* a complicated craft, to be sure, but not a mysterious gift that one is either born with or without. We stressed this point in Chapter 2, but it is important enough to repeat here. If you think of writing as a set of skills that you can learn rather than as an inborn talent, then you can lay aside feelings of defeatism and hopelessness (even those that follow the worst disaster) and dig in.

Ignore any of our advice when you think you have a good reason for doing so. While our experience suggests that you would do well at least to think seriously about our ten points, don't follow them as absolute rules.

ESSAY ASSIGNMENTS

1. Sort through several essays you have written for any one of your classes, and copy out all the passages that you think sound self-conscious, stuffy (as in a poor textbook style), unduly solemn, too easily predictable (no experimentation), faked (sounding as if you picked a subject you knew nothing or cared nothing about), unnecessarily quarrelsome, or euphemistic.
   Now write an essay in which you (1) introduce your selection of unsatisfactory quotations and discuss the faults that you now see in them; (2) revise each of the passages you include; and (3) discuss what you have gained or lost by your revisions. Direct the essay to your teacher.
2. Select an essay or a portion of one from a newspaper or magazine that you think has an offensive or weak voice. Analyze the sources of the offensiveness as you see them (is the writer quarrelsome, self-conscious, pedantic?), and try rewriting enough of the essay to establish a voice that might win readers over rather than put them off.
3. Select a passage from one of your textbooks that you find weak in voice. In an essay directed to your classmates, discuss the passage's apparent faults and try rewriting it. (Refer to our examples in principle #6 if it seems useful.)
4. Select a passage from this book in which you think Wayne Booth and Marshall Gregory sound "like themselves," and write an essay directed at us in which you point out what you see as the strengths and weaknesses of our voice as judged by our own standards.
5. This is not an assignment for a unified essay, but it will take at least as much work. As an experiment, write a paragraph in

which you make some brief point or offer a description of something. Then rewrite the same paragraph in five or six different voices, keeping roughly the same point but trying to capture the sound of a speaker different from yourself. Write a final paragraph in which you discuss what you have learned from the experiment.

Choosing the right "social style"

In addition to the personal voice that emerges as we concentrate on our writing tasks, each one of us also uses several different *social styles:* different ways of speaking and writing that we know will be appropriate to a given occasion. Without thinking about it much (unless English is not our native tongue), we know that different writing games require different social styles. None of us uses the same vocabulary, syntax, or expressions in a job interview that we use in a lunch conversation with a friend. And both of these styles will differ from the style in which we write letters to the editor of the college newspaper, to our families, or to our senators. We use yet a different style in a term paper, and still another in a personal essay. And in each of these instances our style will differ from the style we use to ask questions in class, to give a speech at a college-wide convocation—and so on. We make all of these adjustments more or less automatically, knowing that other people will not only accept a variety of styles from us, but will expect them on different occasions.

A complete discussion of social styles would include a consideration of the illiterate and the homely—styles that reflect minimal education. But since these two styles are not likely to be useful to you in writing essays (either in college or later), we will skip them for now, and talk about those that you can choose from.

Colloquial style

The **colloquial** style is the language of casual, everyday conversation. It is often slangy and grammatically loose but not illiterate. People writing colloquially may be a bit careless about punctuation, may substitute dashes for periods, and may toss in a little slang. But they will not write "I seen" or "we was." Most of us use the colloquial style in letters.

Listen now to the colloquial freshness and pungency of this letter from Gene Henderson, the central figure in Saul Bellow's novel, *Henderson the Rain King* (1958), to his wife, Lily. Henderson is writing from Africa, where he has seen some strange sights, and like anyone writing home, he is catching his reader up on his recent experiences. He, unlike his creator, Bellow, is not trying for special literary effects but rather reaching for intimacy and immediacy.

> That afternoon I wrote to Lily as follows:
>
> Honey, you are probably worried about me, but I suppose you have known all along that I was alive. The flight here was spectacular. We are the first generation to see the clouds from both sides. What a privilege! First people dreamed upward. Now they dream both upward and downward. This is bound to change something, somewhere. For me the entire experience has been similar to a dream. I liked Egypt. Everybody was in basic white rags. From the air the mouth of the Nile looked like raveled rope. . . .
>
> Here [in the jungle] they don't know what tourists are, so therefore I'm not a tourist. There was a woman who told her friend, "Last year we went around the world. This year I think we're going somewhere else." Ha, ha! . . .
>
> I promised [my guide] Romilayu a bonus if he would take me off the beaten track. We have made two stops. . . . I met a person who is called The Woman of Bittahness. She looked like a fat old lady, merely, but she had a tremendous wisdom and when she took a look at me she thought I was a kind of odd ball, but that didn't faze her, and she said a couple of marvelous things. . . .
>
> I wanted to tell the old lady that everybody understands life except me—how did she account for it? I seem to be a very vain and foolish, rash person. How did I get so lost? And never mind whose fault it is, how do I get back?
>
> Then she told me I had grun-tu-molani, which is a native term hard to explain but on the whole it means that you want to live, not die. I wanted her to tell more about it. Her hair

was like fleece and her belly smelled like saffron; she had a cataract in one eye. I'm afraid I will never be able to see her again, because I goofed and we had to get out. I can't go into details. . . .

The attractiveness of the colloquial style is its spontaneity and conversational quality (although that spontaneity when it relies too heavily on clichés may be neither as fresh nor as spontaneous as it sounds at first). When it is handled well, as in Henderson's letter, the colloquial style becomes an open window to character: Henderson shines through his words as an interesting mind and vibrant personality, immediately responsive, immediately approachable.

But when colloquialism is overdone, the writer sounds flip, smug, or self-indulgent. Uncritical colloquialism, for all its chattiness, tends to be stale and hackneyed: "Dear Folks, how ya doin'? I'm fine. Gee, we sure have been getting a lot of static from the profs here at State University. . . ." You get the idea.

A colloquial style is acceptable in informal letters, and of course in conversation, but not in writing that calls for developed ideas and a formal tone. In such contexts, the same features of style that charm us in Henderson's letter would be wrong, even potentially disastrous. (Some of our readers have accused us of using too many colloquialisms in this book. Do you agree?)

Formal style

Formal or standard writing is the language of term papers, business letters, many books (including most scholarly books, and textbooks like this one), reports, memos, editorials, most newspaper reporting, most magazine articles, and so on. Formal language is the language in which most of the world's written information is exchanged. It is grammatically correct, even in minor points, it avoids slang, it insists on a precise but not technically difficult vocabulary, it shows care in sentence construction, and it follows an orderly development of points.

Like you, we would never write our families in formal style. But how should Karen, a college freshman, handle the task of writing to her last summer's employer at the bank? Mr. Sanders, who has taken an interest in Karen's education, has hinted at rehiring her, and has asked her to write with news from college. Conscious of her audience, perhaps she would write something like the following:

Dear Mr. Sanders,

It was good of you to express an interest in my college experiences. You might find campus events fascinating yourself. The variety of personalities and tastes is enormous. Everyone seems to have his or her own way of doing things. It's a big adjustment for me. Sometimes I feel as if I am handling it pretty competently, and at other times I feel a little intimidated—like a hick in the big city. It sort of depends on whom I'm talking to.

My roommate and I come from quite different backgrounds. She is from Boston and reflects her city well: She's both Irish and Catholic. (I asked her if she knows any Kennedys, and she said that that's the same joke all midwesterners make.) Since my midwestern Presbyterianism is also new to her, we have a lot of views to exchange and have already had some stimulating discussions.

If I don't close I'll be stuck at the end of the cafeteria line —a fate worse than being the last customer in the bank at 5:00 P.M. on Fridays. Let me know if you will need help again next summer; I'll certainly be looking for work. Thanks again for your interest.

Sincerely,
Karen

In college, you will probably be expected to use the formal style for all writing except personal essays. The advantages of this kind of writing are obvious. Because the formal style requires complete thought and precise expression, it allows you to present your arguments more clearly than the colloquial style. Personalities emerge less vividly in the formal style, but strong expressions of personality would be intrusive in most formal writing anyway.

The danger of the formal style is its tendency to move into stuffiness and pedantry (using unnecessarily big words or foreign phrases to sound impressive, like the literary scholar we quoted above). Does Karen sound just a bit stuffy—as if she's trying to impress Mr. Sanders with her college vocabulary—or does she really talk this way? Basically, she seems to have hit the appropriate social style pretty clearly: not too intimate or chatty, which would be presumptuous; and not too distant or learned, which would be pompous. Karen avoids the stuffiness that sometimes afflicts writers using the formal style, which itself is nothing compared to the sometimes unbearable tediousness and annoying obscurity of jargon.

Specialists' jargon

Most fields of activity employ technical vocabularies called jargon. Plumbers know all the terms for pipes of different sizes and substances, the terms for how to connect them, the names of special tools, the names for special plumbing problems, and so on. Architects use a vocabulary, specific to their tasks, that only they understand. Baseball fans know all the special terms for different kinds of hits, plays, and pitches. Fly casters have a vast array of terms for different kinds of rods, reels, flies, and fishing situations. Police officers, nurses, carpenters, golfers, and all of the different academic disciplines—each group uses a technical vocabulary, at least for many of its pursuits, that is largely unintelligible to others not in the group.

Jargon is useful as long as the writer who uses it is speaking only to readers already in the club. The following entry from a *Physician's Desk Reference* will be unintelligible to most of us, but to the intended audience of the book, the jargon that a layman would find intimidating and dense is perfectly comprehensible and therefore unobjectionable.

Keflex R
(cephalexin)
USP
DESCRIPTION: Keflex . . . is a semisynthetic cephalospor in antibiotic intended for oral administration. It is 7-(D-a-amino-a-phenylacetamido)-3-e-cephem-r-carboxylic acid, monohydrate.
The nucleus of cephalexin is related to that of other ceph-

alospor in antibiotics. The compound is a zwitterion; i.e., the molecule contains both a basic and an acidic group. The isoelectric point of cephalexin in water is approximately 4.5 to 5. . . . The cephalosporins differ from penicillins in the structure of the bicyclic ring system. . . . Cephalexin is excreted in the urine by glomerular filtration and tubular secretion. . . .

Yeah. That's just what we always say. Couldn't agree more.

You may understand as little of this passage as we do, but nobody could call it really bad writing. Most of the terms that really give us trouble here have no simpler synonyms. (Only once does the author deign to give a definition, of "zwitterion," a technical term that was perhaps not needed.)

But the writer who uses this kind of jargon on readers unprepared for it—or any jargon not strictly necessary—ought to be, if not shot, then at least made to sit through a three-hour lecture delivered in the jargon of a field that the culprit knows nothing about. Writers are especially offensive when they flaunt the contents of their jargon pouch merely to make themselves feel or look intellectually superior, or, even worse, to maintain some kind of advantage over you. When you are asking the right person but still cannot learn how much interest you are paying on a car loan, or how much cash reserve you are accumulating in a whole-life insurance program, and when your questions call forth scores of specialized terms that clarify nothing (to you), then you are the victim of a jargon junky, the kind of person who is so proud of owning an exclusive vocabulary that he would rather talk to himself in a room full of people than take the trouble to become intelligible.

Scientists are often criticized for using excessive jargon, but scholars in the humanities and social sciences are often equally guilty. They sometimes seem to have forgotten the original reason for developing special terms: to allow them to say something important, or at least intelligible, about their fields of study. George Orwell, lamenting this tendency among scholarly and political writers, provides us with the following two examples of excessive jargon in his famous essay, "Politics and the English Language" (1950).

I am not, indeed, sure whether it is not true to say that the Milton who once seemed not unlike a seventeenth-century

Shelley had not become, out of an experience ever more bitter in each year, more alien [*sic*]* to the founder of that Jesuit sect which nothing could induce him to tolerate. [Harold Laski]

On the one side we have the free personality: by definition it is not neurotic, for it has neither conflict nor dream. Its desires, such as they are, are transparent, for they are just what institutional approval keeps in the forefront of consciousness; another institutional pattern would alter their number and intensity; there is little in them that is natural, irreducible, or culturally dangerous. But *on the other side,* the social bond itself is nothing but the mutual reflection of these self-secure integrities. Recall the definition of love. Is not this the very picture of a small academic? Where is there a place in this hall of mirrors for either personality or fraternity? [Essay on psychology in *Politics*]

A final example of scholarly jargon comes from a professional linguist, writing from a different point of view about issues that concern us in this book. He is talking about how the individual's use of language relates to social roles. His use of jargon, while by no means the most extreme that we could quote from scholarly journals, is nevertheless formidable. How many terms do you find that seem to be part of a social code that you do not understand? How many of these terms do you think might have been rendered in less technical, more accessible, language?

The contrastive definition of a finite number of linguistic forms and the rigorous statement of their potentials for co-occurrence constitute an adequate description of the structure of a language. I suggest, similarly, that the cultural forms influencing other than verbal behavior may be contrastively defined and their relationships stated systematically and economically. Furthermore . . . [Philip K. Bock]

Surely there is more obscurity here than necessary—an uncritical indulgence in technical language that necessarily limits the audience to other experts.

*Orwell's *"sic."*

Sometimes jargon may be part of another social style. Consider the case of Mark, a young auto mechanic. He works in the city away from his family and is writing home in a colloquial style, quite appropriately, but he uses so much jargon that his family can only be mystified by the following piece of non-communication.

Dear Folks,

Guess what! I just stole the greatest old car you ever saw. It's a 1953 Packard, one of the classiest cars made in the 1950s, and the guy let me walk away with it for a lousy $200.

Well the first thing I've got to do is replace the old 6 volt system with a 12 volt system so it'll start in the winter. The whole engine is shot, so I've got to grind the valves and put in new piston rings and rods. While I do that I'm going to mill the head and put on a 2-bbl. carb. But here's the best part. I'm also going to slip a racing cam in her! If I don't do a quarter in 10 sec I'll eat all the rust I scrape off.

You know they started coming out with hydramatics about '53, but this car has the old standard trans with a four on the floor stick that comes up at you with a mother of pearl knob that has a silver inlay in it. The drive torque is a real low and mean 3.2, so you can imagine how she'll dig out. People will think I'm a rubber factory.

Say, what I really need is a torque wrench to do the engine work with, but they cost about $40, and now that I've bought the car I'm broke. What's the chances of borrowing $50 from you?

Love,
Mark

If Mark's family understands any more of this than that Mark has bought an old car and wants $50 it will be because the neighbor comes and translates.

Literary style

The literary style is not just one style, but all literary styles share some features: a concern for qualities like beauty, grace, elegance, vividness, evocativeness, and symbolic or metaphorical richness of the kind we discussed in Chapter 8. Literary styles at their best produce a vividness of response unmatched by any of the other social styles. That is in fact what we usually mean by literature: writing that is done so well that we prize it for itself and not just for what it conveys as information or argument. Such writing does not have to be confined to what we usually call literary works—novels, plays, and poems (unfortunately too many novels, plays, and poems have too little of it). When under the control of a master, it can be as appropriate in a political argument as in a poem.

Literary style: An example from John Milton. Here, for example, is John Milton defining the attributes of a true Christian, one who confronts vice in order to strengthen his resistance to temptation and thus increase his spiritual purity. Milton's point is that Christians who shrink from contests with evil and temptation can never have a robust faith. The passage comes from *Areopagitica* (1644), one of the greatest of all defenses of the freedom of speech and press.

> He that can apprehend and consider vice with all her baits and seeming pleasures, and yet abstain, and yet distinguish, and yet prefer that which is truly better, he is the true way-faring Christian. I cannot praise a fugitive and cloistered vertue, unexercis'd and unbreath'd, that never sallies out and sees her adversary, but slinks out of the race, where that immortall garland is to be run for, not without dust and heat. Assuredly we bring not innocence into the world, we bring impurity much rather: that which purifies us is triall, and triall is by what is contrary.

What is specifically literary about Milton's passage? Primarily the careful, detailed attention to language, the way language and meaning are fused into a unity that cannot be altered without altering the character and effect of the whole passage. A paraphrase, even if easier to read, just doesn't have the same effect.

> The person who can look at all the temptations of vice and still prefer virtue is the true Christian. I cannot praise a virtue

that always hides out [fugitive] or lives in religious seclusion [cloistered], a virtue that never rushes out [sallies] and challenges the enemy, but retreats from the dusty, hot contest where eternal life [that immortal garland] is the prize. We are not born innocent but guilty, and what rids us of guilt is the effort to withstand temptation.

This paraphrase is as accurate as we can make it, and we have not deliberately tried to render it ugly or grotesque. But there can be no doubt that it is dull and thin compared to Milton's language. We have reduced the whole meaning to the tired cliché, "A Christian who tries to avoid all temptation is not much of a Christian." The paraphrase loses the evocativeness of the metaphors "fugitive," "cloistered," and "slinks," each in turn creating the picture of a timid and cowardly Christian. When Milton says, "I cannot praise a fugitive and cloistered virtue," his righteous condemnation of cowardly Christians who slink away from contests with evil carries the force of a blow, and prepares us to believe him when he asserts that "we bring not innocence into the world."

One important point underscored by this kind of exercise is that Milton's "meaning" is not like a cooked food put forth in serving dishes. If meaning were something "contained" within words as food is contained within dishes, then meaning might be placed in other dishes without losing any of its identity. But as we have just seen, paraphrases of literary language don't work well —though we cannot avoid using them for some purposes. In writing, if we change the serving dishes we change the contents. Meaning and the words that express it cannot be separated without changing both. Even a simple message like "Help!" does not mean exactly the same thing as "Come give me assistance!" or "Save me!" And what is true of simple utterances becomes even more true when we deal with literature. The more literary a style is, the more obviously impossible it becomes to create exactly the same meaning in different words. Thus, when we say that Milton's passage is literary primarily because of its careful and detailed attention to language, we do not mean that it is literary because he chose elegant serving dishes in which to serve up his meaning. His words are elegant, no doubt, but his language is the meaning and his meaning is the language.

Let us look at some of the further touches by which Milton

renders his prose more forceful and memorable than most of the prose we write or read. He begins by **personifying** vice (*"her* baits"), turning an abstract quality, vice, into a person, a female. At once, then, the passage sets up a little drama that pulls the reader in: The person who is apprehending and considering vice is a "he," a male; thus his contest with vice takes on sexual over-tones that resonate richly throughout the passage. The image of the Christian man being tempted by the woman of vice hearkens back to the primal event in the Christian view of human experi-ence: Adam and Eve's fall from innocence.

Note that he also then personifies virtue as female: either a cloistered nun who shrinks from the race or an athlete who faces the hot, dusty contest for the garland of victory. The symbol of the runner evokes a contrasting picture of our human mortality; we are constantly running a race against time. We cannot wait forever to try to win the garland of immortal life. Next, the rhythmic repetition of "and yet abstain, and yet distinguish, and yet prefer" acts as a kind of ascending triad, a series of three steps, that places the emphasis on "he": *"he* is the true wayfaring Christian." Notice how the repetition of the "and yets" contrib-utes to the emotional resonance. Repetitions, whether of rhythm or of words or both, often indicate great feeling ("To strive, to seek, to find, and not to yield"—Tennyson), or point toward a climax ("Going, going, gone!"; "I shudder, I pale, I bleed to think what he has done"). Milton is a master of this kind of rhythm.

Literary style: An example from James Joyce. Here is an-other kind of literary style. James Joyce, a twentieth-century Irish-man thought by many to be the greatest modern novelist in En-glish, is describing a man's acceptance of his own mortality as he lies in a half-awake, half-asleep state and pictures the snow, a symbol of mortality, extending from his place of sleep outward over the whole world. In this moment of reflection and insight, Gabriel Conroy, the central figure in Joyce's short story, "The Dead" (1916), fully understands for the first time his own partici-pation in the human movement "westward," that is, toward death. He feels that this understanding, hitherto only an intellectual piece of information, now liberates him, for it lifts him above the triviality of Dublin life and gives him a part to play in the general drama of nature's processes, especially death, as symbolized by the

falling snow. The passage we quote here is the last paragraph of
the story.

> [Gabriel Conroy] watched sleepily the flakes, silver and dark,
> falling obliquely against the lamplight. The time had come
> for him to set out on his journey westward. Yes, the newspa-
> pers were right: snow was general all over Ireland. It was
> falling on every part of the dark central plain, on the treeless
> hills, falling softly upon the Bog of Allen and, farther west-
> ward, softly falling into the dark mutinous Shannon waves.
> It was falling, too, upon every part of the lonely churchyard
> on the hill where Michael Furey lay buried. It lay thickly
> drifted on the crooked crosses and headstones, on the spears
> of the little gate, on the barren thorns. His soul swooned
> slowly as he heard the snow falling faintly through the uni-
> verse and faintly falling, like the descent of the last end,
> upon all the living and the dead.

Throughout the story the reader sees Gabriel Conroy caught
up in one petty concern after another. He is usually a bit nervous,
an overly self-conscious egoist, always worried about what people
think of him. But now in a quiet and introspective moment before
falling asleep, Gabriel faces up to what he has been avoiding not
only all evening, but all his life: the triviality of most of his
concerns and fears.

The power of this passage lies mainly in its vision of the
processes of nature, life, and death going on in every part of the
world at once, making Gabriel's absorption in trivialities at last
obvious, even to him. Throughout the story, in ways that just miss
registering in Gabriel's consciousness, the dead have made one
kind of appearance or another. There has been talk of dead relatives, dead opera singers, and dead freedom fighters. Just before
going to bed, Gabriel hears about one last dead soul, the sickly
young boy, Michael Furey, who died many years ago while in love
with Gretta, who later became Gabriel's wife.

The force of the story is subtle, and depends to a large extent
on how vividly we have been made to see the contrast between
the triviality of Gabriel's life and the impersonal vastness of the
processes of nature. If the story said nothing more than, "It doesn't
really make any difference what we think or do because a hundred

years from now we'll all be dead," then there would be little in it to make us think or stir our feelings. This insight is commonplace.

But the story says something rather different. It does not say that all human actions are trivial and useless, but that human beings trivialize their actions through egotism. Instead of seeing life whole, and thus having a backdrop against which we can see the relative importance or triviality of things, we treat even our smallest ambitions and desires as the be-all and end-all of existence. We act, or so Joyce's story says, as if all of life were consciously designing either to fulfill us or thwart us. At the end of "The Dead," the passage you have just read protests against this self-centeredness. As Gabriel thinks about the snow as a symbol of death, and sees it in his imagination falling over the entire universe, he comes to accept his part in the generality of life and death around him without cynicism, resistance, or an egotistical sense of injury. And in this acceptance he finds the generosity and calmness of spirit that all his self-centered flutterings had previously kept him from grasping.

Notice how Joyce plays with rhythms, as in

> SLEEPily the FLAKES,
> SILver and DARK,

and notice how each of the seven repetitions of "falling" echoes the others, with none exactly duplicating any of them. "Falling obliquely" is followed by "falling," which is followed by "falling softly," followed by "softly falling," and so on. The effect is of a delicate stitchery, the same stitches used over and over with minute variations that capture and build upon the effect of previous stitches.

Notice also the expansion of the view, like a camera pulling back farther and farther: Gabriel begins by noticing how the snow falling against his windows is lit by the street lamp; and then, with his mind acting as the camera, he gradually pulls back his view until, at the end, he claims the cosmic view: "the snow falling faintly through the universe and faintly falling, like the descent of the last end, upon all the living and the dead."

Literary style: An example from Loren Eiseley. Masters of literary style may be found among scientists, theologians, philosophers, and historians as well as among novelists and poets like

Joyce and Milton. Perhaps the single most striking example of a consummate literary stylist who was not a fiction writer or poet in our modern sense at all, who in fact condemned most literature as untruthful and corrupting, is Plato. The extended analogies in which he embodied his philosophical views—the twin steeds of passion and desire, controlled by the charioteer reason; the twice-divided line between two kinds of opinion and two kinds of knowledge; the myth of the cave of ignorance; the legend about the origin of the two sexes from an original single sphere jealously split apart by Zeus—these and many more have become a formative part of our culture.

In our own day, many writers carry on the tradition of writing non-fiction prose in a literary style. One of the best recent stylists is Loren Eiseley, a paleontologist and historian of scientific ideas whose work has won a wide popular audience. Here is a paragraph from his essay, "The Hidden Teacher" (1964).

> Because form cannot be long sustained in the living, we collapse inward with age. We die. Our bodies, which were the product of a kind of hidden teaching by an alphabet we are only beginning dimly to discern [the genetic code in DNA], are dismissed into their elements. What is carried onward, assuming we have descendants, is the little capsule of instructions. . . . We have learned the first biological lesson: that in each generation life passes through the eye of a needle. It exists for a time molecularly and in no recognizable semblance to its adult condition. It *instructs* its way again into man or reptile. As the ages pass, so do variants of the code. Occasionally, a species vanishes on a wind as unreturning as that which took the pterodactyls.

Here we see that same caressing of language, that same use of metaphor, symbol, and allusion that we found flowing through the passages of Eiseley's "literary" forebears, Milton and Joyce. Notice the metaphor of the "teaching alphabet": DNA is the "alphabet" carried in a "little capsule" (the cell) that "instructs" each generation what it should be, how it should develop. This metaphor is then followed by another, one that widens the scope of the discussion from biology to philosophy. The metaphor—"in each generation life passes through the eye of the needle"—makes the biological point that all life exists first in a molecular form, but it also makes another point by evoking and building on Christ's earlier use of the same metaphor: Christ's assertion that it would be easier for a camel to pass through the eye of a needle than for a rich man to enter the gates of heaven.

Eiseley picks up on Christ's metaphor to enlarge and enrich his own meaning. He is not talking just about biological *survival,* any more than Christ was talking just about camels. Christ's point is that human beings, specifically the rich, are unlikely to live good lives. Following Christ's emphasis, Eiseley uses the metaphor not to make a biological point about the "improbable" survival of DNA, but a philosophical point about our need to decide how to spend our brief moment before we are "dismissed into our elements." Christ's version of the metaphor implies that *no* form of life could pass through the eye of a needle, but since Christ's time we have learned that, mechanically at least, *all* life takes such a strange journey. Knowing the mechanics of genetic transmission, however, does not solve the problem of destiny and fulfillment— whether human beings will live good or bad, wise or foolish lives. If some species pass out of existence as permanently as the pterodactyls, the question of what we are to make of ourselves in the time allotted to us—both as a species and as individuals—becomes a challenge we cannot avoid. Creatures who can pass through the eye of a needle are strange and powerful, but none of us has unlimited time. Our genetic coding gives us a form, but it is up to us to decide, like the rich man, what kind of creatures we are to be, how we will shape the potentialities of our form in society and history.

Clearly, Eiseley could not have spread the net of his meaning either so wide or so suggestively without the use of literary devices that fuse language and content into one.

Conclusion

In ordering the social styles from colloquial to literary, and in praising the literary styles, we do not mean to suggest that the best writing is necessarily found at the highest point in the ladder of styles. They do not form a strict hierarchy from least to most desirable. The variables of circumstance, audience, and purpose force us to choose different social styles according to criteria that necessarily shift as these critical variables themselves shift. Most of us write very little of what can be called literature; only on rare occasions is a fully literary style appropriate. For most of our occasions we will write in the colloquial, formal, or technical styles —but even in these styles literary devices can be appropriate. Metaphor, allusion, personification, a concern for rhythms, and other literary devices are frequently used by expository writers in all styles to achieve rich and telling effects.

The literary styles we have talked about exhibit an intensity of imagination, a richness of meaning, and a suggestiveness of emotion that differ markedly from writing that reports information *without* raising other kinds of meaning or expectations. Literature responds to the universal human hunger to find a fuller life. From detailed historical novels based on fact to the wildest fantasies of science fiction to Eiseley's kind of ethically based discussion of scientific discovery, we readers ingest literature's pictures of other people's environs, ideas, and passions. Once we have worked these pictures into the fabric of our own memory and thinking, they are likely to stay there forever, not as a diversion from "real" life but quite literally as an enlargement of it.

Because literature addresses such deep and permanent impulses in human nature, it is easy to see why the literary style is the oldest of human society's written social styles. As Sir Philip Sidney said, literature "paints a speaking picture," and the pictures it paints open to us a vivified and expanded view of life's possibilities.

ESSAY ASSIGNMENTS

1. Write two letters (about two or three pages each) directed to two different audiences (one of them your classmates), describing your initial impressions of college, your feelings about your job, your reaction to a specific course, or some other feeling or experience that you would like to talk about. Use two of the different social styles that we discuss in this section of the book.
2. In a two- or three-page essay directed to your fellow students,

translate a hundred words or so from a famous piece of
literature into two or three different social styles. (2 Corinthians
13 or Lincoln's Gettysburg Address might work well.)

3. We have asserted that we are writing this book mainly in the
formal style. But we have also shifted from one social style to
another at different points. Select two or three passages that
you think are not written in the formal style, and tell us in a
letter what other styles you think we have employed.
Document the shifts you think we have made, and evaluate
whether or not we were justified in making them.

10

Tone

So far we have talked about personal *voice*—what makes one writer sound different from another—and the ways in which writers modify their voices to fit different occasions. We turn now to the second main variable in "tone of voice": *tone*. "Tone" is a musical metaphor for writers' relationships with readers that result from writers making two decisions: (1) how they will express or imply their *feelings* about their subject, and (2) how they will place themselves socially, intellectually, or morally with regard to their implied readers—as their superiors, looking down; as their inferiors, looking up; or as their equals, addressing them eye-to-eye.

Part I: Writers share feelings

Tone as the *expression* of feeling should not be confused with the *description* of feeling. Tone expresses or implies the writer's emotional state, the feeling about the subject that the writer desires to share; it will often differ markedly from the feelings expressed by characters who appear *in* the writing. A writer, for example, can describe the cheerfulness of airline flight attendants in a sarcastic tone; or the self-dramatizing gloom of a spoiled child in a scoffing tone; or the pompous pontifications of a political candidate in a tone of good-natured joshing.

Clearly writers need not *say* what they are feeling; tone emerges as a quality of the whole utterance, whether spoken or written. An indignant speaker might say with deep sarcasm, "I'm delighted that you show such contempt for my efforts. Nothing pleases me more than to find honesty where I might least expect it." The speaker does not need to say, "I'm indignant." When Wordsworth says, "But yet I know, where'er I go,/ That there hath past away a glory from the earth," his sense of loss can be heard without his having to say, "I'm sad." It is reported that Mark Twain would never smile as he delivered popular speeches that kept his audiences in stitches.

Tone, then, is the quality of voice that conveys feelings, whether they are stated directly or indirectly. Tone and voice are thus intimately connected—voice will always in part depend on tone—but they are by no means identical. We can always recognize the voices of individual relatives and friends, regardless of whether they speak in anger, amusement, love, or distress. Similarly, widely different tones in writing can be employed by the same writer without affecting a reader's ability to recognize that the various tones spring from the same voice.

Some tones caress, some tones instruct, some tones condemn. With variations of tone we can express love or hate; happiness or grief; comradeship or contempt; compassion or loathing; humor or seriousness; anger, indignation, outrage, or forgiveness. And these tones are only a beginning. Just as a given instrument—a flute or bassoon, say—may express a great range of musical effects yet retain a distinctive "voice," so may speakers and writers.

In order to see this important relationship between voice and tone more clearly, read the following four passages from Charles Dickens, noting how he expresses various tones while retaining a distinctive "presence" that makes him one of the most readily recognizable voices in all of literature. Each Dickens passage will be followed by another passage from an essayist who employs roughly the same tone. By listening closely to each pair, you can see how even "the same" tone will not be really the same from writer to writer. Finally, notice how tone is usually a mixture of tone*s:* anger *and* pity, sorrow *and* hope, and so on.

Be sure to read each passage aloud at least once, or have someone read it to you. Since our surest grasp on language is through speech, we can often discover when reading aloud meanings that escape us when reading silently; hearing the sounds of the words, catching the rhythms, and attempting to recreate a plausible tone for the ear helps us discover the tones that might often escape the eye. Perhaps most useful is to experience several readings, by you to others and others to you, so that differences of reading tones can enter into your discussion of the authors' tones.

Charles Dickens and E. B. White

The first passage is from Charles Dickens's *David Copperfield* (1849–1850). David, the narrator, is looking back as an older man on one of the great loves of his adolescence, "the eldest Miss Larkins."

My passion takes away my appetite, and makes me wear my newest silk neckerchief continually. I have no relief but in putting on my best clothes, and having my boots cleaned over and over again. I seem, then, to be worthier of the eldest Miss Larkins. . . .

I think continually about my age. Say I am seventeen, and say that seventeen is young for the eldest Miss Larkins, what of that? Besides, I shall be one-and-twenty in no time almost. I regularly take walks outside Mr. Larkins's house in the evening, though it cuts me to the heart to see the [army] officers go in, or to hear them up in the drawing-room, where the eldest Miss Larkins plays the harp. I even walk, on two or three occasions, in a sickly, spoony manner, round and round the house after the family are gone to bed, wondering which is the eldest Miss Larkins's chamber (and pitching, I dare say now, on Mr. Larkins's instead); wishing that a fire would burst out; that the assembled crowd would stand appalled; that I, dashing through them with a ladder, might rear it against her window, save her in my arms, go back for something she had left behind, and perish in the flames. For I am generally disinterested in my love, and think I could be content to make a figure before Miss Larkins, and expire. Generally, but not always. Sometimes brighter visions rise before me. When I dress (the occupation of two hours) for a great ball given at the Larkins's (the anticipation of three weeks), I indulge my fancy with pleasing images. I picture myself taking courage to make a declaration to Miss Larkins. I picture Miss Larkins sinking her head upon my shoulder, and saying, "Oh, Mr. Copperfield, can I believe my ears?" I picture Mr. Larkins waiting on me next morning, and saying, "My dear Copperfield, my daughter has told me all. Youth is no objection. Here are twenty thousand pounds. Be happy!"

The tone here is a highly complicated achievement. The older David Copperfield, telling his own story, retains control of the tone, yet he manages to capture the spirit and feelings of his immature, younger self, the one who thinks that to die at the eldest Miss Larkins's feet after acting the hero would be the height of bliss. Clearly, no one-word label could adequately describe a tone that so mingles amusement, regret, nostalgic pleasure, and irony. The older man looking back sees how foolish his younger self was ("sickly, spoony"), but he knows that such foolishness is typical of youth and is not necessarily contemptible. He also sees his youthful innocence, ("I am generally disinterested in my love"), and knows how far he was from having any concrete plans, sexual fantasies, or realistic fears about the future. It is also clear that the older man feels regret—although he never explicitly says so—that he had to relinquish such innocence as a part of growing up. He keeps this flow of strong feelings—nostalgia, affection, regret—from plunging into sentimentality by describing the melodramatic self-consciousness of his passion ("I could be content to make a figure before Miss Larkins, and expire"), and the droll foolishness to which his youthful ardor led him (the fantasy of "dashing through them with a ladder . . . [to] save her in my arms"). The older David's evident belief that such behavior would be worse than ridiculous in anyone over the age of seventeen thus tempers the nostalgic tone of the passage, and lets us enjoy the foolishness without feeling that we've been taken in by mere silliness or sloppy sentimentality.

Compare this tone now with a passage from the essayist, E. B. White, often said to have been the best stylist in contemporary America (he died in 1985). In his essay "Bedfellows" (1956), White, like David Copperfield, is looking back on a time (and a creature) that he has lost. How does White's tone compare with Dickens's?

Fred was sold to me for a dachshund, but I was in a buying mood and would have bought the puppy if the storekeeper had said he was an Irish Wolfschmidt. He was only a few weeks old when I closed the deal, and he was in real trouble. In no time at all, his troubles cleared up and mine began. Thirteen years later he died, and by rights *my* troubles should have cleared up. But I can't say that they have. Here I am, seven years after his death, still sharing a fever bed with him and, what is infinitely more burdensome, still feeling the compulsion to write about him. I sometimes suspect that subconsciously I'm trying to revenge myself by turning him to account, and thus recompensing myself for the time and money he cost me. . . .

I find it difficult to convey the peculiar character of this ignoble old vigilante, my late and sometimes lamented companion. What was there about him so different from the many other dogs I've owned that he keeps recurring and does not, in fact, seem really dead at all? My wife used to claim that Fred was deeply devoted to me, and in a certain sense he was, but his was the devotion of an opportunist. He knew that on the farm I took the over-all view and travelled pluckily from one trouble spot to the next. He dearly loved this type of work. It was not his habit to tag along faithfully behind me, as a collie might, giving moral support and sometimes real support. He ran a trouble-shooting business of his own and was usually at the scene ahead of me, compounding the trouble and shooting in the air. . . .

Fred devoted his life to deflating me and succeeded admirably. His attachment to our establishment, though untinged with affection, was strong nevertheless, and vibrant. It was simply that he found in our persons, in our activities, the sort of complex, disorderly society that fired his imagination and satisfied his need for tumult and his quest for truth. After he had subdued six or seven porcupines, we realized that his private war against porcupines was an expensive bore, so we took to tying him, making him fast to any tree or wheel or post or log that was at hand, to keep him from sneaking off into the woods. I think of him as always at the end of some outsize piece of rope. Fred's disgust at these confinements was great, but he improved his time, nonetheless, in a thousand small diversions. He never just lay and rested. Within the range of his tether, he continued to explore, dissect, botanize, conduct post-mortems, excavate, experiment, expropriate, savor, masticate, regurgitate. He had no contemplative life, but he held as a steady gleam the belief that under the commonplace stone and behind the unlikely piece of driftwood lay the stuff of high adventure and the opportunity to save the nation.

Although the tones in this first pair of passages are not identical, they share at least one important thread of feeling. Each seems dominated by a tone of nostalgic reminiscence: a look backward in time that expresses fondness, a little regret, and amused irony. But there are important differences. Dickens's nostalgia seems a little sadder, White's a little more comic, partly because of theme: The loss of one's youthful foolishness, innocence, and zest is simply a profounder loss than the loss of one's dog. The difference also lies in the fact that the older Copperfield is talking about himself, while White is talking about another creature. White can thus express an admiration for Fred that the older Copperfield cannot easily express for himself without becoming cloying or self-conscious. Fred's independence ("His attachment . . . untinged with affection"), his liveliness and curiosity ("He improved his time . . . in a thousand small diversions"), and his companionship ("My wife used to claim that Fred was deeply devoted to me") turns Fred, without White's ever saying so, into a "person" (see the discussion of "personification" in Chapter 9) whom White appreciates for his vitality and independence. White implies that we could all learn something useful from Fred: Fred never puts on appearances, never acts like the faithful dogs in story books just to please his master, never sacrifices his real interests to the convenience of others. He may be eccentric, but he's authentic.

And note the humor that helps White avoid idealizing Fred, just as it helped the older Copperfield avoid idealizing his romantic younger self. The pun on Fred's version of "trouble-shooting"— "[Fred] was usually at the scene ahead of me, compounding the trouble and shooting in the air"—creates the absurd picture of a six-gun-toting dachshund ripping through the henhouse or the cow pasture shooting in the air while the hapless author trails behind and loses control. This comic reversal of roles makes the dog the master and the master . . . not the master. Finally, note the drollery of that tag, "ignoble old vigilante." Clearly, if White could have ignoble old Fred back—even at twice the amount of trouble—he would close the deal in an instant while laughing at himself for being fool enough to do so.

PARAGRAPH PRACTICE (or Essay Assignment)

Try your hand now at a paragraph of nostalgic reminiscence addressed to your classmates. Like David Copperfield or E. B. White, try to capture your feelings about a particularly happy time or event in your past. You may want to read your paragraphs aloud to other students, comparing the tones for variety and intensity.

Charles Dickens and Maya Angelou

The first of our second set of passages is from Dickens's *Hard Times* (1854), a novel that exposes the poor working and living conditions of laborers in England's nineteenth century manufacturing towns. This passage describes Coketown, Dickens's name for the typically grimy, dreary, depressing industrial town in which the novel is set. In such towns the factory owners made fortunes while the workers lived in squalor and poverty, an injustice that Dickens angrily attacked in more than one tale. What tone(s) seem to dominate this passage?

You saw nothing in Coketown but what was severely workful. If the members of a religious persuasion built a chapel there—as the members of eighteen religious persuasions had done—they made it a pious workhouse of red brick, with sometimes (but this only in highly ornamented examples) a bell in a birdcage on the top of it. The solitary exception was

the New Church, a stuccoed edifice with a square steeple
over the door, terminating in four short pinnacles like florid
wooden legs. All the public inscriptions in the town were
painted alike, in severe characters of black and white. The
jail might have been the infirmary, the infirmary might have
been the jail, the town-hall might have been either, or both,
or anything else, for anything that appeared to the contrary
in the graces of their construction. Fact, fact, fact everywhere
in the material aspect of the town; fact, fact, fact everywhere
in the immaterial. The M'Choakumchild school was all fact,
and the school of design was all fact, and the relations between master and man were all fact, and everything was fact
between the lying-in [i.e., birthing] hospital and the cemetery, and what you couldn't state in figures, or show to be
purchaseable in the cheapest market and saleable in the dearest, was not, and never should be, world without end, Amen.

What emotions emerge through the prose here? Do you find
bitterness and anger? Scorn? Irony? From beginning to end the
pace of the passage accelerates until it suddenly slides ironically,
and with a significant change of tense, into the ending of the
Gloria Patria ("never should be, world without end, Amen"). All
of this suggests an explosive tension quivering just beneath the
surface. The speaker is clearly angry, morally outraged because
nothing counts in Coketown but utilitarian obsessions such as
running the factories and making money, most of which goes into
the pockets of the mill owners. The narrator clearly hates Coketown's monotony and grim "workfulness," and he hopes that
anyone reading his description will also hate it. Between the birth-
ing hospital and the cemetery, the only part of life that "counts"
is just what can be counted. Nothing else is valued in Coketown.
The churches, jails, infirmary, schools—all that might make the
place congenial to human tenderness and compassion—have been
placed in the service of calculation and fact, turning the workers
of Coketown into anonymous numerals playing anonymous roles
in the masters' formula for making money.

In addition to the outrage and sarcasm, other emotions play
around the fringes of this passage without becoming fully or explicitly expressed. We hear tones of ominous warning—a prophetic implication that the human spirit cannot stand Coketown's

deprivations without at last rebelling. Like an evangelist giving a hellfire-and-damnation sermon, the narrator prophesies violent catastrophe as he directly addresses the economists and masters who have created Coketown. These tones explicitly emerge in the passage that describes the forced parting of two factory workers, a man and woman in love.

> It was but a hurried parting in the common street, yet it was a sacred remembrance to these two common people. Utilitarian economists, skeletons of schoolmasters, Commissioners of Fact, genteel and used-up infidels, gabblers of many little dog's-eared creeds, the poor you will have always with you. Cultivate in them, while there is yet time, the utmost graces of the fancies and affections, to adorn their lives, so much in need of adornment; or, in the day of your triumph, when romance is utterly driven out of their souls, and they and a bare existence stand face to face, Reality will take a wolfish turn, and make an end of you.

An explosion of feeling occurs here, ignited by tone. The direct address leaves nothing to implication; the tone is one of frontal assault. The narrator, nearly incandescent, is determined to blast his message into the minds of those who need to know that the dehumanized creatures they are creating in their mills will have no compassion or mercy—feelings that have been ground out of them—when they at last reach the point of rebellion.

In the second passage of this pair, a selection from Maya Angelou's *I Know Why The Caged Bird Sings* (1969), the speaker is a black girl in the South at her eighth-grade graduation, reacting internally to a white commencement speaker who patronizes the young black graduates supposedly being honored. What tone does this passage express?

> It was awful to be Negro and have no control over my life. It was brutal to be young and already trained to sit quietly and listen to charges brought against my color with no chance of defense. We should all be dead. I thought I should like to see us all dead, one on top of the other. A pyramid of flesh with the whitefolks on the bottom, as the broad base, then the Indians with their silly tomahawks and teepees and

wigwams and treaties, the Negroes with their mops and recipes and cotton sacks and spirituals sticking out of their mouths. The Dutch children should all stumble in their wooden shoes and break their necks. The French should choke to death on the Louisiana Purchase (1803) while silk-worms ate all the Chinese with their stupid pigtails. As a species, we were an abomination. All of us.

Is this not a tone of pure rage created by total despair and hopelessness? As the young girl listens to the "polite" insults uttered by the speaker, she suffers a complete loss of hope about the future, and with that loss comes a spasm of hatred, both for the white people whose conspiracy seems the immediate cause of her hopelessness, and for her fellow blacks who sit quietly and take the abuse. Dickens's prediction that the human spirit will eventually rebel against the forces that try to destroy it is borne out in the young girl's imagination as she creates a nightmare image of universal carnage.

This paragraph is the verbal equivalent of an erupting boil. All of the suppressed ugliness of resentment and frustration and hopelessness suddenly surfaces, and threatens to destroy both the victim and the victimizer. A profound sarcasm is invested in the young girl's "Louisiana Purchase (1803)." What good will it do *her* to know the date of the Louisiana Purchase, she who is never to be allowed to rise above the rank of cook, housemaid, field worker? What is the point of going to school, learning about the American way, or trying to have control over her life? What is the point to *anything*? None. And if there is no point, then we may as well all be dead. All we do is hurt and maim each other anyway. We should all die of our own silliness, nastiness, and brutality. The tones of a rage this deep chill the soul, for it is clear that when this tone turns into action, destruction and violence will follow.

PARAGRAPH PRACTICE (or Essay Assignment)

Try your hand now at writing a paragraph in a tone of bitter anger. You might in fact try two paragraphs, one in which you speak, like Dickens, as a third-person narrator, and another in which you speak, like Angelou, as a first-person narrator. Address your paragraph or essay to your classmates, or as a warning to those who are responsible for your anger. You need not "be yourself" in this paragraph. Trying on someone else's voice may work better.

Charles Dickens and Lillian Smith

The Dickens passage here is from the beginning of *Little Dorrit* (1855–1857). It shows Arthur Clennam, a middle-aged business man who has been abroad for many years, sitting in a restaurant on the first evening of his return to London, listening to the Sunday vesper bells and reflecting upon all the Sundays of his growing-up years before he left home. What tones do you hear in this passage? Can you describe how they differ from the tones of earlier passages?

There was the dreary Sunday of his childhood, when he sat with his hands before him, scared out of his senses by a horrible tract which commenced business with the poor child by asking him in its title, why he was going to Perdition?— a piece of curiosity that he really in a frock and drawers was not in a condition to satisfy—and which, for the further attraction of his infant mind, had a parenthesis in every other line with some such hiccupping reference as 2 Ep. Thess. c. iii., v. 6 & 7. There was the sleepy Sunday of his boyhood, when like a military deserter, he was marched to chapel by a picquet* of teachers three times a day, morally handcuffed to another boy; and when he would willingly have bartered two meals of indigestible sermon for another ounce or two of inferior mutton at his scanty dinner in the flesh. There was the interminable Sunday of his nonage†, when his mother,

---

picquet—a picquet is a spray of artificial flowers; thus, Dickens is creating a metaphor: his teachers are stiff and unyielding, like matching artificial flowers, connoting the shallowness and dryness of the religion to which Clennam feels his youth was sacrificed.

†*nonage*—literally, before one has come of age legally; thus, Clennam is older at his nonage than in his boyhood. He is giving an overview of all the Sundays that he spent from earliest memory to the age when he could finally leave home.

stern of face and unrelenting of heart, would sit all day
behind a bible—bound, like her own construction of it, in the
hardest, barest, and straitest boards, with one dinted orna-
ment on the cover like the drag of a chain,‡ and a wrathful
sprinkling of red upon the edges of the leaves—as if it, of all
books, were a fortification against sweetness of temper, natural affection, and gentle intercourse. There was the resentful Sunday of a little later, when he sat glowering and gloom-
ing through the tardy length of the day, with a sullen sense
of injury in his heart, and no more real knowledge of the
beneficent history of the New Testament, than if he had
been bred among idolators. There was a legion of Sundays,
all days of unserviceable bitterness and mortification, slowly
passing before him.

Are these not tones of gloom, sadness, and disappointment
—heartache over a childhood of lost opportunities and lost affec-
tions? The vision of Clennam's cold, Puritanical mother locking up
all his childish need for love between the hard cover-boards of her
Bible expresses a sadness that weighs upon Clennam's spirit like
a deep weariness. As an adult, Clennam seems no longer angry,
but the passage suggests that he feels beaten and old beyond his
years; he has never recovered the springiness and vitality that are
the gifts of a happy childhood.

The repetition of, "There was the dreary Sunday . . . the
sleepy Sunday . . . the interminable Sunday . . . the resentful
Sunday . . . a legion of Sundays," recreates their monotony, dull-
ness, and joylessness. The only thing that changes is that his
feelings grow from childhood fright to youthful resentment. In the
first picture he is little more than an infant "scared out of his
senses" by hellfire-and-brimstone pamphlets. In the second, a
little older, he is marched off to Sunday School like a "military
deserter." In the third, a little older still, he sits all day and watches
his unyielding mother read the Bible. And in the final picture he
is a resentful young man "with a sullen sense of injury in his
heart."

Together these four pictures create a single tone of gloomy

‡*drag* of a chain—the hook on the end of a chain used to drag for bodies in rivers
and lakes.

sadness coming from the heart of a young/old man whose only memories of childhood are of deprivation and disappointment.

The second passage of this pair is from Lillian Smith's *Killers of the Dream* (1961). Like Arthur Clennam, Smith is remembering a childhood with dark shadows lying across it. She is looking back on the place where she was born and raised. As she reflects, like Clennam, on the character of that time and place, compare her tones to his. What expectations about the story do her tones establish in the reader?

> From the day I was born [in the South], I began to learn my lessons. I was put in a rigid frame too intricate, too twisting to describe here so briefly, but I learned to conform to its slide-rule measurements. I learned it is possible to be a Christian and a white southerner simultaneously; to be a gentlewoman and an arrogant callous creature in the same moment; to pray at night and ride a Jim Crow car the next morning and to feel comfortable in doing both. I learned to believe in freedom, to glow when the word *democracy* was used, and to practice slavery from morning to night. I learned it the way all of my southern people learn it: by closing door after door until one's mind and heart and conscience are blocked off from each other and from reality. . . .

The first time Smith becomes aware of these double lessons as a child is when her family adopts Janie, a little girl her own age to whom Smith at once becomes deeply attached. But after three months of companionship the adults discover that Janie has Negro blood in her, and they send her off to live with a black family in shantytown. Notice how the distanced tone of the first passage gradually becomes the frightened, anxious tone of Smith's younger self in the second passage. She still remembers that after being told that Janie was to be taken away she repeatedly cried to her mother, "I don't understand!"

> "You're too young to understand. And don't ask me again, ever again, about this!" Mother's voice was sharp but her face was sad and there was no certainty left there. She hurried out and busied herself in the kitchen and I wandered through that room where I had been born, touching the old

familiar things in it, looking at them, trying to find the answer to a question that moaned like a hurt thing. . . .*

And then I went to Janie, who was waiting, knowing
things were happening that concerned her but waiting until
they were spoken aloud.

I do not know quite how the words were said but I told
her she was to return in the morning to the little place where
she had lived because she was colored and colored children
could not live with white children.

"Are you white?" she said.

"I'm white," I replied, "and my sister is white. And you're
colored. And white and colored can't live together because
my mother says so."

"Why," Janie whispered.

"Because they can't," I said. But I knew, though I said it
firmly, that something was wrong. I knew my father and
mother whom I passionately admired had betrayed something which they held dear. And they could not help doing
it. And I was shamed by their failure and frightened, for I felt
they were no longer as powerful as I had thought. There was
something Out There that was stronger than they and I could
not bear to believe it. I could not confess that my father, who
always solved the family dilemmas easily and with laughter,
could not solve this. I knew that my mother who was so good
to children did not believe in her heart that she was being
good to this child. There was not a word in my mind that said
it but my body knew and my glands, and I was filled with
anxiety. . . .

As I sit here writing, I can almost touch that little town,
so close is the memory of it. There it lies, its main street lined
with great oaks, heavy with matted moss that swings softly
even now as I remember. A little white town rimmed with
Negroes, making a deep shadow on the whiteness. There it
lies, broken in two by one strange idea. Minds broken.
Hearts broken. Conscience torn from acts. A culture split in
a thousand pieces. That is segregation. I am remembering: a
woman in a mental hospital walking four steps out, four
steps in, unable to go further because she has drawn an

---

*All ellipses in this excerpt are Smith's.

invisible line around her small world and is terrified to take one step beyond it. . . . A man in a Disturbed Ward assigning "places" to the other patients and violently insisting that each stay in his place. . . . A Negro woman saying to me so quietly, "We cannot ride together on the bus, you know. It is not legal to be human down here."

Memory, walking the streets of one's childhood . . . of the town where one was born.

In obvious ways Smith's tones are like Clennam's: sadness over lost opportunities and grief over personal and social betrayals. But in addition to these tones, another emerges that is unlike Clennam's: a tone of shame. Smith is not only saddened but shamed that the people she loves breed bigotry into their children, and practice self-deception in their daily lives. The tone of sadness mingled with shame is fully summed up in the final image of people driven mad by contradictions, their madness exhibiting itself as the logical extension of the moral code they once defended with all their hearts. As in the other passages we have examined, the tone is a dimension of the meaning, but cannot be located as the product of any one device or strategy. It is everywhere in general and nowhere in particular, pervading the whole passage.

PARAGRAPH PRACTICE (or Essay Assignment)

Try now to write a paragraph or essay, directed to your classmates, in a tone of gloom or sadness. As we suggested earlier, reading your writing aloud will give you a fuller grasp of the variety of available tones and intensities.

Charles Dickens and Mark Twain

The first passage in our final pair is from *Nicholas Nickleby* (1838–1839), one of Dickens's early novels. The first speaker is Dickens as narrator of the whole novel; the other two speakers are Vincent Crummles, the narrator of the story that is told within this passage (and master of a seedy little theatrical troupe), and Nicho-

las Nickleby, the novel's young hero who has just joined Crummles's band of actors. The group is on its way to its next engagement.

The pony took his time upon the road, and—possibly in
consequence of his theatrical education—evinced every now
and then a strong inclination to lie down. However, Mr.
Vincent Crummles kept him up pretty well, by jerking the
rein, and plying the whip; and when these means failed, and
the animal came to a stand, the elder Master Crummles [the
son] got out and kicked him. By dint of these encourage-
ments, he was persuaded to move from time to time, and
they jogged on (as Mr. Crummles truly observed) very comfortably for all parties.

"He's a good pony at bottom," said Mr. Crummles, turning to Nicholas.

He might have been at bottom, but he certainly was not
at top, seeing that his coat was of the roughest and most
ill-favoured kind. So, Nicholas merely observed, that he
shouldn't wonder if he was.

"Many and many is the circuit this pony has gone," said
Mr. Crummles, flicking him skillfully on the eyelid for old
acquaintance' sake. "He is quite one of us. His mother was
on the stage."

"Was she, indeed?" rejoined Nicholas.

"She ate apple-pie at a circus for upwards of fourteen
years," said the manager; "fired pistols, and went to bed in
a night-cap; and in short, took the low comedy* entirely. His
father was a dancer."

"Was he at all distinguished?"

"Not very," said the manager. "He was rather a low sort
of pony. The fact is, that he had been originally jobbed out†
by the day, and he never quite got over his old habits. He was

---

*low comedy—unsophisticated comedy that relies on physical humor and obvious
jokes (like slapstick), not witticisms or subtlety.

†jobbed out—the pony was owned by a livery stable and rented on a day-to-day basis
to people who could not afford to keep their own horses. Crummles is implying
that under these circumstances the pony would have met a good many "low," that
is vulgar, persons.

clever in melodrama too; but too broad—too broad. When the mother died, he took the port-wine business."

"The port-wine business!" cried Nicholas.

"Drinking port-wine with the clown," said the manager; "but he was greedy, and one night bit off the bowl of the glass, and choked himself, so that his vulgarity was the death of him at last."

What tones do you detect here? What kind of humor? Does it produce the same effects as E. B. White's humorous piece on the fire in his chimney (Chapter 9, pp. 268–269)? Does it rely on any of the same devices?

We hear a tone in both pieces that people often call "dry": a tone of light irony delivered straight, as if the speaker or writer were unaware of being ironic and maybe even unaware of being funny. It's a complicated tone, because the reader has to know that the writer really does intend to be funny, that the lack of awareness is only a pretense. White's piece about the chimney fire is of course designed to be funny, but he never says, "Let me tell you about the funny chimney fire I had." He tells it straight, as if the firemen coming in to socialize (even though they knew the fire was out) were an everyday occurrence.

The humor of Dickens's story is also the product of deadpan delivery. Crummles's tale of the pony's bizarre parentage—the pony's mother and father doing the "low comedy," the pony's father firing pistols, going to bed in nightcaps, dancing, doing clever melodrama, and finally choking to death while drinking port wine—are all delivered in a calm, matter-of-fact tone. The reader can almost see Crummles looking out of the corner of his eye to catch the story's effect on Nicholas Nickleby. To admit that he is telling a funny story would of course ruin the effect. Crummles criticizes the horse's taste in comedy, companions, and wine with uncompromising blandness ("he never quite got over his old habits"), the deadpan delivery only heightening the absurdity. The more solemnly he tells the joke, the funnier it will be.

Our second example in this final pair is another comic story, this one taken from Mark Twain's *Roughing It* (1872), his account of the five-year trip he made out West with his brother (referred to in the story as "the Secretary"). The unsettled West could be a dangerous place in the 1860s; just getting across the plains was perilous in itself. In this passage Twain describes himself and other Easterners arming themselves against the possible dangers of the trip.

The first thing we did on that glad evening that landed us at St. Joseph [Missouri, the edge of civilized territory] was to hunt up the stage-office, and pay a hundred and fifty dollars apiece for tickets per overland coach to Carson City, Nevada.

The next morning, bright and early, we took a hasty breakfast, and hurried to the starting-place. . . . We put our lawful twenty-five pounds apiece all in one valise [which meant that they had to send back most of what they had brought]. . . . It was a sad parting, for now we had no swallow-tail coats and white kid gloves to wear at Pawnee receptions in the Rocky Mountains, and no stovepipe hats nor patent-leather boots, nor anything else necessary to make life calm and peaceful. We were reduced to a war-footing. . . . I was armed to the teeth with a pitiful little Smith & Wesson's seven-shooter, which carried a ball like a homeopathic pill* and it took the whole seven to make a dose for an adult. But I thought it was grand. It appeared to me to be a dangerous weapon. It only had one fault—you could not hit anything with it. One of our "conductors" practiced awhile on a cow with it, and as long as she stood still and behaved herself she was safe; but as soon as she went to moving about, and he got to shooting at other things, she came to grief. The Secretary had a small-sized Colt's revolver strapped around him for protection against the Indians, and to guard against accidents he carried it uncapped. Mr. George Bemis was dismally formidable. George Bemis was our fellow-traveler. We had never seen him before. He wore in his belt an old original "Allen" revolver, such as irreverent people called a "pepperbox." Simply drawing the trigger back, the hammer would begin to rise and the barrel to turn over, and presently down would drop the hammer, and away would speed the ball. To aim along the turning barrel and hit the thing aimed at was a feat which was probably never done with an "Allen" in the

*homeopathic pill—a curative pill, very small.

world. But George's was a reliable weapon, nevertheless, because, as one of the stage-drivers afterward said, "If she didn't get what she went after, she would fetch something else." And so she did. She went after a deuce of spades nailed against a tree, once, and fetched a mule standing about thirty yards to the left of it. Bemis did not want the mule; but the owner came out with a double-barreled shot-gun and persuaded him to buy it, anyhow. It was a cheerful weapon—the "Allen." Sometimes all its six barrels would go off at once, and then there was no safe place in all the region round about, but behind it. . . .

We changed horses every ten miles, all day long, and fairly flew over the hard, level road. . . .

After supper a woman got in, who lived about fifty miles further on, and we three had to take turns at sitting outside with the driver and conductor. Apparently she was not a talkative woman. She would sit there in the gathering twilight and fasten her steadfast eyes on a mosquito rooting into her arm, and slowly she would raise her other hand till she had got his range, and then she would launch a slap at him that would have jolted a cow; and after that she would sit and contemplate the corpse with tranquil satisfaction—for she never missed her mosquito; she was a dead shot at short range. She never removed a carcase, but left them there for bait. I sat by this grim Sphynx and watched her kill thirty or forty mosquitoes—watched her, and waited for her to say something, but she never did.

In these two stories Dickens and Twain both reveal themselves to be masters of the put-on, the leg-pull, the implausible story told straight. Since the tone puts us onto the joke from the beginning, we readers savor the whole story. Notice, though, that if the tone had not given away the joke, the whole experience would be merely baffling or annoying. Dickens and Twain are both experts at telling the joke that pretends not to be a joke.

There are differences between them, however. Twain's tone is not as rigorously deadpan as Crummles's. Twain seems more willing to show an awareness of delivering comic lines. Yet he maintains a near-Dickensian drollness. His amused scorn for the tenderfoot's ignorance and ineptitude parallels the older Copper-field's amused scorn for the romantic excesses of the younger David. The difference is that while Twain openly invites the reader to laugh, Dickens does not allow Crummles to break his deadpan delivery even once. The reader who fails to realize that Crummles's story is a joke gets no explicit clues. Crummles refuses to be either amused or sarcastic about the bizarre details he reports. Twain, however, relies on sarcasm to cue the reader's response. Twain's sarcasm is like a wink at readers as they and Twain the storyteller both laugh at Twain the tenderfoot. The "wink" says something like, "See this tenderfoot? Wait 'til you hear what he did next."

In part, Twain achieves his distinctive tone with a technique we might call "reversal of meanings." He is a master at getting laughs by setting the reader up for kinds of expectations that he then adroitly reverses. The usual form of this move is to make a statement (A) which he then cancels with (B), the following state-ment. "It appeared to me to be a dangerous weapon" (A) is im-mediately canceled by the statement that follows it: "It only had one fault—you could not hit anything with it" (B). Or, "Bemis did not want the mule "(A), "but the owner came out with a double-barreled shotgun and persuaded him to buy it, anyhow" (B). "Per-suaded," is just not the expected word for shotgun coercion. That the Allen, which could threaten all life in a given area, is "cheer-ful," is another reversal. And, finally, Twain's brother carrying his weapon "for protection against the Indians" (A), but leaving it "uncapped to guard against accidents" (B) is another.

Note how Twain and Dickens both rely on absurdity. Twain compares the bullet of the Smith & Wesson to a little pill, and then claims that it took seven "to make a 'dose' for an adult"; Crummles claims that his pony's mother "ate apple-pie at a circus for up-wards of fourteen years." Twain's traveling companion who left the carcasses of 40 mosquitoes on her arm as "bait" is almost as absurd as Crummles's pony choking to death on a wine glass in the circus. The key ingredient that lifts absurdity from stupidity to comedy is tone. Anyone can make absurd statements—people often do—but absurdities are only funny when everyone knows they are part of a joke, and the best clue to a joke is the tone in which it is told.

Conclusion for Part I

Obviously our examples do not begin to cover the whole range of tones resulting from the expression of feeling, but they do suggest some of the variety you can choose from. As we said in Chapter 3 when discussing purpose, you can only achieve a limited number of effects in any one essay. When choosing a tone for a particular writing task, you will probably find it best to stick to one dominant tone—or at least to one dominant mixture—rather than shifting tones significantly within the short space of a single essay.

As we said earlier about voice, *some* kind of tone will emerge from anything you write, for it is almost impossible to speak without conveying some kind of feeling. But tone will not simply take care of itself. When writers fail to think about tone, it will take its revenge by becoming muddy or inconsistent or contradictory or overly vehement.

Unfortunately, working hard on tone involves risks. Like all the other writing virtues we have discussed, a forceful tone can be ruinous when carried to excess. Once we begin to sense the power of achieving a clear tone, we may be tempted to exaggerate it, to push a given tone too hard and hold it too long. The writer who overdoes sarcasm may imply that everyone else in the world is a fool. The writer who overdoes genial good cheer may slide into the sickly sweet or the coy. The writer who maintains a fever of passion becomes as embarrassing as a tenor who tries to make up in volume for being flat. But these problems can be taken care of with revision and practice. Even experienced writers run into them in their early drafts. What marks the mature from the immature writer is the ability to modulate a tone in appropriate ways for different purposes.

ESSAY ASSIGNMENTS

1. Choose two passages of contrasting tone by the same author, or two passages that, like our contrasting essays, are by different authors using the same tone. Then analyze the differences and

similarities, addressing your essay to your instructor. (Be sure to provide a copy of the passages.)

Try to account for the differences in tone by referring to specific details in each passage. You might first describe and analyze the tone of each passage separately before you engage in the comparison. Or you might find it easier to compare them quality by quality, quotation by quotation: A1-B1; A2-B2; A3-B3.

2. Address two different versions of the same event to two different audiences using two different tones. Use the same social style for each essay. Suppose, for example, that you were to write two different explanations of why your grades were disappointingly low last term, one explanation (in either colloquial or standard social style) to go to your parents who are angry with you, and one explanation (in the same style) to go to a good friend who is likely to be sympathetic.

3. Choose some passage from an essay, novel, editorial, or some other source that you think is written in an excessively intense or inappropriate tone. Then alter the tone of the passage by rewriting it, and conclude by discussing the advantages of your version over the original.

4. Pick some famous speech or document (the Gettysburg Address, say, or 2 Corinthians 13, the Declaration of Independence, the Preamble to the Constitution, the opening paragraphs of Charles Dickens's *A Tale of Two Cities* (1859), the opening verses of Genesis, or Winston Churchill's "blood, sweat, and tears" speech), cutting for appropriate length if necessary, and write three different versions of your selection, employing three different tones for each version. Address your essay to your fellow students, and append a concluding paragraph or two in which you discuss the altered effects your changes have created.

Part II: Readers as inferiors, equals, or superiors

In the passages from Part I of this chapter, we have listened to some strong tonal differences that spring from expressing personal feeling. We turn now to the second main source of tonal variety, the writer's diverse relations with readers. We may not think about the matter consciously, but as readers we inevitably respond differently to different tones of address from writers, tones that are conveyed by either overt clues ("You, dear reader, will surely agree with me that . . .") or merely by implication.

The range of possible tones that writers use to establish their relations with readers are as rich as those they use to express personal emotion. As writers we may, for example, appear distant and detached, indifferent to everything but pure rationality, or personal and intimate, trying to earn our readers' love. We may mock, bully, or lash with satire. We may portray ourselves as wise, implying either our readers' relative folly or their potentiality for wisdom; as prophetic, implying their stodgy lack of vision; as fellow-seekers of truth traveling the same road with them; or as fellow human beings asking nothing from readers but understanding and companionship.

The varieties of tone available to us as writers are thus almost overwhelmingly rich, and such riches, as people who suddenly become millionaires often discover, confer problems as well as benefits. If we do not *choose* a tone and carefully establish it, we may *fall into* one that does not really suit our audience, our character, or our purposes. Who among us would like to sound like a wheedler, a whiner, or a bully? Since our tone can convey these impressions as easily as it can convey more favorable or admirable ones, we need to make sure that we are in charge of our tone, that it conveys the impression we have chosen and not one that will surprise or embarrass us.

One way to approach our choice of tones, then, and to avoid inappropriate ones, is to ask ourselves where a given tone places us in relation to the reader. Without simplifying too badly, we can say that all tones place us as writers in one of the following positions: (1) standing on an elevated platform looking down on our readers; (2) standing across from our readers and addressing them as equals, eye-to-eye; or (3) standing beneath our readers and looking up to them as superiors. We can come off as mentors, bosses, or gurus; as friends, buddies, or brothers and sisters; as servants, flunkeys, or supplicants; as superiors or supervisors; as 'jes plain folks; or as seekers of blessings, charity, and favors.

Talking down, or speaking from above

One of the commonest ways a writer may speak from above is simply to know more about the subject than the reader. If you were a scientist or a philosopher who had thought more about certain issues than most of your readers, you would inevitably speak from above in a book or article explaining your views. Obviously, many books are written precisely to present their authors' superior knowledge. You have probably assumed this position in some of your own essays. Whenever you know more than your readers, you are in at least one respect speaking from above.

Knowing more than your readers need not, however, lead to patronizing them. Much of the reading we do is frankly motivated by our desire to learn from others, and much of the writing we do is frankly motivated by the desire to teach—at least to explain, clarify, present arguments, and so on. Knowing more never creates a problem in itself, then, but it may do so if our tone suggests that the reader's inferior knowledge is contemptible, disgusting, or simply inexcusable. Writing that demeans, slights, or ridicules the reader—or writing that scorns the reader's character, education, race, sex, religion, or intelligence—almost always fails (unless the aim is to alienate or infuriate). Only a writer with great moral authority, such as a prophet—we'll meet one or two such writers in a moment—can carry off a scornful tone. And even prophetic voices tend to work best when they do not target their readers directly, but invite them to assume the role of bystanders taking pleasure in seeing someone else get lashed. We can all think of people who deserve annihilating attacks—the sinners and tyrants and cheaters who plague our lives. But the victims of such attacks, whether the attacks are written or spoken, are rarely themselves transformed by the lashings; usually only the bystanders profit.

Talking down: Shakespeare and Socrates. When King Lear curses his daughter, Goneril, the audience takes pleasure in the curse as an appropriate punishment, but Goneril changes neither her character nor her behavior. There is clearly no hope here of improving or educating the listener within the play. As Lear rails against Goneril, Shakespeare addresses us bystanders as moral equals. But there can be no question about Lear's anger or intentions. Only a stone could misunderstand.

> Hear, Nature, hear; dear Goddess, hear!
> Suspend thy purpose, if thou didst intend
> To make this creature fruitful!
> Into her womb convey sterility;
> Dry up in her the organs of increase,
> And from her derogate° body never spring   debased
> A babe to honor her! If she must teem,
> Create her child of spleen, that it may live
> And be a thwart° disnatur'd° torment to her!   perverse/obstinate
> Let it stamp wrinkles in her brow of youth,
> With cadent° tears fret channels in her cheeks,   falling
> Turn all her mother's pains and benefits
> To laughter and contempt, that she may feel
> How sharper than a serpent's tooth it is
> To have a thankless child!

Such writers as prophets, preachers, and social critics, however, working in another vein, have kept alive an ancient tradition of "speaking down" to their actual readers in order to do them good, to condemn their failures and point the way toward improvement. Unlike Lear, such speakers curse not to destroy but to bless. When Socrates was on trial for his life, for example, in fourth century B.C. Athens, a trial that went against him, he spoke down to his listeners (who were also his judges) by reminding them of the flaws in their character, flaws that he had attempted to help them correct all his life.

> If you say to me, Socrates, this time . . . you shall be let off, but upon one condition, that you are not to enquire and speculate in this way any more, and that if you are caught doing so again you shall die;—if this was the condition on which you let me go, I should reply: Men of Athens, I honour and love you; but I shall obey God rather than you, and while I have life and strength I shall never cease from the practice and teaching of philosophy, exhorting any one whom I meet and saying to him after my manner: You, my friend,—a citizen of the great and mighty and wise city of Athens,—are

you not ashamed of heaping up the greatest amount of money and honor and reputation and caring so little about wisdom and truth and the greatest improvement of the soul, which you never regard or heed at all? . . . And if I think that he has no virtue in him, but only says that he has, I reproach him with undervaluing the greater, and overvaluing the less. . . . For I do nothing but go about persuading you all, old and young alike, not to take thought for your persons or your properties, but first and chiefly to care about the greatest improvement of the soul. I tell you that virtue is not given by money, but that from virtue comes money and every other good of man, public as well as private. . . . I would have you know, that if you kill such an one as I am, you will injure yourselves more than you will injure me. Nothing will injure me, not Meletus nor yet Anytus*—they cannot, for a bad man is not permitted to injure a better than himself. . . . I am not going to argue for my own sake . . . but for yours, that you may not sin against the God by condemning me, who am his gift to you. For if you kill me you will not easily find a successor to me, who, if I may use such a ludicrous figure of speech, am a sort of gadfly, given to the state by God; and the state is a great and noble steed who is tardy in his motions owing to his very size, and requires to be stirred into life. I am that gadfly which God has attached to the state, and all day long and in all places am always fastening upon you, arousing and persuading and reproaching you. You will not easily find another like me, and therefore I would advise you to spare me. [Plato, *The Apology*]

In claiming divine support for his criticism, in assuming his own moral superiority in such a clear and untroubled way, and in refusing blankly to modify his behavior or his teachings, Socrates exemplifies a tone of speaking down to his audience. Yet it is also clear that his motive is not to destroy his fellow citizens or to separate himself from them absolutely, but to improve them, to lift their vision of life above the gross materialism into which he sees them sinking.

*Meletus, Anytus—Socrates' accusers.

PARAGRAPH PRACTICE (or Essay Assignment)

1. On the model of Lear's curse to Goneril or Socrates' speech to his jury, write a curse wishing evil upon some hated person, or write a speech criticizing an individual (or a group) for his or her own good. The person may be historical, fictitious, literary, or real.
2. Write a one-paragraph statement or, if this project appeals to you, an essay directed at some group or person on campus whose attitudes, behavior, or beliefs you would like to change. Try to establish a tone in which you let your reader(s) know that you are friendly—a well-wisher—even though you are also a critic.

Talking down: John Ruskin. John Ruskin provides us with another example of one who spoke down to the audience he wanted to reform. The place is England in April 1864, about twenty-five hundred years after Socrates' death, and the occasion is not a trial but a public lecture. Ruskin, a famous authority on architecture, has been invited by Bradford's town fathers, who are planning to erect a grand stock exchange, to give a public lecture advising them on appropriate architectural styles for their new building. But instead of lecturing them about their building, Ruskin, in a speech later published under the title, "Traffic," lectures them about their taste and their morals. His motives are similar to Socrates', but his tone is, if possible, even more scathing. Socrates merely says that the citizen of Athens will suffer more than he if they condemn him to death. But he doesn't specify just *how* bad things might get. Ruskin, on the other hand, prophesies catastrophe if his teachings are not heeded, and he does not make it as clear as Socrates did that he really loves his listeners. He clearly risks eliciting a hostile response in the hope of shaking his audience to the foundations.

My good Yorkshire [County] friends, you asked me down here among your hills that I might talk to you about this [Stock] Exchange you are going to build: but earnestly and seriously asking you to pardon me, I am going to do nothing of the kind. I cannot talk, or at least can say very little, about this same Exchange. I must talk of quite other things. . . . I cannot speak, to purpose, of anything about which I do not care; and most simply and sorrowfully I have to tell you, in the outset, that I do *not* care about this Exchange of yours. . . .

I do not care about this Exchange,—because *you* don't; and because you know perfectly well I cannot make you. Look at the essential circumstances of the case, which you, as business men, know perfectly well, though perhaps you think I forget them. You are going to spend £30,000, which to you, collectively, is nothing; the buying a new coat is, as to the cost of it, a much more important matter of consideration to me than building a new Exchange is to you. But you think you may as well have the right thing for your money. You know there are a great many odd styles of architecture about; you don't want to do anything ridiculous; you hear of me, among others, as a respectable architectural man-milliner [a maker of hats]: and you send for me, that I may tell you the leading fashion; and what is, in our shops, for the moment, the newest and sweetest thing in pinnacles.

Now, pardon me for telling you frankly, you cannot have good architecture merely by asking people's advice on occasion. . . .

You ask me what style is best to build in; and how can I answer . . . but by another question—do you mean to build as Christians or as Infidels? And still more—do you mean to build as honest Christians or as honest Infidels? as thoroughly and confessedly either one or the other? You don't like to be asked such rude questions. I cannot help it; they are of much more importance than this Exchange business; and if they can be at once answered, the Exchange business settles itself in a moment. . . .

Ruskin goes on to make it clear that the question of religion precedes any question of architecture because all art and architecture are expressions of national character. As he sees it, the problem with the English national character is that it worships money, the "idol of riches," before everything else. His listeners should think seriously about

. . . this idol of riches; this idol of yours; this golden image high by measureless cubits, set up where your green fields of England are furnace-burnt into the likeness of the plain of Dura:* this idol [of riches], forbidden to us, first of all idols, by our own Master and faith [i.e., forbidden by Jesus and Christianity]; forbidden to us also by every human lip that has ever, in any age or people, been accounted of as able to speak according to the purposes of God. Continue to make that forbidden deity your principal one, and soon no more art, no more science, no more pleasure will be possible. Catastrophe will come; or worse than catastrophe, slow mouldering and withering into Hades.

Clearly, the speaker is rubbing his listeners' noses in their faults and, like Socrates, he is assuming a position of superior moral authority. Also like Socrates, he bases his authority on religious grounds. He assumes that, as fellow Christians, his listeners (and afterward his readers) embrace the Christian principles that justify his critical tone. As Christians, he implies, *they* should be as scornful of their money-grubbing materialism as he.

Ruskin is frank here to the point of rudeness, and rudeness is risky for any writer. What possible advantage can he see in it? Whether he thought all this out ahead of time is hard to say, but he seems to make rudeness work for him like this: He implies that he cares more for truth than for manners, and more for righteousness than for courtesy. He uses rudeness to portray himself as a bluntly honest man. If the tone works, it forces the reader to respond something like this: "Here is a man who doesn't tell me what he thinks I want to hear; he risks offending me; but because he takes that risk with such passion, ignoring my potential displeasure so bravely, I think he must be speaking truthfully, or at least speaking sincerely and honestly."

The disaster of rejection that Ruskin flirts with can be avoided only by writers who are in complete control of their tone. They must also be—like Socrates, Ruskin, and (in our own day) Martin Luther King—persons whose reputation for integrity remains unquestioned during and after the encounter.

*plain of Dura—where the Babylonian king Nebuchadnezzar set up an image of gold sixty cubits high and six cubits wide.

Talking down: Separating issues from personalities. Whenever readers question either an author's authority or honesty, they will reject any efforts by that author to speak to them from above. But authority and integrity of this kind do not depend primarily on readers knowing details about the writer's life; they are produced by the tone of the writing itself.

To some people, reading a self-help therapy book by an author with a program for happiness, or reading a book of spiritual uplift written by a TV evangelist will seem like reading the naked words of truth. Yet other readers of the same material will be disgusted by what they see as the authors' patronizing tone and unearned claims to authority. To some readers, a scholarly treatise with copious evidence and supporting arguments all in proper order can seem intimidating and "hifalutin' "; they may see the author of a well-documented paper as putting on airs or as pretentious. Yet other readers will expect a scholarly tone in certain kinds of writing.

These varied responses suggest once again why writers must always think hard about their readers: about what they will expect or want, and about their criteria for successful writing. This does not mean that you will always give them what they want to hear. Sometimes you may feel compelled, like Socrates and Ruskin, to write things that you know your readers do *not* want to hear. But not to have some idea of how they are likely to react is to run the risk of simply being ignored—or being tarred and feathered.

To disagree with someone, even to attack someone else's position or research, is not necessarily to put them down with contempt. An attack on people's views and arguments need not imply that they are inferior. Students often seem reluctant to disagree with each other in class for fear they will sound superior or conceited. Many students seem to want to slide around every disagreement by saying something like, "Well, that's OK if that's the way you really *feel*"—as if every position could somehow be validated by sincerity. And if a disagreement does surface far enough to get defined, even then many students exhibit discomfort at following up with arguments and challenges.

Despite some notable exceptions, scientific, philosophical, and literary debates offer us good models for distinguishing attacks on positions from attacks on personalities. At their best these debates are conducted in tones of mutual respect. Opponents give credit for past achievements, and they acknowledge the strengths of the positions they are attacking. Counter-attacks are openly invited. All of this can be accomplished within a context of fundamental disagreement. The following passage is typical of the kind of book review or critique of ideas that one is likely to find in scholarly journals.

> Professor Greenspan's newest book is perhaps the best recent psychoanalytical study of Charles Dickens' novels. Greenspan's position is coherent, she knows what kind of evidence counts for the kind of argument she is making, and she argues well enough to make skeptics come up with counter-arguments as carefully considered as her own. Nevertheless, I think Greenspan has wasted her energy in writing this book, not because she argues poorly, but because Edmund Wilson, Lionel Trilling, and a host of lesser critics have already exhausted the psychoanalytical approach to Dickens. Even though Greenspan employs that approach better than many others, she has nothing new to tell us. Her conclusions seem predictable and stale.

And so on. In a review that promises to be as responsible as this one, the reviewer would go on to summarize Professor Greenspan's main arguments or position, and then lay out the criticisms. Reading the review, Professor Greenspan might be annoyed that the reviewer had rejected her arguments, but the tone could hardly make her feel personally attacked or ridiculed. Such disagreements and responses, especially when conducted in public, help to prevent important issues from being seized as the private property of special interest groups.

Talking down: Satire. A special instance of put-down writing is **satire:** writing designed to ridicule someone or some institution. In *Gulliver's Travels* (1726) Jonathan Swift ridicules the weaknesses of human nature in general, in *Animal Farm* (1945) George Orwell ridicules totalitarian governments, and in *Doonesbury* Gary Trudeau ridicules political figures. In much satire the object of ridicule is *not* the audience. Satire seldom speaks down *to;* it speaks down *about,* inviting the reader to join the writer in ridiculing a person or idea external to them both. In such cases the satirist and the reader are actually eye to eye, and some satirized object or person is being "spoken down" about.

In the following passage from Elaine Morgan's *The Descent of Woman* (1972), Morgan makes fun of male evolutionary biologists who, she claims, use their science to keep women in an inferior position in society.

> According to the Book of Genesis, God first created man. Woman was not only an afterthought, but an amenity. For close on two thousand years this holy scripture was believed to justify her subordination and explain her inferiority; for even as a copy she was not a very good copy. There were differences. She was not one of His best efforts.
>
> There is a line in an old folk song that runs: "I called my donkey a horse gone wonky." Throughout most of the literature dealing with the differences between the sexes there runs a subtle underlying assumption that woman is a man gone wonky; that woman is a distorted version of the original blueprint; that they are the norm, and we are the deviation.
>
> It might have been expected that when Darwin came along and wrote an entirely different account of *The Descent of Man,* this assumption would have been eradicated, for Darwin didn't believe she was an afterthought: he believed her origin was at least contemporaneous with man's. It should have led to some kind of breakthrough in the relationship between the sexes. But it didn't.
>
> Almost at once men set about the congenial and fascinating task of working out an entirely new set of reasons why woman was manifestly inferior and irreversibly subordinate, and they have been happily engaged on this ever since. Instead of theology they use biology, and ethnology, and primatology, but they use them to reach the same conclusions.
>
> They are now prepared to debate the most complex problems of economic reform not in terms of the will of God, but in terms of the sexual behavior patterns of the cichlid fish; so that if a woman claims equal pay or the right to promotion there is usually an authoritative male thinker around to deliver a brief homily on hormones, and point out that what

she secretly intends by this, and what will inevitably result, is the "psychological castration" of the men in her life.

Now, that may look to us like a stock piece of emotional blackmail—like the woman who whimpers that if Sonny doesn't do as she wants him to do, then Mother's going to have one of her nasty turns. It is not really surprising that most women who are concerned to win themselves a new and better status in society tend to sheer away from the whole subject of biology and origins, and hope that we can ignore all that and concentrate on ensuring that in the future things will be different.

I believe this is a mistake. . . .

Who is the real audience here? Is it male scientists? Note that the "we" at the end of the second paragraph and the "us" at the beginning of the fifth paragraph clearly define her audience as women, not those male scientists whose attitudes have robbed women of pride and whose sexism and condescension she despises. And she invites her actual readers—insulted women—to join her in ridiculing and despising them too. (Do you think that she also hopes to convert any male biologists who happen to read her?)

Notice the devices by which she makes fun of males. "She was not one of His best efforts," shows religionists judging God's creation from a narrow, defensive, male point of view. In the third paragraph she ridicules those inconsistent evolutionists who conveniently overlook anything in Darwin's views that justifies a more liberal view of women. And when she describes her enemy as setting about "the congenial and fascinating task" of working out *new* reasons for women's subordination, after Darwin had removed the old ones, she suggests that they are fake scientists, men who would abuse scientific objectivity in order to buttress their phony claims to superiority. In the fourth paragraph, the picture of men viewing women's requests for justice as "psychological castration" suggests that men—or at least men of this stamp—are incompetent, insecure, and defensive. The most scornful put-down of all is her suggestion that men do precisely the kinds of guilt numbers on women that they have always accused women of doing on men: They themselves, the scientists, are "like the woman who whimpers that if Sonny doesn't do as she wants him to do, then Mother's going to have one of her nasty turns."

ESSAY ASSIGNMENTS

1. Write the three following paragraphs as a short essay to be handed in to your instructor.

   First, write a paragraph attacking some objectionable position about a campus issue that you care about, and write it in a put-down tone directed straight *at* your opponents.

   Second, write a paragraph on the same issue, but write it as satire *about* those who hold the position you object to, directed at an audience whom you invite to share your scorn.

   Third, write a paragraph in which you explain (to your instructor) the devices you used to establish your two tones, and assess the strengths and weaknesses of each paragraph as written ridicule.

2. Read Martin Luther King's "Letter From Birmingham Jail" (1964) and, in an essay directed to your classmates, analyze the stylistic devices by means of which King maintains a tone that suggests, as does Socrates' tone, that despite his criticisms, he still loves his readers and wants the best for them. (The essay has been reprinted in hundreds of anthologies, and is in King's *Why We Can't Wait.*)

SENTENCE PRACTICE

Each of the following passages shows a speaker or writer talking down to the audience. In each case try to determine whether the author is speaking from legitimate authority (moral, intellectual, political, and so on), engaging in sarcasm, or talking down in some other way. Discuss your reading of each passage with your classmates.

   After discussion, write a different version of each passage, one that establishes a different kind of relation between the writer and the audience by use of tone.

1. Now see here, Briggs, that's the dumbest idea I've heard in years!

2. Oh yeah, terrific. Since when does "equal marriage" mean that *I've* got to clean the toilet bowl every week?
3. To focus the camera, superimpose the double images in the middle of the view finder.
4. "To err is human, to forgive divine." [Alexander Pope]
5. "A Monk there was, one of the finest sort
   Who rode the country; hunting was his sport." [Geoffrey Chaucer]
6. "The unexamined life is not worth living." [Socrates]
7. "The alternatives before us are clear. Either we must abandon the ideal of freedom or we must educate our people for freedom." [Robert Maynard Hutchins]
8. "Mr. Houghton was given to high-minded monologues about the good life, sexless and full of duty. Yet in the middle of one of these monologues, if a girl passed the window, tapping along on her neat little feet, he would interrupt his discourse, his neck would turn of itself and he would watch her out of sight. In this instance, he seemed to me ruled . . . by an invisible and irresistible spring in his nape." [William Golding]
9. "It is a truth universally acknowledged, that a single man in possession of a good fortune, must be in want of a wife. However little known the feelings or views of such a man may be on his first entering a neighbourhood, this truth is so well fixed in the minds of the surrounding families, that he is considered as the rightful property of some one or other of their daughters." [Jane Austen]
10. "I tell thee, Blockhead, [thy unhappiness] all comes of thy Vanity; of what thou *fanciest* those same deserts of thine to be. Fancy that thou deservest to be hanged (as is most likely), thou wilt feel it happiness to be only shot: fancy that thou deservest to be hanged in a hair-halter, it will be a luxury to die in hemp." [Thomas Carlyle]

As you can tell from examining these passages, some kinds of outside information can be extremely useful in interpreting tone. If you know, for example, that Carlyle wrote *Sartor Resartus,* the book from which Number 10 is taken, in 1833, in the midst of the Industrial Revolution, and that his general aim is to expose to the British their materialism, greed, and lack of religion, then his fervently prophetic tone becomes easier to decipher. But even if you are unclear about these details, the "speaking from above" tone emerges forcefully.

Talking eye-to-eye: Sharing

A second kind of relation that authors can create with their readers through tone is that of equals. As we have seen, speaking from above in one dimension is not always incompatible with speaking eye-to-eye in another. Writers frequently offer explanations or clarifications that their readers are ignorant of, without suggesting that the readers are inferior. But many issues are so complex or ambiguous that none of us can really claim superior knowledge, and we must therefore take care to write about such issues without sounding dogmatic.

Many personal essays rely heavily on the relationship of equality established between writer and reader—the writer's identification with the reader's interests, feelings, or fears. The writer's character and point of view create a community of two: writer and reader sharing the writer's exploration. Even when writers aim to explain or clarify their private feelings, an activity that might be described as speaking from above since no one knows those feelings but the authors, even then their feelings should be made to seem common enough to be recognized by others. As writers, all of us have to assume that even our most private feelings are of the *kind* that others also experience. If we don't, then writing to explain our feelings is never going to work—or even make sense.

Talking eye-to-eye: Denise Levertov. In Denise Levertov's "A Note on the Work of the Imagination" (1961), Levertov describes a vivid dream, a dream that is of course private, as all dreams are, but told in a tone that takes for granted the reader's general knowledge of dreams and how they work. She is telling us about her own unique experience, but she speaks to us on a horizontal plane, recognizing that we have also had experiences of this *kind.*

> I had been dreaming of a large house, set in a flat landscape, and of its history, which is not relevant here. At a certain point I half awoke; and when I returned to the dream I was conscious that I was dreaming. Still close to the threshold of waking, I knew very well that I was lying down for an afternoon nap, in my son's room, because there the street

noises would hardly reach me; that though I had a blanket over me I was cold; and that he would soon be home from school and I must get up. But all this was unimportant: what gripped me was the knowledge that I was dreaming, and vividly. . . .

At length [in my dream] I came into a small bedroom fitted with a washbasin and mirror, and the idea came to me of looking in the mirror as a test of how far in fidelity the dream would go; but I was afraid. I was afraid the mirror would show me a blank, or a strange face. I was afraid of the fright that this would give me. . . .

None of us has had Levertov's dream, but all of us have had her kind of fright in dreams.

Talking eye-to-eye: Karl Popper and intellectual humility. Speaking to your reader eye-to-eye means having respect for the reader and humility about yourself. Though showing respect doesn't mean that you have to avoid all criticism or disagreement, it does mean that you have to be (and seem) reasonable, which further means that you must realize that the other person, not you, may be right. No doubt you have noticed that opinions you find objectionable are believed, or have been believed, by many other people, some of whom are hard to dismiss as merely deluded, crazy, or evil. Persons who never do notice this are sometimes called provincial; they never cease being shocked that the opinions they view as "common sense," or as just "naturally true," are in fact not only rejected by others, but sometimes viewed as vile and unnatural. An education should not make you so blasé or sophisticated that you cannot be shocked by *anything*, but it should introduce you to the certainty that your own views will not seem inevitable to everyone else.

Humility, a necessary intellectual virtue, can be overdone if it slides into a phony "speaking from below," as if to say, "Aw shucks, don't mind me, I'm just a nobody." The humility we are recommending is really nothing more than reasonableness, but since many writers who claim to be reasonable are still arrogant, perhaps humility is an appropriate term for what we have in mind. The philosopher Karl Popper, who has thought as much about this issue as anyone, says in "Utopia and Violence" (1963) that reasonableness lies in a certain attitude,

. . . in an attitude of give and take, in a readiness not only to convince the other man but also possibly to be convinced by him. What I call the attitude of reasonableness may be characterized by a remark like this: "I think I am right, but I may be wrong and you may be right, and in any case let us discuss it, for in this way we are likely to get nearer to a true understanding than if we each merely insist that we are right."

It will be realized that what I call the attitude of reasonableness or the rationalistic attitude presupposes a certain amount of intellectual humility. Perhaps only those can take it up who are aware that they are sometimes wrong, and who do not habitually forget their mistakes. It is born of the realization that we are not omniscient, and that we owe most of our knowledge to others. It is an attitude which tries as far as possible to transfer to the field of opinions in general the two rules of every legal proceeding: first, that one should always hear both sides, and secondly, that one does not make a good judge if one is a party to the case.

Talking eye-to-eye: Matthew Arnold and Edmund Burke.

More than a century ago, in 1865, Matthew Arnold, looking back almost 75 years to 1791, found an impressive illustration of the attitude that Popper recommends in the writings of Edmund Burke. In the passage that Arnold quotes, Burke shows the strength of mind and honesty of character to turn on himself and consider that, in spite of his profound devotion to a particular cause, he might still be wrong. Edmund Burke was a political writer who spent a major part of his career opposing the political and social influence of the French and American revolutions. As a conservative political philosopher and a Tory (the conservative party of his day), Burke had written volumes strenuously objecting to the liberal ideas in France and America at the end of the eighteenth century. Yet, having devoted great energy to arguing against these ideas, and having been the great spokesman of his party, he is still able, near the end of his life and career, to consider that he may have been arguing not only on the losing side, but on the wrong side. He is humble enough to think that future generations may see his opposition to French and American ideas about equality as perverse and obstinate, not firm and resolute. Arnold records and comments on the spectacle of Burke's large-mindedness in this way:

But Burke is so great because, almost alone in England, he brings thought to bear upon politics, he saturates politics with thought. . . . His greatness is that he lived in a world which neither English Liberalism nor English Toryism is apt to enter;—the world of ideas, not the world of catchwords and party habits. . . . At the very end of his fierce struggle with the French Revolution, after all his invectives against its false pretensions, hollowness, and madness, with his sincere convictions of its mischievousness, he can close a memorandum on the best means of combating it, some of the last pages he ever wrote,—the *Thoughts on French Affairs,* in December 1791—with these striking words:—

The evil is stated, in my opinion, as it exists. The remedy must be where power, wisdom, and information, I hope, are more united with good intentions than they can be with me. I have done with this subject, I believe, for ever. It has given me many anxious moments for the last two years. *If a great change is to be made in human affairs, the minds of men will be fitted to it; the general opinions and feelings will draw that way. Every fear, every hope will forward it; and then they who persist in opposing this mighty current in human affairs will appear rather to resist the decrees of Providence itself, than the mere designs of men. They will not be resolute and firm, but perverse and obstinate.* [Arnold's italics]

That return of Burke upon himself has always seemed to me one of the finest things in English literature, or indeed in any literature. That is what I call living by ideas: when one side of a question has long had your earnest support, when all your feelings are engaged, when you hear all round you no language but one, when your party talks this language like a steam-engine and can imagine no other,—still to be able to think, still to be irresistibly carried, if so it be, by the current of thought to the opposite side of the question. ["The Function of Criticism at the Present Time," in *Essays in Criticism, First Series,* 1865]

Talking eye-to-eye *and* from above: Martin Luther King. One of the most rhetorically effective and powerful positions that a speaker or writer can assume *combines* speaking from above with speaking eye-to-eye. In his famous "Letter From Birmingham

Jail," Martin Luther King clearly addresses the white moderates of 1963 from a position of self-acknowledged moral superiority. Throughout his letter (in *Why We Can't Wait,* 1964) he makes it clear that the feeble support of white moderates for his integrationist activities has disappointed, and even outraged, him. "I have almost reached the regrettable conclusion," he says, "that the Negro's great stumbling block in his stride toward freedom is not the White Citizen's Counciler or the Ku Klux Klanner, but the white moderate, who is more devoted to 'order' than to justice; but who prefers a negative peace which is the absence of tension to a positive peace which is the presence of justice."

King's immediate audience is eight fellow clergymen, all white, who had published a statement criticizing him as an extremist. His larger audience, of course, is the world, against whose collective judgment he wants to expose the inadequate reasoning of his local critics. At one point he criticizes their logic: "In your statement you assert that our actions, even though peaceful, must be condemned because they precipitate violence. But is this a logical assertion? Isn't this like condemning a robbed man because his possession of money precipitated the evil act of robbery?" And at another point he denounces his critics as callous and blind: "I had hoped that the white moderate would see this need [for direct, nonviolent action]. Perhaps I was too optimistic. . . . I suppose I should have realized that few members of the oppressor race can understand the deep groans and passionate yearnings of the oppressed race, and still fewer have the vision to see that injustice must be rooted out by strong, persistent and determined action."

Despite this claim to moral superiority, however, King still manages to speak eye-to-eye with his audience. He makes clear that he loves his readers and wishes the best for them even as he criticizes them. He establishes this tone by showing both respect and humility. He shows his respect when he admits that his critics may be "men of genuine good will and that your criticisms are sincerely set forth," and when he admits that their anxiety over King's civil disobedience "is certainly a legitimate concern." By meeting his audience's concerns directly—not hedging or weaseling—King grants that they are worthy of respect.

His humility, revealed throughout, does not undercut any of his criticism. Rather, it acknowledges that he, like his audience, is susceptible to human error, and that he may need their forgiveness as much as they need his. "If I have said anything in this letter that overstates the truth and indicates an unreasonable impatience, I beg you to forgive me. If I have said anything that understates the truth and indicates my having a patience that allows me to settle for anything less than brotherhood, I beg God to forgive me. I hope this letter finds you strong in the faith. I also hope that circumstances will soon make it possible for me to meet each of you, not as an integrationist or a civil-rights leader but as a fellow clergyman and a Christian brother." Insofar as King seems by his tone *not* to have overstated his case, his being willing to consider that he *might* have purchases great credibility. It establishes his character as an honest man, as one who addresses his readers' best judgment, rather than manipulate their weak feelings.

When you approach an issue and an audience with intellectual humility, even being proved wrong does not necessarily discredit you. Most people, for example, would now agree that Burke *was* wrong to oppose the liberal movement that gave to the world the Declaration of Independence and the American Constitution. But because, as Arnold said, Burke's thoughtfulness was genuine, not dominated by party catchwords and predictable clichés, he instructs us *despite* his being wrong. Right and wrong sometimes turn out to be crude categories for assessing the value of what real thinkers offer us. Even if we decide that Burke was wrong about the influence of the French Revolution, he nevertheless teaches us about some of the more sinister sides of democratic society. And in his willingness, as in King's, to allow that others may be more right than he, he offers us a model for addressing our audiences eye-to-eye without having to bend our arguments or compromise our principles. (See Chapter 5, pp. 157–158, for a discussion of knowing your opponents' views as a resource for invention.)

PARAGRAPH PRACTICE

With King's and Burke's paragraphs as background reading, and using the situations we provide for you below, write three concluding paragraphs of your own that show you "irresistibly carried . . . by thought," as Arnold puts it, "to the opposite side of the question."

1. Situation: You are concluding a letter to your parents in which you have been, up to this point, stating the advantages of your marrying a person to whom they object. Now you are ready to take their objections seriously.
2. Situation: You are writing a conclusion to a political speech urging people to vote for your candidate, but you want to close with a reminder that it is even more important for them to vote their consciences.
3. Situation: You are approaching the conclusion of a letter of complaint to the president of a chemical firm that has been polluting your hometown's drinking water; the chemical plant is the town's main employer and thus the foundation of the town's prosperity. You want to condemn but not alienate.

Talking from below, or looking up

Addressing your audience from below is taking a tone that implies your inferiority: You are in your readers' debt, or you must praise them in some way. In each of these cases you are speaking, or writing, "up" to an audience above you. In past periods, in Chaucer's, Shakespeare's, or Milton's day, for example—periods when people took it for granted that both nature and society were unchangeably arranged in a given order—writers could write up to those who were "naturally" above them without a sense of degrading themselves or diminishing their own dignity. Henry Fielding dedicates his novel, *The History of Tom Jones, a Foundling* (1749), to "the Honourable George Lyttleton, Esq.; One of the Lords Commissioners of the Treasury," with the following words (excerpted from a much longer dedication): "If there be in this work, as some have been pleased to say, a stronger picture of a truly benevolent mind than is to be found in any other, who that knows you . . . will doubt whence that benevolence hath been copied?" Having begun his dedication with the admission that Lyttleton had already denied Fielding's request to dedicate the novel to him, he turns even his disobedience into praise for his patron: "In short, sir, I suspect, that your dislike of public praise is your true objection granting my request. I have observed that you have . . . an unwillingness to hear the least mention of your own virtues; that, as a great poet says . . . you 'Do good by stealth, and blush to find it fame.' " Such flattery of readers is not common today.

Almost 150 years prior to Fielding's dedication to his novel, Nicolo Machiavelli had dedicated his great work, *The Prince* (1513), to one of the most powerful men in Europe, Lorenzo De Medici, in tones equally suggestive of the exalted position of the reader, and the humble position of the writer:

> Those who strive to obtain the good graces of a prince are accustomed to come before him with such things as they hold most precious, or in which they see him take most delight: whence one often sees horses, arms, cloth of gold, precious stones, and similar ornaments presented to princes, worthy of their greatness.
>
> Desiring therefore to present myself to your Magnificence with some testimony of my devotion towards you, I have not found among my possessions anything which I hold more dear than, or value so much as, the knowledge of the actions of great men, acquired by long experience in contemporary affairs, and a continual study of antiquity; which, having reflected upon it with great and prolonged diligence, I now send, digested into a little volume, to your Magnificence.
>
> And although I may consider this work unworthy of your countenance, nevertheless I trust much to your benignity that it may be acceptable, seeing that it is not possible for me to make a better gift than to offer you the opportunity of understanding in the shortest time all that I have learnt in so many years, and with so many troubles and dangers. . . .

Talking from below: Everyday examples. In the modern age, with its democratic presuppositions, its social mobility, and its notions about progress, it is hard to imagine any writer speaking in such unqualified terms about anyone else's superiority—at least not in such a public and formal way. But while Fielding's and Machiavelli's mode of speaking from below is no longer fashionable, all of us occasionally face circumstances when speaking from below seems appropriate.

Seeking advice. Whenever we ask another to help us think through an issue or decide what to do, we are speaking from below. Asking for advice does not necessarily involve flattering our advisers, but it is impossible not to admit our lower position when we are reaching upward for help. It is possible, of course, to seek advice on a horizontal plane: Scientists and scholars trade advice about how to find information or how to solve problems without being troubled by the question of who is above or below the other. They tend to focus on the work, not on their relative status. But when seeking advice about personal issues—whether to accept or to offer a proposal of marriage, which job to apply for, what position to take about a religious or moral issue, and so on—the writer clearly looks up to the one from whom advice is being sought.

Requesting help. Clearly, asking for advice is asking for a kind of help, but there is a line in most people's minds between asking for advice and asking for material help: money, time, equipment. When you write to ask someone to cosign a loan, to grant you a scholarship, to help you move, or to paint your house, you are clearly speaking from below in the sense of speaking from a need that the bounty of others can help satisfy.

Expressing praise. When writing award speeches, commemorations to be inscribed on plaques, epitaphs, eulogies, love letters praising our loved one's qualities, or expressions of appreciation for the support of friends, we place ourselves—at least momentarily—in a position below our readers. It is not necessary to believe that we are inferior (although that is possible), but we never insist on our equality within the context of this kind of writing. To praise someone may in fact imply a belief in one's own superiority—but the language will not reveal that fact.

Flattering. Flattery is self-interested praise; even where the praise might be merited, it becomes flattery when writers praise in order to soften up their readers for the sake of gaining something. In addition, flattery is usually duplicitous and exaggerated (flattery always overstates the virtues of the one being flattered). Depending on the writer's aims, flattery may be combined with any of the other modes of speaking from below just described. The injection of flattery, however, will always transform any legitimate relationship with an audience into an illegitimate one. Flattery is basically dishonest, manipulative, and in a more or less subtle way coercive.

Expressing gratitude. Letters or speeches in acknowledgment of favors, gifts, or attention all invite the writer to speak from below. Our notions of graciousness and courtesy include prohibitions about pressing our deserts when we are writing letters of gratitude. You would never write to the civic organization that had given you a college scholarship by congratulating yourself for having won the money, or even congratulating your readers for having had enough good sense to make you their choice. You would, instead, avoid any praise of yourself and stick to expressions of gratitude instead.

Asking forgiveness. At the very heart of requesting forgiveness is an admission of being, or having been, in the wrong, and thus in some sense "below" the readers from whom you ask forgiveness. (Notes to the teacher explaining a missed deadline or a hastily-written paper are in this genre, and in our experience they are usually written with little thought about tone.)

Confessing wrongs. Closely allied with asking forgiveness is making confessions—uncovering some deed(s) that the confessor has hitherto kept secret from those who will view it as wrongdoing. Not all who confess express contrition, remorse, or ask for forgiveness, but even if the confessor does not look up to the audience of the confession, he or she at least knows that the audience looks down on the wrongdoer.

Depreciating oneself. The contrary of flattery is self-depreciation. Flattery always implies self-depreciation, and self-depreciation almost always implies flattery, but in each case the emphasis is different. We say "almost" because there are a few obvious cases—as when asking for forgiveness or making a confession—in which self-depreciation may be genuine, not manipulative, and may not therefore imply flattery. But whenever writers put themselves down in order to give the audience a false sense of superiority, or to purchase generosity or approval that the writer has not really earned, then self-depreciation is being used, like flattery, to manipulate and coerce.

Admitting ignorance. Admission of ignorance can lead to a tone of false humility, and it can also be used as a kind of manipulation. But writers may also acknowledge ignorance in non-manipulative or self-depreciatory ways. Students writing exams or term papers for their professors generally assume that their readers possess more knowledge about a subject than they do. To admit that is not necessarily to flatter or manipulate. The writer may simply be acknowledging that the reader has a right to require the writer to produce certain kinds of information.

PARAGRAPH PRACTICE

Using the following situations, write three different paragraphs in which you "speak from below." Make each one the initial paragraph of a letter or essay that in its fully developed form would be much longer. In other words, don't try to say everything in one paragraph, but do try to establish an authentic tone in each one. Aim to sound like a real person speaking with real feeling.

1. Situation: You are asking a friend to forgive you for some slight or hurt. Your transgression was not accidental; you were angry and lashed out, and you said some stupid, mean, "unforgivable" things.

2. Situation: You and your parents have been sweating out the money for college, not really sure that you will be able to scrape together the necessary funds. Suddenly and unexpectedly, your tight-fisted, distant, but rich uncle offers to pay for one-half of your tuition. You are now at college writing him a thank-you letter. You know from family talk that he likes being flattered, and you also know that his continued support may make all the difference in whether you stay in college or not. You are unwilling simply to flood him with compliments, yet you want to use every honest means to ensure that he continues to think well of you.

3. Situation: You are in the middle of a big research project in an important class—a term paper in history, a lab procedure in biology, or some other activity important to your grade—and you are stuck. You have run into a snag that threatens to bring the whole project to a halt. You have discovered, however, that the person in the whole class whom you like least (and who seems to share your animosity) is the one person who has the information or skill that might help you over your difficulty. You are to write a note asking this person if he or she will help you. You don't want to eat humble pie, but you are willing to meet halfway and to show gratitude for any assistance.

4. Situation: You have quarreled with your spouse or a close friend and are writing to apologize for your part in the fight without accepting all the blame.

ESSAY ASSIGNMENT

In a two- or three-page essay, write four different versions of the same argument in which you speak in turn from above, eye-to-eye, and from below.

The situation is this: You are speaking out in anger on a campus issue of importance, writing a letter to the campus newspaper. The purpose of your letter is to criticize the present arrangements, to show how they are foolish, expensive, inefficient, illogical, or otherwise in need of reform, and thus to win adherents to your cause.

In the first letter assume the tone of one who falls easily into an angry put-down tone, the kind of writer who assumes that everyone who disagrees is an imbecile, and who thinks that the way to get people to do things differently is to make them admit how stupid they are.

In the second letter take the tone of the critic who is willing to stand by his or her criticism, but who is also willing to think that those who hold different opinions may have good reasons for doing so. You want people to see the advantage of your position, but you are willing to grant them the dignity of their own—short of diluting your criticism, of course. Your anger should still show through—but not against your readers.

In the third letter your anger should be disguised under the ingratiating tone of an inferior, a writer who thinks that the best way to move others is to appeal to their generosity and benevolence, even if it is not clear that they have any. Flatter the authorities—not too obviously, of course, but enough to soften them up so that they will accept your view of things.

Conclusion for Part II

The two kinds of tone discussed in this chapter are closely akin. Each of the examples from Part I could be shown to employ tones that speak from above, or eye-to-eye, or from below. A slight change of emphasis would have allowed us to talk about Martin Luther King as speaking from above more than speaking eye-to-eye. On the other hand, taking a given position as superior, inferior, or equal allows for a broad range of emotional tones. Your final tone will almost always be a combination of tones.

Like voice, tone will be important to the success of everything you write. Even if you have developed a powerful, distinctive voice, the wrong tone for the task in hand can make you seem unconvincing and untrustworthy. We should underline that we are not advising you to adopt whatever voice and tone promise to gain you the most approval. But no writer will want to fall into a tone that unnecessarily earns disapproval.

The main problem of tone for most writers, however, is not that of resisting temptations to unethical tones, but that of hitting a tone that will be most useful and appropriate. Usually effective tone emerges as we become clearer and clearer about our purposes as we write succeeding drafts. By thinking about it as we go we can in fact speed up the moment of discovery. Not all purposes are compatible with talking down, not all are compatible with speaking from above; some mixtures of tone simply will not work for some rhetorical occasions, while others in fact *demand* complexity. In short, in our effort to *meet* readers and to share our purposes with them, a mastery of a wide range of different tones can be just as important as developing a recognizably individual voice.

11

Supporting your thesis I: The complex world of "good reasons"

"I know what you're thinking about," said Tweedledum; "but it isn't so, nohow."
"Contrariwise," continued Tweedledee, "if it was so, it might be; and if it were so, it would be; but as it isn't, it ain't. That's logic."
LEWIS CARROLL, Through the Looking Glass

The different demands of different audiences

You have been learning about the many variables that complicate the effort to write well, and you have by now practiced some ways of controlling them. You have learned to think about your purposes as you address the needs of different audiences; about ways of finding something to say; about the importance of careful design and explicit connections that reveal your design; and about personal voice, a variety of social styles, and tone.

While attending to these matters you also no doubt have had to think about the problem that we turn to now, one that we have only touched on so far but that is in some ways the most important of all: how to discover and employ **good reasons** for one's case— how to make our essays more *cogent.* Readers should feel not only that an essay possesses a clear and attractive style, but that its reasoning is so powerful that they *ought* either to accept it, or at least take it into account before replying. The good reasons that it offers—the developed arguments or suggestions that it presents —should seem so well marshaled that every careful reader will feel obliged to treat them with respect.

How can we make our arguments strong enough to produce that effect—not only on our readers but on our own minds as we discover what we want to say and then test our arguments for weakness? How do we develop lines of argument that would in themselves be logically persuasive, even if they were presented in a bad arrangement and in relatively weak prose?

Every skill we have discussed so far will be discounted by any reader who decides that our reasoning is sloppy. It is true that even the most cogent argument—even one that seems logically airtight—can be sorely weakened by bad design, by poor use of connections, or by an offensive tone. But careful readers will view these other elements as less effective, even when we use them well, if they are not grounded in rigorous arguments. In pursuing these, we are returning to the subject of invention, now considered not as merely finding *something* to say but as finding a logical form for it that will hold up under critical scrutiny.

Good reasons cannot be described or listed like the ingredients in good bread. Consider just how many kinds of evidence we actually employ in the arguments we make every day. Very little of it comes from laboratory experiments or mathematical computation—what we might call "hard" or "certain" proof. When we do have scientific proof we would be foolish not to use it, but usually it is unavailable, not just because nobody has done the right study, but because our problems are usually of the kind that cannot be solved scientifically.

Even scientists, except when they are working in their narrow specialties, must often rely for their "hard" proof on second-hand sources (the work of other scientists, taking them as authorities). And like the rest of us, they must rely on comparatively "soft" and unscientific reasoning—a kind of rhetorical proof or informal logic—whenever they think about non-scientific domains. Even what looks like hard calculation or rigorous experiment intended to settle controversial questions often enough leads only to further dispute; even scientists—much less the rest of us—seldom find the kind of "clincher" that will silence every reasonable opponent. Sampling techniques and calculation may tell us, for example, that the average high school graduate has spent more time watching TV than attending classes or studying, but it will not tell us whether this is a good or bad thing in itself, and it will not tell us how to argue for our judgments.

Many kinds of good reasons

In Chapters 12 and 13 we shall consider the range of reasons available for our use (adding to the resources of invention that we discussed in Chapter 5). But first we must emphasize just how much the standard of what makes a "good reason" will vary from context to context and from reader to reader.

In ordinary conversation, the following argument would seem pretty persuasive: "He *must* have seen the eclipse; he was walking from his home to his office when it occurred." The assertion of such a *fact,* one that logically **implies** a strong probability, would convince most of us—for ordinary purposes. But in a court of law further argument would be needed. Was it perhaps raining at the time? Was he so absent-minded that he didn't notice the eclipse, which was after all only a quarter-eclipse? Was his walk *really* taken at the time of the eclipse or just close to it? Is he noted for being inattentive to his surroundings? And so on. On the other hand, if we were talking to friends who trusted our word, and if no great consequences hung on the result, we might get by without even mentioning the walk: "I give you my word that he saw the eclipse." (Note that even such a bare assertion of authority can be analyzed to reveal its logical claim: The unspoken assumption is that, "When I give my word, I do not lie; I here give you my word, so you can believe me.") Every assertion we make can in fact be "unpacked" to make a **syllogism,** just by filling in the unstated terms:

1. You can trust everything I say.

2. I say that he saw the eclipse.

3. Therefore he saw the eclipse.

(If you have had a course in logic, you may have learned another form of logical structure using a different notation, with "p's" and "q's" and "if–then" clauses. Everything that follows can be said just as well in these more "modern" notations as in the syllogistic forms that we have found to be more accessible to students who cannot take a complete course in logic.)

Whether it is always sensible to test our language by its strict logical force is another question. Many—perhaps most—of our beliefs are not arrived at through traceable logical patterns: for example, "I love my mother, my child, my husband"; "I really want to become an educated person"; "It matters a lot to me whether our team wins this Saturday"; "That was a great movie —I cried and cried." To apply strictly logical tests to these statements and reject them if they do not pass would be absurd. People who read our essays are intuitively aware of such differences, and they will expect different levels and kinds of logical force, depending on our different purposes and subject matters.

When Don writes home asking for more money, he might write like this.

> Dear folks,
>
> [After giving the news and chatting a bit, Don gets to the point.] . . . Everything is a lot more expensive here than I thought it would be, and everybody I know needs a larger monthly allowance than I have in order to make ends meet. You know that I don't have time to work and keep up with my studies too, so I hope you agree . . .
>
> > Love,
> > Don

Here we have three claims about "the facts"—none of them supported with anything more than an assertion. Don must decide whether *these particular readers* need the support of more arguments, perhaps of more facts: "The Dean just issued a report showing that the student budget estimate in last year's catalogue was too low." If Don thinks his parents are especially skeptical folks, he might go further and send a xerox of the Dean's report. That would seem like a really hard fact—unless he is known as a confirmed liar and his parents might suspect that it was forged, in which case he would provide a further fact, perhaps getting a notary to sign it. But he will also probably want to enrich his case with arguments of other kinds—not hard facts but perhaps examples or analogies.

> My roommate's parents have just *doubled* his allowance, after he showed them just what things cost here.

Here we have an example based on an **analogy** (see pp. 377–391), one that is intended to lead to the conclusion: *If* more money is needed by one student, *then* it is also needed by another. Note that Don claims to cite a fact—the roommate's allowance was really doubled—and then uses that fact to *imply* the analogy:

> My roommate and his budget situation are enough like me and my budget situation that if *his* parents double *his* money then *my* parents should double *mine*.

If Don is really worried about whether his parents trust his claims, he will do well to add some further claims to support the analogy. "Jack and I have both been extremely economical so far, and his dad actually came to town to look into his spending." Yet if Don's parents are especially generous and trusting, none of this elaboration will be required. A simple note might do—"I'm broke again, and it's not my fault. The Dean just told me that the stupid catalogue budget was too low."

Now suppose that Don is writing to the State Scholarship Commission applying for financial aid. Obviously much of what was accepted as good reasons by his parents will be irrelevant to the Commission, and much more information must be added, including some precise details about expenditures and needs.

Why is there so much variety in reasoning?

One reason that different audiences demand such varying *amounts* of argument is that all the issues we choose to write about have potentially more than one solution. They are all subject to choice as well as necessity. Don does not have an *absolute* need for more money; he is *choosing* to spend his money one way rather than another; he is choosing to stay in college rather than working full time; he is choosing not to work part time; he is choosing to request money from his parents rather than to work or beg on the streets or become a burglar; and so on. That he needs money is in large part a product of his own choices.

Every point we urge upon our readers is similarly based on various choices, many of them unexpressed, and we are placing the burden of even more choices on those readers: whether or not to believe us, whether or not to like us, whether or not to *do* anything about it even if they do believe us, and so on. We write about a question in the first place because there is some choice to be made—of belief, of attitude, of action—and each choice will be related to other choices we have already made.

No significant human choice can be based simply on experimental evidence or mathematical calculation. Both the stuff we write about and the conclusions we come to *could be otherwise*. We write mainly about the maybes of life, not the certainties. If a conclusion is certain, clear, indubitable, and thus already accepted by *everyone* who counts for us, why write about it? Just present the statistical graph or the lab report and be done with it. But in a world of maybes, we are always dealing with matters that might be otherwise, both for us and our readers, and different readers will have different standards for what makes a probable case.

What is the test of a good reason?

The example of the trusting parents who need only a sentence should not suggest that we can decide how many reasons to provide simply on the basis of whether our readers are friendly or unfriendly. The real test is whether the claims we make in our writing, *in particular circumstances,* are likely to need more support depending on the occasion and the audience. On some occasions a simple sentence, presenting a single reason, might be enough to produce total conviction and instantaneous response: "Dear Sir: Unless you pay your bill by Thursday, July 9, 1985, the Ghoule Power Company will cut off your electricity." That will be enough to get me to act, though I know, in one part of my mind, that the letter just *might* be an empty threat; or it *might* be a form letter produced by computer error; or it *might* be a poor practical joke. In short, the situation "might be otherwise," but I cannot afford to act on anything but the probability that the letter means what it says.

The same complexities lurk behind other seemingly simple proofs. "It must be true *because* my father told me about it." "It's the law." "She must love me; she accepted my ring." In some contexts such arguments will be enough; in most contexts they will seem weak.

When simple arguments like, "Pay by Thursday or you'll be sorry," won't do, the problem of defining good reasons becomes even more difficult. If I want to prove or disprove the existence of God or the legitimacy of abortion or the necessity of banning nuclear arms—surely matters of major importance to every thinking human being—the maybes multiply until I find that some readers will probably not be convinced even by whole books, while others who are on the fence might be swayed by a carefully composed page. Computer scientists and philosophers are now producing books and articles "proving" that computers will (or will not) someday handle natural language as human beings do. Obviously even full-length books, stocked with arguments as rigorous as can be found, will not settle such complex matters once and for all.

But we don't have to limit ourselves to such difficult issues as computers and language to recognize that good reasons are often too few or too weak to produce absolute certainty. You have already faced many decisions in your life that you could not settle simply by referring to the available reasons. The reasons at hand were simply inadequate to prove one choice better than another. Sometimes reasons are so evenly balanced that you just flip a coin. Sometimes—as when someone "makes you an offer that you can't refuse"—force or the threat of force "decides." As Huck Finn says, when Colonel Sherburn is pointing the shotgun at the lynching mob that Huck has accidentally strayed into, "I could a staid, if I'd a wanted to, but I didn't want to." On the other hand, you have sometimes found that weighing reasons carefully has led you into genuine opportunities that a simple hunch would have ignored.

Perhaps you can say, for example, that you chose this college. (Or perhaps your parents, or mere chance, decided for you.) If you did choose, your reasons for rejecting all the others were almost certainly weak—weak as compared with the reasons that one would *like* to have before commiting thousands of dollars and four years of one's life. But if you had waited until you had all the relevant evidence, you would never have been able to make your decision at all. (Booth once heard a student say at the end of the fourth year, "If I'd known when I was in high school that this college would be so much hard work, I wouldn't have come." Then, after a considerable pause, he added, "—and it would have been a terrible mistake!")

Such radical uncertainty means that every writer—and every careful speaker too—must exercise a complex kind of judgment about what kinds of situations require what kinds of proof. The right kind or degree of argument for this chapter of our book will not be right for the letter we must write our editor urging him to extend our deadline. The right arguments for your letter home explaining why you have decided to switch from pre-med to English will not be the right arguments, in kind or quantity, for your letter to the dean requesting an extended make-up exam deadline. The right arguments in your letter to your boss requesting a promotion and raise will not work well in your letter to the college dean requesting scholarship aid.

Judgment about the reasons needed in any particular case can be developed only through experience—which is one reason you are asked to write *many* papers rather than just polishing one paper until you "get it right." Through many trials and many errors in different contexts, you improve your hunches about what kinds of readers will require what kinds of reasons.

Suppose a young man has borrowed the family car without permission—though he has been told never to do so—for the very good reason that a friend whose car has broken down on the road has called for help. On the way to help his friend he causes an accident that costs the family several hundred dollars. The family then receives a letter from the insurance company drastically raising the rates. Now suppose that he has to write three letters: one to his parents, with whom he has always been on good terms, explaining his misdeeds; one to an employer who has expressed an interest in hiring him as a delivery boy, but who has phoned to say that she now has reservations about his maturity and driving ability; and a third to the driver of the other car whose collarbone was broken in the accident.

To his parents, he might well write a very personal letter, full of intimate reminders of his past good behavior and personal reassurance about his motives:

> Dear Mom and Dad,
>
> I've been thinking about it and thinking about it, and I still don't feel very clear about exactly what happened. Since I never disobeyed you in the past—at least not in something important like this—I'm just not sure how this happened. And though I'm sure it won't happen again, I'm surprised to find that I don't feel really guilty—it just seems that Jim's trouble was so great that I had no choice but to try to help him.
>
> Of course I see now that what I should have done was explain the whole thing to you . . .

And so on. Notice that when addressing friendly parents, he will probably not need to dwell much on the circumstances of the accident; he'll just say that it *was* his fault, and then spend his time talking about his character and his past relations with them. And he won't need to provide fine-honed proof for each claim. (Of course if we imagine a hostile family, then another level of detail will be required.)

When he turns to the insurance company, he will depend mainly on arguments about his driving record, about the circumstances of the accident ("Though it was technically my fault, the other driver . . ." and so on). And he will try to back every claim with evidence as firm as he can obtain. If he can find a witness to testify that the other driver was partly to blame, he'll dwell on that testimony. Writing to the prospective employer, on the other hand, he will probably emphasize his past good driving record and the reliability of his witness; he may even make some arguments about his own character (though in a different tone from the one used in writing to his parents). He might also think it useful to mention his plans for the future and what he has learned from the experience. Finally, he may use letters of recommendation of a kind that would be entirely irrelevant in writing to the insurance company.

None of this shifting of emphasis or variation in reasons necessarily implies dishonesty or insincerity; it is just that each case requires different arguments for different readers who are looking at the issue from different points of view.

Three general principles

Does all of this variety in kinds and quantity of reasons mean that we must work without rules to guide us? That depends on what we mean by rules. We certainly have no manual of reasons that would lead us step by step toward making infallible arguments. We should all be suspicious of the kind of handbooks of logic that offer decisive tests in choosing the *best* arguments, because *best*, as we have already seen, will vary from occasion to occasion. But there are at least three useful principles implied by all this (we address them to "you," but they apply to every writer):

1. *Always* spend some time, as you work on each writing assignment, thinking about what your likely readers *already* believe about your subject and about the kinds of arguments they are likely to find convincing. Whether your audience is as small as two parents or 25 classmates, or as large as all college students or all educated Americans, you will find, if you think hard enough, that you know *something* about their standards of proof. It will often help to write out a list of the convictions you expect your readers to bring to this subject before they start to read your words. (You might look again at "Your audience as a resource," pp. 131–134.)

2. Don't rest until you think you have met your *readers'* standards, as well as your own. Never be satisfied with a mere string of unsupported assertions that your readers can easily dismiss or contradict. Always try to connect each assertion to some support-

ing *reason* that will justify it, and do not stop in your search for reasons until you find one that you think your reader will accept, either as a "self-evident" assumption or as unquestionable fact. In the language of Chapter 5, you are exploring topics (places) to find where you and your reader already agree.

3. Always adjust the strength of your claim to the strength of your reasons. Don't say, "This proves that . . .," when you are justified in saying no more than, "One possibility is that . . ." Don't say, "It is thus certain that . . .," when you have shown no more than, "It may well be, then, that . . ." (see our list of "modal qualifiers," Chapter 7, p. 207).

The second principle illustrated—"Meeting your readers' standards." To see how we might work to meet our readers' standards, consider the following essay, written by Sandra in response to the assignment, "Write a 'magazine article' on why America has such a high crime rate." Read it carefully, asking whether it is a string of unsupported assertions or a genuine argument. Assume that the student was writing to her composition teacher.

AMERICA'S CRIME RATE

America has the highest crime rate of any country in the world. People live in terror, afraid even to go out into the streets. It is a terrible thing for a so-called civilized country to have so much killing and violence.

There are many reasons for our high crime rate. Lots of Americans are brought up like animals, without ever learning the difference between right and wrong. If you ask them whether crime is wrong they will just laugh at you.

When criminals are caught in this country, they usually are just let off very soon, without any real punishment. Some states still do not even have capital punishment, so that murderers get off scot-free. The courts and police departments are run so that criminals are protected and the victims of crime are often blamed, as if they had asked to be victims.

Poverty is another cause of crime. When poor people see other people with money, they naturally want some of it, so they commit crimes to make up for their poverty.

A friend of mine who was mugged last week told me the

mugger was really scary in the way he talked. He said "Gimme your money or I'll kill you." When such people are loose on the streets, it's no wonder that crime rates are so high.

I don't think that crime rates in this country will go down until people have a change of heart. Only when we decide that we will neither commit crimes nor allow criminals to get away with it can we hope to get rid of crime.

Revising your own first drafts will be easier if you have had a lot of practice in revising other people's. Even on a first reading, you probably see a lot of things wrong with "America's Crime Rate." But which of its faults will seem most serious in the eyes of a thoughtful reader? And how could it be improved? Your task now is to think through what the author might do to turn this meandering diatribe into an *essay*.

First, what is her purpose? Is it to explain why America has a high crime rate? Is it to alarm us? Or is it to get her readers to adopt this or that solution to the problem?

NOTEBOOK ENTRY

Now try out various one-sentence summaries of her purpose. Can you find one that covers her ground? If not, why not?

We are discovering that Sandra has at least three potential essays here, with no clear concentration on any one of them. If she wants to *explain* why America's crime rate is high, her reasons must relate to that purpose. They must be explanations, not mere repetition and exhortation. If she wants merely to *alarm* us, her reasons for alarm should all relate to that purpose, and some of her explanatory material will be irrelevant. If she wants to get us to *do* something, then her reasons must persuade us that this or that action would help reduce the crime rate.

Choose one of these purposes and sketch now an outline of *reasons* that might support that purpose. The outline might read something like this:

Americans must take steps to lower the crime rate—

- because it is disgraceful for a civilized nation to have the highest crime rate;

- because we are being terrorized;
- because crime is immensely costly;
- because . . .

Of all the possible steps for reducing crime, expanding and improving our police departments is the most advisable—

- because it is most effective
- because it is cheapest
- because it . . .

Once you have listed all the reasons you can think of for a given belief, you can then consider each of them, one by one, to see whether (1) it is likely to be accepted by Sandra's readers without further argument, (2) it requires further support, or (3) it is so questionable, to them or to you, as to be useless. For example, no reader is likely to require further proof for the claim that the high crime rate is disgraceful. But most readers will want some further proof for the claim that more police will lower the crime rate more effectively than, say, improving the functioning of our courts or spending more money and energy reducing poverty and improving education.

Now label each of the reasons you have extracted from Sandra's paper:

"OK"=needs no more proof
"add"=needs more reasons
"X"=discard—too weak to be salvaged

Don't be surprised or alarmed if you do not agree with everyone in your class. Consensus is reached on such matters only after long discussion—if ever.

Later on we'll look closely at what you can learn by thinking seriously about all the reasons *against* your case, and *against* each argument you offer for it. Sometimes when one does that kind of thinking honestly, the original thesis looks weaker and weaker and finally must be discarded.

If Sandra does thinking of this kind, she should be able to write a much improved paper. She might—if she thought hard enough—decide to write a paper simply trying to figure out *why* the crime rate is high, saving the exhortation and cure for another essay. It might look like the one that follows, written by another undergraduate as a two-hour in-class essay:

WHY AMERICA HAS THE HIGHEST CRIME RATE

Of all the countries in the world, America has the highest (1) crime rate. In spite of all the so-called advancements of our modern civilization, we are still struggling with the problem of crime in the streets. Why this is and how it can be alleviated is of prime concern to us all.

To begin with, America's violent history plays an impor- (2) tant part in the level of crime today. The days of Jesse James, Wyatt Earp, and the general lawlessness of "the Old West" are glorified in our history books and in the public media. Glorified too, are the gangsters from the "Roaring 20's" era of our history. Who has not heard of Al Capone, John Dillinger, or the "St. Valentine's Day Massacre"? All of these things have enmeshed themselves into our way of life and our national self-image.

Nothing is more important in contributing to violence in (3) our country than violence on television and in the movies. Every day, people are exposed to hundreds of "simulated" violent crimes and think of it as entertainment. Media heroes such as Kojak, Starsky and Hutch, and Baretta are always involved in murder, dope-dealing, rape, and the inevitable fight scene. They are portrayed as vigilante heroes that always win the day using the violence that they claim to defend us from. These things play no small part in violence in the streets.

Another important reason for the prevalence of violent (4) crime in this country is the availability of handguns. Inexpensive pistols known as "Saturday Night Specials" have contributed significantly to murders, aggravated assaults, and armed robberies. It is by their very inexpensiveness and availability that they are such a great problem to law enforcement officials. Handguns have yet to be effectively controlled and therefore our "right to bear arms" can be translated into the "right" to be mugged, shot, and even killed by handguns.

Many have argued that violent crime will not be reduced (5)

until the disparity in the distribution of our economic wealth is corrected. Robberies and armed assaults would be reduced if unemployment were lower and if living conditions in certain areas of our cities were improved. It is the frustration of being jobless and living in squalor that drives many to crime in order to provide stop-gap relief from the problems they face. If we must first correct these conditions to achieve relief from crime, then eliminating violent crime is most certainly a long range goal.

There are those who argue that one reason for crime in the (6) streets is the lack of sensitivity on the part of the man in the street. Kitty Genovese, a woman who lived in New York, was robbed and murdered in front of a large crowd. No one made an effort to stop the criminal and no one offered first aid as she lay dying. Lack of sensitivity and compassion was certainly evident in this rather curious case of social apathy. It may have been due to the bombardment of violence in the papers and on television, producing a desensitizing effect on the general population. People just didn't want to be involved.

All of the above factors contribute to the level of violence (7) in our land. It is essential to point out these causes so we may more quickly produce a cure. The more we know about the problem the easier we can locate the steps necessary to cure it. If this is the case, the first step to take is to care. [Coles/ Volpat, *What Makes Writing Good,* 1985, p. 128]

Do you see how well this essay organizes its reasons to make a coherent case? After mentioning some of its weaknesses, the writer's teacher, John Mellon, had this to say about it:

Looking at paragraphs 2 through 6 we can see that the writer has structured his argument upon three issues. Paragraphs 2 and 3 discuss violence in our national past and present, specifically the Old West and the twentieth-century gangster era, and contemporary violence perpetrated in movies and television by "vigilante heroes." The first issue [cause], then, is the historical and cultural licensing of violence—not only is it permitted in America, it is in a sense "glorified." Then paragraph 4, by rehearsing certain facts about the wide-spread availability of handguns, brings in the issue of the means enabling the commission of violent crime—which is what easily available handguns are. Finally, we see that paragraphs 5 and 6 discuss factors motivating violence: joblessness and economic deprivation of the criminals themselves, together with a lack of sensitivity and of moral outrage and an unwillingness among third parties to act to prevent violence. The complete argument, then, begins with the traditions permitting violence, then gives the principal means enabling it, and concludes by discussing its psychological motivations. [p. 130]

This praise seems justified. The essay works as a quickly written speculation about what *might* be the causes of crime in America, addressed to a teacher who has asked for an essay, not a full-length study or research paper, on the question, "How do you account for the fact that the United States has the highest rate of violent crime in the world?" Most of the reasons seem at least plausible—to that reader in those circumstances.

But if the essay were addressed to readers who had done some research on the subject, or to a group of lawyers, or to scholars who had made a special study of crime, almost every claim in the essay would require much more development—further support with further evidence. That TV violence increases actual violence, for example, is not a universally accepted fact; it is a highly controversial claim. Entire books have been written on both sides of that question. Though the balance of evidence seems to show that the student's claim is justified, some skeptical audiences—let's say a special commission of TV executives—would insist that he cite statistics from the studies supporting that claim. Similarly, everyone knows that the claim about handguns is controversial in some quarters. If the author were writing to members of the National Rifle Association, he would need to spend more than one full essay, or chapter, on this one claim alone. Yet if he were writing a personal letter to those of us who are in favor of handgun control, he could assume our agreement.

If we are right in saying that writers must provide different amounts and kinds of proof for different readers in different circumstances, it follows that no one essay will be good for all occasions and all readers. But there is a great difference between recognizing this general truth and knowing how to apply it.

NOTEBOOK ENTRY

Imagine that you are writing an essay arguing that varsity basketball should not be abolished at your college, even though there have been recent scandals about point shaving, drug abuse, and under-the-table salaries. Consider each of the following reasons for keeping basketball, and try to decide whether you think the offered reasons require further support, *for the specified readers.*

Examples:
(a) You are writing to the head coach, and you say, "To abolish basketball would be terrible; one of the chief reasons for loving this college is its champion basketball team."

Answer: No more support needed. A coach is likely to accept this as a sufficient reason.

(b) You are writing to the local newspaper, making the same case with the same reason.

Answer: Further argument perhaps needed—perhaps about how enrollment is likely to fall and business in the town will be hurt.

1. You are writing an editorial for the student paper—the same case with the same reason.
2. You are writing an editorial for the town newspaper—same case, same reason.
3. You are writing a petition to the faculty, and you say, "We should retain varsity basketball because it has a favorable effect on the academic life of the college."
4. You are writing to the college president, and you say, "We cannot afford to drop basketball, because it both earns a lot of money for the college and attracts a lot of alumni giving."
5. You are writing to the college president, and you say, "Another reason basketball should not be dropped is that like other varsity athletics it helps to build character in the players."
6. You are addressing the local Phi Beta Kappa chapter (the

honorary scholastic society) and you say, "Varsity basketball
should not be abolished, because it provides for both the
athletes and spectators a necessary release from the heavy
academic pressures at this place."

(If you find it more congenial to defend the opposite case—
that varsity basketball *should* be abolished—you can easily make
up a matching exercise for yourself here.)

**The third principle illustrated—"Adjusting claims to the
strength of evidence."** The third principle for helping you decide
how much and what kinds of arguments to use—namely, that you
should adjust the strength of your claims to the strength or weakness of your evidence—is usually a lot easier to follow than the
first two. If you pay attention to the quality of your reasons, you
can usually avoid overstating your case. If you have not in any
way proved a case but only suggested possibilities, say so. "Although nobody can ever arrive at certainty in such difficult mat
ters, it seems probable that . . ."; "Is it going too far to say
that . . .?" On the other hand, if you have assembled what seems
to you a very strong case, you can dramatize that with a good solid
"thus" or "therefore" or, "The conclusion is inescapable."

NOTEBOOK ENTRY

Choose one of your earlier essays and go through it, underlining
every word or phrase that calls attention to the line of argument
or makes an explicit connection between reasons and
conclusions. For example, if you were doing this exercise for
"Why America Has the Highest Crime Rate," you would
underline "Why this is . . ." in Paragraph 1; "To begin with . . ."
and "All these things have enmeshed themselves . . ." in
Paragraph 2; "Nothing is more important in contributing to . . ."
and "These things play no small part . . ." in Paragraph 3;
"Another important reason for . . ."—and so on until, in the
final paragraph, you would underline "contribute to" and "these
causes." Here you are so far mainly making use of the work on
connections that we stressed in Chapter 7.
Now choose two or three of these claims about a "reasoning

Be concise

General conclusion

Support for
Conclusions

connection" and ask yourself whether each of them, *as a claim,* would require more support than you give, for some particular audience. Write a paragraph about one or two of these, like this: "I said that (X) was a reason for believing (Y). This would be a sufficient reason in itself, if I were writing for an audience of (Z) (such-and-such kinds of people), who would take (X), the reason, as needing no further test. But if I were addressing a court of law, or writing to my highly skeptical Aunt Sarah, I would have to present further argument to explain why (X) is true. If I were writing for a professor of logic, I would even have to discuss why I think (X) is a good reason for believing (Y).

Reports, inferences, and evaluations

You have already had a good deal of practice by now in thinking about good reasons. In one sense you have been doing it all your life, as you have made choices, discovered mistakes, and tried again. In most of your writing you have been consciously attempting to support your claims with good reasons rather than with mere hunches or with unthinking prejudices. And in this chapter we have urged you to think hard about the different *kinds* of support that you can offer for your claims. You meet all the kinds every day, just in talking with other people. But it will be useful now to take a more systematic look at all that variety, grouped into three main kinds.

As we talk and write to each other urging agreement, we offer three kinds of statements based on three kinds of judgment: **reports** on what we judge to be verifiably factual or true; **inferences** about what follows (logically) from some established report; and **evaluations** about matters we judge to be good or bad.

you can look it up

deduction

report: Last term this college enrolled 100 more freshmen than the year before (a verifiable fact).

inference: Either the admissions office is doing a better job, or there must be some national trend toward larger enrollments (a logical deduction).

evaluation: If the admissions people are doing a better job, they deserve a bonus (a judgment about what is good).

report: Recent statistical studies have shown that in fact college enrollments are declining nationally (a verifiable
fact).

inference: The admissions office—or somebody here—must be
doing an effective job of selling this college (a logical
deduction).

evaluation: That's wonderful, because this college is a great
place (a judgment about what is good). (or) That's too
bad, because this college does a poor job of educating
those who come here (a judgment about what is bad).

report: It is my firm belief that God exists and is all powerful
(a verifiable fact, not about God's existence, but about
the speaker's "firm belief").

inference: The disastrous earthquake that just occurred was
either not under the control of God, which would mean
that He is not all-powerful, or it was fulfilling some
divine purpose beyond our ken (a logical deduction;
really *two* logical deductions).

evaluation: God's creation reveals more good than evil (a judgment about what is good).

Though the lines dividing these three kinds of statement are
often unclear, not being aware of the differences among them
creates much confusion. Reports, inferences, and evaluations are
all indispensable to our thinking, and though statements from
each class can prove on investigation to be unsupportable, good
reasons can operate in all three classes. Your thinking and writing
will probably suffer if you demand the same kinds of support for
all three kinds.

Reports are of two kinds. Some claim to offer hard facts,
information that in principle can be independently verified by
some sort of direct observation or statistical survey or laboratory
experiment. They are thus often said to be *objective,* that is, not
influenced by the *subjective* opinions or wishes of the reporter.
Other reports are of general truths—principles or assumptions
that are usually offered as self-evidently true, at least for all who
will consider them honestly. Both kinds of report claim to be true
from everyone's point of view, as if those who offer them were
saying, "If you had been there, or if you'll just go out and check,

or if you'll read the same sources I have read, or if you think about this as long as I have, you'll inevitably accept my statement of how things are."

Inferences are claims about what follows logically from reports of either kind. They lead from what is thought to be already known to what is claimed to be shown by the inference. They are about matters that in principle cannot be checked with the senses, with factual surveys, or by direct apprehension of truth. Something is inferred to be true on the basis of something else taken to be more nearly certain. A doctor's diagnosis is a good example. When you call your doctor with a report that you ache all over, that your chest feels tight, that you're running a fever of 102 degrees, and that you can't quit coughing, to you these are factual reports (unless for some reason you are lying or exaggerating; doctors have to learn, as you are doing, when to be skeptical about the accuracy of reports). You are experiencing all of these sensations first hand—your doctor can verify most of them by examining you—and you give as clear a report as you can of how you feel. But to the doctor your report of symptoms is only part of what she has to deal with, and usually not the most important part. She knows that behind the reported facts of your experience lies an invisible condition, perhaps a cold, perhaps the flu, perhaps pneumonia. While she may see your symptoms, she will certainly never see your *condition* as a visible fact. But she can *infer* from your symptoms that this or that condition exists, caused by this or that agent that is probably also invisible. As we all know, doctors' inferences are by no means infallible—in this they resemble most of the inferences that laymen also live by.

In everyday life many of the reports we depend on cannot be firmly and infallibly verified, and our inferences from them are consequently uncertain; we seldom arrive through inference at conclusions that everyone will accept. Good writing depends in part on our ability to show by argument why a given inference is reliable (see Chapter 12), or why the inferences of a given authority or reporter should be trusted without first-hand verification either of the primary report or of the method of inference.

Evaluations express the speaker's or writer's convictions about goodness or badness, reasonableness or unreasonableness, shrewdness or foolishness, and so on. They are sometimes dis-

missed by superficial thinkers who assume that convictions, because they are "subjective," are hopelessly indefensible. That
evaluations are subjective in this sense, however, does not mean
that they cannot be defended with reasons, some strong and some
weak, nor does it suggest that they are so private as to carry no
weight. Other people's convictions are often more interesting to
us than facts, and good writing about evaluations transforms convictions from *mere* opinions into *supported* opinions worthy of other
people's thoughtful attention. I may report, for example, that it is
exactly 33°F outside, which leads me to infer that any ice on the
pond will not be frozen hard enough for ice skating, which leads
me to the evaluation that anyone who risks ice skating today is
just plain stupid—or at best uninformed. After you have reported
the facts of your symptoms to the doctor, she may infer that you
have a viral flu, and she may also think (privately, no doubt) that
you perhaps deserve the flu, since your fall into the lake was not
bad luck but the result of your stupidly going ice skating on a day
when the thermometer read 33°F.

A large proportion of what we want to say to each other is
in the form of evaluation: our views of admirable or contemptible
behavior; of good and bad art; of good and bad movies, books, or
TV programs. Sometimes we offer these judgments as reports on
our own responses, or on the responses of others, or on what we
claim are the plain facts of the case: "Anybody who really looks
at that painting can see that it's a mess." At other times we offer
them as inferences: "Nobody who has a heart could do a thing like
that," followed by the evaluation, "he must be just plain rotten
inside." And sometimes we just try to share them directly, by
pointing or performing or trying to share our appraisals by writing
or speaking effectively on their behalf.

Though reports, inferences, and evaluations can all raise
difficulties for those who think critically about how we know
what we know, evaluations clearly raise the most problems. Some
philosophers have even claimed that they can never be defended
rationally, only asserted. For them, reports and inferences give us
the only real *knowledge* we have; evaluations are "mere opinion" or
"subjective preference." Even if such philosophers are wrong, as
we believe, you can see why you will have your greatest difficulties—and perhaps your greatest rewards—when you attempt to
provide argument in support of your evaluations.

NOTEBOOK ENTRY

Here are 13 sentences that will give you practice in distinguishing among reports, inferences, and judgments. Either in the text itself or in your notebook, label each sentence as follows:

> "R"—a Report of verifiable fact.
> "I"—a deduction that states an Inference.
> "E"—an Evaluation.

For each statement, write a sentence explaining *why* you consider it a report, inference, or evaluation.

If you find that you cannot sharply distinguish—if, for example, you find both evaluations and inferences in what looks like a report—write a sentence or two explaining the problem. Finally, when an inference or evaluation seems to you to require further evidence in its support, it will be useful to write a sentence or two about what kind of evidence that might be. For example, at 3b, you might say, "John spends most of his time either playing tennis or watching sports on TV."

1. (a) The extent of rigor mortis leads me to think that (b) the murder occurred between eleven and twelve o'clock last night. [coroner's statement]
2. (a) The English Channel is twenty miles wide at its narrowest point. (b) Her claim to have swum across in three hours is absurd.
3. (a) Marcie should never have told John that she hates tennis; (b) he's a sports nut.
5. Mt. McKinley, (a) the highest peak in North America, at 20,320 feet above sea level, is (b) not likely to be as difficult to climb as Mt. Everest, which (c) rises to 29,028 feet.
6. (a) These three, then, abide: faith, hope, and charity; (b) and the greatest of these is charity.
7. (a) Ed is a creep. (b) Everyone says so. (c) You should have heard what he said to me yesterday . . .
8. (a) According to information provided by witnesses, on the evening of October 12 at 9:30 P.M. the jewelry store on the corner of LaVista Drive and 12th Avenue was robbed by three youths who locked everyone in the store in the back room and fled in a 1972 two-toned Chrysler. (b) same as "a" except substitute "hoods" for "youths" and add, before "two-toned," the adjectives "junky" and "souped up."

9. (a) We are convinced that the attorney general did an irresponsible job on this (b) difficult and complex case. (c) He went on vacation for two weeks while the hearings were in session.
10. (a) Much solid evidence suggests (b) that the acid rain killing some Canadian lakes is caused by pollution from such cities as Detroit and Buffalo. (c) When will this scandal be faced by our lawmakers?
11. (a) "Peanuts" is the funniest cartoon in the Sunday paper. (b) I even laugh out loud when I read it. (c) And it's been running longer than most of the others. (d) The character I like best is Snoopy, a (e) Beagle dog belonging to Charlie Brown.
12. (a) A human fetus is a human being from the moment of conception. (b) Everybody who has thought about the problem for more than five minutes admits to that.
13. (a) Narrative techniques in the novel as developed in the 1920s and 1930s in America were often based on the assumption that writers should show the action of their stories, not just tell about it. (b) This dogma gave many novelists a lot of unnecessary trouble.

Since some of these statements fall on the borderline between the categories, you may want to discuss with others why that is so.

ESSAY ASSIGNMENT

This assignment is an opportunity to learn something about the way reports, inferences, and evaluations intersect in real life, and about the resulting difficulties in writing about them. Direct your essay to the other students in your class.

Think back to some disagreement or quarrel that you have experienced with some other person—perhaps your parents, employer, brother or sister, work colleague, friend, or teacher. Whether the event occurred long ago or recently, it should be one that you remember vividly.

1. Now write three different accounts of the quarrel, all addressed to the person you quarreled with. Make the first account a report—a narration that is as factual and as objective an account of "what, when, who, where, and how," as you can manage—or an assertion of some general rule, law, or truth that you accept beyond reasonable doubt and that you would like to appeal to in discussing the quarrel further. This version should be quite brief, perhaps no longer than one or two paragraphs, and it

should come as close as possible to being acceptable to the person you were quarreling with.

Base the second account on inferences, especially inferences about the other person's motives and feelings. You might begin like this: "I've been trying to do some sympathetic thinking about what you thought and felt during our crazy fight, and here is what I've figured out about why you said what you said. When you said "X," I figured that must have meant you were feeling "Y," and . . ."

You may feel that you know your own feelings and motives pretty well. But whether you do or not, you certainly have only surface signs and probabilities to go on when you infer other people's motives and feelings. Your account of them will thus necessarily be based entirely on inferences: "Given what I know about your values; given what you said; given your tone, facial expressions, and body language, I infer the following." This kind of exercise should lead you to think hard about how closely or loosely people's real motives and behavior are connected. Be especially careful to write in the tone of someone who is genuinely inquiring, not blaming.

Finally, write a third account that is an evaluation, one that weighs the rightness or wrongness of the two positions in the dispute. The task is to judge where praise and blame should fall, what each of you did right and what you did wrong. This account should include not only an evaluation of what happened at the time of the fight, but of consequences since then. Have you viewed yourself or the other person differently? Did the quarrel muddy the waters or clear the air? Have things been better? Worse? The same? What do you wish would happen now? Are there any possible loose ends still to be tied up? If so, what do you intend to do about them? What, in short, is your evaluation of the overall event?

Obviously you cannot hope that your opponent will accept all of your evaluations. But try to write as fair an account as you can, so that he or she will be led to think hard about the quarrel.

2. If you find it too difficult to write directly to your opponent, write three accounts, on the same plan as that of the first assignment, addressed to some referee whom you both respect. Assume that the referee knows nothing about the quarrel except what your written account provides, so that you must be careful to include all details necessary for clarity.

Writing to a third person, you probably cannot expect that your opponent, if he or she read the account, would accept these

versions as entirely valid or accurate—unless you write very carefully indeed. But you should try your best to be fair at every point.

3. From a current newspaper or news magazine, pick a story
that purports to be factual and see how many evaluations have
gone into the account. If you find the story unnecessarily
evaluative, address your essay to the editors of the publication
itself, criticizing the potential deception they have committed by
parading their evaluations as if they were plain facts. Newspaper
headlines, for example, can slant a story one way or another while
seeming to provide nothing more than an indication of topic. One
could picture a story about the appearance of Billy Graham, the
evangelist, in Atlanta, being headlined differently in newspapers of
contrasting prejudices. A neutral headline might read, "Graham To
Appear In Atlanta," while one slanted in his favor might read,
"Graham To Preach Word Of God In Atlanta," while an
unsympathetic one might read, "Fundamentalists Flock To Hear
Graham In Atlanta," implying that religious conservatives are
mindless migrators.

If on the other hand the piece you select seems to treat its
evaluations responsibly, address your essay to your instructor,
pointing out that despite the author's care in sticking to the facts,
you were nevertheless able to determine the points at which
evaluations were included.

If you have trouble detecting the evaluations, it is always useful
to compare two different newspapers or journals on the same
subject. The sports pages of newspapers in rival towns provide
especially amusing examples of blatant evaluations disguised as
fact, but the same contrast can be found in journals that support
rival political positions. You might, for example, look at the
contrasting editorials and articles on the "Star Wars" military plans
in *The Nation* and *The National Enquirer.* You can find good
help on slanted journalism in many books in your library. A deeply
thoughtful discussion of the ways in which all knowledge is
touched by our personal interests (evaluations) can be found in the
first chapter of Michael Polanyi's *Personal Knowledge* (1958).

How reports, inferences, and evaluations overlap. By this
time you must have noticed that our three kinds of statements
constantly threaten to overlap or merge. A bit of hard thinking
about even the most seemingly objective of reports will usually
reveal that it contains human inferences and evaluations.

Consider for example the apparently factual report on Mt. McKinley's height (#5, p. 358). We obtained this information from the latest edition of the *Encyclopaedia Britannica,* but what does it really mean? Is 20,320 feet an exact measurement? How exact? Is it independently verifiable? Once you start thinking about how such measurements must be made, this "factual" account seems much less assured of its absolute status than it does when it stares out at you as a self-satisfied, uncompromised number in the authoritative pages of the *Britannica.*

In the first place, does Mt. McKinley's height refer to feet above sea level or above its own base? The authoritative *Britannica* does not say. We are sure that many people know the convention for giving mountain heights and thus know what 20,320 feet is higher *than,* but there must be many people as ignorant as we are, which means that the number is more ambiguous than it appears.

Second, if the height is measured from sea level, someone has to judge what sea level *is.* Do we suppose that the measurer is standing on the top of a wave or in the trough of a wave? How big a wave? At high tide or low tide? Since there is never perfect calm on the ocean, mountain measurers must be forced to average out the height and depth of waves to arrive at a figure they thereafter consider, arbitrarily, as sea level. A judgment has been made, an evaluation about how much variability to allow into the calculations. In short, the "facts of the report" are not always as easy to determine as one might think.

Consider another example, #12 in the last Notebook Entry. ("A human fetus is a human being from the moment of conception.") Technically, this statement is an inference; it is a deduction about the status of the known (the fetus) based on the unknown (certain assumptions about biological organisms that the speaker holds to be true; or assumptions based on certain religious views also assumed to be true). But regardless of the assumptions or beliefs upon which the inference is based, it is so tangled up with evaluations that the issue cannot be discussed apart from them. Whether the issue is viewed mainly from a religious or from a biological perspective, there are no self-evident, self-announcing "facts of the case." Questions like, "Is a human fetus a human being?" or, "When does it become human?" cannot be settled by any simple appeal to *the* facts, for there is no such thing as *the* facts of the case. There are many, and different, facts of the case determined by prior inferences and judgments about what will *count* as a fact.

What is more troublesome, not only evaluations but reports and inferences change over the years. Even a matter as supposedly objective as Mt. McKinley's height changes with time. The 1949 edition of the *Britannica,* for example, cites McKinley's height as 20,300 feet, 20 feet shorter than the 1980 edition. The "fact" of McKinley's height is not what it used to be. If this variability is true for issues such as mountain heights, you can see how much more true it is for issues that touch people's deepest beliefs, values, and passions.

You can see, then, that whenever you are tempted to settle a complicated issue by a quick report that refers to a few uncomplicated facts, you may be flying into a hailstorm. Your facts may well be someone else's falsehoods, even someone else's *vile* falsehoods. Your report will almost certainly be based on more inferences and judgments than you realize; nothing is likely to prove quite as simple as you expect.

What does this mean to you as a writer? That you should never commit yourself to anything? That you should stick to clichés and banalities that no one will bother to question? Obviously not. Such an approach would condemn you to a life of terminal indecision and interminable boredom. It would lead to over-cautious writing of the kind we recently found in a history of cognitive science. It was clear from the context that the author thought a given view was an absurd exaggeration. But instead of saying that, he said that the author "ultimately may have carried his own chain of reasoning too far."

Pussyfooting around like this will not protect you from controversy. *Someone* will always disagree with you, even if you stick to clichés and banalities. Controversy, after all, is a part of life. It exists precisely because there aren't enough indisputable facts to settle any important issue to everyone's satisfaction, and because life consists of one judgment call after another.

What tempts us toward blandness is the misguided hope that we can avoid dealing with people who become angry, irrational, and intimidating when they are challenged. But to use this as a reason for trying to avoid *all* controversy would be as self-defeating as trying to avoid cars in a world of automobiles. Some people are dangerous and irrational drivers, but that doesn't keep you

from riding in cars. You simply try to protect yourself by driving
defensively. In writing about controversial issues you should simply try to be more aware of the complexities of the case than the
person who might oppose you. Write defensively: Anticipate the
potential objections to your position by learning about them before you start writing. Read a few essays for background. Talk to
people, especially those who disagree with you. Take your writing
tasks seriously as practice in making changes in the real world.

Conclusion

We live in a sea of assertions and counter-assertions too
complex to be interpreted by any formula or set of rules. Though
we should constantly be seeking to improve our understanding of
what makes a "good reason," we should never forget that different
human situations require different levels of proof. To ask for
mathematical proof when the subject is politics would be as foolish as to accept personal preference when debating the composition of Saturn's rings. All of our reading and writing requires that
we adjust our demands to the possibilities inherent in the world.
And to do that well we need long years of accumulated experience
—we need an education in a broader sense than any one college
course or program can give us.

In the lifetime project of learning how to listen to other
people and "talk back" to them effectively—learning to deal effectively with the complex world of good reasons—a writing course
can at best provide only one small step along a path that you have
been following all of your life. You will take that step more confi-
dently, however, if you steadily remind yourself that informed
argument can change not only the world you live in but the way
you choose to live in it. A senator said recently, as if making a
surprising discovery: "It turns out that words do matter." Writing
that addresses readers with facts, inferences, and evaluations that
they feel obliged to accept changes not only their view of the
world but the way they behave in it—and thus changes the world
itself.

Your world would be a radically different place if it had not
been shaped by the powerful rhetoric of the Bible, of the Greek

classics, of Karl Marx's *Capital,* of Sigmund Freud's *Psychopathology of Everyday Life,* of the "Declaration of Independence," of that terrifying book, Hitler's *Mein Kampf*—a book that helped lead a whole nation into the most destructive war in all history. Whether or not you have read these works yourself, their reports, inferences, and evaluations (many of which would seem silly or vicious to you, reading them from your position in America in the late twentieth century) have influenced people who have in turn influenced your life in fundamental ways. They have thus helped to shape the world you live in as well as the worlds that you have constructed inside your own head.

How you read and write and speak and listen, and thus join in the unending dialogue that is human history, will not only change you in fundamental ways; your own writing and speaking can in turn change the world for others.

12

Supporting your thesis II: Induction and generalization

Now that we have considered some of the inescapable complexities faced by everyone who tries to argue for a case, we are ready to look at the particular kinds of reasoning processes you can use to support your claims. As we've said before, you have used them all in the past—we human beings could not get through even the easiest day without them. But in writing we need to consider them more carefully than we do in everyday speech, not only to avoid logical "fallacies" (Chapter 13), but in order to use them effectively as we think through problems. Though some kinds of poor thinking can be disguised by some kinds of clever writing, in the long run the best writing is done by the best thinkers.

Argument from data to conclusion

Induction: Generalizing from particulars

System by which we classify

The first and perhaps most basic of all our mental operations is generalizing from particulars, often called **induction.** From the day of birth on, we have all learned about the world by observing this or that thing or event, or hearing a report about it, and then "inducing" from it certain regularities that enabled us to predict other events: "Stones—and babies—always fall when dropped." "Steam and hot air rise." "All ice cubes will float in water; metal sinks."

Such **generalizations** are indispensable to our survival. Without induction we could never learn from experience; we would keep on dropping the baby again and again, surprised each time to see it fall. Each time we see, hear, taste, smell, or touch some object, or we observe some event or sequence, or we remember some inference or judgment from the past, our minds are likely to leap to a general rule: "All things of that kind will look, sound, taste, smell, or feel that way"; or, "All people of that kind will behave that way"; or, "All matters of that kind should be judged that way." We could not escape disaster for five minutes without relying on predictions of regular patterns arrived at by induction.

Yet many of our worst mistakes result from *over-*generalizing —assuming that what we have seen or inferred or judged in one case or a small number of cases will be true of all similar cases. We meet two pleasant and helpful Irish cops and then we are shocked, six months later, when we read that a third Irish cop has been caught taking bribes. After driving a Ford that runs well for ten years without repairs, we conclude that Ford is always the car to buy, and then can hardly believe it when our next Ford turns out to be a lemon. Maturing has sometimes been described as one long process of correcting over-generalizations (hasty, over-confident inductions) that we made when we were young. Becoming educated is in large part learning how to resist or correct inductions based on too few cases or on mistaken analogies.

Sometimes, it is true, even one particular can warrant a generalization. A single carving knife that cuts my thumb once provides adequate proof that all sharp knives cut fingers as well as they cut beef. As I am working at my word processor a single lightning stroke causes a brief failure of power; my unit flashes off for a split second and then on again, and I find that I have suddenly lost an hour's work. I then generalize, quite legitimately: "Thunderstorms are always a threat when I am using the word processor." A child takes this same kind of leap from a one-time shock when it "decides" that all hot stoves burn. A dog that cringes before every approaching man because one man once beat it cruelly is no doubt making this same inductive leap.

Nevertheless, inductions based on one or two instances are usually, like the dog's, shaky at best. "This is going to be a hot summer; yesterday was the hottest June 1 on record." "Professor Hickley must hate students; on the first batch of papers he gave mostly Cs, Ds, and Fs." "This is an unfriendly city; the cab driver who brought me from the airport wouldn't even talk with me." Such generalizations go far beyond the evidence.

Obviously the problem for all of us is to determine just how many particulars in a given situation will really justify an induction. If I am lied to by one Basque shepherd (as happened to Booth one summer), am I justified in expecting the next Basque shepherd I meet to be a liar? If I meet one brilliant student from your college, am I justified in expecting all of your fellow students to be brilliant? Obviously not. Yet if I have once grown deathly ill after eating a particular kind of mushroom, I would hardly earn credentials for logical thinking if, after recovering, I justified eating the same kind of mushroom again on the grounds that, after all, I had only been made sick once, and "I learned in college that I should not over-generalize." How can we know when our inductions are based—as the statisticians say—on a "sufficiently large sample"?

NOTEBOOK ENTRY

Label the following inductions as

"Sure"—for "certain" or "nearly certain" or "I'd bet a lot on it";

"Probable"—for "fairly high probability"; "odds are much better than pure chance";

"Possible"—for "very weak evidence, but enough to make me open my mind about possibilities"; "well below 50% chance";

"No deal"—for, "This so-called induction gives no reason at all for drawing one conclusion or another."

1. I've kept a record of my diet for six months, and every time I've eaten strawberries I've broken out in hives. I conclude that I'm allergic to strawberries.

2. Last night I ate oysters and today I am nauseated. I've heard

that you should eat oysters only in months that have an "r" in them; this is June 20. Maybe that's what did it.

3. I think I made a mistake in my choice of colleges. Everybody's so unhappy here.

4. I know that prayer works, because my prayers are always answered.

5. I know that prayer doesn't work, because I prayed sincerely for my mother to recover, but she died.

6. A recent five-year study of 60 white American males between the ages of 18 and 35 showed that suicide was the major cause of death for that group. We conclude that these results hold for American males of all ages.

7. Same statement—but raise the number to 600. To 6000. (Professional statisticians develop elaborate ways of showing how "sampling" can be made reliable by finding the right "representative" cases.)

8. I'm writing worse all the time. I had an A on last week's paper and only a B— on this week's.

9. It is impossible for mammals to fly. To fly, a creature must have wings, and no mammals I've ever seen have wings.

10. A year ago I ate a mushroom with that shape and color, and I nearly died within a few hours. That kind of mushroom is poisonous.

Don't be surprised when you find that some of your classmates disagree with you. About some of these, such as #4, you will always find diverse views.

Cause-and-effect inductions

As the tenth example shows, our strongest inductions are reached when we think we know the real *cause* of something. We have never experienced a fire in a theater, but we have heard of such things, and if we ever see smoke billowing from behind the theater curtain, we will be justified in concluding that there must be a fire back there somewhere. We don't have to experience all fires to believe that, "Where there's smoke there's fire." We know that fires produce smoke, we know something about why they do, and we can know therefore that smoke will almost always come from fire. (Of course there may come a day when we'll be fooled by some artificial smoke produced by a stage technician, just as we might possibly be wrong about getting sick from the mushroom.)

Similarly, we all learned early on that trees have roots. Even if we've seen only a few trees, we can conclude that *of necessity* all trees have roots, because we know the *causal relation* between "being a tree" and "getting nourishment from the ground through roots." It would be foolish for ordinary purposes to hedge our generalization by saying, "Well, of course I don't know that *all* trees have roots, because I've not *seen* them all." On the other hand, if I want to become a botanist who specializes in trees, I'll keep my mind open—some species of tree-like plant may turn up that challenges my ordinary defintion of "tree."

Whether a given inference will be justified by only a few or a great many particulars depends on the context of discovery. Just as children make firm inferences about hot stoves from only one or two instances, so physical scientists often generalize, more or less cautiously, after only one experiment. If particle physicists can perform a single experiment yielding evidence of one unmistakable particle, they will say that such-and-such conditions will *always* produce that particle. The theoretical context of their work, including their careful formulation of hypotheses about what an experiment *might* show, gives them confidence in making maximal use of minimal data.

Of course they may be wrong; other investigators may not be able to replicate the experiment. But if they have a general theory or a hypothesis about a law that would explain *why* a given particle would behave in a certain way, and then it *does* so behave, they will require very few replications of the experiment to convince them that *all* the other billions of billions of billions of instances of that particle will behave in exactly the same way.

They are justified because nature seems to operate in regular, invariable ways—at least at some levels. But human behavior, unlike that of clocks and stars, is caused by so many different variables, and the variables can in turn produce such an enormous variety of effects, that inferring consequences from one or two observations of supposed causes is always risky. In human affairs we seldom know the cause of anything with absolute certainty, and we can thus make serious mistakes when we infer that "X" causes "Y" because we have seen "Y" follow "X" on a few occasions. (See p. 413, the *"post hoc ergo propter hoc"* fallacy.) Does poverty cause crime? Many very poor people do not commit crimes. "The murder was caused by sheer greed." Well, greed may have entered into it, but many very greedy people would not stoop to murder. Love can make some people gentle, others violent. Some people crack under stress, others thrive on it. And so on.

A report spreads that 20 people who took "Marvelcure" were cured of some "incurable" disease. People then rush to buy "Marvelcure," convinced that it must be the cause of the cure. Even if —as is sometimes the case—the reports of renewed health are genuine, we still do not know whether the patients might have got well anyway; or whether some *other* intervening cause could have produced the result. Drugstores are full of useless and even harmful medicines purporting to cure various diseases that in fact cannot be cured without elaborate professional treatment; they make their profit on our willingness to over-generalize: "If George says that WeirdMed cured *his* liver trouble, then maybe, just maybe, it will cure mine." "If 90% of the dentists who were polled say that Corrosodent is the best tooth whitener, then that's the one for me."

The Food and Drug Administration spends much time and tax money trying to decide just which inductions about causes are justified. As we said above, professional statisticians spend their lives trying to determine just how large a sample and what kind of representative cases are required to yield valid inductions about the safety or effectiveness of different products. No wonder we non-specialists often have trouble deciding what's what.

Does cigarette smoking cause cancer? Most people now believe that it does. Millions of dollars have been spent conducting statistical studies, some of them involving thousands of people, trying to determine whether the "statistical correlation" between smoking and lung cancer actually shows that smoking *causes* the cancer. Defenders of the tobacco industry argue that we should not naively blame tobacco until we are sure that it *causes* the cancer. Perhaps it "just happens," they say, to correlate with something else that is the *real* cause.

Even when the evidence for a causal relation is so strong that most people accept it, those who refuse to accept it can seldom be rebutted with absolute certainty, because our knowledge of most causes in everyday life is almost always based on fairly rough probabilities. Just how much more evidence we should demand about causes will depend not only on scientific laws of evidence but on our particular situation, especially on how high the stakes are (an evaluative judgment). The stakes vary from one person or group to another. If my purpose is to protect the tobacco industry as long as scientifically possible, I may go on declaring forever that the relation between smoking and cancer has not yet been absolutely *proved*. It is theoretically possible, after all, although contrary to anyone's expectations, that further studies may reveal unsuspected causes—perhaps smoking causes cancer only when it is combined with riding in automobiles, or with handling newspaper print, or with some other unknown variable. For the tobacco companies, the consequences of losing that escape clause, "theoretically possible," are high. But if, at the practical level, I am trying to decide about smoking, I cannot afford to take *their* skepticism as a guide for *my* choices. Since it is now highly *probable* that the correlation points to a real cause of cancer, I have good reason to avoid or stop smoking. The stakes are much higher for me than for the companies.

Although the tobacco companies often hire scientists who testify that the case against cigarettes has not been yet proved— meaning "with a 100% correlation"—recently they seem to have retreated to the question of whether or not "passive smoking"— breathing other people's smoke—can be harmful. In *The New York Times* of June 29, 1985, a professor of preventive medicine commented on the inductive problem as follows:

> The R. J. Reynolds Company has demonstrated how the quest for profits can distort logic and fact. In its June 11 full-page ad, "The Second-hand Smokescreen," the company condemns zealous opponents of tobacco for saying passive smoking causes disease, in the absence of established scientific fact.
>
> The scientific evidence of adverse effects of passive smoking pales compared with the massive documentation of the ill effects of active smoking. Yet evidence of adverse effects of passive smoking is growing rapidly.
>
> More than 2,000 compounds have been identified in cigarette smoke, and tobacco combustion contributes to levels of carbon monoxide, arsenic and polycyclic hydrocarbons in

the air. Measurable changes in heart rate, lung function and blood pressure have been found in nonsmokers exposed to smoke. Lung function is impaired in children whose mothers smoke, and studies have found higher rates of respiratory conditions, days of restricted activity and bed disability in children in households with adults who smoke. Still other studies have reported excessive occurrences of cancer among children and adults exposed to passive smoke from family members.

Obviously, more evidence is needed, but this should not be used as an excuse to ignore the evidence already accumulated.

> Joseph Feldman
> Professor of Preventive Medicine
> Downstate Medical Center
> Brooklyn, June 18, 1985

Do you find Professor Feldman's argument completely convincing? Partially convincing? Does he give any first-hand evidence? Does his professional title make his case seem stronger than if the letter had been signed "Anonymous"? How strong a piece of evidence is Feldman's title?

PARAGRAPH EXERCISE

Write a paragraph or two either (1) attempting to strengthen Feldman's letter, or (2) constructing a possible reply on behalf of the R. J. Reynolds Company from one of their statisticians, or (3) explaining why you would or would not ask for more evidence in a matter of this kind than you would for a conclusion about, say, the true mating behavior of pygmy chimpanzees.

Consider another example of how our *stake* modifies the weight we attach to evidence: If I already have an "incurable" cancer, and I hear of a new cure that some doctors scoff at and others favor, it is surely not unreasonable of me to take a chance on it. It would be more unreasonable to go to my death saying,

"Well, some scientists *say* there is no cure for this one, so I'll just not try anything."

Because of all these complications, it doesn't help us much to repeat what all the handbooks say: "Do not make unsound inductions," or, "Avoid hasty generalizations." It is true that our inductions should be sound and they should not be hasty. But the problem is choosing our criteria for "sound" and "hasty." For the purposes of scientific thinking, a high degree of probability may not be high enough; for the purpose of choosing a college or major field or religion, of deciding whether to marry or to break up, of voting for a mayor, or of deciding even so trivial a matter as which stereo to buy, we are sometimes lucky to have even a low probability supporting one choice rather than another. Even when we don't really know much about the causes, we still have to make choices on the basis of available evidence, hoping at least to do a bit better than mere chance would allow.

NOTEBOOK ENTRY

Write a sentence or two about the validity of each of the following generalizations. Do you consider it absolutely and uniformly true? Only probable? Possible? Unlikely? How many cases would you need to establish the generalization? How would your judgment be affected by *how much depended on your decision* (e.g., your life or the life of a friend)?

1. On the basis of my own observation, I conclude that all birds can fly.
2. All human beings will sooner or later die.
3. In the temperate zones, winter will always fall in the months between December and March.
4. All tulips grow from bulbs.
5. It is always dangerous to challenge a teacher.
6. On the basis of an experiment with two sections of English Composition at Cardinal University, we conclude that students learn to write better when given individual instruction.
7. Barking dogs never bite.
8. Every cloud has a silver lining.
9. The computer improves writing style. I know because my friend's style has improved since he got his computer.

10. Light bulbs that have been burning awhile should be allowed to cool before you touch them.
11. If you touch hydrochloric acid, it will burn your finger.
12. The sun will rise tomorrow; it always rises.
13. All good writers revise heavily and repeatedly.
14. If you are a careful driver, with good peripheral vision, it is perfectly safe to run a red light at times when traffic is light. I've done it often and never had an accident.
15. I see you have a black eye; you must have been in a fight.
16. He joined a rock band six months ago. I suppose he's really into drugs by now.
17. I have telephoned every tenth student in the campus handbook, and 60% of them favored candidate Wouldrun. I conclude that Wouldrun will get a landslide vote from middle-class voters—the kind of people who send their children to this college.

Guidelines sometimes useful in testing generalizations

1. Do I have a clear idea of the class or group I am generalizing about? How large is it? How homogeneous is it? Do all the members in it share the crucial variable I am considering?

2. Do I know what proportion of the total group is made up of those events, objects, or persons that I have first-hand data about? Have I sampled one in ten, one in a hundred, two out of three?

3. Can I claim a genuine causal link between membership in the group and the quality that my induction depends on? Or is my claim like the following: "The last three customers in this store who were caught shoplifting all had red hair. I now know enough to watch out whenever I see a customer with red hair"?

4. Is there any reason to think that my sample is not typical of the whole? The *Literary Digest* once did an expensive poll of two million voters in the presidential election of 1936, and they concluded that Alfred Landon would easily defeat Franklin D. Roosevelt's bid for a second term. Landon actually won only 8 out of 561 electoral votes. The pollsters had made one grand mistake: They

did their polling all by telephone, and they thus overlooked all of the many voters who in 1936 did not own telephones, most of whom probably voted Democratic!

   a. Does my sample cover a sufficiently long timespan, or is some of it out of date? Statistics about Italian immigrants of 1875 may tell us nothing about Italian immigrants in 1985.

   b. Are there differences of sex, age, or occupation that might bias my sample away from the norms of the group? Statistics about the average salary of wage earners would be drastically skewed upward, for example, if the sample contained only men, who are, on the average, still paid more than women for comparable work.

   c. Does my sample ignore any other causes that might intervene to overthrow my generalization?

How does this generalization strike you? "During the past 30 years the number of scientists in the world has doubled every ten years, which means that about 150 years from now there will be more scientists than people." Mark Twain has a lot of fun mocking people who extrapolate from current statistics to future results without thinking about causes that might intervene:

In the space of 176 years the Lower Mississippi has shortened itself 242 miles. This is an average of a trifle over one mile and a third per year. Therefore, any calm person, who is not blind or idiotic, can see that in the Old Oolithic Silurian period, just a million years ago next November, the Lower Mississippi River was upwards of one million three hundred thousand miles long, and stuck out over the Gulf of Mexico like a fishing rod. And by the same token any person can see that 742 years from now the Lower Mississippi will be only a mile and three quarters long, and Cairo and New Orleans will have joined their streets together, and be plodding comfortably along under a single mayor and a mutual board of alderman. There is something fascinating about science. One gets such wholesome returns of conjecture out of such a trifling investment of fact. [*Life on the Mississippi*, 1883]

For another such satiric poke at scientific over-generaliza-
tion, see "Footnote to the Future," by James Thurber, in *My
World—And Welcome to It* (1942).

Analogy *one of the ways that we learn to deal with the unknown*

When inductions are unpacked to examine their logic, they
all can be shown to be based on **analogy** (though this fact about
them is sometimes overlooked or denied in logic texts):

Hot stove A	produced	Burn B
Hot stove C	will produce	Burn D

Remember that the shorthand way of writing this is

Unknown → Known
Inductive Reasoning

or

$$A:B::C:D$$

$$\begin{array}{ccc} A & & C \\ \downarrow & \rightarrow & \downarrow \\ B & & D \end{array}$$

We read both these as "A *is to* B *as* C *is to* D

$$\frac{\text{Messy paper last week}}{\text{Low grade from teacher}} :: \frac{\text{Messy paper this week}}{\text{Predicted low grade this week}}$$

The strong—and risky—logical claim in every analogy is
carried by that double colon, the "is to," which means, "is related
in the same way." What it really says is that "A bears the same
relation to B as C bears to D." The question we must always ask
is whether there a genuine similarity between the two relations?
    If I say, "This burning light bulb will surely burn me if I
touch it, because I touched one like it yesterday and got a bad
burn," my analogy is pretty strong:

$$\frac{\text{Bulb A}}{\text{Burn B}} :: \frac{\text{Bulb C}}{\text{Burn D}}$$

or

Bulb A:Burn B::Bulb C:Likely Burn D

But if I say, "This 12-year-old will surely behave much better if I give him a good round beating, because when his brother was twelve I beat *him* and he shaped up after that," my analogy is extremely weak, because people differ from each other much more than light bulbs do. Of course even in the case of the bulb, I may stumble if I meet a fluorescent light and refuse to touch it because I think it's hot. But my risk of running into such surprises is much higher when dealing with people. (Here we meet from another angle the same point we made about "knowing the cause.")

PARAGRAPH PRACTICE

In writing this book we have already relied on innumerable analogies, many of them explicit. But we have not until now spelled them out for you in the form

A:B::C:D

In an earlier draft we wrote, "Writing is like having a tooth pulled," but we later cut it out. It reveals itself as a pretty feeble analogy (quite aside from its overstating the pain of most writing), once we unpack it by analysis:

$$\frac{\text{The pain of writing}}{\text{Writing success}} :: \frac{\text{The pain of dentistry}}{\text{Dental health}}$$

About all this analogy tells us is that we should not be surprised when writing is painful, and that the pain will eventually go away. But as soon as we think about the days we may spend on an essay compared to the minutes in the dentist's chair, or think about the gap left when the tooth is gone, or about how much dental health is *not* caused by dentistry, the analogy breaks down.

We made a better one in Chapter 6 when we said that, "Writing an essay is like making any other object in at least this one respect: whatever makes for bad design in any object or procedure—inconsistency, disorder, poor proportions, incompleteness—will also make for bad design in writing."

$$\frac{\text{Bad design in cars}}{\text{Car failure}} :: \frac{\text{Bad design in writing}}{\text{Writing failure}}$$

or

	(a)		(b)

Thoughtful arrangement of parts *is to* effective writing

as

	(c)		(d)

logical design   *is to* well-functioning machinery.

Now, for practice, try your hand at creating one or two analogies that, like our metaphors in Chapter 6, also deal with writing. You might try, "Writing exercises the mind the way breaking rocks exercises the back," or, "A home computer is to pen and paper as cars were to horse and buggy," or, "Sitting in composition class, knowing you might be called on, is like sitting in the dentist's waiting room." (Remember: when an analogy uses "like" it is usually called a *simile*.)

After you have made a couple of analogies of your own, write a paragraph *developing* one of them. In other words, track down some of your analogy's implications and state them in words. You might unpack the home computer/automobile analogy like this:

> Automobiles ushered in new patterns of life for Americans: new opportunities and new frustrations. The "horseless carriage" allowed more families to go more places more often at faster speeds than ever before—as long as the tires held up, the radiator didn't boil over, the transmission didn't drop, and other cars didn't get in the way. Despite the automobile's unpromising initial designs and a shocking number of highway deaths, Americans' basic stubbornness, ingenuity, love of novelty, thirst for speed, belief in progress, and need to show off eventually triumphed: They attached themselves to their automobiles and organized their lives around the opportunities they offered. They killed off public transportation and emptied town centers so that they could drive out to the shopping centers and bring home the groceries in station wagons.
>
> Now Americans seem to be attaching themselves to their home computers in much the same way. They "process" words rather than write them with pens or pencils or even electric typewriters. They send out "personalized" Christmas letters with the name of each new addressee automatically inserted by computer memory. They fall in love with spread sheets that tell them how to do everything from mix a martini to turn a profit. Handwriting, on the defensive since the invention of the typewriter anyway, may now disappear totally. The family that used to argue about who would get to drive the

new convertible now quarrels for individual turns at the computer console. Like the car, the home computer gives every evidence of not only being here to stay, but of becoming increasingly sophisticated, indispensable—and disruptive of previous culture.

And so on, leading perhaps to a comparison of both good and bad effects of this passion for a new technology.

When we talk of "unpacking," "tracking," or "developing" analogies, we obviously are making analogies about analogies:

Unpacking   a container .. a box or suitcase
analogy   its contents   its contents

Tracking   a hunter .. a student
analogy   the prey   a metaphor's contents

Developing   a developer   .. a student
analogy   undeveloped land   a undeveloped metaphor

The unpacking analogy is useful, but it may be unfortunate if it suggests that the meanings are already somehow *in* the analogy, like candy in a box, lying inert and waiting to be picked up passively. Different readers will build diverse interpretations of the "same" analogy, and even the strongest analogy can be ridiculed by any critic who is determined to carry out its possibilities to extremes (see Chapter 8, p. 246). Some analogies tend to freeze this process—they are almost too apt—while others stimulate thought. Would it make a difference if we had said *"unfold* the implications," or *"explore* your mind for relations," or *"invent* a pattern of similarities and differences" instead of "unpack"? (You might want to reconsider here the strengths and weaknesses of our storage analogy when we talked about topics for invention, pp. 120 ff.)

Even the most innocent of words can sometimes carry great analogical force of a surprising kind. Note the word "carry" in that sentence. Do words "carry" meanings? If we ask you to "find the meaning in such-and-such a paragraph," what do the words "find" and "in" mean? Are meanings "in" paragraphs like the meat of a nut *in* the shell? Do we *find* them or *construct* them?

Clearly analogies, perhaps especially hidden analogies like "carry," "in," and "find," can have a powerful effect not just on *what* we think but on *how* we think—how we see the world and how we use the language we inherit. If we think of the meanings as already *in* the analogy, or *in* the words of the analogy, that suggests that our role is more passive (like that of an unpacking clerk), than if we think of meanings as triggered by analogy (the mind as the explosive powder that drives the bullet home), or as a landscape to be explored to far horizons—and so on. What if we had asked you to *invent* or *create* relations, or to *'play* with possible extensions"?

We cannot deal adequately here with the endlessly fascinating, often secret ways in which our minds are molded by the explicit and implicit analogies that we live with. (For a book-length discussion of the power of everyday metaphors to control our thinking, see the book we mentioned in Chapter 8, *Metaphors We Live By,* by George Lakoff and Mark Johnson. Does it make a difference, by the way, whether we say "metaphors we live *with"* or follow Lakoff and Johnson in saying "metaphors we live *by"?*)

When and how to use explicit analogies (or metaphors implying analogy). For now, our problem is to learn to use metaphors and analogies effectively as one kind of support for our claims. (We suggest that before working on this section you review the section on metaphors in Chapter 8, pp. 245–254.) Because most analogies about human experience are weak, yielding at best fairly low probabilities, some guidebooks tell us never to rely on them as real evidence or proof—they are useful at best for clarification or illustration. Some people have even called the use of analogy in and of itself a logical fallacy. It is not hard to find arguments from analogy that are a lot weaker than our use of the dentist's chair. But if, as we have said, our daily life depends on induction, and if all induction depends on analogy (strong or weak), then developing our ability to use and criticize analogies should be one of the most important tasks of our education.

Instead of a blanket condemnation or effort to avoid them

(an effort that could in any case never succeed), we should work at distinguishing strong analogies from weak ones. And we should never forget that when an analogy is especially colorful or witty, it may coerce an agreement that goes far beyond the actual logic of the comparison: "Money is like manure—it's no good until it is spread." The comparison may seem weak, once we analyze it, but in the proper context it could carry great power. Though it "breaks down," as we say, if we push it very far (money is obviously *not* like manure in many ways), we should remember that all analogies will break down if pushed far enough. As we saw earlier, home computers can be compared to automobiles, since they tend to make typewriters obsolete just as cars made horse buggies obsolete. But of course there are more differences than similarities between home computers and cars.

In short, analogies are powerful, indispensable tools of thought (and thus of writing). But they can be both powerfully misleading as well as powerfully insightful. They are far too tightly woven into our thought patterns ever to be extricated, but we should not let them work their ways with us unchecked by critical attention.

NOTEBOOK ENTRY AND PARAGRAPH EXERCISE

Does the analogy offered by the anonymous voice of the narrator in these four lines of Edward Fitzgerald's *The Rubáiyát of Omar Khayyam* [1859] offer us a good reason for taking our pleasures in life *now* rather than postponing them for a better future?

> Dreaming when Dawn's Left hand was in the Sky
> I heard a Voice within the Tavern cry,
> "Awake, my little ones, and fill the Cup
> Before Life's Liquor in its Cup be dry."

Unpack Fitzgerald's analogy in the "is to"/"as" form. How much weight do you see it carrying in a discussion, oral or written, about how we should live our lives?

Write a brief paragraph appraising Fitzgerald's quatrain (four-liner). You might include an alternative analogy, or metaphor implying an analogy. What *is* life like for you?

To us, the analogy here seems muddy at best. Fitzgerald's *Rubáiyát* relies a great deal throughout on the analogy of a cup of wine to life; life must be savored before "it" runs dry, or goes flat, or drains away. Thus life is sometimes the cup itself, sometimes the wine in it. In the four lines here we are asked to fill the cup with "Life's Liquor" before the Cup runs dry, yet the analogy with wine seems to suggest that we should *drink* the wine (our life?), an act that would *empty* the cup (also our life?).

Of course we might figure out some sort of logic here, if we worked long enough at it, but clearly the *emotional* force of the comparison is stronger than its strictly logical force. Somehow the analogy *feels* right, even when unpacking it reveals inconsistencies. No doubt one reason is that Fitzgerald's verse gives it power. If you read the stanza several times aloud, paying attention to the rhymes and rhythm, you find one reason that this poem has always been immensely popular.

A bit of incoherence in a comparison may be acceptable when no great decision is at stake. Fitzgerald is not arguing for much more than a slight change of attitude—a bit less Victorian inhibition and a bit more modern indulgence. But when we are trying to decide more immediate issues, we should expect some better, more persuasive "fit" between our analogies and the situations to which they are applied. The persuasive force of any analogy depends on the degree of genuine similarity between two situations, persons, events, or objects. A politician running for re-election who says, "Don't change horses in the middle of the stream," is claiming that the electorate are in a perilous situation like that of a rider crossing a swift stream on horseback, or perhaps of a horse-pulled wagon; that a political leader is like a horse, the only source of power for the wagon; that the country or city is like the rider or wagon, with no motive power but the horse; and so on. Obviously each of these comparisons is extremely weak—as weak as the claim of a rival that, "It's time for a change—our ship is headed for the rocks, piloted by a captain who is either blind or drunk." Such analogies are weak not only because the points of comparison are shaky but also because the claims are too general to hold up under critical scrutiny. But—and this is important—these kinds of analogy, weak as they may be, are often very forceful in particular circumstances such as elections, in which they operate as a kind of magnet around which public feelings may collect. And each of them could be strengthened if it were preceded or followed by specific details showing how a specific "horse" has in the past demonstrated great power in pulling us through perilous situations, or how a specific "pilot" has plotted a dangerous zigzag course.

In short, our decisions to use explicit analogies must depend on whether or not we think the similarities they dramatize will compel our readers' assent. Most analogies, viewed apart from an authoritative voice or supporting argument, will seem thin and unconvincing, and they seldom reveal strict *logical* cogency. When Thomas Love Peacock, the great satirical novelist of the nineteenth century, wanted to dramatize the pointlessness and irrelevance of poetry in the modern world, he wrote like this:

> A poet in our times is a semi-barbarian in a civilized community. He lives in the days that are past. His ideas, thoughts, feelings, associations, are all with barbarous manners, obsolete customs, and exploded superstitions. The march of his intellect is *like that of a crab, backward.* The brighter the light diffused around him by the progress of reason, the thicker is the darkness of antiquated barbarism, in which he buries himself, *like a mole* . . . [Our italics] [*The Four Ages of Poetry*, 1820]

Peacock doesn't expect us to think that the poet is really much like a crab or a mole, except in the crucial respects of marching backwards and living in the dark. Out of context the analogies (again given here in the form of similes) may seem like mere namecalling. But if they were buttressed with specific examples of poets who *do* seem to look backward or live in the dark, emotionally or intellectually, the analogies can both clarify and strengthen Peacock's charge.

Extended analogies. Sometimes the success of a whole essay will hang on a crucial analogy. In George Orwell's famous essay, "Politics and the English Language" (1946), Orwell constructs an analogy in the second paragraph that controls everything that follows. Taken out of context, it must be considered weak or thin, but it works, if we are to judge by the frequent reprintings of the essay.

Now, it is clear that the decline of a language must ultimately have political and economic causes: it is not due simply to the bad influence of this or that individual writer. But an effect can become a cause, reinforcing the original cause and producing the same effect in an intensified form, and so on indefinitely. *A man may take to drink because he feels himself to be a failure, and then fail all the more completely because he drinks. It is rather the same thing that is happening to the English language.* It becomes ugly and inaccurate because our thoughts are foolish, but the slovenliness of our language makes it easier for us to have foolish thoughts. [Our italics]

The picture of the man who drinks more and more to mask his increasing sense of failure seems to fit. It calls up images of foolish speakers who mask their increasing confusion with a rising tide of babble, but it also *personifies* the English language as a great drunken slob who has no control over what he says. The effect, on those who do not simply reject the picture (and that is not an easy thing to do, once the picture has been implanted), is to make us want to "sober up"; we read on, in the essay, to see how Orwell thinks we might do just that.

While Orwell's analogy serves as a launching pad for his essay, other writers use analogies to summarize their main points. In another essay on writing, James Miller expresses his central point—that decisions about writing become decisions about who the author will be—in the form of a powerful analogy that has been reprinted again and again:

> For writing *is* discovery. The language that never leaves our head is *like colorful yarn, endlessly spun out multicolored threads dropping into a void, momentarily compacted, entangled, fascinating, elusive. We have glimpses that seem brilliant but quickly fade; we catch sight of images that tease us with connections and patterns that too-soon flow on;* we hold in momentary view a comprehensive arrangement (insight) that dissolves rapidly and disappears. [Our italics in second sentence.]

Writing that is discovery forces the capturing, the retrieving, the bringing into focus these stray and random thoughts. Sifting through them, we make decisions that are as much about the self as about language. Indeed, writing is largely a process of choosing among alternatives from the images and thoughts of the endless flow, and this choosing is a matter of making up one's mind, and this making up one's mind becomes in effect the making up of one's self. [*Word, Self, Reality: The Rhetoric of Imagination*, 1972]

NOTEBOOK ENTRY

Copy out (or underline in your text) the metaphors that Miller uses to develop his analogy. Does it trouble you that some of them seem not to fit well with "colorful yarn"? How does a thread "come into focus"? How do you "sift" entangled threads? Try now to rewrite the paragraph with complete analogical consistency. Does your rewriting improve or weaken Miller's paragraph? Can you explain why?

Sometimes entire arguments are conducted on the basis of a consistently maintained analogy. One of the most famous examples occurs in Shakespeare's *Coriolanus* (1607–9?). The citizens of Rome are on the verge of rebellion, and Menenius is trying to talk them out of it.

MENENIUS:
Either you must
Confess yourselves wondrous malicious,
Or be accus'd of folly. I shall tell you
A pretty tale . . .

FIRST CITIZEN:
Well, I'll hear it, sir; yet you must not think to fob off our
disgrace* with a tale. But, an't please you, deliver.

MENENIUS:
There was a time when all the body's members
Rebell'd against the belly, thus accus'd it:
That only like a gulf it did remain
I' th' midst o' th' body, idle and unactive,
Still cupboarding the viand† never bearing

disgrace—the injustices we suffer.

†*viand*—food.

Like* labor with the rest, where th' other instruments†
Did see and hear, devise, instruct, walk, feel,
And, mutually participate, did minister
Unto the appetite and affection‡ common
Of the whole body. The belly answer'd—

FIRST CITIZEN:

Well, sir, what answer made the belly?

MENENIUS:

Sir, I shall tell you. With a kind of smile,
Which ne'er came from the lungs, but even thus—
For, look you, I may make the belly smile
As well as speak—it tauntingly replied
To th' discontented members, the mutinous parts
That envied his receipt§; even so most fitly
As you malign our senators for that‖
They are not such as you.

FIRST CITIZEN:

Your belly's answer? What?
The kingly-crowned head, the vigilant eye,
The counselor heart, the arm our soldier,
Our steed the leg, the tongue our trumpeter,
With other muniments # and petty helps
In this our fabric, if that they . . .
Should by the cormorant** belly be restrain'd,
Who is the sink†† o' th' body—

MENENIUS:

                    Well, what then?

FIRST CITIZEN:

The former agents, if they did complain,
What could the belly answer?

*like—equal.

†instruments—body parts.

‡affection—inclination.

§receipt—intake.

‖for that—because.

#muniments—defenses.

**cormorant—ravenous.

††sink—sewer.

MENENIUS:

I will tell you;
If you'll bestow a small—of what you have little—
Patience awhile, you'st hear the belly's answer.

FIRST CITIZEN:

Y'are long about it.

MENENIUS:

Note me this, good friend;
Your most grave belly was deliberate,
Not rash like his accusers, and thus answered:
"True is it, my incorporate* friends," quoth he,
"That I receive the general food at first
Which you do live upon; and fit it is,
Because I am the store-house and the shop
Of the whole body. But, if you do remember,
I send it through the rivers of your blood,
Even to the court, the heart, to th' seat o' th' brain;
And, through the cranks and offices of man,
The strongest nerves and small inferior veins
From me receive that natural competency†
Whereby they live. And though that all at once"—
You, my good friends, this says the belly,
        mark me—

FIRST CITIZEN:

Ay, sir, well, well.

MENENIUS:

"Though all at once cannot
See what I do deliver out to each,
Yet I can make my audit up, that all
From me do back receive the flour of all,
And leave me but the bran." What say you to't?

FIRST CITIZEN:

It was an answer. How apply you this?

MENENIUS:

The senators of Rome are this good belly,
And you the mutinous members. For examine

*incorporate—belonging to one body.

†competency—income, nourishment.

Their counsels and their cares, disgest* things rightly
Touching the weal o' the common,† you shall find
No public benefit which you receive
But it proceeds or comes from them to you
And no way from yourselves. What do you think,
You, the great toe of this assembly?

FIRST CITIZEN:

I the great toe? Why the great toe?

MENENIUS:

For that, being one o' th' lowest, basest, poorest,
For this most wise rebellion, thou go'st foremost.
Thou rascal, that art worst in blood to run [Thou lean deer not
    worth the hunting, weakest in physical condition],
Lead'st first to win some vantage.
But make you ready your stiff bats and clubs.
Rome and her rats are at the point of battle;
The one side must have bale.‡

Menenius does not "win" this exchange with the citizen; the
citizen is unconvinced. We could argue that he is right to remain
unconvinced, since the analogy—belly is to body as citizen is to
state—is at best extremely loose. But Shakespeare wins his dramatic point: Menenius has revealed to the spectators his argumentative superiority to the rebelling citizens, and has underlined the
folly revealed when one part of the state (body) rebels against the
whole which is "incorporate," a single unity. The argument of
such an extended analogy will probably not change the allegiance
of those who are either passionately in favor of or opposed to
revolution. But it may change their minds in subtler ways: It may
give even opponents a new way of looking at things; the picture
has become part of their mental world even though they reject
it. That will happen even to the most unyielding opponent.
And anyone who is already inclined to Menenius's position
will have that inclination increased by the brilliant analogical
play.

*disgest—digest.

†weal o' the common—public welfare.

‡The one side must have bale—one or the other side must be injured.

ESSAY ASSIGNMENTS

1. We suggest that you now develop an extended analogy that appeals to you. If you can't think of one of your own, try one of the following:

a. The mind is a computer. ("As the circuits on memory chips inside a computer are to computer 'thinking,' so the electrochemical processes of the brain are to human thinking.")
b. My family is a business.
c. This course is a journey through a weird, dangerous foreign country.
d. My last love affair was a roller coaster.
e. This city is a sewer.
f. Students in this college are slaves.
g. Marriage is a sparring match . . .
an adventure . . .
an intricate tapestry . . .
h. Parents are required to be Solomons.
i. My workplace is a snakepit.
j. Cooking is the painting of the kitchen.

Begin by working the analogy into schematic form—A:B::C:D. Then think a bit about which steps in that formula are in most need of development, for some particular audience.

Finally write an essay either entirely devoted to arguing for the validity of your analogy or using the analogy as a primary basis for your case.

2. Some of the most important arguing that we ever do consists in trying to refute bad arguments. Often the best tactic of refutation is to land hard on the weaknesses in an opponent's basic analogies (some of which may not even be stated as analogies).

Write an essay analyzing at least two possible analogies for some thing or event and then criticize one or both of the analogies. You might develop alternatives to those we have mentioned above, or to Menenius's analogy of body and state, or to one you have encountered in recent political or academic argument; or to any analogy we have used in this book. Your comparison might begin like this:

In January of 1986 a group of students at Dartmouth College, in an effort to protest Dartmouth's investments in companies doing business in South Africa, erected some wooden shanties on the College Green. Signs on the shanties read "Apartheid Kills. Divest Now," and "PEACE, DREAM, EQUALITY FOR ALL." Administrators ordered them to remove the shanties; they refused, but when they agreed to move the shanties onto a different part of the Green, away from the spot where the annual Dartmouth snow carnival is held, the administration agreed to take no action against them.

Frustrated by this administrative inaction, a group of conservative students arrived late one night or early the following morning with a flatbed truck and sledgehammers and did all they could to demolish the shanties and haul away the debris. At this point the administration was caught between those who thought the raiders should be punished and those who thought the original protestors should be punished. They had to judge between the rights of two extreme groups, those who were willing to break campus rules to make a point against racism, and those who were willing to wield sledgehammers and destroy symbolic buildings to make a symbolic point about —well, about what? Just how these actions should be described became one of the big issues.

According to *The New York Times* of January 24, 1986 participants could not agree about what analogy best applied to the conservative raid. The "Dartmouth Committee to Beautify the Green Before Winter Carnival" claimed that it was "merely picking trash up off the Green and restoring pride and sparkle to the College we love so much." The vice chairman of the Afro-American Society protested that, "What they did was identical to burning the cross" [as the Ku Klux Klan did in the past]. Rabbi Michael A. Paley, a campus chaplain, saw the early morning raid as a kind of "terrorism." The administration had outlawed both the groups, he claimed, and, "You can't have outlaws without having terrorism."

Of these three analogies—beautifying the campus, burning a cross to terrify blacks, and open terrorism—the weakest [or strongest] seems to me to be . . ., for the following reasons: . . .

Now you take it from there, developing one or more of the analogies and showing its essential weakness or strength.

3. Another possibility: "Despite what students say when pushed to extremes about their pressurized lives, they are not slaves. They are free to leave whenever they choose. Their 'slave drivers' oversee their work only about 12–20 hours a week . . ." And so on.

Conclusion

It has sometimes been said that the greatest of all human gifts is the ability to discover similarities among things that do not appear immediately connected. The gift may even be the basis of our being able to use language symbolically, to do more than point at particulars. I can point to your particular face and call you "Marty," but only when I recognize the similarity between your face and Mary's and Sid's can I employ the *word* "face." Thus our most elementary use of language depends on an induction that also seems to undergird every distinctively human achievement.

Yet induction is also, in its hasty, uncritical forms, a steady, daily cause of disaster. Whenever we fail to discipline our inductive "syntheses" with appropriately critical "analyses," whenever we fail to explore the differences that qualify our eager search for similarities, we distort the rich reality that is to be found in each particular thing or person.

When we write an essay, even one that is primarily analytical, distinguishing differences among the parts of some whole, we always depend on conscious or unconscious generalizations based on past encounters with particulars. We always put together a new synthesis. Thus we can no more hope to write well without thinking about our inductions than we could hope to bat well without learning how to read the spin on a baseball—or to compose music without knowing the character of the different key signatures.

Now what do you think of *these* analogies?

CHAPTER

13

Supporting your thesis III: Deduction, fallacies, and rhetorical reasoning

The second main source of good reasons may at first appear to be the exact opposite of the first. In **induction** we assume that we know something about individual cases and can move from them to a generalization previously unknown. In **deduction,** we assume that we know some general truth and can move from it to new knowledge about certain particulars or individuals. "It is absolutely wrong to kill a human being, *because* the Bible says so." The speaker here assumes the second clause to be true and argues from it, as a *premise,* to the first clause. "It is a fundamental tenet of our democracy, written into our Declaration of Independence, that all men are created equal. How, *then,* can we continue to tolerate practices that discriminate against black people?" Here again the assumption is that if the *general* claim about equality is

393

true, then the *particular* claim about discrimination must also be true. "The second law of thermodynamics says that in any energy system the heat, or energy, can flow from a higher to a lower level but not the reverse. *Therefore* we know for certain that nobody can ever invent a perpetual motion machine—an energy system that feeds on its own energy perpetually." The "therefore" flags a claim to a rigorous deduction, from the first sentence to the second.

Reasoning from general truths

In each of these examples we reason from a general truth—sometimes called the major premise—to conclusions that must follow *if* the premise is true. You may find it useful to look back over some of the arguments we have presented in this book, to see how we have used deduction. For example, on p. 381 in Chapter 12 we said, *"If* . . . our daily life depends on induction, and *if* all induction depends on analogy, *then* developing our ability to use . . . analogies should be one of the most important tasks of our entire education." Each of our "ifs" announced general truths that we thought we had established (at least to some degree), and from them we moved to a claim about a particular task of education. Whenever you meet the "if . . . then" pattern, a deduction is being offered—and your critical antennae should go up: *Is* it logical? *Does* the "then" really follow from the "if"?

Obviously, deductive arguments will work only with readers who accept your initial generalizations. When we are conducting arguments with anyone who rejects the Bible as a guide to behavior, we can't rely on it to prove that killing is wrong. To cite the second law of thermodynamics will almost certainly not persuade the would-be inventor of a perpetual motion machine that he's wasting his time; the very point of his invention is to deny what the law claims. Whenever we argue with people who deny premises that *we* think need no further proof, we must either find ways to make those premises acceptable, or fish around for other general truths that the skeptics *will* accept as starting points. That a given "truth" seems a solid premise to *me* may be personally comforting, and even useful in thinking through where I stand (though it can also be dangerous if it stops my thinking). But in the practice of rhetoric, no premise is useful until I can find someone who shares it.

In fact we all carry around with us an immense collection of these general "truths," more or less unquestioned, from which we deduce consequences that we accept *strictly because logic says so.* If the second law of thermodynamics holds, *then* there can be no doubt whatsoever about rejecting the next applicant for a patent on a perpetual motion machine (the patent office receives—and automatically rejects—many each year). We don't need even to glance at the invention to know that it won't work—*if* we are entirely confident about the law. Similarly, once we have a clear picture of the workings of the solar system, we can deduce from it many precise predictions, including the exact time the sun will rise tomorrow—unless, of course, some monstrous unpredicted intervention confronts the system from outside.

Usually the general truths we rely on in reasoning are not certainties at all but probabilities. Some of them are extremely weak, with no more behind them than a kind of strong hope, wish, or fear: "Every cloud has a silver lining"; "The higher they rise, the harder they fall"; "Don't throw out the baby with the bathwater"; "Never say die"; "The race is not to the swift, nor the battle to the strong, but to him who endureth to the end." And some are even shakier than that, being based on nothing but inherited superstition: "I won't go to work tomorrow; it's Friday the thirteenth!" Many hotels are still built without a thirteenth floor, to cater to customers whose deductions are based on totally groundless major premises. (Have a look at the word "superstitious" in the dictionary).

Almost equally unreliable are the "truths" based on casual or careless induction. Any consequences that we deduce from them will be equally shaky: "He must be rich; he has that great big house on the gold coast." Here the unspoken first premise— "all people who 'have' big houses on the gold coast are rich"— rests on an induction that is highly questionable: Maybe the "owner" is on the verge of bankruptcy, or does not "have" the big house but only rents it, and has borrowed the rent money to make a show.

On the other hand, we live by, offer reports on, and arrive at conclusions from a great number of quite reliable general truths about cause and effect in our day-to-day world—truths that we ordinarily don't even think about unless they are challenged by unusual events. "She can't have come in yet; the door's still locked, and I know she doesn't have a key. Yet her purse is on the mantle, and I saw her carry it out when she left." (Major premises: "People can't go through locked doors without a key"; "Purses can't just come and go by themselves.") Detective stories are often built out of puzzling conflicts among general truths of this kind.

Testing validity of syllogisms

Logicians from Aristotle to the present have formulated highly elaborate ways of testing the validity of deductions from general truths. When we say that reasoning is **valid,** we mean that the logic of a chain of reasons is sound; the conclusion may still be false if the premises are false, but the *reasoning* is valid. On the other hand, a conclusion might be true, on other grounds or by accident, even though the reasoning was invalid. Thus *validity* should always be distinguished from the *truth* of premises and conclusions.

This is not as confusing in experience as it may sound in description. Just as one can accurately follow the best recipe in the world for a black walnut cake but still bake one that tastes terrible if the walnuts are rotten, so one can follow a valid line of reasoning that can still yield false conclusions if the premises are rotten. (Note: By now we would expect you to think critically about that analogy; does it *prove* our point about validity and truth, or merely illustrate and clarify?)

In a valid **syllogism**—the simplest kind of logical chain—we have three propositions, the third of which *must* follow *if* the first two are true. Note that "syl-logism" is a word made of parts you already know, in words like "sym-phony" (sound together), "sym-pathy" (feel or suffer together), and "sym-metry" (measure together). A syllogism puts reasons (from the Greek *logos,* reason or speech) together.

> *Major premise:* All creatures that suckle their young are mammals.
> *Minor premise:* This strange new creature suckles its young.
> *Conclusion:* Therefore this creature is a mammal.

The logic is sound, so the syllogism is valid. The premises are true, so—*since* the logic is valid—the conclusion must be true. But it is easy to construct syllogisms that are valid even though, because their premises are not true, they yield untrue conclusions.

False — *Major premise:* Everyone who subscribes to *Pravda* is a Communist.
   Minor Premise: He subscribes to *Pravda*.
   Conclusion: Therefore he must be a Communist.

Major Premise: Every varsity athlete is a dumb jock. — *False*
Minor Premise: Joe is a varsity athlete.
Conclusion: Therefore he must be a dumb jock.
(Valid but not necessarily true.)

The logic in each of these is absolutely sound; the reasoning is thus valid. What's wrong is a flaw in the major premise (the minor premise might also turn out to be unsound, after checking). We can dramatize this point with a silly but absolutely valid syllogism:

> All airplanes that have red spots on their tails will never crash.
> This airplane has a red spot on its tail.
> Therefore this airplane will never crash.

X *FLAWED MAJOR PREMISE*

Since the major premise is obviously absurd, the conclusion carries no force, even though the logic is valid.

On the other hand, conclusions can be true even when the reasoning is invalid.

> All of our best students come from New Dormitory.
> Louise lives in New Dormitory.
> Therefore Louise is one of our best students.

Louise *may*—for reasons not given in the premises—be one of our best students, but the syllogism cannot really tell us that unless it specifies that *all* the students in New Dormitory are among our best students. (See Fallacies, "Undistributed middle" and p. 400.)

There are many different notation systems used for clarifying logical patterns. Most modern logicians rely less on the syllogistic notation and more on equations in the form: "If A then B; not A; therefore not B". Such equations allow for complex inferences in economical form: "'Not (*p* and *q* and *r* and not −*s*' 'from which we can infer '*p* ((*q* and *r*) *s*).'" With careful notation, problems that are too complicated to be handled with syllogisms become manageable. But they also become too complicated for our consideration here. To see just *how* complicated—and perhaps then to dig in and learn a good deal more about logic than we can even suggest here—you might enjoy a look at James D. McCawley's *Everything that Linguists Have Always Wanted to Know about Logic, But Were Ashamed to Ask* (1980).

The testing of rhetorical logic: Enthymemes

since / because
therefore

abbreviated syllogism

The distinction between truth of propositions and validity of reasoning is a tricky and important one in formal logic, and it can sometimes be important in your writing as well. Formal mastery of technical logic is not as important, however, as developing the habit of thinking hard about how your various claims relate to each other. Using what we say here and in the discussion of fallacies below, you can usually (though not always) spot your own bad logic and that of other people. You can also discover why the "fallacies" are not always fallacious. You can, that is, *if* you really put your mind to it. Your mind has for decades been working ("on its own," we might say) to learn effective reasoning.

The first step in testing anyone's logical claims is to unpack, as we did with analogies, any assertion of logical connection into all of its parts. Sometimes those parts will be just three, forming a syllogism like those we have just looked at. In writing, however, we usually don't meet fully developed single syllogisms but shorter versions, with one of the steps merely *implied.* Then we have what is called an **enthymeme.**

"This can't be sea water; it's not salty."

x = specific professor

You can easily fill in the major premise that has been left out here: "All sea water tastes salty."

If that is a true generalization, and *if* the minor premise is true (this water is not salty), *then* it follows decisively that "this can't be sea water."

Unfortunately for clarity and decisiveness, most of our written logic is, as we have already seen, based on premises much more chancy than "All sea water tastes salty." Usually we reason from premises that are at best only probable:

> "Most pre-meds know something about chemistry, so I assume that Joe can tell us how to find out whether this is poison."

Here we have not one but two enthymemes, curtailed inferences that can be unpacked into syllogisms:

Pre-meds know something about chemistry.
Joe is a pre-med.
Therefore he's likely to know what chemists know.

Chemists know how to detect poisons.
Joe knows what chemists know ("proved" by the first syllogism).
Therefore Joe will know about poisons.

If we are looking for absolute rigor, we can see several big holes in this chain of two arguments (any chain of syllogisms is called a **sorites,** pronounced so-right-ease, though it may sometimes be so-wrong and not at all easy). In the major premise of the first syllogism, "something" is very vague. "What chemists know" is even vaguer. Some chemists may not know how to detect poisons. And so on. But the *logic* is itself sound; all the weakness is again in the premises. In a given argument we might very well have to rely on premises that are just that shaky, but we should know enough not to put much confidence in what Joe says about poisons unless we can come up with better reasons to trust his knowledge than those in our syllogisms.

We don't need to know anything technical about formal logic to see these problems. All we need do is to slow down and *think* about what is entailed in our various claims, or what follows from what. Even if we can only say, "There's *something* wrong here, but I don't quite see what it is," we may have saved ourselves from over-confident, hasty deductions, the greatest source of logical error.

The most frequent and tempting deductive error springs from **faulty distribution:** The two terms in the major premise *seem* to cover the case or cases cited in the minor premise, but they really do not. The trouble is often disguised when we meet it in an enthymeme.

"He must have Communist sympathies; he subscribes to *Pravda.*" People who subscribe to Pravda have Communist sympathies.

Major Premise:

The full syllogism that we gave earlier makes it much easier for us to see that the term "subscribers to *Pravda*" is not "distributed" over *all* subscribers: our premise does not say, as it must to make the syllogism valid, "All subscribers to *Pravda* are Communist sympathizers." As soon as we distribute the term in this way so that it covers the necessary ground, we see that we have in fact simply sneaked our conclusion into our first premise, leaving nothing whatever actually proved. At best we have a suggestion that might be investigated. But only if we had a very large collection of such suggestions would the mounting probabilities lead us to think that our subject just *might* be a Communist. A moment's thought tells us that many people, including scholars and CIA agents, might have reasons to subscribe to *Pravda.*

"John must be an English major, he cares about literature so much." Can you turn this into a testable syllogism? Try it.

All English majors care about literature.
John cares about literature.
Therefore he must be an English major. — Invalid conclusion

Here we have a more serious technical failure in distribution. A device that will sometimes help to clear up what is wrong is to draw circles covering the territory claimed by each premise.

Since the major premise did not say that all who care about literature are English majors, we just don't know how many lovers of literature fall *outside* that inner circle. Since we don't, we have no way of knowing for sure that John "must be an English major." He might be placed anywhere in the larger circle, in or out of the smaller one.

Textbooks in formal logic dismiss any syllogism that suffers from the flaw we have just discovered. But our writing lives are not lived in a world of strict formal logic, and it is easy to see that by carefully qualifying the force of the claims in the premises and the degree of certainty in the conclusion, we can uncover a logic that is quite acceptable—not for absolute proof, of course, but for practical purposes—that is, for those who live in a world of rhetorical, not formally logical, encounters.

> People who care a great deal about literature *are often* English majors.
> John reads a lot of literature.
> Therefore, *it's not unlikely* that John is majoring in *some* field —maybe English, maybe classics, maybe French— where literature is studied.

Thus by observing our third principle in Chapter 11, p. 346 (modulating claims to the force of weakness of support), we can salvage a weak but useful logical case.

We see again here that most of our inferences about human affairs are based on signs or qualities—for example, "He reads a lot"—that give fairly low probabilities that seem either weak or insignificant according to strict logic. But it would be foolish to claim that John's love of literature says *nothing* about the probabilities of his being a literature major. And if we can show a series of such probabilities—"His mother taught literature"; "I know he was considering English when he was a freshman"; "The English Department in this school is one of the most popular"; and so on—the probabilities can rise toward practical certainty.

What this means for our writing is that we can rarely demonstrate our conclusions by laying out pure syllogisms. Most of our logical arguments will consist of trying to show that the premises of particular arguments are highly probable, and of then accumulating probabilities by inventing multiple lines of argument (see again Chapter 5, "Invention").

> "Alyson should be kicked out of college because she has been caught cheating by three different profs, and the college rule says that being caught even twice is grounds for suspension."

The student-faculty disciplinary committee that hears Alyson's case will probably not spend long debating the logic of the statement. *If* she really was caught cheating three times, and *if* the rule applies to her case, she's out. But they will no doubt spend considerable time exploring possible reasons why the rule should not apply in her case. They will consider any available signs that she has learned her lesson, and they will try to make sure that the three professors were justified in their charges. In short, they will not spend much time debating the logic of the main charge, but will instead try out other lines of reasoning. Perhaps like this:

> Some kinds of plagiarism are clearly borderline, especially if a student does not understand the rules.
> Alyson plagiarized, in *one* of the three instances, in only *one* paragraph, and Professor Lax had not explained the difference between plagiarism and legitimate use of sources.
> Therefore, at least one of her offences is partially mitigated.

> If professors create conditions that lead a majority of students in a class to cheat, the offense of any one student is somewhat reduced.
> Professor Crumby (the accuser in the second charge) is notorious for his combination of hostility to students and carelessness about monitoring exams.

Therefore Alyson's second offense is not as serious as it first
appeared.

And so on. Meanwhile those who think she should be expelled or
suspended will be accumulating similar probable cases. "We have
evidence that she cheated in high school, too." (Silent major premise: Second offenders are guiltier than first offenders.) "We have
witnesses who say that Professor Lax did in fact warn about plagiarism." (Silent major premise: Those who know about the law
are guiltier than those who do not.) And so on.

Whether Alyson will be kicked out or not will thus be a
complicated and delicate weighing of many reasons in many logical patterns—just like your weighing of reasons as you choose a
college or major field, accept or reject a job offer, consider making
or refusing an offer of marriage—or write your essays.

NOTEBOOK ENTRY

We suggest that you now try out a few deductions, to get
practice in spotting strengths and weaknesses. Write a couple of
sentences about each of the following items (most of them
enthymemes with one silent premise), and then wherever
possible show how the weak passages could be corrected or
improved. Don't spend time quarreling with the figures or
statistics used in the examples. Some of them are phony,
manufactured for our purposes here. Just assume that they are
reports of actual studies, and try to establish whether they give
you enough information to support the deduction.

1. Statistics show that drivers between the ages of 18 and 21
   have the highest automobile accident rate. They also show
   that consumption of alcohol is involved in more than 50%
   of all driving accidents. Clearly the quickest way to cut
   traffic fatalities is to raise the licensing age either for
   driving or for drinking or for both.
2. Recent studies have shown that college graduates earn on
   average 34% more than high school graduates by the time
   they are 45. What could be a better argument for going to
   college?
3. Our colleges must be failing miserably in their teaching of
   English. I just had a letter of application from a graduate of

a good college, and it was full of elementary errors in spelling and grammar. *Faulty — based on one student*

4. It is really shocking to see that some critics of literature are still using methods and standards that were fashionable 30 years ago. *Current is better?*

5. Some people deny that the world is progressing, but it is evident that progress is real. More new inventions were developed and marketed in the last ten years than in the previous 40! *Number of inventions gauges progress?*

Quality of inventions must be considered

6. The epidemic of pornographic videos, many of them being viewed by children, presents a major moral problem for our society. If we had an epidemic of cholera, the whole country would be up in arms. Why, then, are we so indifferent to this disease that destroys not the bodies but the minds of our young people?

7. It comes down to a simple choice: Either we punish the terrorists or they will destroy our civilization.

8. I suspect that my neighbor belongs to the Mafia. First, he's an Italian. Second, he's from *southern* Italy. Third, he drives a huge black Cadillac. Fourth, whenever I ask him what kind of work he does, he changes the subject.

9. One of the biggest deficiencies in American education is our failure to build vocabulary. Research shows that executives have larger vocabularies than factory workers. We should pass a law requiring every high school to install a course in vocabulary building.

10. I don't see why Americans can't learn to communicate with each other more effectively. We can talk from space shuttle to command post, and we cannot seem to talk with the neighbor next door.

A great scientist reasons to a conclusion. It is time now to look at an extended passage, for practice both in judging the effectiveness of other people's writing and in improving your own use of logical proof. We'll look first at a passage by Charles Darwin, and then at a student's essay. The passage from Darwin is from Chapter 3 of his second famous work, *The Descent of Man,* published 12 years after *The Origin of Species* (1859) challenged the conventional religious beliefs about creation. His thesis in this passage is not about creation, but about animal reasoning. He argues that animals engage in the kind of reasoning we have been talking about in these chapters, but at a lower level. He sees no sharp line between our mental operations and those of our closest animal kin, or between them and the next lowest on the scale of evolution.

Read the passage through once without trying to study it—just get the general lines of thought clear.

Now go slowly through the essay, re-reading each section, and mark in the margin all the reasons Darwin gives to support his thesis. We suggest that you develop something like the following code, but you may want to write out brief statements rather than using abbreviations:

> *Gen. T.,* Unsup. = Report on a general truth unsupported with further reasons
>
> *Gen. T.,* Sup. = Report on a general truth supported by further reasons
>
> *Ded.* = Logical deduction from a general truth or established facts
>
> *Anal.* = Analogy
>
> *Ex.* = Example (remember that all examples can be unpacked into analogies)
>
> *Fact,* Unsup. = Report on facts without providing reasons for accepting them
>
> *Fact,* Sup. = Report on facts supported by further evidence
>
> *Stat.* = Report on statistics
>
> *Auth.* = Report of expert opinion, authority
>
> *Ethos* = Claim to authority or character (*ethos*) in the author himself
>
> *Obj.* = Possible *objections* to the case, raised in order to be answered

Follow the abbreviation with a question mark if you think the reasoning inadequate. (Don't worry when you find categories overlapping.) Then draw arrows between supporting propositions and the propositions they support.

Some such practice as this, if you develop it and apply it to your serious reading for a few weeks, can provide a rough picture in your margins of what each author is up to. (You can perhaps work out one that suits you better.)

insight

₄ Of all the faculties of the human mind, it will, I presume, be
admitted that *Reason* stands at the summit. Only a few persons now dispute that animals possess some power of reasoning. Animals may constantly be seen to pause, deliberate,
and resolve. It is a significant fact, that the more the habits
of any particular animal are studied by a naturalist, the more
he attributes to reason and the less to unlearnt instinct. In
future chapters we shall see that some animals extremely low
in the scale apparently display a certain amount of reason.
No doubt it is often difficult to distinguish between the
power of reason and that of instinct. For instance, Dr. Hayes,
in his work on "The Open Polar Sea," repeatedly remarks
that his dogs, instead of continuing to draw the sledges in a
compact body, diverged and separated when they came to
thin ice, so that their weight might be more evenly distributed. This was often the first warning which the travel-
ers received that the ice was becoming thin and dangerous.
Now, did the dogs act thus from the experience of each
individual, or from the example of the older and wiser dogs,
or from an inherited habit, that is from instinct? This instinct, may possibly have arisen since the time, long ago,
when dogs were first employed by the natives in drawing
their sledges; or the Arctic wolves, the parent-stock of the
Esquimaux dogs, may have acquired an instinct impelling
them not to attack their prey in a close pack, when on thin
ice.

We can only judge by the circumstances under which
actions are performed, whether they are due to instinct, or
to reason, or to the mere association of ideas: this latter
principle, however, is intimately connected with reason.
A curious case has been given by Prof. Mobius, of a
pike . . . *Authority*

When we do this exercise with Darwin's first paragraph, for
example, we are surprised by how many "unsupported" propositions we notice. Reading Darwin rapidly, one gets the impression
of an author who tests every proposition rigorously and accepts
nothing on faith or authority. What our analysis shows is quite
different from that.

Despite the many unsupported assertions, we see here an
author who moves from sentence to sentence exhibiting unusual

care for his logic. His examples are telling, and he knows what they show. The result is not only that we are inclined to believe him when he offers support for his claims; we are inclined to believe him even when he does not. He has earned our trust.

A student reasons his case. Now here in contrast is an essay that illustrates problems with reasoning. Study it carefully and label its reasons, using the same labels that you used for the Darwin essay.

MY CHOICE TO ATTEND WESTERN STATE

I want to explain in this essay why I decided to come to Western State rather than to any other university or college, and why I have decided that my choice was the wrong one.

At first I didn't even think of Western State because I wanted to play football at Central U, where I was offered a football scholarship bigger than the one offered by Western. But then I got to wondering why my parents were so strong for Central, and the more I thought about it the more I started thinking about good reasons to come to Western. Here are the main ones.

First, more of the older kids from my high school came to Western than went to Central. I figured that if so many thought Western was better it must *be* better.

Second, one of my friends a year ahead of me went to Central and he flunked out at the end of his first year. I figured it must be a lot tougher than Western.

Third, I looked at the catalogues of the two places, and it seemed to me that I could understand the course descriptions better in the Western catalogue. Who wants to take a lot of courses if you can't even understand the descriptions?

Fourth, I noticed that in the Western catalogue they said that of 20 state senators polled, 15 said that Western was the best university in the midwest.

Fifth, I liked the representative who came to my high school from Western better than I liked the creep who came from Central. In fact, she was a really good-looking girl who seemed to like me a lot.

For all these reasons I decided that this was the place for me. But now I've about decided that I made a mistake. Western doesn't seem to me as good a place as it was cracked up to be.

First, just about everybody I've met has treated me like dirt just because I'm from one of the smallest towns in the state. Western is just a hard place to make friends.

Second, none of the girls have matched the good looks of the Western rep who visited my high school—far from it. About the only attractive female I've seen was that one they sent out recruiting last year.

Third, the teachers expect too much of us. I'm having to study a lot harder than I did in high school, and I don't seem to be getting any better, either. My grades are no higher now, almost at the end of the first term, than they were at the beginning.

Last, most of the students are radicals here. I've seen a lot of kids in the library reading radical journals, and lots of things that other kids say in class seem to me really unpatriotic. Some of the kids from the big cities criticize America a lot. And one of my teachers said that football has become "destructive of academic values" on too many college campuses. I just don't think I want to be at a place where so many people are flirting with Communist ideas.

NOTEBOOK ENTRY

It's in a way too easy to make up examples of shaky logic, as we just did for this imaginary paper. It's harder to see how to improve a piece of bad logic once we have spotted it. Choose three or four of our poor victim's weakest inferences and write a few sentences about each, either showing why it cannot be salvaged or turning it into an argument that will contribute at least some slight support for his case.

From "fallacies" to "rhetorical resources"

Our subject in Chapters 11, 12, and 13 has been how to find good reasons, reasons that should carry some weight both in our own thinking and in the arguments we present to our readers. But all along we have necessarily talked about the inseparable subject of bad or inadequate reasoning. If we are to think and write well, we must know bad reasons when we see them, in order to resist them in other people's writing and speaking, in order to remove them from our own work, and in order to help us to reply effectively to other people when they reason badly. On every occasion when thinking counts, we need to be alert to the ways in which reasoning goes astray— especially when it manages to *look* persuasive.

We might think that bad reasoning is simply the opposite of what we have been seeking. Bad reasoning in this view would be simply bad induction and deduction, the use of *hasty* generalization, *irrelevant* examples, *loose* analogies, *illogical* enthymemes, and so on. Unfortunately, reasoning does not come in such discrete bundles, with some reasons plainly marked good and others clearly marked bad. From what we learned in Chapter 11, we would expect that many reasons that are worthless or misleading in some contexts will prove useful in other contexts. At certain crucial moments in our lives, weak reasons may be all that we have.

Certain kinds of bad reasons, called "fallacies," have destroyed so many arguments that they have been labeled and banned by logicians and rhetoricians. All educated people know the names of at least some of these, but too often their names are used as unexamined weapons in argument, without sufficient thought about what is bad about them. Booth can remember as a college student being silenced in an argument when an opponent shouted at him, "False dichotomy"; it was the first time he had heard the word "dichotomy," and it was years before he realized that some dichotomies are not false at all but useful.

As we now look briefly at a selected list of the standard fallacies, we shall find that most of them work like "dichotomy": in some contexts the reasoning they label can indeed be weak, misleading, or positively harmful, but most of the processes they label may also prove useful and even indispensable. Any writer who writes about controversial topics—and remember that most important topics *are* controversial—will in all sincerity rely on certain reasons that opponents might call fallacious. If, for example, I conclude my attack on a vicious, murderous tyrant by calling him a vicious, murderous tyrant, his supporters are sure to accuse me of "name calling" or of resorting to "cheap emotional appeal" or of using "slanted language." And I will then perhaps accuse them of "dragging a red herring" across the trail of the argument.

Instead of the traditional list of fallacies-to-be-avoided-at-all-costs, we offer here a list of paired terms, first the fallacy and then the more favorable rhetorical term for the same structure, discussed as potentially useful in argument. You might think of the list as a way of expanding your repertory of arguments and increasing your awareness of when a "forbidden" move might be the best or only move in town.

- **Analogy, false:** forcing an analogy to demonstrate more than it does demonstrate. For some logicians all analogies are false when considered as proof. They are right if by proof we mean "demonstration to the point of certainty"; every pursuit of similarities between any two things or situations will encounter differences somewhere down the line, and at that point hard proof fails. Sometimes that point is reached at the very beginning. "At our last peace conference our enemy's representative, a tall bald man, lied to us. Obviously we can't believe their present representative, another tall bald man."

    Analogy, legitimate. Such easy examples of bad reasoning do not change the fact that analogies are often our best or only resource (see pp. 377–392). The very need for the adjective "false" suggests that some uses must be "*un*false." "My first marriage went bad partly because of such-and-such faults in my husband, Bill, which clashed with such-and-such qualities (which he considered faults) in me. I have not changed *my* nature. It's probably a mistake, then, to marry Hank (though I love him), because his faults are just like Bill's." The analogy is "stretched" pretty far here, but under the pressure of a major decision, it could provide more guidance than blind chance. Indeed, many scientific discoveries result from pursuing suggestions based on analogy.

- **Arguing in a circle** (Latin: *petitio principii;* also called **begging the question**): asserting as a premise the conclusion to be proved. The result is called a **vicious circle** when the arguer supports a conclusion with a premise that depends for its validity on accepting the conclusion in the first place. "I shall prove that English composition is the most important course in the college by showing, first, how it came to be pre-eminent; second, by giving the reasons why other subjects like classics lost their top position; and third, by demonstrating *that nothing could be more important than learning how to write.*" "It seems to me self-evident that he could not be the thief. First, we have no evidence against him. But more important, *he seems totally unlikely as a suspect.*" Such "small circles" obviously accomplish very little—at most the rhetorical force of repetition. At their worst they convey a sense of helpless, hopeless incompetence.

> *Not circles but spirals.* When the circles grow larger, when a long road is traveled between one's statement of the point to be supported and its restatement after prolonged inquiry, circular reasoning becomes much less suspect. Indeed, many theorists from St. Augustine to Kenneth Burke have claimed that all reasoning is finally circular, in the sense that the starting point can never be proved except in terms established from inside the statement itself. ("You must first believe my conclusion before you can even understand my argument for it!") They would argue, for example, that all science is circular (though the circle is very large), in the sense that the assumptions of science cannot be proved by science, yet they are in a sense both proved and depended on by every scientific discovery. (For example, science cannot prove that nature behaves with the same regularities everywhere; yet science depends on the assumption of a uniform nature.)
>
> "Vicious circle" is thus seldom useful except as a term to whip an opponent with. To call a circle vicious is simply a way of saying, "I don't think you have done any more than repeat your claim; you've given no reasons, only assertions." A "vicious circle" gets nowhere. A "productive circle" returns, perhaps more than once, to restate its unproved assumptions, each time carrying new insights that leave us understanding more than the time before: an upward-moving spiral!
>
> Keep your eyes open, in your other courses, for disputes about how unproved "axioms" or "first principles" or "assumptions" are chosen and defended by different disciplines.

- **Argument *against* the man** (sometimes mislabeled *"Argumentum ad hominem"*; one form of this argument is **guilt by association**):

discrediting a position because someone who is already discredited favors it. "Are we going to vote for a measure that is favored by the first and only president ever to be forced out of office for his misdeeds?" "At least three of those who are voting for this measure are known to have been on the take." "I'll not give my support to any symphony orchestra with a clarinetist who is a convicted wife-beater." "Of course I'll vote against that measure; Moscow favors it." Such arguments are often absurdly irrelevant to a discussion.

> *Analysis of character.* One finds many occasions on which the character of supporters tells us what we want to know about a position. Often we not only can but should point out that those who support a position are suspect because of how they have previously behaved. What better clue do we have about future behavior than past behavior? The argument is especially useful when a previously discredited supporter stands to profit if the position we oppose triumphs. "Most of those who are clamoring for a World's Fair in Chicago are notorious for their past wheeling and dealing at the expense of the taxpayers."

• **Argument to the man** (Latin: *"Argumentum ad hominem";* the masculine form is used here because it is established in textbooks, but you may want to try "Argument to the *person*"): argument addressed directly to the emotions, special beliefs, or peculiar situation of specific readers or listeners. "I know that you yourself lost a son in World War II. Are you going to allow our country to get embroiled in Nicaragua?" This appeal is weak or even a "vicious" fallacy when the appeal is irrelevant to the case being argued and is used to deflect attention from arguments of greater relevance to a decision. You should note that the "ad hominem" label is increasingly applied to the previous argument (argument against the man) as if it meant "attack on the opponent" rather than "appeal to the opponent's personal situation and feelings." If this trend in usage continues, we should probably just avoid the Latin terms, or bring in another one, "argumentum ad invidium," for the attack on personal motives. Or we might invent a hybrid, "argumentum ad sneerum," for the silent look that says, "My opponent is beneath contempt."

Accommodation to the audience. Some of the most important writing and speaking rightly succeeds precisely because it *is* directed to actual people, their needs and beliefs. If you were urging fellow students to oppose a tuition rise, would it be irrelevant to appeal to their empty wallets or mounting debts? Is the loss of a son in war really irrelevant to one's thinking about wars? In short, accommodation to the audience has an ancient and respectable history; you will ignore it at your peril.

• **Assuming a cause from temporal sequence** (Latin: *Post hoc ergo propter hoc: "After* the thing, therefore *as a result* of the thing."): The simple fact that one event (B) *follows* another (A) never establishes certainty that (B) was *caused* by (A). "Every time I travel to my hometown, we seem to have a thunderstorm." We all seem inclined to infer causes whenever we see a sequence, and we often infer them quite fallaciously.

    Causal sequence. As we saw in Chapter 12, we depend on temporal sequence for most of our clues about causes. When the first event is invariably followed by the second, we have sufficient reason to *suspect* causal connection. To chant "post hoc" whenever someone infers cause from sequence is as naive as to assume that sequence absolutely proves the causation.

    If a friend consistently asks me for an "emergency" loan just after my payday, I may begin to suspect, although I don't know for sure, that his emergencies are caused by his knowledge about my paydays, not by any circumstances in his life. If I want to prove that my college president is a sleazy opportunist, surely it is legitimate to point out that each year, just before the salary non-increases are announced, he proclaims a budget crisis, yet each year, just after the Board's budget meeting, he announces a balanced budget. The probability that the upcoming Board meeting was a cause for canceling salary raises is fairly high. See **cause** below.

• **Authority, irrelevant:** reliance on experts in cases where more telling evidence is available, or when the authority is clearly irrelevant to the issue at hand—Refrigerator Perry, the football star, as an authority on which car to buy; Cliff Robertson, the movie star, testifying about the superiority of AT&T service. When Dr. Spock, the famous author of books about child-rearing, uses his position to speak against nuclear armament, we have a right to ask whether he knows any more about nuclear policy than we do.

Authority as valid testimony. We could never have survived until now if we had not learned to attend to the authority of those whose experience preceded ours. Everyone must depend on authoritative testimony, especially in matters that require some expertise. Indeed, most of our beliefs are based not on personal experience, but on "testimony" received from others. Even scientists, who in our society are thought to be the most independent inquirers, could never prove on their own most of the scientific beliefs that they share; only a few experts in each tiny field perform the front-line investigations and the rest of the scientific world accepts their results mainly on reputation—or authority.

Because appraising the legitimacy of authority is always chancy and difficult, we offer here a little checklist of questions that are usually helpful in testing an authority's usefulness in an argument:

1. Is the authority *known* to the relevant audience?
2. Is the authority genuinely expert on the subject in hand, or merely well known in some other domain?
3. Is the authority known to be trustworthy? As Senator Sam Irwin said about ex-President Nixon, winning a point in the Watergate hearings, "It is not entirely unlikely that a man who has been found lying when under oath would lie when *not* under oath!"
4. Is the authority *representative* of the more authoritative opinions in the subject being discussed? Would other authorities concede that this person *is* an authority?

• **Bandwagon** (Latin: *Argumentum ad populum*): "Everybody's doing it." "It must be the best 'soap.' It's at the top of the ratings." "Thirty million Frenchmen can't be wrong" (a slogan popular earlier in this century). This appeal is especially subject to abuse in any democracy, where to oppose the majority is often essential yet sometimes thought of as wicked.

Tradition, folk wisdom, convention, common sense. Whenever many people agree on any point, that point should not be dismissed lightly. If a view has been held by many people, especially over many decades or centuries, that is surely one good reason to take it seriously, unless we have very good specific reasons to believe it false. When we have no other evidence one way or another, it would be silly to ignore folk wisdom, common sense, or the experience of those who have gone before.

The rule in appraising common beliefs has too often been, "Doubt them if you possibly can." Instead we should ask, "Do I have a *good reason* to doubt what so many have believed. If I do not, it is more reasonable to assent than to doubt." (For an extended discussion of this reversal of emphasis, see Booth, *Modern Dogma and the Rhetoric of Assent,* 1974.)

- **Begging the question:** see **arguing in a circle.**

- **Causes, simplification of:** assuming fewer causes than are actually at work. (For example, assuming that there is *either* one cause *or* another for an event, rather than a possible combination of many causes. See "Either/Or Thinking.") All human events result from many causes of different kinds. What is *the* cause of the next sentence you will write in your notebook? You could say, "My decision about what to write." Or you could say, "My enrolling in this course." Or you could say, "My earlier experiences that led me to come to college." Or you could say, "The true cause was those authors who wrote this book."
  Or:

  The teacher's assignment.
  The pattern of electrical activity in your brain.
  Your genetic inheritance.
  The working of your alarm clock in getting you out of
  bed this morning.
  The pencil or pen with which you will write.
  Your knowledge of whatever subject you write on.

And so on. If you remove any one of these things, the sentence will not get written, so in one sense or another they are all required if the writing is to be done. Logicians sometimes distinguish such **necessary causes** from **sufficient causes.** Everything in your past and your present surroundings *could* be considered necessary, but only your precise decision about what to write, the mental process that chooses the words, would be sufficient to produce a particular sentence.

Differing purposes will dictate highlighting different causes. But we usually think badly when we forget that all human events are what social scientists call "over-determined": They depend on many different kinds of precedent and on innumerable configurations of causes. To pretend that we have located *the* one cause is always an error, except when conditions are precisely defined by a context: "The car crashed because of a blowout."

Causes, argument based on knowledge of. We depend at every moment on notions of causal lines that are unquestionably chancy, over-simplified. In many writing and speaking situations, perhaps most, our audience lacks either the time or the capacity to take in everything we may know about a subject. Especially in emergencies, when time does not allow for weighing alternatives—warfare, hostage crises, delicate peace negotiations—we must simplify causes in the sense of emphasizing only those that pertain to our problem.

The line between legitimate and illegitimate here is perhaps even hazier than in our other procedures. Perhaps a good rule of thumb is this: Writers are justified in suppressing complexities only when they are convinced of two points: that the welfare of the audience depends on a quick decision, and that members of the audience would come out on the right side *if* they had time to look at other possible causes. See **deck stacking**

- **Composition, false:** assuming that what is true of individual members of a group will be true of the group collectively. "If my money could buy more goods, I would be better off; therefore we would all benefit if prices were lower." "No single man in that mob would dare murder someone. We can rest easy: the group will never carry out a lynching."

Composition, legitimate. Again, the very need for the adjective "false" shows that logicians have recognized a legitimate kind of "lumping": the passage from a concept or assertion true of individuals taken separately to a concept or assertion about the class that they belong to. As a teacher I would be in real trouble if I could not infer *something* about next year's students from the behavior of students I have known before. Exactly *what* I can infer without committing this logical fallacy is never easy to determine, but much of the most important thinking and writing about the world's problems would be impossible without inferring what groups are like from knowing individuals.

• **Deck stacking:** suppressing arguments or evidence against your own case or for opposing cases. Other terms for it: **riding your thesis; one-sided presentation.** This abuse is perhaps more widespread than any other, probably because committing it in the name of a good cause can feel like the moral thing to do. Few people ever achieve the objectivity and discipline required to be fair to an opposing case. One sign that a person is getting an education is an increasing *effort* to avoid stacking the cards. When the stacking becomes actual cheating, it is sometimes called **fudging,** or **cooking your data.** See **strawman.** (Note that we have no defensible version of this one.)

• **Dichotomy, false:** see **either/or thinking.**

• **Dilemma, false:** a version of **false dichotomy** in which both the "either" and the "or" suggest unpleasant consequences. A dilemma offers two paths, or "horns," both of them threatening or undesirable (like the horns of a bull) the two seeming to exhaust the possibilities. "So we must choose the lesser of two evils (since there are only the two possibilities)." The general form is this: "If we do X, then A (a bad thing) will happen; if we do Y, then B (another bad thing) will happen. Yet X and Y are the only possibilities. So let's bite the bullet, and choose the least painful course." The dilemma is false, obviously, when more than two paths are in fact available—when one can, by taking thought, "pass between the horns of the dilemma." In current debates over armament build-up, for example, proponents of increasing nuclear stockpiles like to say, "If we don't continue to make more new bombs, we either leave ourselves too weak to defend against attack, or we invite attack by giving evidence of being too weak." If these are really our only two alternatives, then there is no escaping the conclusion: We must have more bombs. But the dilemma is false, as anyone who reads much in the debate soon discovers.

> *Dilemma.* Whenever there are indeed only two possibilities, both unpleasant, to dramatize the dilemma can be a useful way of assisting choice: Of the two painful directions, which is *less* painful? A rotten tooth must come out or stay in.
>
> Still there are probably more mistakes made from accepting dilemmas prematurely than from ignoring them when they are real. Some of your most original thinking can result from discovering paths through dilemmas that others present to you.

- **Division, false:** the opposite of **false composition.** Attributing the qualities known to apply to a group to every individual in the group. "I would expect him to be both rude and excessively talkative. He comes from New York City." "As a Seventh-day Adventist, she'll probably live a long time. They have a fantastic longevity rate." Some uses of this argument have been strongly and rightly attacked by civil rights activists. Nothing is more unfair to any individual than to assume that you can predict his or her precise behavior on the basis of generalizations you hold about some group.

> *Legitimate reasoning about individuals as sharing group properties.* It's hard to find the right name for what we do when we rightly predict what an individual will do by knowing his or her group identity or group affiliations. And yet we can hardly deny that *for some practical purposes* we often do so—even while knowing how easy is to make mistakes on this line. Simple survival in life often requires us to generalize about groups on the basis of individual behavior **(composition),** and then act on the the resulting *low* probabilities of how individuals will behave **(division).**
>
> Just when such inferences should be called prejudice is never easy to determine. But while we think about the ethical issues that such questions raise, we should remember that there *is* a threatening fallacy here: the confident assumption

that qualities found in a group will be found, in the same sense, degree, and kind, in all individuals of the group.

- **Either/or thinking** (also **false dichotomy**): speaking or acting as if one must choose between two and only two positions, taken as opposites, when in fact there are alternatives. "Are we going to be men and fight or are we going to crawl like rats into our holes?" "Elijah Muhammad was either the greatest prophet or the greatest fraud who ever lived." In most human affairs we find that such binary thinking—"the switch must be either on or off"—is misleading; a third or fourth or fifth possibility can be discovered if we think hard enough.

    Hard choices. There are, after all, times when two and only two alternatives are available: juries must decide between "guilty" and "not guilty"; young men must decide either to register for the draft or not to register. One cannot both marry and not marry (short of breaking the law or cheating in some way). One cannot both write a paper for this week's assignment and *not* write a paper. See **dilemma.**

- **Equivocation (shifting the terms; quibbling; deliberate ambiguity):** capitalizing on ambiguity; punning in a deceptive way; allowing a term to have two quite different meanings in two parts of a proof.

    No man has four legs.
    One man has two more legs than no man.
    Therefore one man has six legs.

    "You couldn't have it if you *did* want it," the Queen said. "The rule is, jam to-morrow and jam yesterday—but never jam *to-day."* "It *must* come sometimes to 'jam to-day,'" Alice objected. "No, it can't," said the Queen. "It's jam every *other* day: to-day isn't any *other* day, you know." [Lewis Carroll, *Through The Looking-Glass,* 1872]

Of course it is not these joking kinds that give us real trouble but the kind that sneak up on us and seem to yield plausible results. A good example is given in the fine book, *An Introduction to Reasoning* (1984), by Stephen Toulmin, Richard Rieke, and Allan Janik:

    One historical example of the fallacy of equivocation occurs in an argument by which Lorenzo Valla, an Italian Renaissance humanist, attempted to justify free love. His argument was based on the dual meanings of the Latin word *vir,* which means both "man" and "husband." Exploiting the fact that this single word has both these meanings, he claimed that *Every man is a husband* and concluded that marriage is therefore a superfluous institution. . . . [But] you cannot switch from one sense to another in midstream, as it were; that would be no better than perpetrating a pun on the two senses of the word *pitcher:* "This team needs a new pitcher. So go and get one from off the shelf in the kitchen."

Sensitive respect for ambiguities. Without some forms of equivocation, the world would come to a grinding halt within 24 hours. All language is inherently ambiguous, and all human affairs allow for more than one clear, unequivocal interpretation. Some of our best thinking and writing will be done when we manage somehow to get more than one voice into our prose. The sound of equi-vocation—debating two equally defensible views—is often the sound of real thinking.

- **Force, threat of** (Latin: *argumentum ad baculum*): To say, "Your money or your life," can hardly be called an argument. Yet it seems a bit strange to call it a fallacy: It's surely worse than that. You will have little temptation to use this "fallacy" in your essays, but you may very well encounter it used against you outside the classroom. For many people—thank goodness not for all—it is the only argument they can think of for obeying laws and paying taxes. The threat of force simply stops all genuine argument—it is a confession to the failure of argument. To win an argument with a gun or fists is to lose it in a much more serious way: You lose your humanity. To make someone "an offer you can't refuse" (implying "I'll kill you") is another "fallacy" that we cannot turn to legitimate uses in our writing. If studied at all, it would be studied under "strategy" or "politics," not under "rhetoric."

- **Genetic fallacy:** assuming that what a thing or person is or says *now* can be attacked or defended on the basis of origins (genesis). "That formula can't be any good; I know that Smith was stoned out of his mind when he wrote it out." "There's no use taking that church seriously. It is based on the visions of its founder, and he was known to be both an epileptic and a fraud." "Theodore Roethke was in and out of mental institutions throughout his life. His poetry can't be much good." "We needn't pay attention to his arguments; we know that as the son of a rich man he could only defend the establishment." "I don't have to listen to your arguments; I know your motives." (See **argument against the man**.)

> *Consider the source.* There are times when origins make a genuine difference. "I'm suspicious about that plan for a city hall. The developer who originated it owns the land on which it would be built." Ancient rhetoricians liked to ask *"Cui bono?"*—who is likely to benefit?—before approving any project. Their reasoning was by no means fallacious. It is not unreasonable to be more suspicious of the arguments about cigarettes and cancer when they come from a tobacco company spokesman than when they come from someone who is not paid to take a position. Some of the arguments may turn out to make sense, but their *genesis* is not irrelevant to how we consider them.

- **Hasty generalization (faulty induction):** any "leap" from facts to general claims across "too large a gap." Its forms are many (see above, pp. 367–377). Any generalization is hasty if it ignores relevant evidence that might be obtained.

  > *Legitimate induction.* Our lives depend on generalizing before *all* the evidence is in. The double bind this puts us in when we think about practical affairs is nicely illustrated by the two opposing proverbs: "Look before you leap," and, "He who hesitates is lost." Which one should we follow? The answer is both, even though they seem to contradict each other. They are both based on an almost infinite number of experiences—of disaster that results from incautious leaping and disaster that results from delaying the leap.
  >
  > The fallacy consists, then, in believing, or in trying to make our readers believe, that our evidence justifies more confidence in our generalization than is justified. See also **composition, false,** and **sample, inadequate.**

- **Ignoring the burden of proof:** forgetting or concealing the fact that the chief task is to establish *your* case. The question of

which side of a case carries the "burden of proof"—the primary
responsibility to establish a case positively rather than simply
refuting opponents negatively—is always complicated. In the
courts, the burden of proof is on the accuser: We are supposed
to be assumed innocent until proven guilty. In contrast, in scientific matters we are told to assume that any new theory is
"guilty" until proven innocent; the mark of the true scientist is
habitual skepticism pending proof. In speaking and writing
about most human problems, the fallacy consists in refusing to
look at the weaknesses in one's own position. If I claim to have
a special wisdom, or to have had some extraordinary and inherently dubious private experience (such as "projecting" myself to
the planet Venus and back, as some have claimed to do), the
burden of proof is on me, and it would be foolish of me to say
to doubters, "Well, you can't *prove* that I didn't do it."

Shifting the burden of doubt. A great deal of mental confusion (and too much mental anguish) has resulted from a
modern habit of assuming that in *all* of our deepest beliefs,
the burden of proof is on the believer and the initial advantage with the doubter. "Believe nothing that you cannot
positively prove," or "Doubt everything that in theory *can* be
doubted": These two mottos, if followed to logical conclusions, would leave us stranded in the middle of life with no
important beliefs whatsoever. Our most important convictions
and feelings (about love as opposed to hate, kindness as
opposed to cruelty, fairness as opposed to injustice, knowledge as opposed to ignorance, and so on) can all be doubted
by anyone who puts the burden of proof on "the affirma-
tive," asking for some sort of laboratory experiment or statistical, "solid," "factual" evidence. The burden of proof
should in such matters be put back upon the apostle of
doubt: Which is more reasonable, to go with our deepest
convictions (except where we have *specific* and strong reasons
for doubting), or to apply a blanket rule that says we should
doubt everything we cannot positively prove? (Again see
Booth, *Modern Dogma,* especially Chapters 1 and 2.)

In practice, we do not work with general rules for or
against systematic doubt. We do our actual thinking in complicated patterns of give and take: (1) We accept the burden

of trying to "prove"—that is, finding the best case for—our own precious convictions; (2) we insist that our opponents do the same—they should meet standards as high as our own, *but no higher;* (3) we accept then the "burden," though it is no longer a burden, of relating their reasons to our own, hoping that perhaps all of us may come out of the encounter different from when we went in. Once again a labeled fallacy turns out to be an invitation to thought rather than an easy path to victory.

Name calling (Latin: *Argumentum ad invidium;* **invective**): unjustified labels flung at an opponent or opposing position. Again we must begin by admitting that one writer's name calling is another writer's fair description. In some situations no names can be too strong. Would we say that to call Hitler a vicious assassin was irrelevant name calling? Still, in most of our arguments it is fallacious—and ineffective—to introduce invective against our opponents. The same goes for any form of sarcasm, including heavy irony: "No one could esteem the worthy president of this university more than I do. He is no doubt a paragon among doorbell ringers, a wonderful companion at an expensive banquet, a fabulous teller of racist anecdotes when the white folks are safely gathered together . . ." Such stuff can work for some audiences on some occasions, but it usually shuts off any honest consideration of issues.

One form of name calling consists of applying terms that have a polite look about them but that really carry negative connotations: "He's a good bourgeois apologist"; "She's one of the most pious people I know"; "Your solid, steady, clear-headed logic is highly admirable, but you forget just one thing: your conclusions stink."

Precise epithets. Though invective wrongly applied can be unfair, cruel, and destructive, every writer needs an arsenal of epithets, perhaps most of them unfavorable, for use when the occasion warrants. See **slanted language.**

• **Non sequitur:** general term (from Latin, "it does not follow") for any fallacious deduction.

Imaginative or "creative" structure. Though it would be silly to defend sloppy tracking in anyone's writing—stuff that claimed to follow logically and did not—the truth is that the phrase *"non sequitur,"* like its cousin "bad logic," is not of much use except as an epithet attacking the *other* person's logic. New kinds of design, new organizing principles will look like *non sequiturs* to readers who are wedded to old designs. The fallacy consists only in claiming any kind of sequence that you do not achieve.

- **Petitio principii:** see **arguing in a circle.**

- **Post hoc ergo propter hoc:** see **assuming a cause from temporal sequence.**

- **Red herring:** dragging an irrelevant issue across the trail of an argument—like dragging a smelly herring across a trail pursued by hounds. Almost any rhetorical device can become a red herring. Deflections from the point can be especially insidious when they *look* like stuff even more serious than the issue at stake. Unscrupulous lawyers learn how to change the subject, and the issue, without seeming to have done so.

  Lateral thinking. Some of the most powerful and creative thinking is done precisely when someone recognizes that the whole discussion has been pursuing the wrong line, and that a new direction is needed. "Instead of thinking about all this *that* way, why don't we try thinking of it this way?" Nobody can tell you in advance whether an apparent red herring will turn out to be a stroke of creative genius.

  This is one more case when we and our friends use favorable names for what we do and label what our opponents do—even if it is structurally identical—with pejorative terms.

- **Reduction to absurdity** (Latin: *Reductio ad absurdum;* one form is sometimes called **domino argument**): pursuing any line of thinking beyond its useful application; "extrapolation" from current trends or arguments to an absurd point beyond any likely development. "Don't you see that if you say 'X' [some fairly reasonable proposition], first thing we know we'll have 'Y' [something obviously awful or absurd, but remotely **analogous** to 'X']?" In the prolonged cold war between the United States and the Soviet Union, both sides have depended a great deal on the *"reductio":* "If Viet Nam falls, the whole of Asia will go with it." "If Afghanistan is allowed to rebel, none of our satellites will be safe."

Insight into the true connections among things. One rhetorician's *reductio* is another rhetorician's "looking ahead to discern where all this leads." Without our capacity to imagine consequences, to *extend* our vision into unknown territory, we would live a hand-to-mouth existence. The fallacy consists only in going beyond all possibility or probability; drawing the line where excess begins will always be a controversial matter.

- **Reification:** treating an abstraction as if it were something real or concrete. "Are we going to let the terrible *vices* of *Communism* triumph over the traditional *virtues* of the American *dream?*" "People worry about *unemployment.* What they forget is that *a rising gross national product* requires a certain *level* of *unemployment.*" But the "gross national product" is not an agent that can "require" us to do anything. If the sentence were rewritten to get some actual unemployed people into it, and some figures on income, it would have an entirely different effect. The reification hampers thought.

    Rising above the particulars. Again we find constructive uses of a fallacy under other names. We cannot get along without abstractions, and some abstractions are as real (in the sense of having real effects in the world) as nails or concrete. The fault here thus cannot be cured simply by turning abstract terms into concrete terms, as Orwell suggested (pp. 245–252)., and as we ourselves may seem to have suggested in Chapter 8. The fallacy enters when you let "reified" concepts become so "real" that they do your thinking for you and seem to be doing your acting for you.

- **Sample, inadequate:** see **hasty generalization.**
- **Slanted language:** words or phrases that load on more emotional charge than a situation warrants. (See pp. 236–244.)

    Appropriate expression of human feeling. On most subjects, writing that is purged of all emotional overtones is considered dull, cold, and even unreadable. All the art is in learning how to match feeling with occasion. To avoid emotional language at a funeral or political rally would be as absurd as to pour it on in a laboratory report.

- **Strawman:** stereotyping or caricaturing an opponent in order to "fix the fight"; portraying a weaker opponent so that your arguments will look stronger. (See **name calling; slanted language; deck stacking**). If we report an opponent's position in simplified, absurd terms, we can easily make our own case look better—until, that is, some intelligent reader starts asking questions. It's easier to slay a figure made of straw than one of flesh and blood. This is perhaps the most difficult of all fallacies to avoid—at least for those of us who are sincerely trying to deal with opposing views. The only "medicine" for it is to try to state our opponents' cases so clearly that they would be forced to say, "Yes, you have understood my position."

  Here is one more for which we can think of no defensible use. It is true that everyone builds "straw persons," willy-nilly. But the deliberate construction of weak versions of our opponents is no more a genuine *rhetorical* device than is lying.

- **Stretched analogy:** see **false analogy.**

- **Undistributed middle:** failure to ensure that a key term in a syllogism or enthymeme appears in both premises in the same form, covering the same ground.

  > Some red-headed people are irascible.
  > George often gets angry too easily.
  > That's because he's red-headed.

  Reliance on weak probabilities. See pp. 400–401, where we discuss the ways in which an argument that depends on a failure to "distribute" can sometimes be turned into a genuine though weak argument.

ESSAY ASSIGNMENTS

1. This assignment will probably not lead to a well-organized, polished essay but to extended notes toward improving a past essay.

Read over the essays you have written during this course, and choose one that depends heavily on deductive argument.

Write an analysis and evaluation of the *argument* of that essay; address it to your teacher. You might want to begin with the procedures we suggested in analyzing the selections by Darwin and the student (pp. 406–408). Be sure to include at least the following:

* A clear description of any premises that the paper *assumes* to be true without further argument.
* A clear and detailed breakdown of each step in your reasoning, including the steps that are buried as enthymemes within single sentences.

For example:

> My main point, my purpose, was to stir my readers, fellow students and teachers, to act against the threat of cuts in federal aid to education. My thesis was the claim that unless students and faculty members unite across the country to protest to Congress, disastrous cuts will follow.

A. My argument thus depended on several assumptions that I did not try to support:

  1. College education is a good thing—whatever harms education is bad.
  2. Education should not be confined to those who can pay for it; rather, a society should make it available to all.
  3. Congress is susceptible to letter campaigns from constituents; in a democracy we are not helpless.

> Instead of arguing for these "self-evident" assumptions, I spent my space on arguments for believing that aid to education is now threatened. I offered three lines of evidence for that claim.

  (a) the President's recent statements;
  (b) the recent bill mandating a balanced budget regardless of harmful effects;
  (c) the seeming decline in popular concern about higher education.

My essay could thus be analyzed as built on one basic syllogism (there are a lot of incidental ones) and one sustained induction:

> *The syllogism:*
> Whatever harms higher education is bad and should be
>   opposed.
> Cuts in federal aid will harm higher education.
> Therefore all cuts should be opposed.

> *The induction* (necessary if my minor premise is to carry a
> full threat):
> Cuts are coming unless we act quickly:
> (a) Because . . .
> (b) Because . . .
> (c) Because . . .

B. In addition to this central structure, I find one other main
deduction, hardly mentioned on the surface, but relied on
heavily:

> Whatever harms me and my kind (fellow students) is bad for
> the country, regardless of what it may do to other
> people.
> Cuts in federal aid would mean a harmful cut in my loan.
> Therefore . . .

On close examination, I find nothing whatever either to support
this implied claim about myself or to refute those who might raise
it as an objection (attacking my ethos by accusing me of the
fallacy of **argument to the man**). In other words, I do nothing in
the essay to answer the likely charge an opponent would level at
me: You're just worried about protecting your own hide, and your
appeal is only to the selfish interests of a narrow (though large
group), not to a consideration of the general welfare of a country
buried in debt.

And so on.

After you have said as much about the logical structure as
makes sense to you, write a final section in which you suggest
what you might have done to strengthen your argument. For
example:

> An obvious step in any extended revision I might write would
> be to meet the conservative budget-worriers head on; they're
> sure to notice that I don't even mention the economic welfare
> of the country.
> A second obvious step would be to deal directly with the
> likely charge that I'm thinking only about my personal interest. I
> should add a strong statement of the truth: I myself do not
> have or need any student loans; I have no immediate personal
> stake in this—it is the future of the country I am thinking of.
> Another possible revision would be . . .

In thinking about these improvements in argument, don't worry
about the possible length of the stronger paper you are planning.
Just think of what would strengthen it, in some ultimate statement
that would probably be much longer than any essay you have
written before.

2. Choose one of your essays that has depended, either throughout or only in part, on what looks to you now like a weak deductive claim. Write an improved version, attending to one or all of the following, in each deduction that seems relatively weak:

- Strengthen your reader's acceptance of the major premise.
- Underline the obviousness of the minor premise.
- Reinforce your reader's willingness to accept the logic leading from your major premise to your minor premise to your conclusion.
- Add further enthymemes that will support your case (e.g., testimony of noted authorities)

3. All daily newspapers of any quality publish columns by nationally known journalists (around 700 words each—about the size of many of your essays); many also have an "op-ed" page in which visiting commentators argue for national or local policies. Choose one of these from any recent newspaper, on an issue that you consider to be of vital importance. Analyze the logic of the writer's argument, as you did with Darwin (you may now want to make use of some of the terms for good and bad arguments that we have just listed).

Now write an essay on one of the following:

- Attack the argument by refuting the logic of one or more of its central arguments;
- Extend or improve the argument by strengthening or dramatizing the logic of one or more of its central arguments;
- Appraise the strong and weak points of the argument, and discuss how it might have been improved.

Conclusion

By now you have probably realized that if we had the space to cover all the issues involved, almost every point we have discussed in this book could easily be developed into a long article or even a book-length study. Some scholars spend lifetimes studying many points that we have had to skim over with a paragraph or two. But of all the subjects that would require more space for full treatment, the logic of argument most strongly resists brief discussion. We naturally hope that you will be tempted to take full courses in logic or advanced composition, in which you can continue to work at judging good and bad reasoning.

But more important than any course will be your own determination to learn to think for yourself. The terms you have learned in these chapters give you a good starting point. The rest depends on your determination to pay *close attention* to the arguments that come your way and to practice, every day, some critical writing and thinking about them.

The rhetoric of research papers: Weaving other people's ideas into your own

Introduction

So far in this course you have probably been asked to write only short essays. We have stressed the importance of cutting back to the essentials rather than padding out a thin idea. Many writing occasions, however, require a more sustained effort. Perhaps you have already been required in some other course to write a 10- or even 20-page paper—still an "essay" in our sense of the word, but one that is built on the results of extensive reading of other authors' works. That kind of requirement, calling for what is usually referred to as *research,* will become more frequent as you progress through college, and the skills it calls for will be valuable throughout life whenever you are asked to make use of what other people have written.

Some colleges require "research papers" of all first-year students; others do not. But even if you are not asked to do the traditional "fifteen-to-twenty-pager," you will face many writing occasions when you need the help of other writers. The basic problems of research are simply these: How can I get the most help from others, and how can I acknowledge that help most efficiently? Though an assignment to "do research" can lead to mere drudgery and empty busywork if you think of it as merely accumulating evidence of hours in the library, at its best it can lead you to discover new resources and new interests.

What are the special opportunities and problems that we encounter when we grapple with a subject that calls for research? How do we assemble larger bodies of material, much of it not originally our own, into essays that are still genuine *attempts at inquiry,* not merely passive reports?

Finding help with the mechanics of library work

We do not pretend to offer you a complete guide to the mechanics of research documentation and proper form. Instead, we shall concentrate on the *rhetoric* of the research paper. Most of what we will say should apply to the writing of any paper that leads you to seek help from outside sources. But it will not solve for you the dozens of technical problems, such as proper footnoting and bibliographical form, that arise whenever we are obliged to acknowledge our borrowings.

You will find help with the mechanics of research available in many handbooks. The three that are perhaps most commonly used by college students are the *MLA Handbook for Writers of Research Papers,* published by the Modern Language Association, and two books by Kate L. Turabian, *A Manual for Writers of Term Papers, Theses, and Dissertations* (4th ed., The University of Chicago, 1973), and *Student's Guide for Writing College Papers* (3rd ed., The University of Chicago, 1976). A good recent guide is *The Research Paper: Sources and Resources,* edited by John T. Hiers, James O. Williams, and Julius F. Ariail (Lexington, Mass.: D. C. Heath, 1986). We suggest that you purchase one of these, or one recommended by your teacher. They give detailed coverage of many points that we discuss briefly here. The opening chapters of such books should be especially useful as you begin any major research project; their advice can save you many hours trying to find information that is readily available in standard bibliographical guides. With one of these books on your desk, you will be able to find quick answers to such questions as, "Should the comma go here or there?" or, "How should I alphabetize my footnotes?" Without such a reference, you will need to memorize many minor details of documentation style.

The point of scholarly research

We do not do research in order to master research skills; we master research skills because we have a problem that we want to solve, a case that we want to make, or an idea that we want to develop with the help of outside sources. We then learn the skills of scholarly *presentation*—that is, how to write a research paper—not for their own sake, but in order to share our results in the clearest and most efficient manner. In other words, the motives for doing a research project—whether a Ph.D. dissertation or an essay that relies on only one or two books or articles—are the same as the motives for any other kind of public writing: They are basically *rhetorical.* Such essays are designed as a sharing of ideas that matter to both their authors and their readers.

This means that when you attempt longer essays, with or without elaborate research, you will need to think even harder than before about your purpose and your thesis, about your design, tone, and style. The main difference will be the kinds of topics you will cover and the devices of invention and discovery you will employ. In the full-fledged research paper, the kind of probing for topics that we performed with Carol Bly's essay (pp. 124–130) becomes habitual and extensive; we locate our best sources and then we raid them with as much intelligence and skill and honesty as we can muster.

As you face these longer, more ambitious tasks, the most dangerous temptation is to go out and "do some research" merely as a mechanical task or because you were asked to, rather than to seek out a problem that you can solve only by using the library. Sometimes a writer's research projects spring spontaneously from curiosity, but often they are "assigned" by someone else: a teacher, an employer, a judge, or some other official. If you have been asked to "do a research paper" by your teacher, you may have been given a list of possible problems to work on. Or you may be free to find a problem of your own. In either case, your first task is to probe as hard as you can to find, among all the unlimited possibilities for research, some angle or issue about which you can hope to make yourself an expert in a few short weeks.

This means that you should start *now* (even if "now" is months before the paper is due) to probe your own interests, your questions about how the world works or ought to work, and your beliefs that might be buttressed by gathering further evidence. Which of the many possible questions can you hope either to solve or to clarify by delving into what other people have already written? (You may later get a chance to do original research of another kind, exploring the world not through books but through laboratory experiments or statistical studies. Many of the techniques that you will now learn in doing a "research paper" will be useful to you in that kind of specialized research.)

Four guidelines in seeking help from books and articles

The essential problem that we face when we move from our writing desks into the library stacks is this: "How can I make use of other people's ideas to improve my own?"

Writing based on research is in one way like weaving. Using strands from other people's writing and conversation and from one's own thinking, one weaves a new fabric, one that could never have been predicted even by someone who knew every thread in advance. None of the strands may in themselves be original in the sense of being brand-new inventions, but each is respected for what it is, and in good research each one is finally incorporated into a pattern unpredictable except by the weaver.

The one trouble with that analogy is that in genuine research the final pattern is likely to seem new and perhaps surprising *even* to the researcher. Perhaps a better analogy for research would be that of a chemical reaction produced by some especially brave (and not very scientific?) chemist who dares to throw chemicals together without being quite sure what will happen. He (all *mad* chemists, as you may have noticed, are males!)—he knows something about the ingredients, perhaps something about how they have behaved in the past. But he cannot know in advance precisely what will happen when *this* one is mixed with *that* one.

Working with ideas from books and articles she has not read before, the sane but open-minded researcher cannot know for sure how those ideas, highly volatile substances, will transform her original problem. Gathering them from here and there and throwing them into a pot that is already bubbling and fuming, she risks coming out of the encounter not only with a new idea but with an entirely different way of looking at the world.

The pursuit of genuine research is thus by its nature a bit dangerous—if what we want most is to protect our present notions. But if we want to come out of the effort a bit further along on the road to an education, then we need to know how to avoid at least the four dangers lurking here:

1. The danger of not defining your problem clearly enough to decide what help you need;

2. The danger of not finding the help that is in fact readily available (in books, articles, conversation);

3. The danger of not learning what your sources have to teach, once you have found them—a failure of **critical reading** and **reporting;**

4. The danger of not giving clear, adequate, and correct credit or thanks for what you borrow.

Each of these dangers can be transformed, when we think about them, into guiding principles.

Finding a purpose

Everything we said in Chapter 3 about finding a clear purpose becomes doubly important here. As we authors write this final chapter, we are troubled by a mental picture of thousands of miserable college students slaving away in libraries, "doing research" without the slightest idea *why.* Too many of them are filling notecard after notecard, accumulating stacks of carefully labeled quotations—all to accomplish *what*? To meet a requirement and nothing more? To fill up a given number of pages? To prove that they have worked hard?

The first rule here is *don't start taking notes until you have a reason to.* Spend your time first in *thinking* about what you might do and reading fairly rapidly in works that seem related to your still-vague interests. This kind of exploration is best done at the time of day when you are most alert—rapid reading is in one sense superficial reading, but it nevertheless demands your total attention. While you are doing it, your mind will be stirring about, at several levels, both taking in the book in hand and playing with its possible uses.

Even if your teacher provides a list of possible subject areas or questions for you to choose from, these will almost always point in highly *general* directions. The assignment itself will almost never give you a *slant* on the subject precise enough to be called a purpose, and it will almost certainly never provide you with a specific thesis. You will always need to shape the subject yourself, and if you are doing genuine research, you won't know your precise thesis until fairly late in the game. Obviously you will learn more from the assignment (partly because you'll enjoy it more) if you can find some problem that fascinates *you,* some hypothesis or hunch that *you'd* like to test, and—somewhere along the line—some thesis that you'd like to persuade other people to believe.

Remember: Whatever subject you choose will be your companion for many hours and many days. Choosing one that seems dull or a waste of time will bore you and frustrate you—for weeks! On the other hand, apparently boring subjects often become interesting as you learn something about them. This means that you may have to give an apparently boring subject the chance to get its hooks into you, rather than just dismissing it out of hand. Try to be open-minded; remind yourself that most of those hundreds of thousands—perhaps millions—of books in your campus library are written on subjects that proved interesting at one time to *someone,* their authors, and that they might prove similarly interesting for you once you get into them. In short, you will find more reward, and open yourself to more education, in widening your own interests than in dismissing other people's.

If you can't think of a subject or problem that really attracts you at first, pick whatever seems least remote and start browsing —in an encyclopedia, in the card catalogue, in the indexes to periodicals (see the research manuals we mentioned)—and see what happens. The important thing is to *start today.* You'll need lots of time for this initial exploration, and the more time you spend in finding and sharpening your thesis, the less trouble will lie ahead. To start right out with note cards, taking quotations without knowing why, may *feel* like making progress, but in the long run it can be worse than useless. It's easy to get swamped in a flood of notes.

Many research papers are simply factual reports on what experts today say about a subject. They are very much like encyclopedia articles: summaries of current knowledge and opinion on specific subjects. In one sense this is the easiest kind of research paper to do, and there's nothing wrong with it—except that it's not likely to be very interesting to anyone, not even to the author. If you choose a subject like "home insulation for energy conservation" you can find information about how to improve insulation and then simply report what you have found, carefully documenting your sources. To do even that job accurately and concisely would be no mean achievement. But if you start *thinking* about what you read, you'll soon discover that disagreements among the experts, even about basic information, opens up more interesting possibilities. "How to insulate a house" will quickly expose to the thoughtful researcher lively controversies about health and politics. No one knows, for example, just how *much* insulation is good, because recent research shows that every house is full of internal pollutants; the possibility that some houses have more dangerous pollutants *inside* than *outside* suggests that too much insulation may be bad for your health! What starts out, then, as a mere report on insulation may quickly turn into an inquiry about an important medical and political problem. At this point you will no longer be asking yourself, "How can I fill up a 10- to 20-page paper about 'How to insulate a house'?" but rather, "How can I *think* about *two values* that seem to conflict: economy and health?"

Once you have a genuine problem to think about, you will have a good reason for seeking the best-qualified experts to testify —in your quotations and notes—about the problem's various angles. On the subject of home insulation, you can find experts who will tell you that the "tighter the house the better," and other experts who will warn against closing *in* the pollution while you're trying to close *out* the cold air. You may or may not find more thoughtful experts who will help you decide how to weigh health and economy against each other. In either case, you will find that you now *need* some research to help clarify your thinking and thus enrich your writing. The reading that you report on will not seem like mere busywork to your readers; they will welcome the help that the experts can provide.

In other words, research is important when it helps to turn the researcher into some kind of expert not just on a subject but on a problem. To repeat: Merely doing a "book report" on what the experts have said on a subject is usually of no use at all. Hard thinking about conflicting reports, on the other hand, is always in short supply.

Refining your purpose. As you move into any given subject area, try to foresee the possibilities and dangers that lie in your formulation of the problem, just as you might have done in narrowing your subject and purpose back in Chapter 3. It is often useful to write out your thinking in the form of notes, like this:

Subject Area: Big-Time College Athletics.
Question: "How much corruption has been uncovered?"
> *Comments:* That question is too large. "Corruption" is not defined. The time span is not specified. To cover all the sports over many decades would require a whole book. So try again, this time moving toward something more manageable.

Question: "What forms of corruption have been discovered among varsity basketball players in the last ten years?"

Comments: Much better, but I still don't say what I mean by corruption. Can I hope to cover drug use, under-the-table payments, point-shaving, gambling, fixing of grade records, admission of under-qualified athletes? It's still too big.

Question: "What caused the point-shaving scandal at West Gamblin State?"

Comments: How could I ever decide for sure about the true causes? Even people on the scene don't agree about them. I'd have to know too much to make that kind of decision, even after a year of research. Better try again.

Question: "What are the most likely explanations of recent point-shaving scandals?"

Comments: This one looks pretty good. It gives me an immediate motive to go to the library to find out what explanations have *already* been offered, in magazines, newspapers, and books, and it gives me the interesting job of thinking about whether the explanations make sense. It doesn't require me to come to an absolute decision, but I would like to *think about* how the different factions—the athletes themselves, the coaches, the college presidents—have responded to the scandals. The research I'll do now has a clear purpose.

NOTEBOOK ENTRY

Here is a list of possible subject areas that might provide any number of hypotheses or theses that would require research. Choose the one that seems most immediately interesting to you and try to formulate either a clear question that might be completely or partially answered in a week or two of library probing. Then write a sentence or more about the difficulties that the question raises. (You might put your question in the form of a hypothesis: *"If* the corruption was caused by _____, *then* I should expect to find _____." Your expected difficulties would probably run like this: "I have been told that the legal record has still not been made public." "Our library periodicals room, where much of my data should be found, is a shambles; too many current journals have been stolen." And so on.

> The decline of baseball as the national pastime
> The history of this college
> How good writing should be taught
> The American steel industry
> The rise of Japanese industry after World War II
> Hitler and the Nazis
> The Vietnam War
> American art museums
> The conflict between government tobacco subsidies and
>   government antismoking programs
> College sports as big business
> How books are reviewed in American periodicals
> The early life of William Shakespeare
> Rock music in the sixties
> Charles Dickens as a storyteller
> Modern domestic architecture

How did you do? Did you recognize that every one of those subjects is still much too large and loose as it stands?

Here is an example of how our thinking might run if we started with one of these monstrous subjects. Consider the last one. We might go about refining "Modern domestic architecture" this way:

> *Question:* "What are the dominant styles of home building in modern America?"
>   *Comment:* Still much too broad. "Modern" is not defined —it could mean anything from 1900 to 1985. This one would still require a large book.
> *Question:* "What were the dominant styles of home design in Chicago (or in my hometown) in the 1930s?"
>   *Comment:* I probably could learn enough about this in a week or two to make a good report on it. I would have to go out and do some research in the form of *looking,* not just reading—and I'd enjoy doing that. But it doesn't seem to call for any *thinking* on

my part—and I must decide whether that's good or bad for me at this point.

Question: "Do the recommendations for remodeling in current do-it-yourself magazines yield interiors that undermine or support harmonious relations between parents and children?"

Comments: Well, that's a tough one, asking for a lot of judgment calls. A lot of people wouldn't know what to do with this question, but it happens to interest *me*, because I've always felt that our family apartment made living together almost impossible—yet it was in exactly the "handsome open style" that I not long ago saw praised in *Better Homes and Gardens.* My research would be more at the magazine racks than in the library—I would have to ask the teacher if that's OK. But at least this one would be *interesting.*

Question: "Have the styles of houses portrayed in *Better Homes and Gardens* since World War II changed drastically from decade to decade?"

Comment: Surefire—but too obvious? I know that the claim is true even before I begin, and I don't want to busy myself simply finding evidence for what I know already. Besides, who will want to read about that? Nobody. Would the question be improved if it read, *"How* have the styles changed?"

Question: "Have the styles of houses portrayed in *Better Homes and Gardens* since World War II accurately reflected Americans' changing conceptions of the good life?"

Comment: More interesting—but I've opened a can of worms. Conceptions of the "good life" would require a year's work in itself. So this one is even worse than the last.

Question: "Is there a sharp contrast between the 'dream house' portrayed in popular do-it-yourself remodeling magazines today and the ideas about domestic architecture that professional architects recommend when they are writing in their professional journals?"

Comment: Probably *still* too big, unless I already know quite a bit about architecture.

At the end of such probing you can go back over the list and see if any one thesis will do. Certainly you would reject most of these, and you might simply decide that since none of them looks good you should start over, probing some other subject.

Of course we do not expect that our trial comments would be the same as yours. Our point is that in such detailed thinking you are likely to raise questions with yourself that can help you avoid trouble later on. Though you shouldn't prolong the preliminary thinking so long that you never get started, it is generally true that an hour of hard thought *now* can save many hours of pointless labor later on.

It is usually, though not always, a good idea to complete such thinking with a clear statement of a thesis. "I shall argue, with such-and-such readers in mind, that *this* is the case." Again your research will often be focused better if the statement is in the form of a testable hypothesis: "My hunch is that such-and-such is true. *If* I am right, *then* I should be able to discover, looking at such-and-such sources, such-and-such kinds of evidence. If I am wrong, I am likely to find, on the contrary, that . . ."

Finding help through research

Once you know what question you want to answer, the trick is not just to locate any kind of help that may be hiding somewhere in some library, but to find the best help most efficiently. And it is not an easy trick, even with the aid of the published guides such as the various bibliographies and indexes you are led to by the handbooks. There are far too many of these book lists, organized by subject, for us even to begin to list them here; even the lists provided by the research manuals are almost brutally selective.

Before you are done, you will have constructed your own bibliography—a list of books and articles that you have used in your work and that might be helpful to anyone who wants to pursue your problem further. But meanwhile, how do you get started? How do you make your way through the millions of books and articles available to you either on campus, on microfilm, or through inter-library loans? Which guides through this maze are most helpful?

Card catalogue. A useful first step is a visit to your closest resource, your own library's book list, whether it is in the card catalogue or on the computer. Books will be listed by author, by title, and by subject matter, and you can get a start on your subject—especially on the question of whether it is unmanageably large—by moving back and forth among the cards or computer entries. For example, if you look up something as general as "Environment," you will find so many listings that you won't know where to start. But if you then look closely at the titles, you can sort out those few that sound closest to your interest. Then, when you look up the individual authors of those works, you will find that the listings tell you whether a given book has a bibliography. You have really hit pay dirt when a book that appears to be close to your problem turns out to have a good bibliography—especially if the entries are *annotated,* that is, described and evaluated by the author. Check out that book—especially if it was published recently. Though authors' annotations are never to be trusted absolutely, they can often point you in the most fruitful directions. Remember: Your task is not to accumulate titles—that's all too easy. Your task is to find those few special books or articles— perhaps no more than one or two—that will give you the help you need. (Note the additional information that the catalog entries contain: Most entries tell you at the bottom, for example, which additional subjects in the catalogue will list related titles.)

You will probably not find any book that specifically argues for the same thesis you are now exploring, if you have narrowed that thesis sufficiently. But if you do, and if the book seems convincing to you, you must, unfortunately, find some other thesis; otherwise you will just end up writing a "book report" as you did in grade school. Most likely, you will find many books and articles on the same *general* subject as yours, but none that argues your precise case. A quick look through their tables of contents or indexes may turn up a chapter or section that borders on your narrower interest but still doesn't steal your problem out from under you.

Encyclopedia articles. Another step in this brief initial survey is a quick reading of encyclopedia articles on subjects close to your own; such articles usually give short bibliographies of authoritative sources. (But *beware:* some of the items in the bibliography may be sadly out of date.)

General bibliographical guides. In the research handbooks you will find lists of bibliographical guides that cover all subjects, works like the *Reader's Guide to Periodical Literature* and *Books in Print*, as well as works that list the major guides to particular subjects. (You can find "indexes" for almost every subject—for example *Art Index, Humanities Index, Social Science Index,* the *Modern Language Association Bibliography,* which indexes over 6000 periodicals dealing with literature, *Music Index, American Statistics Index,* and so on.) In the two guides to student research that we mentioned at the beginning, you will find lists of bibliographies dealing with particular subjects. If your problem has to do with dancing, for example, you'll find in Turabian six works on the subject, including *A Bibliography of Dancing.* If you are interested in religion, you'll find two-and-a-half pages of titles, including *A Reader's Guide to the Great Religions,* the *Index to Religious Periodical Literature,* and *A Bibliography of Bibliographies of Religion.* It may surprise you (or even depress you) to learn that such bibliographies are so overwhelmingly plentiful that there is now a flourishing business in bibliographies of bibliographies, and even of bibliographies of bibligraphies of bibliographies—lists of those books that contain lists of those books that contain lists of books! You can see again that if you are not careful you will find yourself overwhelmed with too much *non-*information—long lists of books that nobody could hope to master. If that happens, start over and do some more thinking about your thesis. See if you can sharpen it further, in order to reduce the amount of material you will have to wade through.

It would be absurd for us to try to give you in a few pages the kind of guidance you *might* need to get through the maze of compilations that *might* be useful to you in working on your problem. Our point is simply that many people have probed your general subject area before you, and that, if you persist, the library will yield information about who those people are and about the location of their work.

Reference librarian. When you get really stuck, you can always turn to the reference librarian. "Do you happen to know of any bibliographical source specifically devoted to my problem?" or, "Where would *you* go if you wanted to find out such-and-such?" Reference librarians have spent years learning what is available, and even if they do not happen to know the best sources for your particular problem, they know *how to find* those sources. Do *not* ask overworked librarians for help in choosing a subject. It is not their job to help you decide what you should write about.

Helpful as these various resources will be, they cannot perform *your* special selection of references. Only your specific problem, question, thesis, or hypothesis, gradually coming into sharper focus, can dictate just which helpers you should seek out from the crowd.

Learning to do research is a little like learning to write: You can't do it all at once, and you can never master it completely. Throughout your college work you will continue to learn how to seek out those rare "good friends" in the library who can teach you what you want to know. Only when you look a given source in the eye and make a specific request can it respond to *you*. You do that by finally finding the precise books and articles that come closest to your interest.

Using your sources, once you find them: "What does this really say?"

Once you have found a source that looks as if it might be helpful, how do you conduct your request for help? The book or article will lie there useless until you do something with it. Even as you start reading it will not announce clearly just *how* to use its information or line of reasoning. You can turn its passive offer of help into active hostility if you don't find out what it really has to say. In other words, the problem of great floods of useless information is only partially solved by sharpening the subject as we recommended in Chapter 3 and in the first section of this chapter. Even when you have narrowed down your sources to the best ones, few enough to be covered, problems still remain. Just as no food yields nourishment until you eat it, no research source yields intellectual nourishment until you have digested its contents. So the question remains: How *do* we obtain the nourishment that other writers may offer?

The painful truth is that most of us most of the time fail to read with sufficient critical attention to find out what is really *there*. Partly because the ocean of books and articles is so vast, we often skim over subjects too fast, doing *only* the kind of rapid preliminary reading that was advocated at the beginning of this chapter, and thus we give superficial or misleading reports on what we have read. The problem is magnified by the impulse to take notes on every partial point that we find interesting. Your notes on a hastily read paragraph may in fact reverse the author's meaning if it happens to be the author's report on an *opponent's* beliefs.

A common form of misrepresentation in notes goes like this. A given source, *The History of U.S. Policy in the Middle East,* may say something like the following:

> It has often been believed that the United States has followed a consistently pro-Israeli policy during the past four decades. It is true that many of our actions have been taken to help the young nation survive and prosper. We have given both military and industrial aid in great quantities, and at the diplomatic level we have often offered necessary support. But what is often forgotten is that we have also tried in every conceivable way to maintain a genuine neutrality in the various conflicts that have erupted. In fact, one could cite almost as many examples of aid to Egypt as to Israel.

(Warning! Almost nobody can copy so much as a paragraph with absolute accuracy, on the first try. If you don't believe us, make a copy of the previous paragraph and then have a friend check its accuracy, word for word, punctuation mark by punctuation mark. The results may suggest that you should be cautious even about trusting your own notes. Because of this universal human tendency to make mistakes, it is a good idea to photocopy any passage that is almost certain to appear in your final draft. But be careful not to flood your study with photocopied material that you will never have time to master.)

Even if accurate in one sense, a hasty reader's notes on this paragraph might go astray like this:

> . . . the U.S. has followed a consistently pro-Israeli policy during the past four decades. . . . Many of our actions have been taken to help the young nation survive and prosper.

After accurately labeling the quotation card with the title of the author and book, the student then files the note away. Returning to it a few weeks later, he or she has no memory and no clue that the author was actually arguing that America has been equally pro-Israel and pro-Arab. The notes, with their reversal of the original, then get frozen into the research paper like this:

Many authors believe that the United States has followed a policy unfairly biased against the Arabs. As Arthur Blailer puts it, in *The History of U. S. Policy in the Middle East,* "The U.S. has consistently . . . [worked to] help the young nation survive and prosper." [Blailer, p. 72]

The result *looks* scholarly. In one sense it *is* scholarly: a "scholar" did some library work and made notes in a seemingly conscientious and accurate manner. But by unconsciously *quoting out of context,* such scholars mislead themselves and their readers.

What this means is that for most research projects, you should include only sources that you have mastered. Spend as long as you can getting familiar with the terrain. Once you have located the small number of discussions that seem closest to your needs, read them carefully, each one *at least twice*—and only *then* start taking notes on the passages that you may want to quote. And be sure that you report what the author wanted to say, not just random words or a message you would *like* the author to say! Be especially careful with **ellipses**—those marks that show an omission (. . .). Used skillfully and unscrupulously, they can make any source seem to say almost anything. Does not the Bible say, "Thou shalt . . . kill" and "Thou shalt . . . commit adultery"?

NOTEBOOK ENTRY

Here are the opening words of a book about capitalism, by Michael Harrington. Read it through once, at your usual reading pace.

Western capitalism is in crisis.
During the two decades from 1950 to 1970—from the reconstruction of Europe to the Great Recession-Inflation of recent years—that statement would have been perceived as absurd everywhere but on the socialist left. Conservatives, liberals, even social democrats agreed: capitalism had transformed itself, resolving those of its internal

contradictions which had exploded in the catastrophes of the 1930s. For many it had become postcapitalism, a new society, which, though vaguely defined, was supposed to be free from the destructive cycles of boom and bust.

But then, even now, in the tumult of the middle seventies, when a sense of foreboding and fear has seeped through the Western consciousness, it still does not seem that these new troubles are the product of an economic system. Rather, one might blame these things on a remarkable outbreak of bad luck. The Organization of Petroleum Exporting Countries (OPEC) was accidentally unified in response to the Yom Kippur War of 1973 and thereby discovered that it could quadruple the price of oil. Bad weather in Russia and other countries caused prices for agricultural exports to rise on the world market and sent the cost of food soaring. Even the spectacular ineptitude of the economic management in the Nixon and Ford administrations could be understood as a matter of political chance, not of structural necessity [resulting from inherent flaws in capitalism]. On all these counts, there was no need to have recourse to an outmoded category like capitalism. One simply cursed the accumulation of misfortune and looked for ways to muddle through. [*The Twilight of Capitalism,* 1976]

Try now to write, without reading the passage again, a one-sentence summary of the two paragraphs; try to state, in your own words, Harrington's precise meaning.

Take a few moments during class or afterward to compare your summary with other students'. Do you find large differences? (If you do not, yours is the most remarkably unified class we have ever encountered.) How can we account for large differences? You all read "the same passage." You all wrote what you *thought* it said. Yet the results look (we predict) as if many of you had read an entirely different passage.

Every scholar ought to remember such conflicts whenever he or she begins to take notes. *"Will my notes be of any use to me, or to anyone else?"* Certainly not unless they have *some* connection with the original. Consider for a moment the reading of Harrington by the classmate who seems to you to have distorted the passage most. Of what use would a research paper by that student be to you if you read it hoping to learn whether Harrington would be worth reading, or what he really thought?

NOTEBOOK ENTRY

Now *study* the Harrington passage, reading it as many times as
you need to achieve confidence about what Harrington really
says. Write a new summary in a sentence or two.

Again take a few moments to compare at least a few of
the results. Did you change your mind on a second or third reading? Is there still disagreement among your fellow students?
Do you think that if you all studied the passage long enough
you would come to identical summaries? That seems extremely
unlikely. Can you think of reasons why even with the greatest of care we are likely to give different reports on our
reading?

These new readings, however, should be much more closely
related to each other, and it should be possible to discuss the
grounds of difference by referring to details in Harrington's text.
You may now find that some of your classmates' readings are
helpful in improving your own.

The point, then, is obvious but too often forgotten: Notes
based on hasty reading are likely to be useless, except in some
form like "looks worth studying" and "obviously not relevant";
more careful notes can be helpful both to yourself and other
readers. Too many research notes are made like those first ones,
from memory after one reading—sometimes long after. One of our
teachers, a famous scholar, preached two simple rules: Never discuss any work that you haven't read at least twice, and never
discuss any work that you have not read again recently. He taught
that our minds play tricks on us; we convince ourselves that a book
has said what we would like it to say rather than what the author
intended to say.

Here are some possible notes on Harrington. By now you
should be fairly confident about what he was *really* trying to say.
Which of these summaries would you want to have in your collection of notes, a month from now? One way to think of the question is to imagine Michael Harrington himself reading these notes,
and grading them according to the following scheme:

A   = Accurate. Right on. Just what I was trying to say.

OK = Catches at least one of the points I was trying to make, but the emphasis is questionable.

O   = A fairly accurate report of what my *opponents* would say, not what I believe.

F   = Failure. Completely off the mark.

1. Harrington begins *The Twilight of Capitalism* with an admission that by the 1960s capitalism had pretty well solved its problems.

2. Harrington begins with a claim of three genuine causes of capitalism's troubles in the 1970s: OPEC's raising oil prices; bad weather in Russia; and bad management by American presidents.

3. Michael Harrington argues in the opening pages of *The Twilight of Capitalism* that by the 1960s, "Capitalism had transformed itself, resolving those of its internal contradictions which had exploded in the catastrophes of the 1930s. . . . It had become postcapitalism, a new society, . . . free from the destructive cycles of boom and bust."

4. Michael Harrington's point in the opening paragraphs of *The Twilight of Capitalism* is that when things were going well in the capitalist nations, it was easy to think that the problems of capitalism had been solved, and even when things went bad in the seventies it was still easy to blame troubles on bad luck rather than on an economic system.

5. Harrington argues in the opening paragraphs of *The Twilight of Capitalism* that, in the 1970s, "There was no need to have recourse to an outmoded category like capitalism."

6. In *The Twilight of Capitalism,* Harrington argues that "Western capitalism is in crisis," even though most people in the 1960s and 1970s have thought the very notion of capitalism as an economic system was an "outmoded category."

7. In *The Twilight of Capitalism,* Michael Harrington confesses that even in the 1970s, when capitalism began to run into visible troubles, he "simply cursed the accumulation of misfortune and looked for ways to muddle through."

Which summaries look best to you? We consider #6 best, and #4 not bad; perhaps both would be better if they incorporated the points reported on, in distorted form, in #2. Notice that some of the worst ones (#5 and #7) *look* better, because they include direct quotations.

What qualities does #6 have that make it best?

1. It emphasises Harrington's main point, using his own words economically but crucially.

2. It gives an accurate summary of his subordinate point— why people have thought that the very notion of capitalism as an economic system subject to collapse is outmoded.

3. It is brief. Notes are not much use if they take as much time to read as the original. If the brief summary is accurate, it will tell me whether I want to go back to the original for a fuller reminder.

This exercise with Harrington is of course highly artificial. Ordinarily no reader would read only the opening paragraphs. You can test your own reading of those paragraphs, however, by a quick look now at Harrington's next sentences:

This means that the real history of the crisis of the seventies is still a secret kept from most of the people who must suffer from it. All the explanations to the contrary notwithstanding [an obvious reference to the paragraph about the 1970s], it is a crisis of the capitalist system. Outrageous as the truth may seem, those years of prosperity and expansion [the 1960s] were preparing the recent calamities even as they gave rise to the understandable illusion that the old problems of capitalism had finally been eliminated.

No doubt the worst summaries above seem to you outlandish or unlikely. Would *anyone* read as badly as the author of #7? Unfortunately, yes. Many a printed, would-be scholarly work reverses the meanings of sources in just this way. We must be as skeptical about printed authorities as about our own hasty first reports—the ones we make before careful re-reading.

Misreporting to your readers in your final draft is not the

most serious harm that results from hasty note-taking. The greatest damage is done to your own learning. Our minds always tend to accept or reject materials according to whether they fit our previous experiences, prejudices, or expectations. They take the easy path of trying to fit each new statement into the container of familiar old concepts, instead of taking the harder but more profitable path of opening out to new challenges. Most books and articles worth reading will say something that we have *not* heard before. They challenge us to think afresh, and when we resist that challenge, when we simply grasp at this or that phrase that fits our preconceptions, our own education remains exactly where it was. Any essay we write, using a source that has been abused in this way, will not differ essentially from what we could have written without doing any research at all.

The final suggestion about dealing with sources, then, is this: Begin by ranging widely and quickly over many possible sources; zero in on as few sources as possible, *study* those sources seriously, and then *report them accurately.*

Thinking critically of your sources

It would make our lives as researchers simple and easy if all printed sources were equally trustworthy. Most of us are probably too much inclined to trust whatever we find in a book, especially if it is published by a famous press. The nasty fact is that most sources are *to some degree* untrustworthy; in most books and articles you will discover, if you check closely, that the authors have misquoted, summarized carelessly, and committed errors in the documentation. If you have ever been quoted in a newspaper, you probably have discovered that reporters tend to get things wrong. Professional scholars are only slightly less subject to careless reporting.

Even standard reference works often get dates and names wrong, because they simply borrow them from other sources without checking. In one recently published bibliography of the works of a famous critic, for example, we have found, through careful checking, an average of two plain mistakes per page. It is a little harder for us to confess our own errors, but one of us— Booth—must admit that in one article that he wrote with some care, he made at least four crucial errors of fact, including an eight-year mistake in the date of death of a close friend! When we add to such errors, produced without intending to deceive, those made by all the authors who set out to mislead us, we see that we can never take for granted the reliability of any source.

How, then, can we hope to pick out those sources that are "the best"—the most comprehensive, the most accurate, and the most reliable? Unfortunately, there are no easy criteria. The most effective way of evaluating sources is to become well read on the subject. The more you know, the more readily you will spot the relative strengths and weaknesses of various sources. To some degree, different sources will act as checks on others. Without your becoming an expert on a subject, a bit of concentrated reading will soon give you a sense of which sources are most trustworthy and knowledgeable.

This is such a complicated issue that we can only expand slightly here on what we said about testing authorities in Chapter 13 (pp. 413–414). We rely partly, of course, on the reports of other people: Some scholars earn a reputation for being trustworthy, while others are known to be careless or deeply biased. Such reports can never be absolutely decisive for us, but we all have to use them as we begin to make our way into a subject.

In digging into any source on our own, we can always make some use of the following clues, though no one of them will ever tell us that a given source is *always* to be trusted, or that another one is *always* untrustworthy:

- What does this author hope to gain from me? Is it merely my attention and agreement, or does he or she profit in some way if I agree? (The more profit, the greater the reason for suspicion.)
- Is there a clear connection between the reasons offered and the conclusions? Does the author seem to be at least trying to *argue* a case and to respect the data, or am I given merely a collection of assertions?
- Does the author try to meet any obvious objections that I can think of? (If *I* can think of them, the author probably could, too, and if they are not brought out into the open, is it possible that some deliberate distortion is taking place?)
- Can I, in a few spot checks, verify the quotations and documentation the author offers? (If I find that out of the first five pas-

sages I check on, three are misquoted and one apparently does not even exist, I do not need any more evidence to make me suspicious of the rest of the author's work.)

- Does the case made here either fit what I have learned from other sources, or if it does not, does it give good reasons for doubting those other sources? (Too many authors set out to make a splash with outlandish theories about this and that, knowing that many readers prefer to enjoy a sensational account than to read a sober assessment of evidence.)
- On the other hand, does what the author says fit my previous beliefs so neatly that I am a "sitting duck" for his or her case? (Some of our most foolish mistakes in the use of sources come when we find books and articles that confirm our fondest beliefs. The most difficult task in educating ourselves is that of recognizing when our approval of a statement is caused only by our predisposition to believe it.)

We could continue to list guidelines indefinitely; almost every point we have made in this book could be turned into a point about trust of sources; all of our advice to you about how to write well is in one sense advice about how to make other readers trust *your* writing. An author's characteristic way with design, with connections, with varieties of tone, and with patterns of argument —all these can give us clues about whether to grant our trust. This being so, we should not be surprised to discover that the most difficult problem of all in doing research is this sorting out of degrees of trustworthiness.

It has sometimes been said that the goal of education is to learn to recognize a trustworthy person when you see one. Certainly one goal of practice in research is to learn to recognize a trustworthy source when it comes your way.

Giving credit and the problem of plagiarism

The two main reasons for giving credit to others are: to help your readers, if they want to pursue your ideas further, and to be fair to your helpers—to pay your debts.

We have already talked a bit about fairness, and the plagiarism that violates it (Chapter 1, pp. 27–28). In an ideal society, people might not worry about who "owned" a given idea or phrase. Surely the product of brainwork is not like a piece of jewelry, sharply defined as *mine* and therefore *not yours*. Who, after all, "owns" the ideas that we all share—the fundamentals of addition and subtraction, the grammar of our sentences, the hope for peace rather than war? We sometimes approach this ideal of sharing when we're in a friendly discussion; nobody then worries about "mine" and "thine." Yet the truth remains that, even at our best, even in the freest discussions, we usually find it only fair to be clear about which of us is responsible for which views.

Whatever our feelings about communal sharing, the society in which we "publish" our ideas draws sharp boundaries between *your* intellectual property and *mine*. It treats the labor of writing as a kind of property, and it protects each author's property rights. Writers thus commit not just a technical or moral fault when they steal structures of language or thought that were created and are thus "owned" by others; they run a great personal risk. If the results of plagiarism are published, the plagiarist can be subject to damage suits and even imprisonment. At least two college presidents have been publicly disgraced in recent years when someone discovered that large sections of their published research had been simply copied from out-of-the-way sources.

Since almost everything we think or say has been learned from others, the decision about just how much citation is required by honesty and practicality is often unclear. Should we (Booth and Gregory) cite all of the freshman rhetorics we have learned from, beginning as freshmen years ago, and on through our teaching years and concluding with those we have reread during the two years spent writing this book? A bibliography for such borrowing —even the part of it about which we are conscious—would fill many pages, so many that it would not help anyone understand our ideas or know where to go to pursue them further. We thus refrain from giving such a bibliography here—but we might be obliged to give one for a different audience and purpose. Should you give a footnote every time you are aware that the seed of your idea was planted in a given teacher's class? To do so would make your pages look absurd.

Despite the fuzziness of the borderline between fair and

unfair borrowing, you can generally rely on the following guidelines.

Quoting directly. Acknowledge *all* uses of *any* printed wording. Even a short phrase should be credited to its owner:

> "In William James's phrase, we need to find activities that are 'the moral equivalent of war'."
> "As T. S. Eliot's Prufrock puts it, the evening sky looked to me 'like a patient etherized upon a table.' "

You need not provide the sources of generally known quotations. It would be excessive to write, "As Shakespeare's Hamlet says, 'To be or not to be.' " But quotations, long or short, that are not generally known should be credited. "W. H. Auden offers a wonderful comment on competition: 'The slogan of Hell: Eat *or* be eaten. The slogan of Heaven: Eat *and* be eaten.' " Even two or three words, if they are original and distinctive, should be identified: " 'conspicuous consumption' (Veblen)"; "Eliot's 'dissociation of sensibility.' "

Just how much additional identification you should offer will depend on the kind of help you think your readers will want or need. In a research paper, you will probably be asked to give complete publishing information. That can be done in many different ways, depending on what your teacher or editor requires. Here are three standard procedures, but there are others and you should be sure to follow closely whatever model your teacher suggests:

1. *The in-text "author-date-page" method.* You can give a reference in your text to a bibliographical entry, with the page number following the date:

> "In the early books on cosmology, particularly those written by Jeans and Eddington in the 1920's and 1930's, the second law of thermodynamics occupied a prominent place" (Bonnor 1964, 171).

Then, in your bibliography, you give the full information:

Bonnor, William. *The Mystery of the Expanding Universe.* New York: Macmillan Publishing Co., 1964.

2. *Footnotes.* You can give the full information in a footnote, using above-line numbers immediately following the passage you want to acknowledge:

William Bonnor tells us that some of the cosmologists in the 1920s and 1930s gave a prominent place to the second law of thermodynamics.[1]

---

[1] *The Mystery of the Expanding Universe* (New York: Macmillan Publishing Co., 1964), p. 171.

3. *Endnotes.* You can give all identifying information in consecutively numbered endnotes listed at the end of your paper. Such a note should include everything that would appear in a footnote, plus the author's name.

Remember that the purpose of such notations is to help readers do what you think they will want to do. You have probably noticed that in this book we have given full publishing information for very few works, because we have assumed that as students of writing, you would not be primarily interested in checking up on whether we have quoted accurately from Charles Dickens, say, or Michael Harrington. To document every quotation would clutter up this book with unused information. But if we were writing an essay or book on the subjects treated in our quotations, we would offer readers full references.

Summarizing. Whenever you borrow the order or structure of ideas, *say so.* Summaries should be labeled as summaries, even if you do not quote a single word from the passage. "His argument boils down to this, in my view: _____"; or "In short, what Jones claims is _____." To see how this might work, consider the following passage—four paragraphs from a work that you might want to refer to in writing a research paper with the title, "The Powers and Limits of Human Memory":

The first person to propose an experimental test of the span of a man's instantaneous grasp seems to have been Sir William Hamilton, a nineteenth-century Scottish metaphysician. He wrote: "If you throw a handful of marbles on the floor, you will find it difficult to view at once more than six, or seven at most, without confusion." It is not clear whether Hamilton himself actually threw marbles on the floor, for he remarked that the experiment could be performed also by an act of imagination, but at least one reader took him literally. In 1871 the English economist and logician William Stanley Jevons reported that when he threw beans into a box he never made a mistake when there were three or four, was sometimes wrong if the number was five, was right about half the time if the beans numbered ten, and was usually wrong when the number reached fifteen. . . . Refined [modern] techniques serve only to confirm his original intuition. We are able to perceive up to about six dots accurately without counting; beyond this errors become frequent.

But estimating the number of beans or dots is a perceptual task, not necessarily related to concepts or thinking. Each step in the development of an argument [on the other hand] is a particular thing with its own structure, different from these other steps and quite different from one anonymous bean in Jevons' box. A better test of "apprehension" would be the ability to remember various symbols in a given sequence. Another Englishman, Joseph Jacobs, first performed this experiment with digits in 1887. He would read aloud a haphazard sequence of numbers and ask his listeners to write down the sequence from memory after he finished. The maximum number of digits a normal adult could repeat without error was about seven or eight.

From the first it was obvious that this span of immediate memory was intimately related to general intelligence. Jacobs reported that the span increased between the ages of eight and nineteen, and his test was later incorporated by Alfred Binet, and is still used, in the Binet intelligence test. It is valuable principally because an unusually short span is a reliable indicator of mental deficiency; a long span does not necessarily mean high intelligence.

A person who can grasp eight decimal digits can usually

manage about seven letters of the alphabet or six monosyllabic words (taken at random, of course). Now the interesting point about this is that six words contain much more information, as defined by information theory, than do seven letters or eight digits. We [human beings] are therefore in a position analogous to carrying a purse which will hold no more than seven coins—whether pennies or dollars. Obviously we will carry more wealth if we fill the purse with silver dollars rather than pennies. Similarly we can use our memory span most efficiently by stocking it with informationally rich symbols such as words, or perhaps images, rather than with poor coin such as digits. . . .

A person who can repeat nine binary digits ["bits"—the smallest unit of information exchange] can usually repeat five words. The informational value of the nine binary digits is nine bits; of the five words, about fifty bits. Thus [we have] a quantitative indication of how much we can improve the efficiency of memory by using informationally rich units. [George A. Miller, *The Psychology of Communication,* 1967]

If you decide to summarize this account, paragraph by paragraph (as you might want to do if the details are important to your own case), you should give Miller credit, even if you do not use any of Miller's phrases or sentences. Similarly, if you write a short summary, you must be sure that credit is clear. Perhaps your acknowledgment will be handled like this:

George A. Miller explains why our minds are more efficient with "informationally rich units" than with nonsense units by giving the history of experiments on memory. They all show that the mind can grasp in a flash and retain only a maximum of about nine or ten meaningless units and about five or six units that are rich in information, such as words. But five words will carry about fifty "bits," while the nine nonsense units carry only nine bits.

Whether you should then give the precise publication data and page number will again depend on the kind of writing you are doing. If it were a newspaper article, no citation would be expected. But in any kind of academic research, you should add either a footnote at the bottom of the page or at the end of the paper:

17 George A. Miller, *The Psychology of Communication.* New York: Basic Books, 1975, pp. 7–9.

Or again you can give a citation in your text itself (Miller 1975, pp. 7–9), referring to the title as listed in your bibliography. For details about how to handle special problems in the main ways of acknowledging sources, and for the preferred style of these citations, refer to the manual recommended by your writing teacher (or those we mentioned at the beginning of this chapter).

Paraphrasing. A paraphrase is more detailed than a summary. It attempts to give most or all of the structure of the argument found in the original. Obviously any paraphrase must be documented clearly, because it follows the author's original design. When paraphrasing, as when summarizing, be sure to put quotation marks around every copied phrase or sentence.

For example:

Miller's account is so incisive that I will paraphrase it here:

Starting in the nineteenth century, Scottish and British experimenters learned that human beings could take in at a glance no more than about six or seven random beans or marbles or dots. Later experimenters worked not with objects but with symbols. They found that the maximum number of random numerals that could be repeated after a single, quick hearing was about seven or eight. . . . Finally in the twentieth century experimenters found ways of proving that the mind uses "informationally rich units"—words, phrases, sentences—to increase its efficiency, each additional load of meaning multiplying by many times the amount remembered (Miller 1967, 7–9).

A completely illegitimate kind of paraphrasing is performed by moving through a passage and "translating" it line by line into your own words—without acknowledgment. This practice is almost as bad as using quotations as if they were yours. Nothing whatever is accomplished, for you or for your reader if, for example, you paraphrase a sentence by Miller—"Refined techniques serve only to confirm his original intuition"—into, "His creative hunches were confirmed by the refinement of later methods."

Borrowing ideas. If you learned your basic idea, the central thesis of your work, from a source, be sure to give the source credit. There are many ways of doing this: "As George A. Miller shows, in Chapter 2 of *The Psychology of Communication,* the mind has special ways of . . ."; or, "The mind has special ways of . . ." (I borrow here from George A. Miller's *The Psychology of Communication,* Chapter 1); or, "George A. Miller has summarized well what we now know about . . . (Miller 1975, Chapter 1) . . ."—and then list Miller in your bibliography.

Assisting your reader with documentation

We turn now from the *duty* to acknowledge your debts to your desire to be *helpful* to readers. A considerate scholar will want to observe the following guidelines.

Making things as easy as possible. The fewer flourishes of scholarship the better, provided you give as much guidance as the reader needs. Your task is not to prove that you have done a lot of research, but to help your readers decide whether your views are based on accurate information, and to help them explore your ideas further if they so desire. The requirements of this rule will usually be met adequately if you have abided by our suggestions about fairness, *unless* you have overdone the citations. As you do your final draft, you may find that it is weighted down with duplicated documentation; if so, cut whatever you don't need. Beginning researchers sometimes make the mistake of giving multiple footnotes on the same passage, often using the Latin abbreviation "ibid" ("in the same place"). Usually you don't need "ibid"; once a source has been identified, you can just put further references as page numbers into your own text.

Later on in his book Miller seems to contradict himself when he says that . . . (p. 231).

Think of what your readers already know, and adjust your citations accordingly. Will they know so much about the *OED*, for example, that they'll think it silly if you provide a full title and bibliographical information? Will they think that "the *Encyclopaedia Britannica,* 15th ed." is sufficient, or will they want *'Encyclopaedia Britannica, The New,* 15th ed., 30 vols. Chicago: Encyclopedia Britannica, Inc., 1974"? Only in the rarest of tasks will the latter form be needed (in an essay on encyclopedias, perhaps?). Will your probable readers recognize some famous quotation from Shakespeare or Yeats or should you document it? *Unless you have a clear answer to such questions, give the fuller citation.*

Notice that we have often not given exact locations for the literary quotations sprinkled throughout this book. We have assumed—perhaps wrongly—that with your mind on learning how to write, the precise location of a poem by Yeats or a quotation from E. B. White would just get in your way. But if we had been writing about Yeats or White, full citation would be helpful—and thus required. In a research paper, it is always better to give more than *some* readers will need, so long as there is a chance that most of them will want the assistance.

How much use of sources—and when? We've already warned against simply throwing in references to make your work look scholarly. But how do you decide just what kind of support and documentation to offer?

Again there are no simple rules, but the principle is clear enough: Think of your reader and your purposes, and all else should follow. But the application is often difficult. We offer here only a few pointers to get you started on a process that is never perfected.

• Pay close attention to the practices of other authors working in your new "field" (the general subject in which you are doing research). Pay especially close attention to what they take for granted and what they assume needs documentation. Writing to readers trained in literature, you would not give a source or footnote to your assertion that Shakespeare was a great writer, or that he lived in the sixteenth century, or that he wrote tragedies and comedies, or that he wrote *Hamlet.* But if you chose to argue for one or another of the offbeat theories about Shakespeare's works—that they were written by Christopher Marlow, or by Lord Bacon, or by the Earl of Essex—you would probably want to support almost every sentence with some kind of reference. In short, skeptical readers require more documentary support than friendly readers.

- Don't use long quotations when a short sentence will do. Long quotations tend to make your reader skip. On the other hand, if a fine author has made one of your points more effectively than you can do, a longer quotation may be justified, if you precede it with a brief clue to your reader about why it is important: "David Stockman has put this scandalous point so well that he deserves to be read in full."
- Use only a brief desciption, not a quotation, when all your reader needs is a reminder that an authority is on your side. "The three members of the commission have all at different times agreed with this obvious point (Gilbert 1981, 46; Harrison 1975, 13; Smith 1980, 102)."
- Use a *summary* whenever you need to include many points made by an author but don't need to take the space for a full quotation. *Don't* use long summaries just to show that you have actually read the whole book or chapter.
- Don't use paraphrase—detailed, line-by-line "translation" of points from the author's language to your own—unless for some reason you are not allowed to quote directly. Since in your course work you are legally allowed to quote almost anything without permission, the need for paraphrasing will not arise until the day when you may want to publish what you have written. At that point authors are sometimes forced by copyright law to paraphrase.

None of these points will work if separated from careful thought about the particular problems you face in your particular project. What we said in Chapter 1 about the unique problems faced in every writing task applies here as well. One can conceive of a research paper that would offer documentation of some kind for every line, and of other papers that might offer only a few footnotes and a brief bibliography.

After all this advice, the fact remains that decisions about documentation always call for delicate judgment. If, for example, you think of teachers as the main or only readers of your essay or research paper, you will make guesses about what they will need and require; if you think of fellow students as your primary readers, you will provide the help you think *they* will need. If we thought of ourselves as writing for a scholarly journal—*Publications of the Modern Language Association,* say, or *Daedalus*—we would offer much fuller documentation than would be suitable if we were writing for readers of *The New York Times Book Review* or *The Atlantic.*

Finally, you must decide for yourself just what sort of reader you are trying to assist. When you submit an assigned paper with imaginary readers, it is a good idea to indicate to your real reader (your teacher or fellow students) just what kind of audience you are writing for. You can do that on the title page, like this:

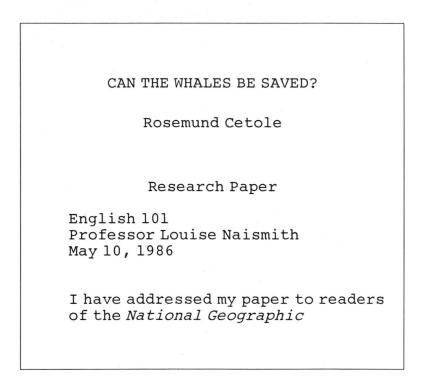

CAN THE WHALES BE SAVED?

Rosemund Cetole

Research Paper

English 101
Professor Louise Naismith
May 10, 1986

I have addressed my paper to readers
of the *National Geographic*

Conclusion

Doing research can be either a meaningless chore, performed for the sake of learning a mechanical skill, or a major step in your education, a way of learning how to learn. Compared with taking in the world through travel or happenstance conversation and casual reading, research is a relatively formal, disciplined way of learning. Generations of careful scholars have evolved rules designed to reduce misunderstanding to a minimum (it is never removed entirely) and to ensure that a wider community, continuing through time, can share what is already known or believed to be true, and then continue to learn.

When you do the best kinds of research, then, you are participating in, and profiting from, an ancient tradition of careful inquiry. Every discipline that you encounter in college, every course and every major field, has been built largely through the *discipline* of careful research. What is more, most professions have developed in the same way. Each of them would soon become routine, hidebound, and lifeless if it were not continuously nourished and replenished by the work of good scholars.

You are joining that band of scholars whenever you take seriously the task of reading any book or article with full attention, reporting on what it says with full responsibility, and *thinking* about where it leads you as you compare it with other possible scholarly sources. Systematic, disciplined research is only one of many ways in which you can educate yourself. It builds on other ways that are often even more important: conversation, classwork, carefree reading of books that are *not*, as in research, confined to a narrow subject, and—most important—learning how to express (and thus test) your ideas in writing.

But there is no substitute for the discovery, through such research, of what it means to dig deeply into some one subject. Many of us come to our first humble awareness of how little we know as we follow the strands of a subject from one new discovery to another, discoveries of facts or knowledge that other people have known all along. Even in the most narrow discipline, nobody learns everything. The resulting humility can be discouraging, if our purpose has been to win points or to display mastery over other people. But it can be invigorating if we remember what it teaches us about future inquiries: There's always more to be learned, pattern after pattern of meaning awaiting discovery and explanation by the rightly trained inquirer.

Afterword

Having worked through this book, having completed the course, are you ready to write the perfect paper? By this time you know that such a question is absurd, because the answer is obvious. The essay that cannot be improved simply does not exist. You can now write *better* essays—much better than you wrote at the beginning of the course. You have learned systematic approaches to revision that you can use when you work on every new paper, and *that* means that you can go on improving throughout your college career and after you leave college. Such long-term improvement is all that any of us can hope for. To fix our gaze on perfection as an abstract goal will always blind us both to the practical steps we can take right now, and to the progress we are actually making.

We are all in the never-ending business of trying to make ourselves understood. Perhaps if we all thought alike, if we were programmable like computers, we could write a perfect paper—by computer standards—on every try, a paper suitable for all occasions, perfectly understandable by readers who would also be duplicates of each other. There may be some people who would prefer to live in a world like that, a world reduced to programmed certainty. In such a world, writing as we are trying to learn it here would have no place. In fact, a perfect essay, in one sense perhaps possible in such a world, would be no *essay* at all, not an attempt but a fixity; it would leave us with nothing more to say.

If you and I thought exactly alike, what would we say to each other? If we were programmable, all of the fierceness and compassion and joy in life would evaporate. Conversation, spoken and written, would stop. The open-ended world that so often presents itself as confusing or threatening would turn into a world of closed doors and settled issues. If, finding ourselves in such a world, we could then look back, as programmed creatures, on our lives as agents who were once free to dispute with each other, would we not miss our former lives, miss even the uncertainties and fears— and the writing problems—that we non-programmed creatures must cope with? Would we not feel that freedom had been too high a price to pay for such security?

We address each other, and try to change one another's minds, because we all know that nobody *is* perfect, either in knowledge or behavior. In learning to write better—without the hope of perfection—we join the age-old, never-ending human project of trying to make life better for us all.

Index

About the Authors

Wayne C. Booth is the George M. Pullman Distinguished Service Professor of English at The University of Chicago. He has degrees from Brigham Young University and The University of Chicago, where he received his Ph.D. He has taught Freshman English 33 times (he counted), and he still finds it "the most challenging and most important course in the college curriculum." His publications include *The Rhetoric of Fiction, A Rhetoric of Irony, Modern Dogma and the Rhetoric of Assent,* and assorted essays on writing and on the teaching of writing. He is co-editor, with Professor Gregory, of *The Harper & Row Reader.*

Marshall W. Gregory is an associate professor at Butler University in Indianapolis. He received his Ph.D. from The University of Chicago. Like Professor Booth, he has taught Freshman English throughout his career. His academic interests include 19th century British literature, literary theory, liberal education theory, the teaching of writing, and faculty development. He has published numerous articles in such journals as *Change, Liberal Education, Journal of General Education,* and *ADE Bulletin.* From 1983–1986, Professor Gregory was national director of the Lilly Endowment Post-Doctoral Teaching Awards Program. He is co-editor, with Professor Booth, of *The Harper & Row Reader,* and is currently working on a book on ethical criticism.